ALFRED THE GREAT

THE MEDIEVAL WORLD
Editor: David Bates

ALFRED THE GREAT

War, Kingship and Culture in Anglo-Saxon England

Richard Abels

LONGMAN
London and New York

Pearson Education Limited
Edinburgh Gate,
Harlow, Essex CM20 2JE, United Kingdom
and Associated Companies throughout the world.

Visit us on the World Wide Web at:
http://www.pearsoneduc.com

First published 1998

ISBN 0-582-04048-5 CSD
ISBN 0-582-04047-7 PPR

British Library Cataloguing in Publication Data

A catalogue entry for this title is available from the British Library

Library of Congress Cataloging-in-Publication Data

Abels, Richard Philip, 1951—
Alfred the Great : war, kingship, and culture in Anglo-Saxon
England / Richard Abels.
p.   cm. — (The medieval world)
Includes bibliographical references and index.
ISBN 0-582-04048-5 (hc.). — ISBN 0-582-04047-7 (pbk.)
1. Alfred, King of England, 849-899.   2. Anglo-Saxons—England—
Wessex—Kings and rulers—Biography.   3. Great Britain—Kings and
rulers—Biography.   4. Great Britain—History—Alfred, 871–899.
5. Military history, Medieval.   6. Civilization, Medieval.
I. Title.   II. Series.
DA153.A2   1998
942.01′64′092—dc21   98–20930
CIP

Set by 35 in 11/12 pt Baskerville
Produced by Pearson Education Asia Pte Ltd
Printed in Singapore (JBW)

5   4   3   2
04 03 02 01 00

TO MY MOTHER AND FATHER, BLANCHE AND
MILTON ABELS, WITH LOVE AND DEVOTION

CONTENTS

GENEALOGICAL TABLE, MAPS AND FIGURES

ABBREVIATIONS

AB	*Annals of St-Bertin* [cited by year]. F. Grat, J. Vielliard and S. Clémencet, eds (Paris, 1964); J. Nelson, trans., *Ninth-Century Histories: the Annals of St-Bertin* (Manchester, 1991)
Æthelweard, *Chronicon*	Æthelweard, *Chronicon*, ed. A. Campbell (Oxford, 1962)
Alfred 4 § 2	Alfred's law code [cited by chapter and section]. Ed. F. Liebermann, *Die Gesetze der Angelsachsen*, vol. 1 (Halle, 1903)
Alfred's Boethius, ed. Sedgefield trans. Sedgefield	*King Alfred's Old English Version of Boethius De Consolatione Philosophiae,* ed. W.J. Sedgefield (Oxford, 1899) *King Alfred's Version of the Consolations of Boethius Done into Modern English, with an Introduction,* trans. W.J. Sedgefield (Oxford, 1900)
Alfred's Pastoral Care, ed. Sweet	*King Alfred's West Saxon Version of Gregory's Pastoral Care,* ed. and trans., H. Sweet, 2 vols, Early English Text Society, Original Series 45 & 50 (London, 1871–72)
Alfred's Soliloquies, ed. Carnicelli	*King Alfred's Version of St. Augustine's* Soliloquies, ed. T.A. Carnicelli (Cambridge, MA, 1969).

trans. Hargrove	*King Alfred's Old English Version of St. Augustine's* Soliloquies *Turned into Modern English,* trans. H.L. Hargrove (New York, 1904)
ASC	*Anglo-Saxon Chronicle* [cited by year]. D.N. Dumville and S.D. Keynes, gen. eds, *The Anglo-Saxon Chronicle: A Collaborative Edition,* 23 vols (Cambridge, 1983–). Trans. in *EHD* I.
ASE	*Anglo-Saxon England* [periodical], (Cambridge, 1972–)
Asser	Asser's *Life of King Alfred* [cited by chapter]. Trans. S.D. Keynes and M. Lapidge
BCS	W. de G. Birch, ed., *Cartularium Saxonicum* (London, 1885–93) [cited by charter number]
EHD I	*English Historical Documents, vol. I: c. 500–1042,* ed. D. Whitelock, 2nd edn (London, 1979) [cited by number and page]
EHR	*English Historical Review*
Harmer, ed., *SEHD*	F.E. Harmer, ed., *Select English Historical Documents of the Ninth and Tenth Centuries* (Cambridge, 1914)
HE	Bede, *Ecclesiastical History of the English People* [cited by book and chapter]. B. Colgrave and R.A.B. Mynors, eds (Oxford, 1969)
Keynes and Lapidge	*Alfred the Great: Asser's Life of King Alfred and Other Contemporary Sources,* trans. with an introduction and notes by S.D. Keynes and M. Lapidge (London, 1983).
MGH: SRG; Capit	*Monumenta Germaniae Historica: Scriptores rerum germanicarum in*

	usum scholarum; Capitularia regum Francorum
Old English Orosius, ed. Bately	*The Old English Orosius,* ed. J. Bately, The Early English Text Society, Supplementary Series, 6 (London, 1980)
Plummer, *Chronicles*	C. Plummer, *Two of the Saxon Chronicles Parallel,* 2 vols (Oxford, 1892–9; repr. 1952)
S	P.H. Sawyer, *Anglo-Saxon Charters: An Annotated List and Bibliography* (London, 1968) [cited by charter number]
Stevenson, *Asser's Life of King Alfred*	W.H. Stevenson, ed., *Asser's Life of King Alfred together with the Annals of Saint Neots erroneously ascribed to Asser* (Oxford, 1904)
TRHS	*Transactions of the Royal Historical Society*

. . . . .

EDITOR'S PREFACE

The personality, career and achievements of Alfred, king of Wessex (871–899), have always been of central importance to historians of medieval England and Europe. Alfred's successful resistance to the vikings and his initiation of a process which seems to lead inexorably to the creation out of the debris of the viking raids of a single English kingdom have always identified his reign as a crucial turning point in British history. Not only this, his personality has been seen by many as containing elements of greatness. In particular, his patronage of culture and learning clearly indicates a man who was much more than an early medieval warrior, and whose behaviour was profoundly influenced by a great range of intellectual and moral influences.

Richard Abels's new treatment of the reign is timely and refreshing. There are now so many controversial problems of interpretation associated with the reign that a balanced and careful overview which takes them into account is a near necessity for the non-specialist. Among other things, the authenticity of the central source, the *Vita* attributed to Asser, is once more under discussion. Many of the most complex problems associated with the cultural renaissance are the subject of specialised articles which are difficult to access for student and general readers. Archaeological and numismatic evidence has added a great deal to the available *corpus* of knowledge. The continental context of Alfred's policy and achievement have been extensively analysed. It is one of the most powerful features of Professor Abels's book that he presents all these discussions with notable clarity, providing a careful commentary of them and his own considered views. Asser's *Vita Alfredi* is carefully rehabilitated as a crucial, contemporary source for the reign. Alfred himself emerges as an immensely capable man; on the one hand, a warrior and a pragmatist, with an acute and ruthless understanding of power, and on the other, a king with an increasing awareness of the moral and educational aspects of rule and an ability to recruit very capable churchmen to his cause. The patronage of culture and learning, in line with most modern thinking, is identified as a central aspect of kingship, and is provided in its full continental and Christian context. The portrayal of Alfred's personality is notably sensitive and searching. As Richard Abels admits in his conclusion, he perceives Alfred in terms which the Victorians once found appealing, a thinking soldier. But the assessment is also a thoroughly modern one, with an emphasis on dynastic politics, leadership, and the adroit presentation of policy to persuade his people to unite with him against the vikings. The book is also very much a study in *mentalité*, purposefully setting out to portray how Alfred understood the world around him and how he tried to make sense for himself and others of his personal history.

Richard Abels brings an extensive expertise in the interpretation of early medieval sources to his task. A scholar well known for his publications on warfare, military institutions and the statistical interpretation of Domesday Book, his *Alfred the Great* both builds on this background and displays a notably wide-ranging approach to all types of available evidence. This book is an extremely welcome addition to the Medieval World series. It presents a persuasive and original overview of one of the most important reigns of the medieval period, which will be exceptionally valuable. It also provides an exceptionally accessible insight into the complexities of early medieval kingship, politics and rule.

AUTHOR'S PREFACE

Thucydides observed that if the city of Sparta became deserted, so that only its temples and the foundations of its buildings remained, a visitor would find it difficult to believe the tales of Spartan glory and power. One would be equally hard pressed to appreciate the greatness of King Alfred of Wessex (871–899), on the basis of the physical artefacts that have survived from his time. A tour of 'King Alfred's Wessex' will disappoint a tourist expecting monumental remains and scenic ruins. The ditch and earthen rampart defences of Wareham and Wallingford still stand, though the former has been cut and recut over the ages and the latter is usually crowded with children on bicycles. They suggest the effort and expense that went into Alfred's creation of a network of fortified towns to defend his kingdom, but, frankly, seem primitive and slight compared to the massive Roman stone fortifications at Richborough Castle and Chester or the great stone castles of the High Middle Ages. The 'Alfred Jewel' in the Ashmolean Museum, with its gold, pear-shaped decorated frame, its cloisonné enamel design of a male figure, and its late Antique crystal, and the magnificent Fuller Brooch in the British Museum are lonely testimonials to the vanished craftsmanship of the age; their fame is due as much to their rarity as their artistic quality. Alfred is absent even from the towns and places most associated with him. His place of refuge at Athelney today is marked only by a working farm. The only indication that it ever had anything to do with Alfred is a small monument erected there in 1802. In his birthplace at Wantage, Oxfordshire, Alfred is represented only by Count Gleichen's statue, erected there in 1877, and by the King Alfred's Head pub nearby. Winchester, long regarded as

Alfred's 'capital' city, is equally frustrating to the Alfred-hunter. One can find some Anglo-Saxon artefacts in the city museum, but Alfred's tracks have long since been eroded by time and human construction.

That is, until one climbs to the top of St Gilet's Hill and looks down over the town and realizes that the layout of Winchester's High Street still reflects the plans of Alfred's architects. Alfred is there, but hidden from sight. Like the buried foundations of a building, Alfred's influence underlies much of English history. His reign proved a watershed in England's political and cultural history. Alfred advanced the process of political consolidation and unification that would, two generations later, culminate in the creation of the kingdom of England. His success in fighting the vikings not only preserved Wessex from conquest but kept Britain from becoming an outlier of Scandinavia. His administrative and military innovations provided the tools with which his son and grandsons conquered the Danelaw and established a precocious royal administration that shaped the governance of medieval England. The spiritual and literary renaissance he spearheaded helped create a tradition of vernacular prose and learning that would blossom a century later in the works of men such as Wulfstan, Ælfric, and Byrhtferth. As Alfred remarked in an autobiographical aside he inserted in his translation of Boethius's *Consolation of Philosophy*, he desired to live a worthy life and to leave to posterity his memory in good works. This is precisely what he accomplished.

The scholarly debts I have incurred in writing this book are many. Simon Keynes, Patrick Wormald, Janet Nelson, D.R. Pratt and Robin Fleming not only read and commented upon various chapters of this book in manuscript but generously shared their own unpublished research. Their insights and criticisms forced me to rethink and clarify my ideas and caught many errors. (Of course, I alone am responsible for any that remain.) I also learned much from discussions and correspondence with Mark Blackburn, John Clarke, D.M. Metcalfe, Janet Bately, David Howlett, Bernard Bachrach, Stephen Morillo, Carroll Gillmor and Chris Lewis. The late Warren Hollister, who helped so many younger historians, was responsible for initiating my involvement with Longman's *Medieval World* series. There I benefited greatly from the thoughtful comments (and extraordinary patience in awaiting a finished manuscript) of the series editor, Professor David Bates, and the editorial director, Andrew MacLennan.

Mary DeCredico, David Appleby and Craig Symonds, colleagues in the history department of the United States Naval Academy, and Barbara Manvel of Nimitz Library read much of this book in manuscript. I am grateful not only for their helpful editorial and substantive suggestions but for their encouragement and friendship, as I also am to the other members of our history department's works-in-progress seminar, who kindly yet critically read and commented upon rough drafts of four separate chapters. The Naval Academy Research Council provided generous financial support for travel and research.

Major Jason Wilson (ret.), proprietor of the Wessex Bookstore in Westbury, showed kindness to a lost American visitor. When he learned that I was writing a biography of Alfred, he closed his shop and took me for an informative and stimulating tour of Bratton Camp, sharing local traditions concerning the battle of Edington. Major Wilson also introduced me to John Peddie, also a retired British infantry officer and himself the author of a fine study of Alfred's military campaigns. Mr Peddie graciously invited me into his home, where he and I spent an evening chatting about Alfred. His practical insights into the military challenges that faced Alfred and his identifications of the locales of battlefields helped shape my ideas on these subjects. Frederick Morgan, the owner of Athelney Farm, was kind enough to allow me to tramp through his fields and to view the ceramic and stone artefacts he has uncovered in the course of farming.

As with my first book, my greatest debt is to my family. My wife, Ellen, not only indexed the book, but read and critiqued every word, draft after draft. She suffered through my self-doubts and tolerated my obsession with a man who has been dead now for eleven centuries. She remains my best critic and my best friend. Without her support, forbearance, and patience I could not have written this book. My parents, Milton and Blanche, to whom this book is dedicated, also provided encouragement. My children, Paul and Rebecca, aged twelve and ten respectively, did not read or comment on the book, but they helped nonetheless by reminding me throughout about what is truly important in life.

ACKNOWLEDGEMENTS

The publishers would like to thank the following for permission to reproduce copyright material: Routledge for extracts from D. Whitelock (ed.), *English Historical Documents, Vol. 1* (London, 1995) and Dr Simon Keynes and Penguin Books for extracts from S. Keynes and M. Lapidge, *Alfred the Great: Asser's Life of Alfred and Other Contemporary Sources* (London, 1983).

Whilst every effort has been made to trace copyright holders, in a few cases it has proved impossible, and so we take this opportunity to offer our apologies to any copyright holders whose rights we may have unwittingly infringed.

INTRODUCTION

In the year 876 King Alfred tried to solve a problem that had plagued all Christian kings who had the misfortune to deal with pagan vikings: how could one force men who had no fear of damnation to fulfil their sacred oaths? His army was besieging a viking raiding party that had barricaded itself in the town of Wareham. He could not force his way in, and the vikings inside could not escape. The obvious solution was to obtain a pledge from the marauders to depart in exchange for safe passage out of the kingdom. Anglo-Saxon kings traditionally secured such agreements with an exchange of hostages and solemn oaths. Unfortunately, Alfred had learned through hard experience how lightly vikings regarded such oaths and how expendable hostages could be. He had to get these heathen raiders out of his kingdom, but how? If the Danes did not fear God and damnation, whom or what did they fear? Alfred chose a pragmatic and logical solution. Oaths upon Christian relics were obviously worthless. But if the vikings were made to swear upon their own 'holy ring', they might be bound to their word. The vikings in Wareham agreed and in a solemn ceremony swore to Alfred upon Thor's ring that they would quit his kingdom without further destruction. They exchanged hostages as a further guarantee and Alfred probably sweetened the deal with a gift of cash.

That night the Danes slaughtered the hostages Alfred had given them and stole out of Wareham under cover of dark. By the time Alfred realized what had happened, the raiders were riding as fast as their mounts could carry them into the West Country. Alfred pursued but could not overtake his treacherous enemy before they had seized and fortified Exeter. Fortunately for Alfred, in relocating their base

1

the Danes lost a large fleet off the coast of Swanage. Weakened by the loss of ships and men, the vikings were finally willing to negotiate a peace in earnest.

When Bishop Asser, Alfred's Welsh mass-priest and court scholar, came to relate these events seventeen years later, he faithfully followed the account given in the recently compiled *Anglo-Saxon Chronicle* with one small but interesting change. Where the Chronicler had proudly declared that the vikings had sworn to Alfred on 'the holy ring – a thing which they would not do before for any nation', Asser altered the text to read 'they took an oath on all the relics in which the king placed the greatest trust after God Himself'.[1] *His* 'Alfred', a Christian warrior-king waging a holy war against a heathen foe, would never have participated in or profited from a pagan ritual. The process of sanitizing Alfred's image had begun.

Hamo Thorneycroft's monumental statue of King Alfred looms over a row of parked cars in the middle of the Broad Way of Winchester, the busy thoroughfare at the foot of the town's High Street. The 2.7 metre bronze sculpture rests upon a one tonne granite pedestal of equal height. Alfred, his face etched with resolution, surveys the High Street of the city that the Victorians regarded as his capital. In his upraised right hand he grasps a large downward-turned sword by its blade a few centimetres below its guard, transforming it into a cross. Here we have the very model of a Christian warrior – and Englishman.

The unveiling of the Winchester statue on 20 September 1901 was the culmination of a millenary celebration in memory of 'Alfred the Good, Alfred the Truth teller, Alfred the father of his country, and of ours'.[2] The year for the commemoration had been established by a national committee of government officials, educators, and prelates, based upon the traditional, though erroneous, dating of Alfred's death. William H. Stevenson, a distinguished Anglo-Saxon historian who in 1904 would publish what is still the standard edition of Asser's *Life of King Alfred*, protested in a letter

1. *ASC* s.a. 876; Asser, ch. 49, trans. Keynes and Lapidge, p. 83.
2. Address by the Earl of Rosebery, in A. Bowker, *The King Alfred Millenary. A Record of the Proceedings of the National Commemoration* (London, 1902) p. 112.

to the *Athenæum* that Alfred had actually died in 899.[3] But Stevenson's reservations came too late to affect the preparations, which proceeded as planned.

Filled with naval and military parades, high-flown oratory, and music and poetry composed for the occasion, the commemoration was intended to be 'a striking patriotic manifestation marked by every circumstance and ceremony that could impress the popular mind'.[4] After a prayer by the Bishop of Winchester and a Chorus of Praise composed by G.B. Arnold, the organist of Winchester Cathedral, former Prime Minister Rosebery arose to address a cheering crowd:

> The noble statue which I am about to unveil can only be an effigy of the imagination, and so the Alfred we reverence may well be an idealised figure. For our real knowledge of him is scanty and vague. We have, however, draped round his form, not without reason, all the highest attributes of manhood and kingship. The Arthur of our poets, the paladin king, without fear, without stain, and without reproach, is to us the true representation of Alfred. In him, indeed, we venerate not so much a striking actor in our history as the ideal Englishman, the perfect sovereign, the pioneer of England's greatness.[5]

In this Rosebery echoed the judgement of Sir Walter Besant, best known for his panegyrics on Victorian progress, for whom Alfred represented 'the typical man of our race – call him Anglo-Saxon, call him American, call him Englishman, call him Australian – the typical man of our race at his best and noblest'.[6] The millenary celebration of Alfred had less to do with the historical personage – Rosebery in a toast at the luncheon following the unveiling freely admitted that his knowledge of Alfred was 'comparatively elementary as

---

3. Bowker, *The King Alfred Millenary*, p. 42. W.H. Stevenson, 'The date of King Alfred's death', *EHR* 13 (1898) pp. 71–7. The problem arose because of discrepancies and temporal dislocations in the numbering of the annals in the various recensions of the *Anglo-Saxon Chronicle* and a failure to recognize that, starting with the entries for the mid-ninth century, the chronicler(s) began the new year in September.

4. Ibid., p. 107.

5. Ibid., p. 109.

6. Bowker, *The King Alfred Millenary*, p. 9, quoted by C.A. Simmons, *Reversing the Conquest. History and Myth in Nineteenth-Century British Literature* (New Brunswick and London, 1990) p. 189.

regards facts'; indeed, he could not even 'stretch [his] tongue to pronounce with any familiarity the diphthong which learned men announce to the name of our familiar Alfred' – than with national self-congratulation on having developed into such a splendid nation and empire. As Rosebery put it, 'How is it that we have gone back a thousand years to find a great hero with whom we may associate something of English grandeur, and the origin of much that makes England powerful? Is it not the growing sense of British Empire, the increased feeling, not for bastard, but for real Imperialism?'[7] Alfred, the 'founder of the Royal Navy', was for Rosebery and his contemporaries not only the father of England but of the British Empire.

Another image of Alfred had been captured in stone a quarter of a century before by Count Gleichen, an artistically gifted cousin of Queen Victoria. His statue of Alfred, erected with much less fanfare in 1877, graces the Georgian town square of the king's birthplace, the Oxfordshire market town of Wantage in the Vale of the White Horse at the foot of the Berkshire Downs. In some ways this less well-known statue epitomizes the Victorian ideal of the king. Wantage's Alfred gazes into the distance just as resolutely as at Winchester, but here we find him clutching to his bosom with his left hand a scroll. His right hand rests upon the handle of a great war axe. The scroll represents Alfred the teacher and law-giver, the activities given pride of place on the statue's inscription:

> Alfred found learning dead, and he restored it. Education neglected, and he revived it. The laws powerless, and he gave them force. The Church debased, and he raised it. The land ravaged by a fearful enemy, from which he delivered it. Alfred's name shall live as long as mankind respects the past.

Gleichen's Alfred is a royal warrior-scholar, learned in studies, courageous in war and pious in all his actions. This image of Alfred informed Victorian biographies of the king, from the popular works of Thomas Hughes and Walter Besant to the scholarly endeavours of Beatrice Lees and Charles Plummer. Typical is Plummer's encomium for

7. Bowker, *The King Alfred Millenary*, pp. 126–7.

4

Alfred. After nearly two hundred pages of serious critical, and often sceptical, scholarship concerning Alfred's life and works, Plummer concludes his work by comparing his hero to 'Marcus Aurelius, the imperial saint of paganism, Louis IX, the royal saint of mediaevalism, Charles the Great, and our own Edward I'.[8] Of these, only St Louis approaches Alfred in his perfection of character and accomplishments, and even he is found wanting, his very saintliness having 'shed a consecration on an evil despotism, which finally exploded in one of the most hideous convulsions in history'. Alfred, on the other hand, was 'one of the very few rulers whose work in life, and whose memory after death have been, as far as may be said of anything here below, an unmixed blessing to their peoples'.[9] For the great Whig historian of the Norman Conquest, E.A. Freeman, Alfred was simply 'the most perfect character in history'.[10]

The Victorian cult of Alfred flourished because men like Besant and Plummer understood Alfred to be the First Englishman, the founder of the Navy, the Empire and British greatness. He was a reminder that the blood that flowed in Prince Albert's veins was the same as that of his bride, that all the Anglo-Saxon races shared a common ancestry and destiny. Though Alfred had lived a thousand years before, he was relevant, if not as a historical personage, at least as a type. But times change. The Christian heroism that Alfred embodied for the Victorians – patriotic, honest, stubbornly resolute but tinged with humility – has gone out of fashion in our more cynical and knowing age. The British Empire has long since entered its autumn, and attitudes and assumptions about imperialism, nationality, and race have changed. As one recent author put it, 'The Alfred Memorial still dominates Winchester, but perhaps less as a commemoration of the ninth-century king than as a relic of the nineteenth-century imperial dream.'[11] When I undertook my own

8. C. Plummer, *The Life and Times of Alfred the Great* (Oxford, 1902) p. 200.
9. Ibid., p. 202.
10. E.A. Freeman, *The Norman Conquest of England*, 5 vols and index, 3rd edn (Oxford, 1877) p. 49; cited by J. Campbell, 'Asser's *Life of Alfred*', in C. Holdsworth and T.P. Wiseman, eds, *The Inheritance of Historiography, 350–900* (Exeter, 1986) p. 133 n. 90.
11. Simmons, *Reversing the Conquest*, p. 191.

'Alfred pilgrimage' in 1989, visiting the various sites associated with Alfred, I quickly discovered that for the average
English person the name Alfred evokes little more than a
vague memory of burnt cakes. He has become the property
of academic historians and literary scholars rather than
popular essayists.

Nothing better illustrates changing sensibilities than a
controversy that arose over a third statue of Alfred. This
one has stood since 1990 in Alfred University in Alfred,
New York. The comparatively modest 1.7 metre figure stands
on a 2.7 metre base in the centre of the main quadrangle of
the University. Like the Winchester statue, the king stands
with his left hand resting on a shield. He holds in his right
hand an open book engraved with the motto, '*Fiat lux*' ('Let
there be light'). This clean-shaven, youngish Alfred wears
what looks like Roman armour decorated with designs inspired by the Book of Kells and the Sutton Hoo ship burial.
His shield rests upon the ground to indicate stability and his
sheathed sword points downward to symbolize 'peace with
strength'.[12] For the sculptor, William Underhill, Alfred was
a convenient subject for a project that he had had in mind
since the early 1980s, to create a traditional statue of a heroic
figure.[13] What it became was the subject of intense debate
within the campus community. A number of the faculty and
students questioned the desirability of representing the
school with the image of a 'Dead White European Male',
even one so closely associated with education and cultural
revival. As Dr Linda Mitchell, a professor of medieval studies
at the university, observed, 'If the university is claiming a
dedication to diversity it would be foolish to choose a symbol
so exclusive and effective in emphasizing the straight white
male power structure of history.'[14]

There may not be as much distance between Rosebery's
eulogy of Alfred and the criticism of Alfred as a 'D.W.E.M'
as one might at first think. The Alfred University protest, as
even the most ardent opponents admitted, had less to do with
a historical personage than with what Alfred symbolized.

12. Description from Alfred University website (www.alfred.edu/campus/
   kingtxt.html).
13. Personal communication from Professor Underhill.
14. *New York Times*, Campus Life Sunday Supplement, 15 December 1991,
   p. 69.

Rosebery's ideal Englishman has come under attack for being an ideal English man. In the eleven centuries since Asser and the authors of the *Anglo-Saxon Chronicle* began the process, each age has defined Alfred in its own terms. The Victorian portrayal of 'good, kindly, earnest Alfred' says more about late nineteenth-century ideals than it does about the man himself. The same, of course, is true of the depiction of Alfred as a 'Dead White European Male'. Over the centuries, Alfred has been portrayed as a royal Job, meekly accepting reproof from a peeved peasant woman for allowing her cakes to burn; as a forerunner of Elizabethan Protestantism; as the author of Tudor and Stuart royalist policies; as the father of the English constitution and champion of English liberty against the oppression of tyrants; as the founder of both the Royal Navy and of Oxford University; and, in myriad plays and poems – most of them dreadful – as the epitome of British patriotism.[15] To recover a portrait of the historical Alfred one must remove many layers of weathered varnish accumulated over centuries of myth-making, beginning with Alfred's own attempt to shape his story.

The effort is worthwhile, for the real Alfred was a far more interesting character than the paragon of traditional accounts. He was a hero, to be sure, but a hero of the Dark Ages, closer in spirit to Charles Martel and Charlemagne than to Plummer's ideal Englishman. He was certainly pious, but he was also practical, willing to use pagan rituals to get his way if he had to, and capable of snatching land from the Church if it would help the defence of his kingdom. He may not have fathered the 'English nation', but he did begin a process that was to culminate in the creation of the kingdom of England two generations later, even though he himself little realized what the outcome would be. Pragmatic, flexible, innovative, and at times brutal, he did whatever was necessary to save his kingdom, please his God, and advance his blood-line.

To understand Alfred and his policies as king, it is necessary to appreciate how tenuous his hold on the monarchy was in the early years of his reign. In a sense, the kingdom that was to be known as 'England' was forged in the furnace

---

15. Simmons, *Reversing the Conquest*, pp. 25–41; L.W. Miles, *King Alfred in Literature* (Baltimore, 1902); Keynes and Lapidge, pp. 44–8, 197–202.

of the viking invasions; certainly, Alfred's kingship was tempered and strengthened by it. Eighth-century England had been dotted with petty tribal kingdoms. The viking invasions changed all that. By 879 the vikings had extinguished all native English dynasties except for the West Saxon House of Cerdic. To survive, Alfred had to strengthen the defences of his kingdom, and this meant not only building fortresses and ships but also developing a powerful new ideology of kingship that would bind the West Saxon nobility more closely to him.

But that was not in itself sufficient. To be *worthy* of survival, Alfred believed it necessary to rededicate himself and his people to God. The vikings, for Alfred, were not merely human predators, but a scourge sent by God to recall His wayward people. In diagnosing the moral failings of his contemporaries, Alfred focused upon their indifference to the pursuit of wisdom, which he contrasted with their pious forefathers' love of learning. 'Remember', Alfred wrote, 'what punishments befell us in the world when we ourselves did not cherish learning nor transmit it to other men. We were Christians in name alone, and very few of us possessed Christian virtues.'[16] No people could flourish without God's favour. The vikings had come in response to the moral and spiritual failures of the English. Alfred was determined to restore his kingdom to what he believed it had once been, a place of learning and religious devotion, ruled by kings who 'obeyed God and his messengers; and preserved peace, morality and authority at home, and at the same time enlarged their territory abroad'.[17] He was determined to succeed in both warfare and wisdom. Indeed, for him the two went hand in hand. For these reasons, Alfred sponsored an ambitious literary, cultural and spiritual revival based on the translation of key Latin texts into the vernacular. In doing so, Alfred demonstrated a talent for scholarship as well as law. He himself rendered the first fifty Psalms and works by Gregory the Great, Boethius, and Augustine into English, often glossing the texts with his own insights. Alfred became the only English king to write a book before James I in the early seventeenth

---

16. *Alfred's Pastoral Care*, ed. Sweet, p. 4; trans. Keynes and Lapidge, p. 125.
17. *Alfred's Pastoral Care*, ed. Sweet, Prose Preface, p. 1.

century. He has as great a claim to be considered the father of English prose literature as of the English nation.

The boroughs and ships he built, the texts he chose to translate and disseminate, the chronicle he sponsored, and the great law code he issued were all meant to aid King Alfred in his efforts to defend his realm, extend its borders, and make him and his people worthy of God's grace. The measure of Alfred's success is that by his death he was no longer merely 'king of the West Saxons' but 'king of the Anglo-Saxons'. What Alfred sowed was to be reaped by his son Edward, and his grandsons, Æthelstan, Edmund, and Eadred. Alfred did not merely preserve the kingdom of Wessex; he transformed it.

. . .

SOURCES

The sculptors of Alfred faced the challenge of depicting a man of whose physical appearance they had not the least knowledge. Their 'Alfreds' were ideal images, much as were the classically proportioned Greek gods and human athletes fashioned by Phidias and Praxiteles. The only contemporary 'portraits' of Alfred that have survived (or that probably ever existed) are 'his' visage on coins, crude and stereotyped imitations of the imperial portraits on Roman exemplars. This sufficed. They represented the king's power, which is what mattered. That we do not know what Alfred looked like is perhaps not important, but it does underscore the difficulties of writing a biography of even a famous ninth-century man. Biographers of early medieval men and women must make do without many of the tools of the trade, memoirs, diaries, private correspondence and the like. The endeavour is much like trying to reconstruct a mosaic from shattered and scattered fragments. Fortunately, the evidence for Alfred's reign is unusually rich for a person of his times. Not only do we possess a biography of the king by a clerical member of his household, Asser, and a contemporary chronicle of the events of his reign, the so-called *Anglo-Saxon Chronicle*, but also a number of works that were either written by Alfred himself or, at least, issued in his name: a will, a law code, a few charters, and, most remarkably, English translations of the first fifty Psalms and Latin works by Pope Gregory the Great, Boethius, St Augustine. Scattered through these translations are personal additions and asides that open a window on to the world-view of the man.

For most historians, the starting point for understanding Alfred has been Asser's *The Life of King Alfred (Vita Ælfredi regis Angul Saxonum)*, written in 893 at a time when Alfred was fighting off a second viking invasion of his kingdom.[18] Much of what we know about Asser comes from autobiographical asides in the *Life*. He was 'raised, educated, tonsured and, eventually, ordained' at St David's, a monastery in Dyfed in the farthest reaches of southwestern Wales. A kinsman of a bishop of St David's – the Welsh church at the time, like that of Ireland, was organized along monastic rather than Roman diocesan lines – Asser himself may have been the monastery's bishop in 885 when King Alfred first summoned him to his court.[19] Alfred was then in the process of gathering a coterie of international scholars to help him implement an ambitious programme of spiritual and educational renewal. With the approval of his fellow monks, Asser agreed to serve in Alfred's household for six months in each year. As presented by Asser, this arrangement was to benefit both parties: the monks were to gain a powerful lay protector against the depredations of the king of Dyfed, who had recently submitted to Alfred's lordship, and Alfred was to profit from 'the learning of St David' in the person of Asser. Alfred also made it clear to the Welshman that he would find the king a most generous patron. Over the next few years, King Alfred bestowed upon Asser two monasteries in Somerset, Banwell and Congresbury, and, some time later, a far larger monastery in Exeter with its various dependencies in Cornwall and Devonshire. Sometime between 892 and 900, Asser succeeded Bishop Wulfsige in the see of

18. Asser, ch. 91; the date may be calculated from Asser's statements that Alfred was born in 849 and was in his 'forty-fifth year' at the time of composition; trans. Keynes and Lapidge, pp. 269–70, n. 218.
19. Ibid., ch. 79. Alfred calls Asser his bishop in the preface to his translation of *Pastoral Care*, though Asser was not yet bishop of Sherborne. It is possible that Asser served as a suffragan bishop at Exeter under Bishop Wulfsige, but it is more likely that Asser's episcopal office was in Wales. In ch. 79 of the *Life*, Asser associates himself with the bishops of St David's expelled by King Hyfaidd of Dyfed in disputes with the monastery over jurisdiction.

Sherborne. He survived into the reign of Alfred's son, Edward the Elder, and died in 908 or 909.

Asser earned his rewards through pedagogical and scholarly service. He read to the king from the Bible and other salutary Latin works, and explored with him their hidden meanings and subtleties. In doing so, he helped Alfred acquire the competency in Latin that enabled the king to translate these works into his native tongue. In his prose 'Preface' to his translation of Pope Gregory the Great's *Liber Regulae Pastoralis* Alfred credited Asser, along with the Mercian Plegmund, archbishop of Canterbury, and the mass-priests John the Old Saxon and the Frank Grimbald, with aiding him in the work. The historian William of Malmesbury, writing in the twelfth century, believed that Asser also had a hand in Alfred's translation of Boethius, and he may have been right.

If Alfred rewarded Asser with ecclesiastical offices and land, Asser answered the king's generosity with loyalty and love. The *Life of King Alfred* was a manifestation of this love. Asser's *Life of King Alfred* is an authentic and invaluable source, but it is also a problematic text that must be used critically.[20] No medieval manuscript, let alone a contemporary copy, survives and we must content ourselves with reconstructions based upon early modern transcripts of a lost manuscript. The *Life*'s loose organization, repetitions, inconsistent use of verb tenses, and lack of conclusion suggest a work in progress rather than a polished text, and what we call the *Life of King Alfred* may be no more than an imperfect copy of an incomplete draft.[21] The *Life* is not an easy read, at least in its original Latin. Like other ninth- and tenth-century Insular writers, Asser wrote in a florid style designed to display the author's erudition; the meaning of a passage

20. On the question of authenticity, see Appendix.
21. See Stevenson, *Asser's Life of King Alfred*, p. cxxxi; M. Schütt, 'The Literary Form of Asser's *Vita Alfredi*', *EHR* 62 (1957) pp. 209–20, esp. 210; Keynes and Lapidge, p. 56; Campbell, 'Asser's Life', p. 115. D.P. Kirby explains perceived discrepancies in the *Life* as the result of an imperfect conflation of separate compositions dating from between 885 and 893 ('Asser and his Life of Alfred', *Celtica Studia* 6 (1971) pp. 12–35). D. Howlett, on the other hand, argues that Asser's work reveals a sophisticated underlying structure relating to what he calls 'Biblical Style' (*The Celtic Tradition of Biblical Style* (Blackrock, 1995) pp. 273–333).

is sometimes 'obscured by a cloud of verbiage'.[22] But the greatest stumbling block is the nature of the work itself. The *Life of King Alfred* is not a biography in the modern sense. Asser did not strive for historical accuracy and objectivity. Rather, like Einhard's *Life of Charlemagne*, upon which it drew,[23] the *Life* was meant to be an encomium, a celebration of Alfred's greatness for the edification of its multiple audiences: the monks of St David's, the royal court, the king's sons, and, not least, Alfred himself, to whom the work was dedicated.[24] Like Einhard's 'Charlemagne', Asser's 'Alfred' is a model ninth-century Christian king: a lover of wisdom, truthful, patient, munificent in gift-giving, just, a defender of the poor and weak, incomparably affable, intimate with his friends, faithful to his God, and, to top it all off, a victorious warrior in a holy war.[25] Early medieval writers were inveterate plagiarists. Asser 'borrowed', Aldhelm from Einhard and Bede, and it is possible that he shaped his Alfred along the lines of Einhard's presentation of Charlemagne, just as Einhard modelled his Charlemagne on Suetonius's Augustus. Even Asser's personal reminiscences may have been influenced by a desire to follow a model. His reluctance to join Alfred's court without the permission of his people and the gifts that Alfred gave him recall Alcuin's entry into Charlemagne's service as recounted in the anonymous Frankish *Life of Alcuin*, a comparison flattering to both author and patron.[26] But one can take scepticism too far. The details

22. Stevenson, *Asser's Life*, p. lxxxix.
23. Asser, ch. 73, trans. Keynes and Lapidge, p. 88; Stevenson, *Asser's Life of King Alfred*, pp. 54, 294. Cf. *Eginhard, Vie de Charlemagne*, ed. L. Halphen, 4th edn, Les classiques de l'histoire de France au moyen âge (Paris, 1967) p. 2.
24. Campbell, 'Asser's Life', pp. 122–5; A. Scharer, 'The writing of history at King Alfred's court', *Early Medieval Europe* 5 (1996) 185–206. Cf. Kirby, 'Asser and his Life of King Alfred', pp. 12–35, Keynes and Lapidge, p. 56, and S.D. Keynes, 'King Alfred and the Mercians', in M.A.S. Blackburn and D.N. Dumville, eds, *Kings, Currency, and Alliances: The History and Coinage of Southern England, AD 840–900* (Woodbridge, forthcoming), who argue for a principally Welsh audience.
25. Asser, chs 13, 42, 76, 80, 81, 88, 91, 99–106. See Scharer, 'The writing of history', pp. 194–9.
26. Keynes and Lapidge, p. 265, n. 195. Cf. A.P. Smyth, *King Alfred the Great* (Oxford, 1995) pp. 225–7.

Asser provides are not derived from Continental sources, and there is no real reason to doubt that they substantially represent the truth as Asser knew it.

Though historical accuracy is of paramount concern to modern historians, it may have been less critical to Asser and his audience. As with Eusebius and Bede, Asser's truth was moral rather than empirical. Underlying his 'Alfred' were biblical examplars of virtuous kingship, Solomon in particular, Carolingian mirrors for princes, and the teachings and personal example of Pope Gregory the Great.[27] Even Alfred's weaknesses, a carnal nature against which he struggled and lifelong bouts with illness, are presented so as to reflect credit upon Alfred. The king's haemorrhoids become a divine gift, a scourge of God intended to strengthen his devotion to chastity. When Alfred prays for a less agonizing and visible condition that would still temper his carnal lusts, he is miraculously cured, only to be visited by another God-given ailment years later on his wedding night.[28] Asser's intention was not to remake Alfred into a saint, but to glorify him as a Christian king without blemish, a lord who deserved love and obedience. This was how Alfred himself wished to be perceived. Although Asser used Carolingian models, much of what he added to the *Life* came from his own knowledge of Alfred and the court. He repeated the king's favourite stories, such as the tale of the wicked Queen Eadburh and how she came to a wretched end, and wrote of Alfred's love of learning and methods of governance from first-hand experience. Asser was an image-maker, to be sure, but the image he devised came ultimately from Alfred himself.

Asser's *Life of King Alfred* belongs to what was then a recent genre, which combined chronicle history with anecdotal biography. Though Asser's debt to Einhard is made obvious through quotation, his work is actually closer in structure and content to two other early ninth-century Frankish historical

---

27. J.M. Wallace-Hadrill, *Early Germanic Kingship in England and on the Continent* (Oxford, 1971) p. 141, and, much more fully, Scharer, 'The writing of history', pp. 188–200. Scharer emphasizes Asser's debt to Sedulius's *Liber de rectoribus Christianis*, a mirror for princes composed for King Charles the Bald around 870.
28. Asser, ch. 74.

works, Thegan's and the Astronomer's 'lives' of the Frankish emperor Louis the Pious (814–840), both of which combine annalistic and biographical materials.[29] Asser used a number of historical texts in writing the *Life*. In addition to Einhard and perhaps Thegan and the Astronomer, Asser drew upon Bede's *Ecclesiastical History*, the early ninth-century Welsh *Historia Brittonum*, the anonymous *Life of Alcuin*, and the *Anglo-Saxon Chronicle*.[30] About half of Asser's *Life* is, in fact, a Latin translation of the *Anglo-Saxon Chronicle* for the years 851–887. The *Chronicle* served as a tailor's form upon which Asser could drape his stories and anecdotes. It enabled Asser to place Alfred within a historical context, so that his audience would appreciate Alfred's true greatness: his providential rise to the West Saxon kingship, his victories over a heathen enemy who had destroyed the kingdoms of his neighbours, his founding of a new kingdom of 'Angles' and 'Saxons', and (with a touch of hyperbole) his triumphant emergence as 'ruler (*rector*) of all the Christians of the island of Britain'.[31] Fortunately for Asser, the *Anglo-Saxon Chronicle*'s presentation of history was conducive to the biographer's purposes.

The *Anglo-Saxon Chronicle*, a work so important that Anglo-Saxon history would be virtually impossible to write without it, was a product of the vernacular literary renaissance fostered by Alfred. The *Chronicle* has come down to us in seven manuscript recensions, which scholars conventionally designate

29. D.A. Bullough, 'The educational tradition in England from Alfred to Aelfric: teaching *utrisque linguae*', *Settimane di studio del centro italiano di studi sull'alto medioevo* 19 (1972) pp. 453–94, reprinted in D.A. Bullough, *The Carolingian Renewal: Sources and Heritage* (Manchester, 1991) pp. 297–334, esp. pp. 297, 317–18, n. 3; Campbell, *Asser's Life*, pp. 118–19. Thegan, the Astronomer, and Asser also share the use of biblical quotations.
30. Asser's report that the eclipse of 878 occurred 'between nones and vespers, but nearer to nones', if not simply a trick of memory, must come from an east Frankish source, perhaps a set of annals from Fulda or the oral testimony of John the Old Saxon. Stevenson, *Asser's Life*, p. 285–6; cf. A.P. Smyth, 'The solar eclipse of Wednesday 29 October AD 878: ninth-century historical records and the findings of modern astronomy', in J. Roberts and J.L. Nelson with M. Godden, eds, *Alfred the Wise: Studies in Honour of Janet Bately on the Occasion of her Sixty-Fifth Birthday* (Cambridge, 1997) pp. 205–6.
31. Asser, dedication, ed. Stevenson, p. 1.

with the letters A–G.[32] None of these is the 'original'. The earliest, MS. A (also known as the 'Parker Chronicle'),[33] is a composite work by a number of different scribes, the earliest of whom wrote in the late ninth, or, more probably, the early tenth century. Even 'A' is at least twice removed from the original text of the *Chronicle.* The version that Asser used, which was closer in its variant readings to 'B', was itself no more than a copy of a copy. Study of the *Anglo-Saxon Chronicle* becomes immensely complicated when one considers the tenth- and eleventh-century histories of the manuscripts. Fortunately, matters are simpler for the annals relating to the ninth century and before. The main stock of the *Chronicle* down to 892 is substantially the same in all surviving manuscripts. Historians are in basic agreement that the original *Chronicle* extended to at least 890 and that the annals for 893 to 896, with their detailed war reporting, are an addition by a new author who wrote in 896 or very soon after.[34] The version of the *Chronicle* that Ealdorman

32. For general introductions to the *Anglo-Saxon Chronicle,* see D. Whitelock, 'The Anglo-Saxon Chronicle', in *EHD* I, pp. 109–25; Keynes and Lapidge, pp. 275–81; Smyth, *King Alfred the Great,* pp. 455–64. The notes to C. Plummer's *Two of the Saxon Chronicles Parallel* (1899) remain of utmost value, though *The Anglo-Saxon Chronicle, A Collaborative Edition,* gen. eds D.N. Dumville and S.D. Keynes (Cambridge, 1983–) has now superseded it as an edition.

33. After Matthew Parker, Archbishop of Canterbury (1559–75), its one-time owner, the manuscript is now at Corpus Christi College, Cambridge, MS. 173. For studies of MS. A, see *The Anglo-Saxon Chronicle: A Collaborative Edition,* gen. eds D.N. Dumville and S.D. Keynes, *Vol 3: MS. A,* ed. J.M. Bately (Cambridge, 1986) pp. xiii–lxxi; D.N. Dumville, 'The Anglo-Saxon Chronicle and the Origins of English Square Minuscule Script', in his *Wessex and England from Alfred to Edgar: Six Essays on Political, Cultural, and Ecclesiastical Revival* (Woodbridge, Suffolk, 1992) pp. 55–139.

34. Whether it went down to 891 or 892 is still a matter of debate. Janet Bately's analysis of the *Chronicle's* language and syntax suggests a common stock of multiple authorship down to 890, with the first Alfredian compilation ending in the closing years of the 870s. J. Bately, 'The compilation of the Anglo-Saxon Chronicle 60 BC to AD 890: vocabulary as evidence', *Proceedings of the British Academy* 64 (1978) pp. 93–129; idem, 'The compilation of the Anglo-Saxon Chronicle once more', *Leeds Studies in English* 16 (1985) pp. 7–26. That MS. A changed scribes in the middle of the annal for 891, after the first scribe apparently believed that he had completed that entry, might suggest that the 'original' ended there. The claim for 892 is based on

Æthelweard translated into Latin in the 980s contained a different set of annals for the last years of Alfred's reign. As these emphasize the roles played by Alfred's son, Edward, and his son-in-law, Ealdorman Æthelred, in securing the victory (at the expense of Alfred), it is possible that they derive from a lost extension of the 'basic' *Chronicle* composed in the early years of Edward the Elder's reign.[35]

Who wrote the *Anglo-Saxon Chronicle* and why remain open questions. Much depends upon how one answers them. The central controversy has revolved around the role, if any, of Alfred and his court in the compilation of the *Chronicle* and whether it was intended as 'propaganda' for Alfred and his house. A century ago it was widely believed that Alfred himself had a hand in the composition of the *Anglo-Saxon Chronicle*. The careful lexical studies of Janet Bately have proved otherwise.[36] Sir Frank Stenton, on the other hand, thought the *Chronicle* to be a private compilation originating in the southwestern shires, perhaps at the behest of one of Alfred's ealdormen.[37] The arguments for the private origins of the *Anglo-Saxon Chronicle* are less persuasive than the view that it was a product of Alfred's court.[38] Not only does the latter account better for the early distribution of the work (and its use by Asser), but it makes good sense in terms of its content. For the *Chronicle* is less a history of the English peoples than of the rise of Wessex and the house of Alfred. Cobbled together from earlier annals, regnal and episcopal

---

the fact that all extant recensions contain the annal for that year. It has also been suggested that the Chronicler's interest in the movement of viking armies on the Continent in the 880s is best explained by his knowledge that they would return to England in 892. See Keynes and Lapidge, pp. 278–9; Dumville, 'The Anglo-Saxon Chronicle', pp. 89–90.

35. Keynes and Lapidge, p. 189. Smyth, *King Alfred the Great*, p. 492.
36. Plummer, *Two Saxon Chronicles*, II, p. civ, cvi–cviii. Cf. Bately, 'Vocabulary', pp. 116–29.
37. F.M. Stenton, 'The south-western element in the Old English Chronicle', *Preparatory to Anglo-Saxon England*, ed. D.M. Stenton (Oxford, 1970) pp. 106–15; idem, *Anglo-Saxon England*, 3rd edn (Oxford, 1971) pp. 692–3; D. Whitelock, *EHD* I, pp. 123–4.
38. C. Plummer, *Life and Times of Alfred the Great*, pp. 11–12; R.H.C. Davis, 'Alfred the Great: propaganda and truth', *History* 56 (1971) pp. 169–82, repr. in his *From Alfred the Great to Stephen* (London, 1991) pp. 33–46. Cf. Keynes and Lapidge, pp. 40–1.

lists, genealogies, records of eclipses, the works of Bede, Isidore, and Jerome, and various other materials, the *Chronicle* retells in secular terms and from a distinctly West Saxon viewpoint the story that Bede began about the growth of unity among the tribes and peoples of England. As commentators have observed, the *Chronicle* begins with parallel histories of the major kingdoms and gradually focuses more and more upon Wessex, culminating in Egbert's defeat of the Mercians and Alfred's holy war against the heathen vikings. The reigns of Alfred's grandfather, Egbert, and father, Æthelwulf, are treated more fully than those of their predecessors. The Chronicler celebrates Egbert's victories, which foreshadow Alfred's own, by adding him to Bede's list of kings who had enjoyed hegemony in England.[39] The *Chronicle*'s detailed reporting of Alfred's campaigns against the vikings contrasts starkly with the often laconic manner in which it had recorded the Great Heathen Army's conquests of Wessex's neighbours. The narrative is constructed to place Alfred in the best light possible. This section of the *Chronicle* reaches a climax in the elaborate annal for 878, which leads the reader from the despair of Alfred's flight into the fen-fastness of Somerset to his triumph at Edington and its fruit, the conversion and baptism of the Danish King Guthrum with his leading men at Aller and Wedmore. The entries for the 880s, with the exception of the critical annal of 886 telling of Alfred's reoccupation of London, read like a denouement; they deal mostly with the movements of viking armies on the Continent, apparently in the knowledge that the vikings would return to England in 892.

Whether this constitutes 'propaganda' depends upon what one means by that term. A clear theme emerges from the *Chronicle*'s account of political and military developments among the 'English' peoples in the British Isles, that Alfred's reign was the culmination of English history. To impress this upon his readers, the Chronicler slighted the achievements of the great eighth-century Mercian kings in imposing their hegemony over much of southern Britain. The triumphs of Alfred's grandfather and father, on the other hand, are trumpeted, and the legitimacy of their rule

---

39. *ASC* s.a. 829. For parallels between Egbert and Alfred, see Scharer, 'Writing of history', p. 181.

underscored by the inclusion of Æthelwulf's genealogy in the annal for 855/858. (The West Saxon genealogical regnal list that serves as a prologue to MS. A makes the same point in relationship to Alfred, concluding as it does with Alfred's accession after 'twenty-three years of his life were passed, and 396 years from when his race first conquered the land of the West Saxons from the Britons'.) The Chronicler's treatment of members of the house of Egbert, however, was not even-handed. Alfred's brothers are given short shrift so that Alfred should appear all the greater. The Chronicler's focus upon Alfred, emphasis upon loyalty to lords, and insistence upon the legitimacy of Alfred's authority suggest an apologia for the political status quo of the early 890s. The practical purpose of the *Chronicle* may have been to persuade its audience to fulfil new and onerous burdens laid upon them as a war necessity. The dramatic account of Alfred's flight into the Somerset marshes and the obsessive tracking of the depredations of the vikings on the Continent in the 880s served to remind Alfred's subjects how close they had come to viking rule and how much danger still remained. Alfred was a king who lacked, for the most part, the means of coercion. To get his way he had to persuade and cajole his nobles and officials. The *Chronicle* may have been one tool of persuasion.[40]

The *Chronicle* presents other, more mundane, problems for those who would use it as a framework for Anglo-Saxon chronology. All surviving manuscripts (except for the excerpts included in the early twelfth-century 'Annals of St Neots') suffer from a dislocation of two or, in some cases, three years between 756 and 845. Given the conditions of composition, it is understandable how a compiler might place an entry in the wrong year, or how a scribe might overlook a blank annal in the manuscript from which he was copying.[41] To minimize confusion, all citations are to the corrected dates as determined by Dorothy Whitelock. Even the 'correct' dates can be a bit misleading. The chroniclers began their annals with Christmas until 851, when they shifted to an autumn new year, in accordance, perhaps, with the Caesarian Indiction, 24 September. The change reflects

---

40. Davis, 'Propaganda', p. 182.
41. Whitelock, *EHD*, I, pp. 124–5.

the military preoccupation of the writers, who seem to have been 'thinking in terms of a campaigning year rather than a calendar year'.[42] As a result, Alfred's death, which occurred on 26 October 899, is recorded in the annal for 900.

Alfred's own writings afford unique insight into the mind of the king, but they are no less problematic a source than Asser's *Life* or the *Chronicle*. The scholarly consensus is that Alfred personally translated Gregory the Great's *Pastoral Care*, Boethius's *The Consolation of Philosophy*, St Augustine's *Soliloquies*, and the first fifty Psalms of the *Paris Psalter*. The attribution for the first two is based on Alfred's own claim to authorship in prefaces he wrote to these works, and the vocabulary and syntax of the latter two make it likely that they were composed by the same man responsible for the Old English *Pastoral Care*.[43] Alfred was also responsible for the issuance of a law code and a brief preface to Bishop Wærferth's translation of the *Dialogues* of Gregory the Great, undertaken at his behest. Other late ninth-century texts once attributed to Alfred – the Old English translations of the histories of Orosius and of Bede – have been purged from the canon on the basis of syntax and language, although, along with the *Anglo-Saxon Chronicle* and Gregory's *Dialogues*, they may have been inspired by Alfred's programme to revive learning through vernacular translation of Latin works 'most necessary for all men to know'.[44]

Alfred's writings are what allows one to write a biography of the man rather than a mere history of his times. His law code, with its elaborate literary preface that in itself is a treatise on divine and human law, provides a glimpse into Alfred's own understanding of the nature of his authority and the duties of kingship. The translations, at first glance less promising material, are filled with what appear to be personal asides and additions. The temptation is to read

42. K. Harrison, *The Framework of Anglo-Saxon History to AD 900* (Cambridge, 1976) pp. 117–18.
43. A.J. Frantzen, *King Alfred* (Boston, 1986) pp. 7–10; J. Bately, 'Lexical evidence for the authorship of the Prose Psalms in the Paris Psalter', *ASE* 10 (1982) pp. 69–95.
44. *Alfred's Pastoral Care*, ed. Sweet, p. 7. Keynes and Lapidge, p. 33, and Smyth, *King Alfred the Great*, pp. 529–30, point out that the histories of Orosius and Bede and the *Anglo-Saxon Chronicle* complement one another and together 'form a coherent body of historical writing' (Smyth).

them as expressions of the king's innermost thoughts and feelings, which is perhaps not unreasonable. Yet our expectations of personal revelation must be tempered by awareness that differences between a Latin text and its translation can be accounted for in many ways. We do not know, for instance, whether the manuscripts from which Alfred made his translations are the 'standard' texts of the works that we have today. Nor do we know whether he used glosses, and if he did, what they contained. And then there is the problem of what 'authorship' meant in the communal world of early medieval scholarship. Alfred himself in the prose preface to the *Pastoral Care* credited Asser and other court scholars with helping him render Gregory's treatise 'sometimes word for word, sometimes sense for sense'. The coherency of style that enables us to identify Alfred's authentic writings also permits us to believe that what we have are Alfred's own dictated words, but which insights were his and which were suggested by his helpers cannot be known. Still, there is a consistency of thought that flows through these texts, the sense of a single mind at work, and whether or not Alfred was being taught the meaning of the texts as he 'translated' them, from what one knows of the man it is unlikely that he would have included anything with which he disagreed.

Charters, coins, and archaeology round out the sources for Alfred's reign. Only a handful of Alfred's charters survive. Altogether there are twenty-six charters that purport either to have been issued by the king or are associated with him. Only six or seven of these survive in original form, and all of those are, oddly enough, of Kentish rather than West Saxon provenance.[45] The others were preserved in the cartularies of medieval monastic houses. Forgery was almost a cottage industry in the monasteries of medieval England, as monks attempted to right the vagaries of historical preservation. Some of the forgers were quite good, modelling their work on genuine exemplars, and it is not always easy to determine whether a charter in a cartulary is genuine or

---

45. S 287, containing Alfred's confirmation of an earlier grant of King Edgar; S 344; S 350; S 1203, a private grant attested by Alfred; S 1276, which may be a tenth-century copy; S 1508, the will of Ealdorman Alfred; and S 1445, the 'Fonthill Letter', which though from late in the reign of Alfred's son, Edward the Elder, contains an important reference to Alfred's judicial activity.

fraudulent. The technical criteria used for assessing authenticity differ from scholar to scholar, so that a diploma judged to be trustworthy by one expert may be deemed an outright forgery by another.[46] Still, there is good reason to believe that nine of the Alfredian charters preserved in cartulary copies are substantially genuine.[47] One is Alfred's will, a document of the utmost importance for understanding Alfred's personal relations with his brothers and nephews and political conditions in Wessex in the 880s. The will and the 'Fonthill Letter' (S 1445), a legal memorandum from the reign of Alfred's son, are especially informative, but we can learn a great deal even from ordinary diplomas. Their witness lists preserve the names of Alfred's ecclesiastical and secular officials and of his household thegns and chaplains, many of whom would be otherwise unknown. The transactions they describe allow us a glimpse of royal patronage and the economic basis of kingship. One can also learn much about Alfred's political aspirations from the royal titles found in the superscriptions and attestations.

The iconography of coins is also important for understanding the ideology of kingship. Coins were also, of course, instruments of economic exchange, and are equally important for analyses of economic activity in ninth-century England. But, much like charters, the evidence of the coins is difficult to interpret. Numismatists are often forced to render judgements based upon incomplete and unsatisfactory evidence. The experts assure us that Alfred's minters struck tens of millions of pennies, but, in fact, this is an inference drawn from study of a handful of surviving coins and dies. Archaeology, of which numismatics is a subspeciality, is the one field in which new evidence is constantly being discovered. Archaeology allows us to understand the material

---

46. The variety of opinion concerning the authenticity of charters is clear from the references listed by P.H. Sawyer in his invaluable *Anglo-Saxon Charters: An Annotated List and Bibliography*, Royal Historical Society Guides and Handbooks, no. 8 (London, 1968).

47. S 344–348, S 350, S 352, S 355. See D. Whitelock, 'Some charters in the name of King Alfred', in M.H. King and W.M. Stevens, eds, *Saints, Scholars and Heroes. Studies in Medieval Culture in Honour of Charles W. Jones*, 2 vols (Collegeville, Minnesota, 1979) I, pp. 77–98; S.D. Keynes, 'The West Saxon charters of King Æthelwulf and his sons', *EHR* 109 (1994) pp. 1134–41. Cf. Smyth, *King Alfred the Great*, pp. 371–400, and the review of the charter criticism in Sawyer.

reality underlying documents such as the Burghal Hidage and Alfred's law code. But like other sources, artefacts must be interpreted and are susceptible to different constructions. If historians look to archaeologists for evidence, the archaeologists look to the historians for an interpretive framework to make sense of their findings.

Asser wrote his *Life of King Alfred* 'to say something (albeit succinctly and briefly, as far as my knowledge permits) about the life, behaviour, equitable character, and without exaggeration, the accomplishments of my lord Alfred, king of the Anglo-Saxons'.[48] The words are largely Einhard's but the intention was shared by virtually all classical and early medieval biographers. In many ways, it remains the goal of those who write biography today: to understand, as well as the sources allow, a person within his or her historical milieu, and to determine the true historical significance of that life. What has changed, perhaps, are the reasons for choosing our subjects, and the manner in which we pursue our investigations. Asser's purpose was to extol and magnify Alfred, to portray him to his friends, followers and subjects as one worthy of love and obedience. Much like a thirteenth-century scholastic theologian, the ninth-century biographer sought to demonstrate a truth already known to him. A modern biographer, on the other hand, begins by questioning the very possibility of discovering the 'truth' about one who has been dead for eleven centuries. In some ways, the choice of subject is itself a legacy of the past. We write about those whose accomplishments were deemed in their own day worthy of encomium. Though we must rely on the information from these sources, we must also be aware of their tendentious nature. A modern biographer must thus begin with scepticism and suspicion. He must also guard against seduction, not only by the sources, but, perhaps more insidiously, by the desire to justify the decision to devote so much time, study and thought to the chosen subject.

Having lived with Alfred now for nearly as long as Asser did when he wrote, I have, gradually, grown less and less resistant to the idea of Alfred's 'greatness'. I am not sure that I would have liked Alfred. The man, as I have come

---

48. Asser, ch. 73, trans. Keynes and Lapidge, p. 88. Cf. preface to Einhard's *Life of Charlemagne*.

to understand him, had a maddeningly professorial quality to him, an obsession with details and a conviction that he was duty-bound to share with others his opinions and truths. He was also convinced that he was performing God's work and that his successes and setbacks were divinely ordained. Though he lauded mercy and forgiveness in his writings, he was nonetheless capable of great brutality, of exulting in the defeat and slaughter of enemies. But he was also voraciously devoted to learning and believed that to be worthy of rule one must seek wisdom. He was an intellectual as well as a warrior, but, above all, he was a pragmatist who did what was necessary to fulfil 'the tasks that he was commanded to accomplish'. Alfred's greatness is perhaps even clearer in retrospect; his monuments survive not only in libraries but in the very fabric of our history and language. But it was the greatness of a Dark Age king. To understand and appreciate Alfred we must attempt to recover, as well as we can, the world in which he lived.

Chapter 1

ALFRED'S WESSEX

To his companion and biographer Asser, Alfred was 'my venerable and most pious lord, ruler of all the Christians of the island of Britain, Alfred king of the Anglo-Saxons'. In choosing this royal style, *Angul-Saxonum rex*, Asser echoed formulas used in Alfred's charters from at least the late 880s.[1] In its entry for the year 871 the *Anglo-Saxon Chronicle* reports that 'Alfred, the son of Æthelwulf, succeeded to the kingdom of the West Saxons'; twenty-nine years later it records the death of Alfred who 'was king over the whole English people [*cyng ofer eall Ongelcyn*] except for that part which was under Danish rule'.[2] This was more than a mere change in diplomatic formulas. When Alfred's father and brothers asserted that they were kings of the West Saxons and also of the people of Kent, the political statement was clear. The West Saxons were a 'people' with a common 'history' (even if largely mythical), inherited customs, and a sense of shared biological descent. The 'Anglo-Saxons' were not. They did not exist as a people, a tribe, or a nation. The phrase itself was foreign, coined by Continental writers to distinguish the 'Saxons' who had gone to Britain from those who had remained at home. Yet Alfred chose to be called 'King of the Anglo-Saxons', and in doing so distinguished his kingship from that of his forebears. On the most literal level the title celebrated Alfred's rule over Anglian Mercia. It also suggested something more, perhaps a consciousness of a profound political transformation in the making,

1. Asser, preface, trans. *EHD* I, no. 7, p. 289. Keynes and Lapidge, pp. 227–8 n. 1.
2. *ASC* s.a. 871, 900. Cf. *ASC* s.a. 886; Asser, ch. 84, trans. Keynes and Lapidge, p. 98.

the gradual and halting emergence of a new kingdom that extended beyond the territorial or tribal confines of the ancient kingdoms of Wessex, Kent, or Mercia. For Alfred's achievement was to lay down the foundations upon which his successors were to erect a new and lasting state, one that was to give political substance to the spiritual, linguistic and cultural unity of the 'English people' first posited by the Venerable Bede in the early eighth century.[3]

That at least is how it looks in retrospect. In the course of the tenth century Wessex was transformed into England, and Alfred's reign was the critical precondition for this process. But this must not mislead us into endowing Alfred with a prescience he could not have possessed. What Alfred ruled and how he ruled it had far more in common with the kingship of his father and brothers than with that of his great-grandson, Edgar the Peaceable (959–75), who could justly claim to be 'king of the English' and 'governor and ruler of all of Britain',[4] let alone with the Norman and Angevin monarchies of medieval England. The very language used by Asser and the Chronicler in describing Alfred's political world possesses an archaic flavour, especially to those accustomed to the concepts and jargon of modern political scientists. It removes us to a Dark Age world defined not by 'nation states', 'citizens' and 'political institutions' but by lords, followers, Christian kingship, and tribes.

To understand Alfred's life and accomplishments, we must begin with what he inherited, not only the kingdom over which he came to rule, but the social structures and cultural assumptions that governed his thinking about kingship and defined for him the possibilities of action. We must also appreciate the legacy of military glory and political success to which he fell heir. From his grandfather, Egbert, and his father, Æthelwulf, Alfred inherited a prosperous and powerful West Saxon hegemony. Their labours provided Alfred with a foundation for his own efforts; they gathered the 'timber and staves' with which he built the kingdom of the

3. See P. Wormald, 'Bede, the *Bretwaldas* and the origins of the *Gens Anglorum*', in P. Wormald, D. Bullough, and R. Collins, eds, *Ideal and Reality in Frankish and Anglo-Saxon Society: Studies Presented to J.M. Wallace-Hadrill* (Oxford, 1983) pp. 99–129.
4. *ASC* s.a. 975A; S 687. Cf. *EHD* I, no. 110 (S 693); *EHD* I, no. 113 (S 773).

West Saxons into the germ of what would become 'England'. It is with an examination of the political and material world into which he was born that our study of Alfred should begin.

. . .

THE RISE OF WESSEX

Alfred, the fifth and youngest son of Æthelwulf, king of the West Saxons, was born some time between 847 and 849 on a royal estate at Wantage, Berkshire, in what had until recently been Mercian territory. Too few charters have survived for us to make sense of the movements of the ninth-century West Saxon royal court, or to venture even a guess as to why Alfred's mother, Osburh, happened to be at Wantage at his birth. That she was there, however, is historically significant, for it provides clear evidence that by 848 King Æthelwulf's dominion extended over the long-disputed middle Thames valley.[5]

Between the mid-eighth and mid-ninth century, the kings of Wessex and Anglian Mercia, the dominant kingdom of the Midlands, had contended for control of the rich agricultural lands of Berkshire. In 844, only a few years before Alfred's birth, Ceolred, bishop of Leicester, had given an estate at Pangbourne, Berkshire, to Berhtwulf, king of the Mercians, in exchange for the 'liberty' of Abingdon and other monasteries of the see. King Berhtwulf, in turn, had granted this land to his ealdorman, Æthelwulf.[6] Four years later all of Berkshire was in the hands of King Æthelwulf and its Mercian ealdorman in the service of the West Saxon king.

King Æthelwulf's acquisition of Berkshire was the final chapter in a long and involved history of relations between Mercia and Wessex in the middle Saxon period, a story of alternating conflict and diplomacy that was to culminate in Alfred's own marriage to a Mercian noblewoman and the marriage of their daughter to a powerful Mercian ealdorman.

5. Cf. A.P. Smyth, *King Alfred the Great* (Oxford, 1995) pp. 3–9. Smyth's rejection of Wantage as Alfred's birthplace seems to arise less from a careful consideration of the evidence than the desire to undermine the historical credibility of Asser's *Life of King Alfred*, which he regards as a forgery. His argument that Wantage was somehow vulnerable because of viking raids along the coasts of Wessex in the 840s is particularly unpersuasive.
6. S 1271.

The basic thrust of the tale was a shift of power south of the Humber from Mercia to Wessex during the first half of the ninth century. By Alfred's birth West Saxon power had outgrown the boundaries of the ancestral realm; his father, Æthelwulf, ruled a composite kingdom that stretched from beyond the River Tamar in the west to the isle of Thanet in the east and which embraced the once independent kingdoms of Cornwall, Surrey, Sussex, Kent, and Essex. Just as Alfred's own son and grandsons were to build the kingdom of 'England' upon foundations that he laid, Alfred himself was heir to a legacy of military glory, conquest, and prosperity, much of which had been achieved at the expense of the Mercians by Alfred's celebrated grandfather, King Egbert.

Egbert's story has the quality of a saga. Exiled in his youth, he was to achieve not only kingship in his native Wessex, becoming the first of his line in nine generations to sit on the throne of Cerdic, but dominion over all the English peoples south of the Humber by crushing the Mercians in battle. The West Saxon Chronicler, looking back from his vantage point in Alfred's reign, celebrated Egbert's achievement by adding him to Bede's list of kings who enjoyed *imperium* over southern England, making him the eighth such 'bretwalda'.[7] Alfred must have grown up listening to tales of his grandfather's heroic deeds, learning from them what it meant to be a good king. Like *Beowulf*'s Scyld Scefing, from whom Alfred and his kindred claimed descent, Egbert had risen from inauspicious beginnings to be a mighty king who took

> mead-benches away from enemy bands, from many tribes, terrified their nobles . . . [and] lived to find comfort from that, became great under the skies, prospered in honours until every one those who lived about him . . . had to obey him and pay him tribute.[8]

7. Literally, 'ruler of Britain'. *ASC* s.a. 829 A (but cf. B,C,D,E: 'brytenwealda', 'wide-ruler'). Cf. *HE* ii.5. The term, which clearly has imperial connotations, was possibly coined during Alfred's reign. *ASC* s.a. 829A. Cf. Wormald, 'Bede, the *Bretwaldas* and the Origins of the *Gens Anglorum*'.

8. *Beowulf, A New Prose Translation*, trans. E. Talbot Donaldson (New York, 1966) p. 1; *Beowulf and the Fight at Finnburg*, ed. F. Klaeber, 3rd edn (Boston, 1950) ll. 4–11.

For these accomplishments Scyld won the praise of the *Beowulf*-poet – '*þæt wæs god cyning!*' – and by this measure Egbert was at least the equal of his legendary forebear. Leadership in war was a basic function of kings in eighth- and ninth-century England.[9] Though the clergy were wont to emphasize the sacral quality of kingship and the king's duty to defend the Church and maintain justice, the secular sources portrayed kings largely as warlords and measured their greatness in terms of victory in battle and conquest. Military success brought not only glory but wealth through the acquisition of new territories and the imposition of tribute upon the defeated. The wealth Egbert won through war not only helped establish his dynasty within Wessex but secured West Saxon hegemony over all of southern England.

The rise of Wessex was of recent vintage at the time of Alfred's birth and its long-term prospects were uncertain. West Saxon hegemony had been hard won in battles fought within living memory. Nothing guaranteed that West Saxon glory would prove any more lasting than Mercian, and to judge by the fatalism that is so prominent a leitmotif in Anglo-Saxon poetry and Christian historiography, neither Æthelwulf nor his sons would have expected their efforts to bear permanent fruit. *Wyrd*, destiny (or God's providence, as the mature Alfred would view it), had already greatly favoured the dynasty established by Egbert, the 'Ecgberhtings', raising them above their royal predecessors in power, wealth, and glory. But, as the proems to their charters reminded kings, all earthly things are transitory and 'the wanton fortune of this deceiving world . . . is shamelessly fickle'.[10] What God had given, He in his providence could as easily take away.

By Alfred's birth, the probable instrument of God's providence was no longer the traditional enemy, Mercia, but an external threat. Relations between Mercia and Wessex had improved, largely because of the arrival of a common foe, the pagan Danes, who threatened the survival of both kingdoms. From 836, when King Egbert suffered defeat

9. R. Abels, *Lordship and Military Obligation in Anglo-Saxon England* (Los Angeles, CA, 1988) pp. 11–12, 33–4; B. Yorke, *Kings and Kingdoms of Early Anglo-Saxon England* (London, 1990) pp. 157–67.
10. E.g., *EHD* I, nos 69 (S 255), 70 (S 262), 104 (S 407).

at Carhampton at the hands of a viking force of thirty-five ships, until 851 when Alfred's father, King Æthelwulf, and his two eldest brothers, Æthelbald and Æthelstan, defeated the vikings on land at *Aclea* and at sea off Sandwich, the West Saxons were preoccupied with fighting off the increasingly virulent raiders. Mercia was also ravaged mercilessly by the pagan raiders. Faced with a common foreign enemy, Æthelwulf and the Mercian King Berhtwulf forged a lasting alliance between their kingdoms. Under Berhtwulf's successor, Burgred (852–874), relations between the two kingdoms grew even closer. In 853 Æthelwulf sent an army against the Welsh in response to a Mercian request for aid. Later that same year Burgred took Æthelwulf's daughter, Æthelswith, as his wife.

Berkshire passed permanently into West Saxon hands sometime before Alfred's birth at Wantage in 848 or 849. What in the past had required sword and fire now took place peacefully, as King Berhtwulf acceded to the wishes of his more powerful neighbour to the south. In practical terms little probably changed in Berkshire. Even the ealdorman remained the same. The Mercian Æthelwulf, whose family came from Derbyshire, bowed to the West Saxon king of the same name and received from him rule over the shire that had been his under Berhtwulf. He held it as a loyal retainer of King Æthelwulf and his sons until his death in 871. London, on the other hand, remained a Mercian emporium. King Æthelwulf apparently had no intention of reducing Mercia to subjugation or even of weakening it significantly. Wessex's acquisition of Berkshire left the River Thames as the border between the kingdoms and made defence of the upper Thames a joint responsibility. This may well have been the strategic thinking behind the boundary changes.

. . .

THE POLITICAL CONTOURS OF ALFRED'S KINGDOM

The kingdom that Egbert patched together through claims of hereditary right and conquest has been called 'Greater Wessex' by modern historians. It is, to be sure, a convenient label for discussing the conglomerate realm that Æthelwulf and his sons ruled, but it is also misleading. Nothing in its history or geography lent coherence to this large, disparate region. In terms of claimed tribal descent, tenurial custom, and even agricultural organization, the lands and kingdoms that Egbert had won in the southwest and southeast differed significantly from Wessex.

The traditional land of the West Saxons embraced the shires of Hampshire, Wiltshire, Somersetshire, and Dorset.[11] A large expanse of chalk downlands, stretching from the Hampshire Downs in the east through Salisbury Plain and the Berkshire Downs to the Dorset coast near Abbotsbury, unified the region geologically and politically through the ancient ridgeway tracks exploited by both the Romans and Anglo-Saxons. The fertile countryside, rich in woodland and rivers, was dominated by large villages, open-field farming, and large manor-like estates. Each shire was administered for the king by an ealdorman of noble birth who served at the king's pleasure, and by royal reeves responsible for maintaining law and order and collecting at royal villas the food rents and services owed to the king. The king's presence was visible throughout these shires in the numerous royal estates, palaces, and farms that dotted the West Saxon landscape, and it was here that the itinerating king's court could most often be found.

The region that lay west of Selwood, encompassing Cornwall, Devonshire and parts of Somerset, seems to have formed a separate political region, reflecting its historically later settlement by Anglo-Saxons and integration into the West Saxon kingdom. Here, as in the southeast, the landscape was dominated by homesteads and hamlets rather than open-field villages. The West Saxon colonization of Cornwall and perhaps even Devonshire was still an ongoing process during the reign of King Alfred. Certainly, the British presence grew stronger as one moved west, and much of the peninsula, with the exception of western Somerset, must have still been dominated by native British landowners in the late ninth century. The region 'west of Selwood' gained much of whatever political coherence it possessed from its ecclesiastical organization. The huge diocese of Sherborne in the ninth century stretched over Dorset, Somerset, Devonshire

11. B. Yorke, *Wessex in the Early Middle Ages*, Studies in the Early History of Britain Series, N. Brooks, gen.ed. (London & New York, 1995).

and Cornwall. In Alfred's youth, Bishop Ealhstan was undoubtedly the most politically powerful force in the southwest and one of the most influential magnates in all Wessex.

Despite the distinctive character of the region, the shires of the southwest, with the possible exception of Cornwall, had been fully incorporated into the West Saxon kingdom by the mid-ninth century. This was not true of the southeast. Neither Egbert nor Æthelwulf seems to have thought in terms of a lasting political union between Wessex and the southeast. Their efforts at territorial consolidation were limited to merging the once independent kingdoms of Kent, Sussex, Surrey, and (with less success) Essex into a 'Greater Kent', which, for most of their reigns, was ruled by underkings chosen from among their sons. This is not to say that they restricted their own rule to Wessex. None of the underkings apparently had the right to issue coinage or charters in his own name, while Egbert and Æthelwulf exercised unfettered royal authority over the southeast whenever the royal court travelled there. It is equally clear that Egbert and Æthelwulf maintained two separate royal establishments through which they ruled their composite kingdom. In Wessex the kings met largely with West Saxon ealdormen, prelates, and thegns, and in Kent, with the Kentish elite.[12]

In short, Egbert and his immediate successors were, as they claimed in their Kentish charters, kings 'of the West Saxons and also of the people of Kent'. That the two kingships remained partible is underscored by King Æthelwulf's will, in which he divided the realm between his two eldest sons, the older receiving Wessex and the younger the southeast. As we shall see, it was not until the ascension of Alfred's brother, King Æthelberht, in 860 that the two realms began to be regarded as halves of a single kingdom.[13] Alfred

---

12. S.D. Keynes, 'The Control of Kent in the Ninth Century', *Early Medieval Europe* 2 (1993) pp. 120–30. One hundred and seventeen laymen below the rank of ealdormen are named in the witness lists or main texts of King Æthelwulf's surviving charters. Of these only a handful – Æthelheard, Æthelred, Ceolmund, Dudda, Milred, Osmund, Wulfhere, Wulflaf and Wulfred – witnessed charters in both the western and eastern parts of the kingdom, probably as members of King Æthelwulf's itinerating household.

13. See below pp. 93–4. Cf. N.P. Brooks, *The Early History of the Church of Canterbury* (Leicester, 1984) p. 327 for royal styles.

himself, interestingly, did not distinguish in his diplomas between his rule over Wessex and Kent. In both he issued charters in the early years of his reign as 'king of the Saxons' and later, after he added part of Mercia to his dominion, as 'king of the Anglo-Saxons'.

Egbert's assumption of power in Kent and the southeast was facilitated by the support of a large segment of the local nobility, who became the mainstay of West Saxon rule in the region. The transfer of political rule entailed the eclipse of many who had prospered under the Mercians and the rise of 'new men' among the elite of the southeast as Egbert and his son, Æthelwulf, the new underking of Kent, in good Anglo-Saxon fashion rewarded their friends and punished their enemies.[14] Local landowners who supported the West Saxon takeover did well, as one would expect in a society shaped by the ethos of reciprocity. One charter that has survived in an early eleventh-century copy demonstrates one mechanism used by the new West Saxon kings to secure and reward the loyalty of the Kentish thegnage.[15] In 844 King Æthelwulf granted land at Horton, Kent, to Ealdorman Eadred and gave him permission to transfer it to a series of local landowners, each of whom kept part and passed the remainder to others, 'to be enjoyed in perpetual inheritance'. The king's presence was felt at each level of the donation, since the land was not merely lent out but 'booked', that is, conveyed as a hereditary property and freed of many onerous services and dues normally owed the king. In the gift-giving culture of ninth-century England, King Æthelwulf's grant not only reinforced his ties with Eadred and Eadred's with his neighbours, but confirmed or created bonds of mutual obligation and friendship

14. The flow of gifts to Canterbury dried up, not to be restored until Egbert, near death, sought the support of Archbishop Ceolnoth for his son's succession. BCS 421 (*S* 1438), discussed by P. Wormald, 'The Ninth Century', in J. Campbell, ed., *The Anglo-Saxons* (Oxford and Ithaca, N.Y., 1982) p. 140; Keynes, 'Control of Kent', pp. 129–30. See also R. Fleming, 'History and Liturgy at Pre-Conquest Christ Church,' *Haskins Society Journal* 6 (1995 for 1994) p. 75, for the apparent pruning of Christ Church's obituary lists to remove names of benefactors with Mercian connections.

15. S 319 (BCS 538). For what follows see R. Abels, 'The devolution of bookland in ninth-century Kent: a note on BCS 538 (S 319)', *Archaeologia Cantiana* 99 (1983) pp. 219–23.

between the king and the lesser landowners who benefited from the gift.

The four-level transaction described in the Horton charter is unique among surviving diplomas. Nevertheless, the process it describes was probably commonplace. King Æthelwulf and his sons enriched local supporters through generous grants of land and by 'booking' properties they already possessed. By doing so, they created a solid core of supporters in the southeast upon whom the rule of Kent, Surrey, Sussex and Essex rested. Rather than impose West Saxon ealdormen upon the eastern shires and settle West Saxon supporters upon royal lands there, Æthelwulf opted to rule through the native nobility. This meant gifts of land and offices. The more precarious the West Saxon king's position, the more generous he had to be. In 855 Æthelwulf, who planned to go on a pilgrimage to Rome, 'booked' a tenth of his royal lands in the southeast to local thegns and churches in the hope of winning the favour of God and retaining the loyalty of the local thegns during his absence.[16]

In short, 'Greater Wessex' under Æthelwulf was actually two realms, a western kingdom that comprised what had traditionally been Wessex along with Cornwall, and an eastern kingdom that embraced Kent, Sussex, Surrey, and Essex. Like his Carolingian counterparts, Æthelwulf planned on dividing his kingdoms between his two eldest sons. Only the threat of the vikings and the accident of underage heirs compelled the sons of Æthelwulf to unify the kingdoms.

. . .

WESSEX, ITS LAND AND PEOPLE

King Alfred, meditating upon the tools and responsibilities of kingship, observed that no king could govern effectively or honourably without a well-populated land; the service of praying men, fighting men, and working men; and the wealth and resources to maintain all three with land, gifts, weapons, food, ale, clothing and other necessities.[17] This, of course,

16. See below pp. 68–70.
17. *Alfred's Boethius*, ed. Sedgefield, ch. 17, p. 40. For possible sources for Alfred's tripartite schema, see T.E. Powell, 'The "Three Orders" of society in Anglo-Saxon England', *Anglo-Saxon England* 23 (1994) pp. 103–32, esp. pp. 104–9.

is a king's-eye view of society and a highly simplified one at that. Alfred's intent was to describe the human tools and material resources essential for kingship rather than to analyse the class structure of ninth-century Wessex. His point was that a king ruled not only over a land and its people but through them. They had been entrusted to him by God so that he might through them 'virtuously and worthily administer the authority' committed to him.

To appreciate Alfred's accomplishments and to understand the nature of his kingship, we must consider at least briefly the 'tools' of governance he inherited, the land and people of Wessex. The law code that Alfred issued in the latter part of his reign, supplemented by the translations of Alfred and his contemporaries and the evidence of the charters, provides the most illuminating window onto the society over which he ruled, though it is heavily tinted by Alfred's conception of Christian kingship. Royal majesty is the unstated theme of the law code, which depicts West Saxon society as a hierarchy of status, wealth, and power under a king who is both a theocratic monarch and a royal lord.[18] Even more than the late seventh-century West Saxon law code of Ine, which Alfred appended to his own, Alfred's code recasts customary law and previous promulgations as royal law. In it the king stands securely at the apex of society. One who plots against the king's life or gives shelter to plotters, for example, is made to pay with his life and property, unless he can acquit himself of the charge by giving an oath equal to the king's wergeld, that is, by producing a group of oath-helpers the sum of whose wergelds would equal that of a king.[19]

For Alfred, royal authority had been established by God to promote justice and ensure stability and harmony. Lordship and kinship were the primary personal bonds which cemented and helped order the West Saxon polity, and Alfred in his exercise of Christian kingship claimed to stand above both. The idea that it was the king who guaranteed the rights of lord and man, oversaw kinship obligations, and determined what those rights and obligations ought to be,

18. See discussion below, pp. 246–53.
19. *Alfred* 4, § 1.

had been gradually developing in Wessex since the late seventh century. Whereas Ine decreed that a man who left his lord without permission was to be returned and fined sixty shillings payable to the lord, Alfred restated this law to emphasize royal authority, declaring that a man could only leave his lord with the cognizance of the king's ealdorman in whose shire he served. If he departed without informing the ealdorman, any lord who accepted his services was liable to a fine of 120 shillings payable to the king.[20] Though Alfred accepted the validity of vendettas, he also claimed the right to supervise and regulate them, determining who was and was not a valid target for vengeance. A commended man, for instance, was permitted to fight on behalf of his lord and a lord on behalf of his men without precipitating a feud. Similarly, a man could fight on behalf of wronged blood kin, unless that entailed going against his lord, which Alfred absolutely forbade.[21] (The idea that the lordship bond was more sacred than kinship also colours the heroic tale in the *Chronicle* of the deaths of King Cynewulf and the rebel *ætheling*, Cyneheard.[22]) The king even claimed half the wergeld if a kinless man were slain, the other half going to his 'associates' (*gegildan*), presumably sworn friends obliged to avenge his death.[23] Here we see the king as the protector of the defenceless, a role that perhaps also explains Alfred's decree that slaves were to be granted holidays during the Wednesdays of the four Ember weeks so that they might sell to whomever they wished any goods given them as alms or earned in their spare time.[24]

Social rank and dignity in Alfred's Wessex were determined in part by birth and in part by service to God and king. The law code refers to three ranks of free men, whose deaths were to be compensated with payments of 1,200, 600, and 200 shillings. Elsewhere, it categorizes all free men as either 'husbandman or noble' (*ge ceorle ge eorle*).[25] To judge by the laws of Ine, the 1,200- and 600-shilling men comprised

20. *Ine* 39; *Alfred* 37, § 1–2.
21. *Alfred* 42, § 1–7.
22. *ASC* s.a 757.
23. *Alfred* 30, § 1; 31.
24. *Alfred* 43.
25. *Alfred* 4 § 2.

the nobility, the former perhaps being landed nobles and the latter landless or of Welsh descent. The 200-shilling men apparently described all free commoners, *ceorls*, regardless of the size of their holdings or the extent of their economic and personal freedom.

An even more basic division was between freedom and servitude. Alfred's Wessex was a slave society. No one can even begin to estimate how many slaves (or free men, for that matter) there were in ninth-century Wessex, but from Alfred's laws it is clear that even ceorls owned slaves.[26] Since the routes to slavery included war, the penal system, and voluntary renunciation of freedom in time of famine, it would not be surprising if slaves outnumbered the free. What separated a slave from a free man was that the latter, whether commoner or noble, possessed certain legal privileges and obligations, most notably the rights to take oaths and to defend and avenge his person, honour, kin, and dependants. The right to give an oath meant that a free man was 'law-worthy'. He could answer an accusation or defend his right to property by swearing a solemn oath aided by a requisite number of oath-helpers. Unlike a slave, a free man enjoyed a blood-price, a 'wergeld'. If a slave were killed, his owner could demand compensation for the loss of his property, but neither a master nor a slave's kinsman was obligated to ransom him from a vendetta or guarantee his safety. In contrast, if a free man were killed, his kinsmen, usually his immediate family – there is little evidence for the existence of extended kindreds in Alfred's Wessex – and his lord had the legal right and moral obligation to take vengeance upon his enemy and his enemy's friends, or accept from them monetary compensation fixed by custom and law. It was no coincidence that the medieval English manumission ceremony marked the transition from servitude to freedom by ritual bestowal of arms. That a man had a wergeld also meant that he could compound most offences by payment of fines, culminating in the payment of a sum equal to his wergeld in lieu of the loss of life and limb, and could expect monetary payments for outrages committed against him. A slave, on the other hand, faced corporal punishment for his misdeeds, and any compensation for violence committed

26. *Alfred* 25.

against him or her was to be awarded to the master and the king.[27]

Since Alfred's law code was an expression of regality, it is little wonder that it accorded greater protection to the persons and honour of the king's bishops and ealdormen than to ordinary nobles. Not only were offences against the dignity of an ealdorman to be punished more severely than those against other nobles, but an ealdorman apparently enjoyed a double wergeld, 1,200 shillings for his noble birth and a second 1,200 for his office, the latter presumably to be paid to the king.[28] From the earlier laws of Ine we know that royal household dependants were similarly accorded high status and protection because of their familiar relationship with the king. The implicit distinction between a nobility of blood and one of service, however, had eroded by the ninth century, as aristocratic landholders were incorporated into a more vigorous and all-embracing conception of royal governance. Even the terminology of nobility changed to reflect the altered relationship between noble and king. *Gesith*, the term for a nobleman in seventh-century Wessex, meant 'companion' and, like the Latin *comes*, emphasized that noble blood made a man worthy of a king's fellowship. In Bede's *Ecclesiastical History of the English People* (AD 731) we encounter great aristocrats leading their own troops in battle on behalf of their royal lords and living like kings on estates attended by military retainers and domestic servants.[29] Such men also dominated the West Saxon countryside in the late ninth century, but they were now more often called 'king's thegns', royal ministers or servants.[30]

Ninth-century West Saxon nobles were expected to follow the king into battle and to aid in his administration of justice and public order. In return they looked to receive from him land, gifts, honours, and power. As landholders they were responsible for policing their dependants and peasant tenants, collecting and supervising labour upon roads and

27. See, for example, *Alfred*, 11, § 1–5; 25; 25, § 1 (penalties for rapes committed by and upon the free and slaves).
28. S 1508 (will of Ealdorman Alfred, AD 871–889), trans. *EHD* I, no. 97, p. 538.
29. Bede, *HE* IV.22.
30. H.R. Loyn, *Anglo-Saxon England and the Norman Conquest*, 2nd edn (London and New York, 1991) pp. 216–27.

fortifications, supplying troops to the king's army, providing hospitality for the king and his agents, paying suit in the royal household when it ventured into their localities, and attending local folk moots where the king's will was announced and justice done under the watchful eyes of royal ealdormen and reeves. For Egbert and his successors, nobility entailed honourable service to the king.

The key to successful kingship was bending the nobility to one's will, and this was achieved more through love and generosity than threat and force. In a world shaped by the ethos of reciprocity, a good king was by necessity an openhanded lord. Even ecclesiastics such as Alcuin, whose vision of kingship was shaped by Scripture and patristic biblical commentators, praised the kings they served not only for their defence of the faith, enrichment of the Church, and pursuit of justice, but for their zeal in war and generosity to their followers. To Asser Alfred's generosity was nothing short of astounding; to Bishop Wulfsige of Sherborne, Alfred was the 'ring-giver', 'the greatest treasure-giver of all the kings he has ever heard tell of, in recent time or long ago, or of any earthly king he had previously learned of'.[31] Indeed, much of the wealth enjoyed by nobles, the land, stock, and peoples they held as *folcland* or *lænland*, had been granted or confirmed to them by the king. Such land belonged to the royal fisc, to be granted out by the king as he saw fit, though the presumption was that *folcland* and royal loans would pass from father to son, as the son came of age and proved his worth in the king's service. That nobles or noble kindreds in early England possessed hereditary lands and wealth apart from that which they received from the hands of kings has often been posited. There is little positive evidence, however, for such tenures, and a great deal to suggest that without royal favour many young nobles could not establish households or families of their own.[32] By the eighth century, royal followers who served the king especially well could hope for a royal charter that would transform their precarious holdings into the hereditary property known as 'bookland'. Bookland tenure had been introduced

---

31. Bishop Wulfsige's Preface to the Translation of Gregory's *Dialogues*, trans. Keynes and Lapidge, p. 188.
32. See Abels, *Lordship and Military Obligation*, pp. 22–5, 28–33.

into England in the seventh century by churchmen concerned with the security of their landed possessions in an age of political and religious instability. Within a century of its invention, bookland had ceased to be the preserve of the Church, though the conservative diplomatic formulas continued to preserve the idea that chartered land was held by 'ecclesiastical right'.

As Alfred observed in his preface to his translation of St Augustine's *Soliloquies,* 'every man desires that, after he has built a cottage on his lord's loanland and with his lord's help, he may sometimes rest himself therein, and go hunting, fowling and fishing; and provide for himself in every way from that loanland, both on sea and land, until such time as he shall earn bookland and an ever-lasting heritage through his lord's kindness'.[33] The *quid pro quo* of reward for service is clearly expressed here, together with intimations of the king's gratuitous power. For Alfred the conversion of loaned land into a permanent endowment was a metaphor for man's exchange of the unstable happiness of this transitory life for the eternal bliss of heaven. A king and his power, it is implied, are earthly reflections of God and his full plenitude. Nor did earning bookland conclude the transaction between king and follower. The recipient was still expected to serve the king in his court, in his folk moots, and on royal military expeditions (*fyrds*). Indeed, a bookholder was obliged by virtue of his tenure to provide peasant labour to repair bridges and fortifications and to produce a contingent of warriors for the king's armies based upon the assessed value, 'hidage', of his land.[34] Though the essence of bookland was the right of free disposal, Alfred nonetheless decreed that the holder of inherited bookland could not alienate it from his kindred if those who had acquired it originally or those from whom he had received it had enjoined that it remain within the family.[35] While heaven may be eternal, a 'book' was not necessarily so. Ninth-century kings, Alfred included, maintained the right of reversion over bookland in case of lack of heirs and could

33. *Alfred's Soliloquies,* ed. Carnicelli, p. 48; trans. Hargrove, p. 2. (I have freely revised and 'modernized' Hargrove's translation throughout.)
34. Abels, *Lordship and Military Obligation,* pp. 43–63. See below, pp. 206–7.
35. *Alfred* 41.

revoke a 'book' if its holder committed repeated serious crimes.[36] The possession of a book, like the possession of 'loanland', bound the noble holder firmly to the Crown.

The gulf between king and noble can be exaggerated, despite the ideology of theocratic kingship found throughout the writings that originated in Alfred's court. Kings, whatever their status with God, were in origin nobles who had thrived. All men descended through the male line from a previous king were 'throne-worthy', and this dignity was probably claimed by a goodly segment of the hereditary nobility. Egbert himself had come from a royal lineage richer in ealdormen and thegns than in kings. What transformed him from an exiled *ætheling* into a king was his acceptance by the lay and spiritual magnates of the realm as their lord. This, even more than anointing and royal inauguration rituals, was the decisive event in the making of a king, although by the ninth century royal consecration was undoubtedly expected and sought by new kings. Nor was a new king safe until all the magnates had bowed to him or been disposed of by exile or death. Whatever appeals Alfred made to the divine foundations of kingship and no matter how prominently theocratic kingship appears in his writings, Alfred and his advisors understood that the key to successful rule was to 'carefully and cleverly exploit and convert his bishops and ealdormen and nobles, and his thegns most dear to him, and reeves as well (in all of whom, after the Lord and the king, the authority of the entire kingdom is seen to be invested, as is appropriate) to his own will and to the general advantage of the whole realm'.[37]

It would be tempting to identify the nobility with the 'fighting men' of Alfred's *Boethius*, bringing Alfred's use of the tripartite scheme in line with later medieval conceptions of the Three Orders. There would be some justice in this, since the West Saxon nobility was a hereditary military aristocracy, trained from youth to ride horses, handle weapons, and face the horrors and hardships of war. Nobles not only led the armies of Egbert and his successors but provided the best trained and most professional element of

---

36. E.g., S 1445, trans. *EHD* I, no. 102. See below pp. 278–82.
37. Asser, ch. 91, trans. Keynes and Lapidge, pp. 101–2. See discussion pp. 258–74 below.

those forces. The heart of a king's army (as with any magnate's military retinue) was his hearth-troop, comprised of
young household thegns, the sons of landed nobles, who
feasted and slept in the king's hall and accompanied him as
he and the court travelled about the countryside. Such were
the king's 'followers' whom Alfred rewarded with money at
regular intervals and to whom he left 200 pounds in his will,
to be 'divided between them, to each as much as will belong
to him according to the manner in which I have just now
[at Easter] made distribution to them'.[38] One suspects that
it was men such as these that Alfred had in mind. Yet the
majority of warriors on any particular royal expedition in
the ninth century were likely to have been commoners. Some,
the *gafolgeldan* or 'tribute payers', held estates from the king,
perhaps a hide or two of land, amounting to 100 acres (forty
hectares) or more. These were hardly 'peasants', but well-to-
do rural notables, the forerunners of the Domesday sokemen,
whose lands were worked by poorer peasants and slaves.
Others served as the commended men of nobles, as members of the military retinues of their social betters. War may
have been the arena in which a thegn displayed his characteristic virtue and won honour and rewards, but it was not
the special preserve of nobles.

Still, when Alfred thought of the commoners he must
have considered them, as a group, to have been 'working
men'. The place of the ceorl, the ordinary free man, in
Anglo-Saxon society has been a subject of controversy among
historians for generations. The dominant historiographical
school would place the ceorl at the centre of the Anglo-
Saxon legal and social world, at least in the earliest centuries of Anglo-Saxon England before the rise of a powerful
centralized monarchy in the tenth century depressed his
status and paved the way for the further levelling of the
Norman Conquest. Other historians have questioned the
centrality of the ceorl even in the settlement period, suggesting that his freedom was greatly circumscribed by economic and judicial obligations to noble lords.[39] For Alfred's

38. S 1507, trans. Keynes and Lapidge, p. 177.
39. F.M. Stenton, *Anglo-Saxon England*, 3rd edn (Oxford, 1971) pp. 277–
314; T.M. Charles-Edwards, 'Kinship, Status, and the Origins of the
Hide', *Past and Present* 36 (1972) pp. 3–33; H.R. Loyn, *The Governance of
Anglo-Saxon England, 500–1087* (Stafford, 1984) pp. 50–3. Cf. E. John,

Wessex, at any rate, the latter view comes closer to the mark. A fortuitous mistranslation in the *Old English Orosius*, a work apparently commissioned by Alfred as part of his educational programme, suggests that even in ninth-century terms the ceorl was not completely 'free'.[40] The translator relates that the Volscians 'had freed some of their slaves and also became too mild and forgiving to them all. Then their ceorls [Latin: *libertini*, 'freedmen'] resented the fact that they had freed the slaves and would not free them.' The less-than-free status of the 'ceorl' in this text is echoed in Alfred's treaty with the Danish king, Guthrum. There 'the ceorls who occupy tributary land' are imputed the same 200-shilling wergeld as Danish freedmen rather than the higher wergeld of free viking warriors.

In what way were ceorls unfree? The key lies, perhaps, in the relationship between the ninth-century husbandmen and their lords, especially if the lord was also a landlord. The West Saxon royal dynasty, even before Alfred, promoted the rights and obligations of lordship as a mechanism through which the king could rule the realm more firmly and securely. From the late seventh century on, the freedom of the West Saxon ceorl was bounded by the rights of his lord over him. The ceorl of Ine's day, in fact, was so tightly bound to his lord that if he attempted to seek another, the law prescribed that he be returned and fined sixty shillings, payable to the lord from whom he had fled. A ceorl who held land from his lord could be obliged to labour under the lord's command. Indeed, if he had accepted a dwelling-place when he covenanted for his yardland, he became tied to his tenancy. Because he had accepted the gift of a house, he was no longer free to leave his holding, even if his lord were to demand increased services from it.[41]

It is unlikely that the condition of the lesser free peasantry improved substantially between the late seventh and the late ninth century. From an extremely interesting vernacular

Orbis Britanniae (Leicester, 1966) pp. 135–6; H.P.R. Finberg, 'Anglo-Saxon England to 1042' in Finberg, ed., *The Agrarian History of England and Wales*, vol. 1, bk. 2 (Cambridge, 1972) p. 443.

40. *Old English Orosius*, ed. Bately, IV.3, p. 87. I follow here the exposition of H.P.R. Finberg, 'Anglo-Saxon England to 1042', p. 451.

41. *Ine* 3, § 2; 39; 67. See discussion in Abels, *Lordship and Military Obligation*, pp. 18, 210–11, n. 28. Cf. Loyn, *Anglo-Saxon England*, pp. 170–6.

memorandum attached to a royal charter of Alfred's son, Edward the Elder (AD 901), we learn that the tenure of the ceorls of the royal estate of Hurstbourne Priors in Hampshire in the last years of Alfred's reign and in the first of his son was heavily burdened with labour services. The body of the charter relates the complex tenurial history of the estate and stipulates that the land pass to Winchester with all the people who had been on it when Alfred was still alive. The memorandum attached to the charter enumerated what was expected from them. From each 'hide' (an assessment of tax liability equivalent to a notional 120 acres (forty-nine hectares)) the ceorls were to pay forty pennies at the autumnal equinox, and six church-measures of ale, and three sesters of wheat for bread. They were to plough three acres (1.2 hectares) in their own time and sow them with their own seed and bring it to the barn in their own time, and give three pounds (1.36 kilograms) of barley, supply split wood and poles for fencing, and mow half an acre (0.2 hectares) of meadow in their own time as rent. At Easter they were to render two ewes with two lambs, which they were first to wash and shear in their own time. They were to work as bidden every week except for one at midwinter, a second at Easter, and a third on the Rogation days. (Curiously, Alfred was more generous in his law code than to his tenants, allowing all free men some thirty-seven days of rest.)[42] In the onerous obligations of their tenure, the ceorls of Hurstbourne prefigure the villeins of the Domesday Book. They are cousins to the humble *geburs* of Wynflæd's will and similar tenth-century testaments who also were bequeathed along with the estates in which they held land.

The condition of the ceorls of Hurstbourne does not prove that all men below the rank of noble were heavily burdened with rent and labour services, free men in name but 'trembling on the verge of serfdom'.[43] The actual social structure of Alfredian Wessex was even more complex and highly stratified than suggested by his law code, and the general

42. S 359, discussed by Finberg, *Agrarian History*, pp. 452–3. Cf. F. Maitland, *Domesday Book and Beyond* (Cambridge, 1897) pp. 330, 331. Cf. *Alfred* 43.
43. Stenton, *Anglo-Saxon England*, p. 475, referring to the *geburs* of the eleventh-century treatise known as the *Rectitudines Singularum Personarum*.

category of 200-shilling men embraced men and women of quite disparate fortune and rank. The most prosperous ceorls may well have possessed more land and wealth than many young nobles striving for a place in a lord's household. Ceorls as well as nobles fought in Alfred's armies and attended his folk moots. Their main function in Alfred's eyes, though, was to be the king's 'working men', whose labours helped feed those who prayed and those who fought. The 'lord' of Hurstbourne, after all, had been Alfred himself; it was to a royal reeve that the ceorls of the estate had rendered their labour services and rents. In this they served the king in the same capacity as other king's ceorls, settled in Charltons appended to nearby royal manors, who worked the king's demesne and rendered to his reeves the food rent upon which the king and his court depended.[44] They were, as Alfred's tripartite scheme recognizes, an integral part of a closely knit society, bound to one another by ties of kinship and to the nobles and the king by bonds of lordship.

44. Finberg, *Agrarian History*, pp. 453–4.

Chapter 2

MEMORIES OF CHILDHOOD, 848–858

All we know of Alfred's youth is what he as a mature adult chose to tell his intimates. As with so much else about Alfred, the story of his childhood rests largely upon the testimony of the king's courtier and confidant, the monk Asser. From Asser's *Life of King Alfred* one can recover only fragments of Alfred's early years – a handful of names and dates and a few charming though problematic stories that must have held special meaning for the king as he looked back upon his life. Too little survives to allow more than a brief glimpse of a much-idealized vision of the young Alfred. Yet Alfred's own memory as mediated by his faithful biographer affords us insight into how, decades later, the king and those closest to him made sense of his early years.

'Now, what I want is, Facts', lectured Dickens's Mr Gradgrind. 'Stick to Facts, sir!' But what are the facts about Alfred's childhood? Despite Asser's good intentions, and to the despair of Gradgrinds and modern biographers, reliable facts are few and far between. Even the date of Alfred's birth is in dispute. Asser begins his biography by informing the reader: 'In the year of the Lord's Incarnation 849, Alfred, king of the Anglo-Saxons, was born at the royal estate called Wantage, in the district known as Berkshire (which is so called from Berroc Wood, where the box-tree grows very abundantly).'[1] We have a 'fact', then, and one so well established that the British nation celebrated the thousandth anniversary of the hero's birth in 1849, issuing in that year a 'Jubilee Edition' of translations of Alfred's literary corpus as well as a commemorative medal.

1. Asser, ch. 1, trans. Keynes and Lapidge, p. 67. Wantage is now in Oxfordshire.

Unfortunately, Asser may have been out by a year or two.[2] A contemporary West Saxon genealogical regnal list thought to be the product of Alfred's court states that Alfred was twenty-three years old when he became king, and the *Anglo-Saxon Chronicle* dates his accession to after Easter in 871.[3] Taken together, these sources indicate that Alfred would have been born sometime between the Easter celebrations of 847 and 848. How, then, did Asser arrive at 849? While the list states that Alfred 'took the kingdom when there were gone of his years three and twenty winters', Asser has him ascend the throne in 871 'during his twenty-third year', that is, at the age of twenty-two.[4] Simple subtraction would have then led Asser to erroneously place Alfred's birth in 849.

Or, perhaps, Asser was right and the compiler of the list wrong. Alfred himself was likely indifferent to the question. The compiler of the *Anglo-Saxon Chronicle* dutifully recorded the accessions of kings and bishops and their deaths, but never their births. The Christian calendar in the ninth century revolved around deaths rather than birthdays; the lives of saints and the benefactors of the Church were remembered on the anniversaries of their deaths, their true 'births' into eternal life. The confusion over Alfred's birth date, however, reminds us how little we can know about a 'Dark Age' figure, even one as well documented as Alfred. We ought to begin, then, with a caveat. Like an archaeologist reconstructing a ninth-century royal mead hall from the dark stains of post holes in the ground, the biographer of Alfred is engaged in an endeavour of imagination based on logical possibilities. We can expect no more certainty than the sources allow.

. . .

ALFRED'S FAMILY

For Asser a mere narrative of deeds did not suffice to capture the essence of the man. As with King Solomon and

2. C. Plummer, *The Life and Times of Alfred the Great, Being the Ford Lectures for 1901* (1902, reprinted New York, 1970) pp. 69–70; B.A. Lees, *Alfred the Great, The Truth-Teller, Maker of England, 848–899* (New York and London, 1915) pp. 61–3.
3. D.N. Dumville, 'The West Saxon Genealogical Regnal List: manuscripts and texts', *Anglia* 104 (1986), p. 25; Keynes and Lapidge, p. 228, n. 2.
4. Asser, ch. 35.

Jesus Christ – and, for that matter, Julius Caesar – one could only truly comprehend Alfred through reference to his ancestry. Even before the youth had acted and the man had won glory, his destiny was determined by what he was – the scion of a royal dynasty that traced its ancestors back through the mists of Germanic myth to the biblical progenitors of the human race.

Asser introduces Alfred by reciting his pedigree: 'King Alfred was the son of King Æthelwulf, the son of Egbert, the son of Ealhmund, the son of Eafa, the son of Eoppa, the son of Ingild', and so forth. Along the way we encounter the magical and necessary names of Ingild's 'famous brother Ine', whose reign in the late seventh century lent a patina of royal dignity to his brother's descendants; Ceawlin, son of Cynric, who, by Bede's testimony, had enjoyed overlordship over all the southern English; Cerdic, the founder of the West Saxon royal house; Woden, the Scandinavian god transformed into the font of Germanic royalty by Christian clerical genealogists; and Woden's own biblical 'ancestors', Seth, son of Noah, son of Lamech, son of Methuselah, son of Enoch, down to Adam himself. To the modern reader this may seem reminiscent of the interminable lists of 'begats' in Genesis, or, perhaps, even of *Monty Python's* wonderful parody of viking sagas. Asser undoubtedly wanted his reader to recall the Bible, but the texts he had in mind were the tables of descent of Jesus and of Solomon from the House of Jesse in Matthew 1 and I Chronicles 1–3.[5] Alfred's genealogy thus fixes his place equally within West Saxon, Germanic, and Christian history.

Asser's is not the only pedigree of the 'Ecgberhtings' that has come down to us. The *Anglo-Saxon Chronicle* under the year 855 preserves the ancestry of King Æthelwulf, as does a late ninth-century West Saxon genealogical regnal list that survives in a number of manuscripts. The inclusion of 'Woden' and 'Adam' in these pedigrees warns us against relying too heavily upon the accuracy of 'folk memory'. Anglo-Saxon royal genealogies, a genre that can be traced back to eighth-century Mercia and Northumbria, were not intended as 'factual' presentations of historical memory. Rather, they were ideological documents intended to establish the

---

5. D. Howlett (personal communication on Ansaxnet).

political legitimacy of the current king and his line, a crucial endeavour given the uncertain nature of succession in
middle Saxon England. As political circumstances changed,
so did royal genealogies (a phenomenon, interestingly enough,
also observed in near-contemporary France and by anthro-
pologists in modern preliterate societies).[6] The manipula-
tion of genealogies to create a useable past could be radical.
In the seventh or early eighth century, for instance, the
upper reaches of the Bernician pedigree were grafted onto
the West Saxon royal genealogy, as the eponymous Saxon
god, Seaxnot, was ousted in favour of the Anglian font of
regality, Woden.[7] A close comparison of the various late
ninth-century pedigrees of the 'Ecgberhtings' reveals subtle
differences that may have had profound, if today obscure, contemporary political implications. In middle Saxon England,
as in Orwell's *1984*, he who controlled the present controlled the past, and he who controlled the past had a chance
to control the future.

Asser also included a brief notice on the ancestry of
Alfred's mother, Osburh, 'a most religious woman, noble by
temperament and noble by birth'. Osburh, we are told, was
the daughter of King Æthelwulf's famous butler, Oslac. This
is all we know for certain of Alfred's maternal kin, though
ealdormen Osmod and Osric, and the Osferth who received
from Alfred a generous bequest of eight estates in Sussex,
possibly belonged to this side of the family.[8] That Alfred's
grandfather was his father's 'butler' should not mislead us;

---

6. D.N. Dumville, 'Kingship, genealogies and regnal lists', *Early Medieval Kingship*, ed. P.H. Sawyer and I. Wood (Leeds 1977) pp. 85–8 (and references). See also P. Geary, *Phantoms of Remembrance: Memory and Oblivion at the End of the First Millennium* (Princeton, New Jersey, 1994) pp. 50–1.

7. K. Sisam, 'Anglo-Saxon royal genealogies', *Proceedings of the British Academy* 39 1953) pp. 302–5; see also Dumville, 'Kingship, genealogies and regnal lists', pp. 79–81.

8. For Osmod, see *ASC*, s.a. 836; S 270, 271, 278. For Osric, Asser, ch. 18; *ASC*, s.a. 845 (as ealdorman of Dorset), 860 (as ealdorman of Hampshire); S 290, 294, 298, 299, 308, 317, 326, 327. [These represent, perhaps, two different men.] For Osferth, see Alfred's will, trans. Keynes and Lapidge, pp. 177, 322; S 350, 364, 367, 378, 1286. On Alfred's possible maternal family connections, see J. Nelson, 'Reconstructing a royal family: reflections on Alfred, from Asser, chapter 2', in I. Wood and N. Lund, eds, *People and Places in Northern Europe 500–1600: Essays in Honour of Peter Hayes Sawyer* (Woodbridge, Suffolk, 1991) pp. 47–66.

royal 'domestics' were important men who enjoyed power, wealth, and influence. Asser, indeed, takes pains to connect Oslac to the West Saxon royal house itself: 'Oslac was a Goth by stock, for he was descended from the Goths and the Jutes, namely from the line of Stuf and Wihtgar, two brothers – indeed, ealdormen – who having received authority over the Isle of Wight from their uncle King Cerdic and from Cynric his son, their cousin, killed the few British inhabitants of the island whom they could find on it.'[9] Much of Asser's information is drawn, though in a confused fashion, from the *Anglo-Saxon Chronicle*'s entries for the years 530 and 534. The reference to the 'Goths' has attracted a good deal of scholarly discussion; some have even seen it as an attempt to establish Alfred's ancestral authority over the invading Danes, though this may be stretching matters. What may be more significant is the mention of Stuf and Wihtgar, said by the *Chronicle* to have been 'kinsmen' of Cerdic and Cynegils.[10] By highlighting these maternal ancestors, Asser emphasized that Alfred was of royal descent on the 'spindle' as well as 'spear' side. Osburh's 'Jutish' descent was also politically important. Æthelwulf may have claimed authority over Kent by virtue of his grandfather's election as king by the native nobility, but the hard reality was that he ruled the kingdom because his father had defeated and driven out the Mercians. The charters issued by Egbert and Æthelwulf (as underking) in the late 820s and 830s indicate their desire to appease and accommodate the local nobility, in particular the powerful archbishop of Canterbury. Under these circumstances, a marriage between the young underking and the daughter of an influential Kentish or South Saxon magnate would undoubtedly have helped secure local support for the West Saxon dynasty against the possible resurgence of Mercia. In 893, when Asser penned this chapter, the reference to Alfred's Jutish blood would still have been

9. Asser, ch. 2, trans. Keynes and Lapidge, p. 68.
10. Cynegils, who was Creodda's son and Cerdic's grandson in Asser's first chapter, now becomes Cerdic's son. David Howlett has made the intriguing suggestion that Asser included Creodda in his extended genealogy so that the number of generations between Alfred and Cerdic would equal that between Solomon and Abraham. See D.R. Howlett, *The Celtic Tradition of Biblical Style* (Blackrock, 1995) pp. 273–333.

of value in helping legitimate West Saxon rule over the southeast.

Though Alfred's blood was royal, that he ever became king was surprising. His parents already had four sons, Æthelstan, Æthelbald, Æthelberht, and Æthelred, and a daughter, Æthelswith. Why they named him 'Ælfræd' rather than choosing another name beginning with 'Æthel-' is unknown, and its significance, if any, unclear. The 'Aelf-' element is found in Northumbrian and East Anglian genealogies, but not in the West Saxon, and the name Alfred was uncommon in the mid-ninth century. Names of the Anglo-Saxon elite were usually made up of two elements, each a word in itself. Ælfræd literally means 'elf counsel,' while Æthelred means 'noble wolf'. However, while it would be romantic to see Alfred's name as preserving a belief in ancient wood spirits, his parents were probably as little influenced by the literal meaning of names as our own.

Alfred's oldest sibling, Æthelstan, must have been at least in his mid-twenties when Alfred was born, since he had been ruling Kent, Surrey, Sussex, and Essex under his father for almost a decade by 848. This has led some historians to suggest that he must have been Æthelwulf's younger brother (unlikely) or the son of an undocumented first marriage. He apparently died some time between 851 and 855. The second brother, Æthelbald, first appears in the historical record in 841, as a witness to a grant of land in Dorset, and was old enough to fight alongside his father in the battle of *Aclea* in 850/851.[11] If, like Alfred, Æthelbald began to attest charters when he was about six years old, he was born around 835, making him a dozen or so years older than Alfred. Æthelberht, who ruled jointly with Æthelbald during their father's pilgrimage to Rome in 855, presumably was about ten years Alfred's senior, as was their sister, Æthelswith, who married in 853. The fourth brother, Æthelred, who may have been acting as an underking as early as 862,[12] was closest to Alfred in age; his name appears, along with the young Alfred's, in the witness list to a charter issued in 854.[13]

11. S 290; *ASC*, s.a. 851. See also S 344, 319. On the date of the battle of *Aclea*, cf. *AB* s.a. 850.
12. S 335, 336; S.D. Keynes, 'The West Saxon charters of King Æthelwulf and his sons', *EHR* 109 (1994) pp. 1129–30.
13. S 308.

Unsurprisingly, Asser singles Alfred out for special praise: 'Now, he was greatly loved, more than all his brothers, by his father and mother – indeed, by everybody – with a universal and profound love, and he was always brought up in the royal court and nowhere else. As he passed through infancy and boyhood he was seen to be more comely in appearance than his other brothers, and more pleasing in manner, speech and behaviour.'[14] Asser's assertion that Alfred was greatly loved, if not simply a literary topos or political 'propaganda', might reflect the affection lavished by aging parents upon their last born.[15] Osburh was certainly no Sarah and Æthelwulf no Abraham, but given life expectancies at the time, the royal couple, in or near their forties,[16] were advanced in years when their youngest son was born. They may well have regarded him as a special gift from God. That he was more highly esteemed than his brothers probably ought not to be taken as factual. Asser's purpose here was to mark the boy for future greatness. As with the biblical David and Joseph, the love lavished upon this youngest son prefigured and was justified by his accomplishments as a man.

Asser's insistence that Alfred was brought up only in the royal court and nowhere else is clearly meant to contrast with the upbringing of his siblings, who by implication had been fostered in other noble households. This does not mean that Alfred's early years were placid. Life in an itinerating royal court peopled with dozens of men, women, and children must have been anything but. One can imagine the king and his entourage, with a caravan of wagons stuffed with treasure, coins, household goods, and amenities, slowly making their way along the earthen trackways

14. Asser, ch. 22, trans. Keynes and Lapidge, p. 74.
15. The same claim is made for St Boniface in the *Life* by Willibald. Cf. also Thegan's *Life of Louis the Pious*.
16. If Osburh was Æthelstan's mother she must have been at least forty when Alfred was born. This has led some to see her as a second wife, but perhaps unnecessarily so. In four generations of Charlemagne's descendants, the average age of women at death was thirty-six, and about 40 per cent lived into their forties. S.F. Wemple, *Women in Frankish Society: Marriage and the Cloister, 500 to 900* (Philadelphia, 1985) pp. 101–2, 199–201. Perhaps more importantly, Osburh would have been most politically attractive to Æthelwulf when he was still ruling the eastern region under his father, between around 825 and 839.

and poorly maintained Roman roads of the Wessex countryside, pausing for a week or two at monasteries, royal estates
and towns along the route, to feast on the food-rent owed
the king or enjoy the hospitality of an abbot, and to conduct whatever royal business was to be done in the locality.[17]
Though King Æthelwulf issued charters from places as far
east as Canterbury and Wye, in Kent, his court favoured the
royal estates and timbered palace complexes of Hampshire,
Wiltshire, Somerset, and Dorset, the shires that comprised
ancient Wessex. Here is where the young Alfred would have
felt most at home.

Once the court had taken up residence, its numbers would
have swelled with visitors. The local ealdorman, bishops,
abbots, and great thegns, all accompanied by retinues, would
come to pay court and provide counsel. Others would seek
out the king to solicit justice in their disputes. Foreigners,
including perhaps the occasional overseas merchant willing to brave the risk of viking pirates, might also pay their
respects, bearing and receiving gifts and enjoying the king's
hospitality in return for regaling him with tales of exotic
places and adventures. Alfred would have seen emissaries of
foreign rulers and prelates, from as near as Mercia and as
far as Francia. In 852, for instance, Æthelwulf received a
messenger from Lupus, abbot of Ferrières, petitioning him
for lead to roof his monastery in return for the monks'
prayers.[18] A year later the court was swarming with Mercian
messengers, as King Burgred sought Æthelwulf's support
for a campaign against the Welsh and his daughter's hand
in marriage.

· · ·

EARLY EDUCATION

Alfred as a child must have witnessed a great deal that he
did not understand, as he feasted in the royal hall with his
brothers and the noble youths entrusted to the king's care

17. In the fourteenth century the normal travelling distance for the
    royal household, which undoubtedly was many times larger than
    Æthelwulf's, was about fifteen miles a day. C. Given-Wilson, *The Royal
    Household and the King's Affinity. Service, Politics and Finance in England
    1360–1413* (New Haven and London, 1986) p. 33.
18. *EHD* I, nos. 217, 218. See below, p. 63.

by their fathers. He would have comprehended little of the furious preparations for war against the vikings that must have occupied the court in 851, other than a dim awareness of the disturbance to his routine. But a king's son assumed a 'public' persona early in life. By the age of six at the latest Alfred was attending his father's assemblies and lending his name to the witnessing of charters.[19]

Public duties aside, Alfred's childhood was little different from that of other noble boys. He played with his young companions at 'riding sticks and manifold other games imitating their elders'[20] and shared with them the literary and physical education proper to noble boys. As a youth he loved to listen to English poetry and hunt, and his passion for both continued throughout his life.

Hunting was more than recreation for an *ætheling*, teaching riding and use of weapons, the necessary skills for a martial aristocracy. Alfred presumably rode with his father and older brothers on their hunting expeditions, observing and learning from them and the royal huntsmen the skills of the chase. Through the hunt Alfred also became familiar with the terrain of his kingdom's forests and wastelands, lessons in topography that were to prove invaluable later in life in his war against the Danes. The royal hunt took him as far west as Cornwall, but much probably took place in the familiar environs of Selwood, with its roebuck, hares, and wild boars, and along the hidden watery trackways of the Somerset levels, where waterfowl could be found in abundance.

Alfred regarded the hunt as a craft to be mastered, which, like kingship itself, required skill, knowledge, and proper tools. And master it he did. 'He strives continually in every branch of hunting', Asser observed, 'and not in vain; for no one else could approach him in skill and success in that activity, just as in all other gifts of God, as I have so often seen for myself.'[21] In later years, hunting was to be his main escape from the cares of kingship and the infirmities of the flesh, and he was to maintain in his household a complement of royal falconers, hawk-trainers, and dog-keepers.

19. E.g., S 316 (a contemporary charter, issued perhaps in 853, but more likely in 855); 303, 308, 315, 317.
20. As he says in an aside in his translation of Boethius. *Alfred's Boethius*, ed. Sedgefield, ch. 36, p. 108; trans. Sedgefield, p. 124.
21. Asser, ch. 22, trans. Keynes and Lapidge, p. 75.

Characteristically, he prided himself on being able to instruct these experts upon the finer points of their professions.[22]

Alfred believed that a nobleman worthy of his rank should possess both wisdom and 'manly skills'. When as king he established a court school for the education of his own children and the young nobles committed to his foster care, he planned that the boys should be able to read and write in both English and Latin 'even before they had the requisite skill for manly skills (hunting, that is, and other skills appropriate to noblemen)'.[23] In beginning literary studies before 'manly pursuits', Alfred was in step with ninth- and tenth-century educational practice. Odo of Cluny, writing in the first half of the tenth century, explained how the saintly layman Gerald of Aurillac 'applied himself to the study of letters' (restricted to learning the Psalter) before going on to instruction in the physical activities proper for the warrior class, riding to hounds, archery, and learning to fly falcons and hawks.[24] Where Alfred differed from Gerald's parents was in insisting that education in letters ought to continue even while a youth was mastering the skills necessary for a martial life. For Alfred, the pursuit of wisdom was a lifetime activity that complemented the manly arts. Alfred, indeed, compared learning to hunting. In his famous preface to the *Pastoral Care*, he lamented the decline of learning in the Wessex of his youth with a metaphor from the hunt. Of the books that lay unread because of the illiteracy of the men of his day, Alfred declared, 'Here we can still see their tracks, but we cannot follow it up, and therefore we have lost both the wealth and the wisdom, because we were unwilling to incline our minds to that track.' The same simile appears also in an original passage in Alfred's translation of Boethius in a chapter awash with language drawn from the hunt.[25]

22. Asser, ch. 76.
23. Asser, ch. 75, trans. Keynes and Lapidge, p. 90.
24. Odo of Cluny, *Vita sancti Geraldi Aurillacensis comitis*, ed. J.P. Migne, *Patrologia Latina* 133 (Paris, 1844–55) col. 645, trans. G. Sitwell, *St. Odo of Cluny* (London, 1958) p. 97, discussed by R. McKitterick, *The Carolingians and the Written Word* (Cambridge, 1989) pp. 217–8. Cf. A.P. Smyth, *King Alfred the Great* (Oxford, 1995) pp. 205–10, 274–7.
25. *Alfred's Pastoral Care*, ed. and trans. Sweet, prose preface, p. 5. Cf. *Alfred's Boethius*, ed. Sedgefield, ch. 38, p. 121. Cf. S. Lerer, *Literacy and Power in Anglo-Saxon Literature* (Lincoln, Nebraska, 1991) pp. 77–82; Smyth, *King Alfred*, p. 572.

Later in life Alfred was to decry, perhaps with some exaggeration, the abysmal state of learning in Wessex when he came to the throne, and lament that 'at the time that he was the right age and had the leisure and capacity for learning, he did not have the teachers'.[26] That he had some tutors, however unsatisfactory in retrospect, is attested by a famous but problematic story. One day, as Asser relates the tale, Alfred's mother showed him and his brothers a beautifully decorated book of English poetry. 'I shall give this book to whichever one of you can learn it the fastest,' she said. Alfred, attracted by the beauty of the initial letter in the book and 'spurred on by divine inspiration', quickly spoke up, forestalling the older boys, 'Will you really give this book to the one of us who can understand it the soonest and recite it to you?' Smiling with pleasure, his mother reassured him that she was in earnest. 'He immediately took the book from her hand, went to his tutor and read/learnt [*legere*] it. When it was read/learnt [*Quo lecto*], he took it back to his mother and recited it.'[27] This simple story served multiple purposes for Asser. Not only did it establish Alfred's childhood love of learning and innate superiority to his slower brothers, but it prefigured Alfred's efforts as an adult to revive learning. Still, the tale raises a great many questions, not the least being when did this competition occur? As we shall presently see, Alfred went on two pilgrimages to Rome between the ages of five and seven. By the time he had returned from the second, his mother, Osburh, was dead and his father remarried to the twelve-year-old daughter of the West Frankish king, Charles the Bald. It is unlikely that the young Carolingian princess, Judith, would have read poetry in English, let alone that Asser would have termed her Alfred's 'mother'. So if the event really did occur, it must have been before 855, perhaps in 854, between Alfred's two trips to Rome. That a precocious six-year-old could learn to read a book of vernacular poetry is possible, though Classical and early Christian authorities deemed the age of seven to be the proper time to begin literary studies. The problem is that, if Asser is to be believed, Alfred was illiterate

---

26. Asser, ch. 25, trans. Keynes and Lapidge, pp. 75–6. Cf. chs 88–9, where Asser depicts his own more successful efforts to instruct the king in wisdom.
27. Asser, ch. 23, trans. Keynes and Lapidge, p. 75.

at the time of the competition. In the preceding chapter Asser makes a point of saying that Alfred, because of the 'shameful negligence of his parents and tutors', 'remained ignorant of letters until his twelfth year, or even longer'. Could Asser have been so incompetent, or indifferent to the truth, as to have contradicted himself so flatly in the matter of a few lines? Or is the inconsistency merely apparent? With all its problems, the tale sounds as if it were based on a genuine childhood memory of Alfred. Nor is it reasonable to think that Asser would have fabricated it. The *Life*, though it may have been intended for an audience of Welsh monks, was addressed to King Alfred and undoubtedly was meant to be read by him. Alfred, better than anyone, would have known when he had first learned to read. So what are we to make of the tale? The most reasonable solution is that the child took the book to his tutor, who read it aloud to him until the boy had committed it to memory and could recite it to his mother. Alfred, for all his complaints, thus had at least one fond memory of a childhood tutor, one literate in the vernacular and patient enough to help a six-year-old boy memorize an entire book of poems.

This interpretation of the tale finds support in the preceding chapter of Asser's *Life*. Although lamenting Alfred's poor childhood education, Asser praises him for having listened so carefully to the English poems recited in his father's court that he had no problem retaining them in his memory as an adult.[28] He assures us that Alfred was from birth manifestly superior to his brothers, in large part because of his noble character as revealed through his life-long pursuit of wisdom. Surely, this charming story is meant to illustrate these qualities. We are given a demonstration of Alfred's youthful love of poetry, the power of his memory, and his natural pre-eminence. Asser even subtly hints that the boy, drawn as he was to the book's mere physical beauty, could not yet appreciate in his illiteracy and immaturity that the true treasure lay *in* the words.[29] (Implied is also a

28. Asser, ch. 22.
29. Lerer, *Literacy and Power*, pp. 64–70. Alfred draws a contrast between the possession of books as 'treasures/wealth' and the wisdom contained in them in his Prose Preface to the *Pastoral Care*. See T.A. Shippey, 'Wealth and wisdom in King Alfred's *Preface* to the Old English *Pastoral Care*', EHR 94 (1979) pp. 346–55.

contrast between Alfred's childhood tutors, who trained him to memorize, and Asser, who taught him to understand.) Nonetheless, ill-equipped as he was, the young Alfred was already keenly on the track of wisdom. The 'memory' of this competition was both thus a demonstration of Alfred's innate love of learning and a harbinger of what was to come.

. . .

SPIRITUAL SON TO ST PETER

Youthful 'memories' can be deceptive.[30] For Asser, one of Alfred's outstanding qualities was his truthfulness. Yet Alfred seems to have misremembered or misrepresented the most extraordinary event in his early life: his reception by Pope Leo IV during the first of his childhood pilgrimages to Rome. Almost everything about Alfred's pilgrimages is problematic. Enough scholarly ink has been spilled on the subject to drown a colloquium of graduate students. The 'facts' are recorded in the *Anglo-Saxon Chronicle* and by Asser, who, in this instance, departed from his source. The former records in typically laconic fashion that in 853 'King Æthelwulf sent his son Alfred to Rome. The lord Leo [IV] was then pope of Rome, and he consecrated him king and stood sponsor to him at confirmation.' Asser adds that Æthelwulf brought Alfred back to Rome with him when the king undertook his own pilgrimage a couple of years later.[31]

Rome and the papacy held special meaning for the Anglo-Saxons. Bede's celebrated *Ecclesiastical History of the English People* provided the English kingdoms with a common spiritual history derived from Rome. As Bede taught, the 'Angli' had been rescued from damnation through the love of Pope Gregory the Great (590–604), the 'Apostle of the English', who had dispatched to these heathen shores St Augustine and his band of Roman missionaries. St Peter's love was reciprocated. Seventh- and eighth-century popes called upon

---

30. For a discussion of memory as a process of active creation, see Geary, *Phantoms*, pp. 19–20, and references there, especially F. Bartlett, *Remembering: A Study in Experimental and Social Psychology* (New York, 1932), and J. Bransford, *Human Cognition: Learning, Understanding and Remembering* (Belmont, Calif., 1979).
31. *ASC*, s.a. 853, 855–58; Asser, chs 8, 11. Cf. *AB*, s.a. 855.

devout Englishmen such as Willibrord, Willibald, and, above all, St Boniface to bring Roman Christianity to Frisia and Germany and to reform the Frankish Church in accordance with Roman sacramental discipline and ecclesiological ideas. Anglo-Saxon devotion to Rome manifested itself, among other ways, in the English Church's strict adherence to Roman liturgy and customs, in the popular veneration of SS Peter, Andrew, and Gregory, and in a flood of pilgrims.

Rome, city of the apostles, burial ground of martyrs, boasted more relics than any place in the West, among them the bodies of SS Peter and Paul. For the rationalist medieval historians of the late nineteenth century, the cult of the saints, with its veneration of fragments of bone and human tissue, was a grisly confirmation of the barbarism and superstition of the 'Dark Ages'. Such a view fails to appreciate the spiritual need met by relics. These were not mere mementos of the dead, any more than the Mass was a mere reminder of Christ's sacrifice. A relic placed one in the presence of the sacred. The supernatural power that suffused it was as real and immediate to Alfred's contemporaries as the current that flows from an electric socket is to us. The saint's living presence and the force of his sanctity were manifest in each fragment of his physical remains and even in objects he had touched.[32] The possession of relics secured for a church the protection and patronage of saints and attracted to it pilgrims bearing gifts in hopes of winning supernatural favour.

As a repository of the holy, Rome was a spiritual magnet for devout Christians. To pilgrims it was 'noble Rome, red with the blood of martyrs', a treasure-house of the sacred, where sinners could hope to win the favour of saints and from which the pious might acquire relics to sanctify the churches of their homelands. Anglo-Saxons in particular seem to have felt the lure of the Eternal City. From the late seventh century on, 'many Englishmen, nobles and common, layfolk and clergy, men and women' undertook the difficult journey to 'the threshold of the apostles', so that they might 'be thought worthy to receive a greater welcome

---

32. P. Brown, *The Cult of the Saints: Its Rise and Function in Latin Christianity* (Chicago, 1981) p. 88. See also Brown, *Society and the Holy in Late Antiquity* (Berkeley and Los Angeles, 1982) pp. 222–50, 317–19.

from the saints in heaven'.[33] Among them were two West
Saxon kings. The first, Caedwalla (686–688), was the sort
of character who reminds us how alien the past can be. He
had been a pagan until his twenties, when, as a rebel *ætheling*
leading a warband in the forests of *Andredesweald* and the
Chilterns, he suddenly sought out St Wilfrid, then also in
exile, to be his 'spiritual father'. Conversion did nothing to
moderate his ferocity. Brutal even by seventh-century standards – he is said to have exterminated the entire native
population of the Isle of Wight – he abruptly abdicated at
the age of thirty to receive baptism in Rome, motivated
possibly by illness.[34] On Easter Day 689 he was baptized in
the presence of Pope Sergius, who received him from the
font and gave him the Christian name Peter. He died seven
days later and was buried in St Peter's church, where his
tomb became an essential attraction for later English pilgrims. Caedwalla's successor, Ine (688–726), later reputed
to be the founder of the *Schola Saxonum,* the 'Saxon quarter' near St Peter's, also abdicated to make the pilgrimage
to Rome, where he and his wife, Æthelburh, are said to have
died. Ine was a highly successful ruler remembered as a
benefactor of the Church and as a law-giver. Because the
Ecgberhtings could cite remarkably few kings in their direct lineage, they incorporated Ine, the brother of Egbert's
great great-grandfather, Ingild, into their pedigree. Ingild
may not have ruled, but he was the brother of a man 'who
held the kingdom for thirty-seven years and afterwards went
to St Peter's and ended his life there'.[35] Ine not only helped
legitimize the Ecgberhtings but provided them with a model
of kingship. Alfred appended a copy of Ine's laws to his own
legislation, and Æthelwulf paid homage to his great predecessor by following in his footsteps to Rome.

33. Bede, *HE* V.7, ed. and trans. Colgrave and Mynors, p. 473. St Boniface,
    writing in 747 to Archbishop Cuthbert of Canterbury, was less con-
    vinced of the salutary effects of pilgrimages, especially for women.
    The Letters of Saint Boniface, ed. and trans. Ephraim Emerton (New
    York, 1940) no. 78, p. 140. See P.A. Halpin, 'Anglo-Saxon Women
    and Pilgrimage', *Anglo-Norman Studies* 19 (1997) pp. 97–112.
34. Bede, *HE,* IV.15–16, ed. and trans. Colgrave and Mynors, pp. 381–5;
    v.7, pp. 469–73; *ASC,* s.a. 686, 687, 688.
35. *ASC,* s.a. 855–858. Ine is also named in the Alfredian West Saxon
    Genealogical Regnal List and in Asser's pedigree.

It is nonetheless puzzling that Æthelwulf would have sent Alfred on pilgrimage at the tender age of four or five. For the Chronicler and Asser, the answer was to have the boy consecrated king. Certainly, popes performed similar services for Carolingian rulers,[36] but it is unlikely that Æthelwulf would have singled out his youngest son for such an honour while passing over his three older living brothers, thus risking their disaffection and possible rebellion. [37] Why, then, was Alfred sent to Rome in 853 and what happened to him there? A letter sent by Pope Leo IV to Æthelwulf, which has been preserved in extracted form in a twelfth-century collection of papal letters, sheds much-needed light.[38]

> To Æthelwulf, king of the English. We have now graciously received your son Alfred, whom you were anxious to send at this time to the thresholds of the Holy Apostles, and we have decorated him, as a spiritual son, with the dignity of the sword [or military belt; the Latin word is *cingulum*] and the vestments of the consulate, as is customary with Roman consuls, because he gave himself into our hands.[39]

Apparently, Leo IV received the young Alfred in grand fashion. He was feted and honoured in a way calculated to impress the English boy and his entourage and guarantee the good will and gratitude of his father. The pope stood sponsor for the boy at his confirmation, becoming his 'spiritual father', and invested him as a Roman consul in a ceremony that

36. Charlemagne's grandson, the Emperor Lothar, had asked (or permitted) Pope Sergius II in 844 to consecrate his eldest son, Louis, king. *AB*, s.a. 844, 850. See discussion by Stevenson, *Asser's Life*, pp. 180, 183–5.
37. Cf. C. Plummer, *Alfred the Great*, pp. 73–4; J. Nelson, 'The Franks and the English in the Ninth Century Reconsidered', paper presented to ISAS, July 1991. Nelson suggests that Alfred's anointing was part of a short-lived succession strategy devised by Æthelwulf to divide his kingdom among all his sons, again following the lead of the Carolingians.
38. Doubts were raised about the authenticity of the letter by J. Nelson in 'The Problem of King Alfred's Royal Anointing', *Journal of Ecclesiastical History* 18 (1967) pp. 145–63, reprinted in her *Politics and Ritual in Early Medieval Europe* (London, 1986) pp. 309–27. Professor Nelson has since reconsidered her objections and is now persuaded that the fragment is more likely genuine. 'The Franks and the English in the Ninth Century Reconsidered', paper presented to ISAS, July 1991.
39. *EHD* I, no. 219, p. 880.

may have somewhat resembled, at least in some of its trappings, the papal consecration of kings. But this was hardly a hallowing to kingship. By the mid-ninth century the Roman consulship was no longer an office of state. It survived in a vestigial form as a mere title, borne even by some merchants and notaries, the perfect honour to confer on a visiting Northern prince. What Pope Leo IV actually bestowed on Alfred may have been, in the words of W.H. Stevenson, 'little more than a brevet of Roman nobility'.[40] Even so, the early medieval papacy excelled at pomp and circumstance, and the ceremony by which Alfred was made a 'consul' was undoubtedly impressive, especially to a young boy. Apparelled in magnificent robes, perhaps even in the purple cloak of a triumphing consul, Alfred would have stood before the Holy Father as he girded a decorated sword around his waist, undoubtedly to the accompaniment of suitable chants.

If this is all that happened, how did the Chronicler and Asser get it so wrong? Even more to the point, why did Alfred, the 'truth-teller', not correct their sycophantic error? What is at issue here is no less than the credibility of our sources, including the king's own veracity. The problem has so disturbed historians that some have rejected the *Anglo-Saxon Chronicle* as a private compilation originating far from the king's court and Asser's *Life* as a forgery. Others have taken the opposite tack and seen the error as Alfred's clever use of 'propaganda'. The truth of the matter is, of course, impossible to establish. But it seems to me that Alfred, looking back from the vantage point of the early 890s, may have come to believe that he had, indeed, been anointed king as a boy. Experts on early medieval liturgy and inauguration rituals are sceptical that anyone could mistake the rite of confirmation for a royal consecration. But an aging man recalling an event from his early childhood, forty years before, might well have done so. One can easily imagine Alfred reshaping the memories of his youth to conform to the realities of his adult life.

For the pious Alfred only divine providence could adequately explain his success. Ill from at least adolescence, he had not only survived into manhood, but had succeeded to the kingship as a fifth son and had defeated the vikings

40. Stevenson, *Asser's Life of King Alfred*, pp. 183–4. See also Lees, pp. 83–5.

when his contemporaries in Mercia, East Anglia, and North-umbria had fallen prey to them. For Alfred it could have been hardly coincidental that his life bore striking parallels to that of King David, in whose Psalms he found special solace and meaning.[41] Like David, he had soared above his older brothers and achieved greatness as king after being driven into the wastelands. And like the Hebrew king, he had smashed his heathen enemies and restored the worship of God in his kingdom. Alfred knew from Holy Scripture that David had been marked out in his youth by the prophet Samuel, who had selected him out of all of his brothers to be anointed king, years before he actually ascended the throne. Possibly Alfred 'remembered' the ceremony in Rome decades before as similarly prefiguring his unexpected and divinely ordained kingship. Alfred, like Bede, understood the 'true law of history' as revealing the underlying spiritual truth in human actions.[42] This, of course, is speculation, but it fits well with Alfred's vision of himself and his life as revealed through his writings.

Whatever Alfred may have come to believe forty years later, his father's objective in sending him to Rome had little to do with prognostications of future glory. It is more likely that his presence in the embassy was intended as a gesture of good will toward the papacy, whose favour the king hoped to win. Alfred was sent to Rome, at least in part, to prepare the way for the grand pilgrimage his father planned to take.[43]

In 853 Æthelwulf was at the height of his power and pres-tige. It was a propitious time for the West Saxon king to claim a place of honour among the kings and emperors of Christendom. At *Aclea* two years before, Æthelwulf had inflicted, in the words of the Chronicler, 'the greatest slaugh-ter on a heathen army that we ever heard of until the present day'.[44] News of the battle spread far. Bishop Prudentius, writ-ing the so-called *Annals of St-Bertin* at Troyes, concluded a dismal annal concerned largely with the devastations wrought by the Moors and Northmen by giving thanks to God for the English defeat of the Northmen 'with the help of our Lord

41. As Beatrice Lees noted, p. 84. See below, p. 239.
42. R.D. Ray, 'Bede's *Vera lex historiae*', *Speculum* 55 (1980), pp. 1–21.
43. Lees, p. 80.
44. *ASC*, s.a. 851.

Jesus Christ'.[45] Lupus, abbot of Ferrières, also took notice
of the victory, and around 852 sent a letter to Æthelwulf
praising him for the good reports he had heard about his
rule and the 'strength conferred upon [him] by God against
the foes of Christ'.[46] Actually, Lupus's blandishments were
merely a prelude for his real purpose. The abbot needed
lead to roof the church of St Peter in his monastery. Having
heard of Æthelwulf's generosity from his Frankish secretary,
Felix – also the recipient of a letter on the roofing project
– and undoubtedly aware of the rich mineral resources
of Devon and Cornwall, Lupus besought the king 'to share
in the work'.

> Help, therefore, to complete this in God's honour, not for our
> merit, but in consideration of the divine reward. For we, who
> intercede for you without your generosity, will be the more
> eager if we receive a gift which will so greatly profit you and us,
> regarding only the remedy of the soul. We shall, however, as we
> have already signified, be ready in anything possible that you
> may enjoin on us.[47]

Lupus's last phrase may have been meant to proffer hospitality
to the prospective pilgrim. This, at any rate, would explain
his odd choice of titles in addressing Æthelwulf. Lupus
wrote to the king as abbot of St Judoc (Saint-Josse-sur-mer in
the Pas-de-Calais near Étaples) rather than claiming the far
higher dignity of abbot of Ferrières.[48] The cell of St Judoc,

45. *AB*, s.a. 850, trans. Nelson, p. 69.
46. *EHD* I, no. 217, p. 878.
47. *EHD* I, no. 217, p. 879. Cf. no. 218, to Felix. Lupus also sent letters
at this time to Archbishop Wigmund of York (*EHD* I, no. 215),
and Ealdsige, abbot of York (*EHD* I, no. 216). For the Latin texts,
see *Servati Lupi Epistolae*, ed. P.K. Marshall, Bibliotheca Scriptorum
Graecorum et Romanorum Teubneriana (Leipzig, 1984), nos. 13, 14,
61, 62.
48. Lupus addresses the Northumbrian recipients of his letters as abbot
of Ferrières, and Felix as abbot of both Ferrières and St Judoc. The
importance of St Judoc to the English and to Alfred's family is underscored by the transfer of the saint's relics to Edward the Elder's
New Minster, Winchester, soon after its foundation. *ASC* s.a. '903' F
(probably referring to events of 901); *Liber Vitae of the New Minster and
Hyde Abbey, Winchester*, ed. S.D. Keynes (Copenhagen, 1996) p. 81 and
comments on pp. 17–18 on the popularity of the cult of St Judoc at
the New Minster.

which lay near the great port of Quentovic, had been founded half a century before by the English scholar, Alcuin, as a hospice for English pilgrims on their way to Rome.[49] Lupus undoubtedly wished to remind the West Saxon king of the services he and his predecessors had rendered English pilgrims and offer future service. In the gift-giving societies of early medieval England and Francia, one gave in expectation of receiving. Not only would Æthelwulf's gift of lead be repaid by the monks' prayers for his soul, Lupus assured the king, but the abbot would serve the king 'in all things'.[50] Æthelwulf and his emissaries could expect the hospitality of the monks on their journey to Rome.

Lupus may have written in response to news of a planned embassy to Rome; he seems to have been well informed about such things. Lupus's allusion to Æthelwulf's reputation for piety and generosity may have been self-serving, but it was not exaggerated. The king had planned a pilgrimage to Rome in 839 as one of his first acts after ascending the West Saxon throne and had gone so far as to secure safe passage from Louis the Pious. The *Annals of St-Bertin* preserve an interesting letter that, if genuine, sheds light on Æthelwulf's religious motivations. According to Prudentius, then resident in the emperor's household and in a position to know, Louis the Pious received envoys from 'the king of the English' requesting permission to travel through his lands on a pilgrimage to Rome. The English messengers also admonished the emperor to 'devote even more careful attention and concern to the salvation of the souls of those subject to him'.[51] The king's request and warning were motivated by a terrifying vision experienced by an English priest, an extended account of which he entrusted to the envoys for

---

49. *Lupi Epistolae*, ed. P.K. Marshall, no. 11, p. 20; trans. Graydon W. Regenos, *The Letters of Lupus of Ferrières* (The Hague, 1966) no. 19, p. 34. See W.J. Moore, *The Saxon Pilgrims to Rome and the Schola Saxonum* (Fribourg, 1937) p. 87; P. Stafford, 'Charles the Bald, Judith and England', in *Charles the Bald, Court and Kingdom*, ed. M.T. Gibson and J.L. Nelson, 2nd edn, revised (Great Yarmouth, Norfolk, 1990) p. 140.
50. He repeats this twice in the letter. *EHD* I, 217, pp. 878–9.
51. *AB*, s.a. 839, trans. Nelson, p. 43. Given the date of the annal, it is conceivable that the 'English king' was actually the dying Egbert rather than his son, but the priest's vision quoted in the annal seems to point more to a new king anxious about impending disasters.

the emperor's edification. The priest, in his vision, was taken to a land with myriad wonderful buildings. His guide brought him into a church, where he saw many boys reading books written in alternate lines of ink and blood. Horrified, he asked his guide what this meant, and was told that the lines of blood represented the sins of the Christian people, 'because they are so utterly unwilling to obey the orders and fulfil the precepts in those divine books'. The boys were the saints, whose constant intercession with God was the only thing that stayed the divine wrath. The guide reminded the priest that in that very year an abundant crop of fruit had withered on the trees and vines. This was but a harbinger of the terrors that were to come. If the Christian people did not do penance quickly:

> a dense fog will spread over their land, and then all of a sudden pagan men will lay waste with fire and sword most of the people and land of the Christians along with all they possess. But if instead they are willing to do true penance immediately and carefully atone for their sins according to the Lord's command with fasting, prayer and alms-giving, then they may still escape those punishments and disaster through the intercession of the saints.[52]

For whatever reason, Æthelwulf did not make a pilgrimage to Rome in 839. And, as the priest had warned, pagan men came to 'lay waste with fire and sword' the Christian lands. Throughout the 840s Danes raided along the coasts and rivers of England and Francia, as Æthelwulf and his ealdormen fought one pirate band after another from Romney Marsh to Carhampton. *Aclea* provided a respite after a decade of sporadic warfare. By 853 the time may have seemed propitious to the king to begin preparations for his long-delayed pilgrimage by dispatching an advance party to make his intentions known to the pope.

But why did he include Alfred among the 'great number of nobles and commoners' he sent ahead? The journey was an arduous one, not to be undertaken lightly even by robust adults, let alone a boy of four or five. It took about two months to traverse the 1,600 or so kilometres separating

52. *AB*, s.a. 839, trans. Nelson, p. 43.

Wessex from Rome. The itinerary was a veritable obstacle course, beginning with the brief but hazardous Channel crossing and continuing with the great trek through Francia and northern Italy. The pagan Danes who ravaged, burnt and enslaved along the Seine and Loire valleys in the spring and summer months of 853 operated far enough away from the main pilgrim routes to offer little threat, and the coastal areas of northern and central Italy were relatively peaceful following the victory of a combined Roman and Neapolitan fleet over the Sardinian pirates in 849.[53] But Alfred and his companions still faced many perils. Road conditions throughout ninth-century Francia were abysmal and robbers lurked in the forests and defiles through which travellers had to pass, making retinues of armed men desirable not only for prestige but safety's sake. Abbot Lupus, writing to a friend around 856/8, urged him to pick a safe road to the abbey and to surround himself with 'a company of travelling companions large and strong enough to keep brigand gangs at bay, or, if necessary, to drive them away'.[54] And then there were the Alps. The itinerary of Archbishop Sigeric of Canterbury, who journeyed to Rome in 990 to obtain his *pallium*, names seventy-nine places along the route, spaced at about twenty-kilometre intervals, most the sites of pilgrim hospices.[55]

Still, Æthelwulf committed his youngest son to the hardships of the sea, road, and mountains. One can only speculate why. Undoubtedly, he was motivated at least in part by his love of the boy. From at least adolescence, Alfred suffered sporadic attacks of illness. If they began earlier in his childhood,[56] Æthelwulf may have sent Alfred to the Apostle to be healed in body as well as spirit. Asser, chapter 74, says he suffered from haemorrhoids (*ficus*) from 'early youth' (*ab infantia*), but in the same chapter implies that Alfred's piles began after he had reached puberty. But love of Alfred may have been only part of the story. The inclusion of a

53. *AB*, s.a. 853.
54. *Lupi Epistolae*, ed. P.K. Marshall, no. 104,
55. Veronica Ortenberg, 'Archbishop Sigeric's journey to Rome', *ASE* 19 (1990) pp. 197–246, especially pp. 228–46.
56. M.J. Enright, 'Disease, royal unction and propaganda: an interpretation of Alfred's journeys to Rome, 853 and 855 AD', *Continuity* 3 (1982) pp. 1–6.

king's son in the embassy was undoubtedly intended as a sign of respect, and of the king's four living sons – Æthelstan had probably died before 853 – his youngest was the most expendable in a year marked by a major expedition against the Welsh, battles with the vikings, and a marriage of state between the Mercian King Burgred and Æthelwulf's daughter, Æthelswith, 'conducted in royal style' (*nuptiis regaliter factis*).[57] In concentrating upon the meaning of the political ritual performed by Leo, historians may have missed the real significance of Alfred's reception by the pope. He was not only made a 'consul' but, more importantly, was confirmed, with Leo himself standing sponsor. Æthelwulf may have sought to create spiritual bonds between himself and the papacy. In sending Alfred, Æthelwulf offered a profound gesture of love for St Peter and the Holy See, into whose care he had committed his son. By anointing the child with the chrism of confirmation and receiving him as his 'spiritual son', Leo IV returned the gift in kind, creating a spiritual affiliation extending not only between himself and his 'son' but between the two 'fathers'.[58] The ritual bound in friendship and equality the two men who now called Alfred son. This, I believe, was Æthelwulf's true purpose in sending Alfred to Rome.

57. Asser, chs 7–9, trans. Keynes and Lapidge, p. 69. There is some reason to think that King Æthelwulf also sent Alfred's older brother, Æthelred, then a child of about eight. The medieval monks of Brescia commemorated among the benefactors of their abbey an Æthelred (*Ederath*) who is paired with an Alfred (*Elfreth*). A column of entries later it names *Elfreth* again and Æthelwulf (*Ædeluulf*) 'king of the English'. This might suggest that Æthelred was with Alfred when the English embassy rested in Pavia at 'St Mary of the Britons', a pilgrims' hostel that belonged to the monastery of Brescia. See H. Becher, 'Das königliche Frauenkloster San Salvatore/San Giula in Brescia im Spiegel seiner Memorialüberlieferung', *Frühmittelalterliche Studien* 17 (1983) pp. 299–392 (pp. 377–82), and S.D. Keynes, 'Anglo-Saxon Entries in the "Liber Vitae" of Brescia,' in J. Roberts and J.C. Nelson with M. Godden, eds, *Alfred the Wise: Studies in Honour of Janet Bately on the Occasion of her Sixty-Fifth Birthday* (Cambridge, 1997) pp. 99–119. That Pope Leo IV's letter to King Æthelwulf fails to mention Æthelred, however, is problematic.
58. For spiritual affiliation, see J.H. Lynch, *Godparents and Kinship in Early Medieval Europe* (Princeton, NJ, 1986) pp. 162–218, especially pp. 211–15. Hadrian's baptism and sponsoring of Charlemagne's sons, Carloman and Louis, provided a model for the exchange.

. . .

ÆTHELWULF'S 'DECIMATION' AND HIS PILGRIMAGE TO ROME

Alfred was back in Wessex in the spring of 854 and celebrated Easter with his family at the royal 'palace' at Wilton.[59] King Æthelwulf presided over a large Easter assembly, attended by Bishops Ealhstan of Sherborne and Swithun of Winchester, the king's four sons, at least three ealdormen from the western shires, two abbots, a priest, and about a dozen king's thegns then resident at the court. The business conducted included issuance of a number of land grants and charters confirming ecclesiastical privileges, implementing a remarkable decision by the king to 'book' [i.e. convey by charter] 'the tenth part of his land throughout all his kingdom to the praise of God and his own eternal salvation' before he departed for Rome 'with great state'.[60] As Asser interpreted it, the king had 'freed the tenth part of his whole kingdom from every royal service and tribute and as an everlasting inheritance he made it over on the cross of Christ to the Triune God, for the redemption of his soul and those of his predecessors'.[61] By 'booking' the donations Æthelwulf not only alienated them permanently from the royal demesne (and his family holdings) but freed them from all fiscal obligations to the Crown except for the three necessary military 'common burdens': host duty, repair of fortifications and bridge work.

This was 'gift-giving' on a lavish, even extravagant, scale, and though Asser and the *Chronicle* emphasized the religious motive behind this donation, it is clear from the charter evidence that the beneficiaries included the secular nobility as well as the clergy. A Kentish charter dated to 855 relates

59. S 303, 308, 310, 311.
60. *ASC*, s.a. 855–8. See S 302–5, 307–8, and 314, for general grants of privilege to the Church; 306 and 309–12, for (suspicious) grants to Malmesbury and Winchester; and 315, for a grant to a Kentish thegn. Cf. S 290, 1862. The authenticity of these charters, which survive in later copies, has generated a good deal of discussion. The scholarly consensus seems to be that many of them preserve a genuine substratum. See H.P.R. Finberg, *The Early Charters of Wessex* (Leicester, 1964) pp. 187–213; Keynes, 'West Saxon charters', pp. 1119–22; S.E. Kelly, 'King Æthelwulf's Decimation of 854' (forthcoming). But cf. Smyth, *King Alfred the Great*, pp. 382–4.
61. Asser, ch. 11, trans. Keynes and Lapidge, pp. 69–70.

how Æthelwulf endowed his thegn, Dunn, with a village and ten yokes of land near Rochester 'in consideration of the decimation of the lands, which God giving, I have ordered done for my other thegns'.[62] The last clause suggests the sweep of the king's generosity.

Such heroic munificence requires explanation. A lord gave because it was expected of him; but in expectation that his generosity would be returned through loyalty and service. In the case of the clergy, this meant spiritual service, specifically their prayers. A series of charters detailing the general fiscal privileges Æthelwulf bestowed upon the Church explains how the clergy expressed their gratitude.[63] They pledged that every Saturday the monks of the realm would sing fifty Psalms on his behalf and each priest perform two masses, the 'Deus qui iustifias impium' for the king (while he lived; a different mass was chosen for him after his death) and the 'Pretende domine' for his bishops and ealdormen. 'We have done this', Æthelwulf is made to say about his gifts, 'in honour of our Lord Jesus Christ, and of the Blessed and always Virgin Mary and of all the saints, and out of reverence for the Paschal celebration, so that omnipotent God may deign to grant pardon to us and our posterity.' Æthelwulf also looked for a return on the part of his thegns. He may have hoped that the land he gave them would eventually find its way into ecclesiastical endowments, benefiting their souls as well as his own. But his gifts to them (and to his churchmen) also had a more mundane political purpose, to secure, in the words of a contemporary Kentish charter, their 'humble obedience and fidelity [to the king] in all things'.[64] This sentiment is echoed in an earlier charter preserved in the archives of Sherborne Abbey, the language of which is strongly reminiscent of King Egbert's and King Æthelwulf's agreement with Archbishop Ceolnoth at Kingston-upon-Thames in 838, when the dying king and his heir were electioneering for ecclesiastical support for Æthelwulf's succession.[65]

62. S 315 (BCS 486); A. Campbell, ed., *Charters of Rochester. Anglo-Saxon Charters I* (London, 1973) no. 23, pp. 26–7.
63. E.g., S 304 (BCS 468); S 308 (BCS 469).
64. S 316 (BCS 467).
65. S 290. Cf. S 1438. *Charters of Sherborne*, ed. M.A. O'Donovan (London, 1988), no. 3. See discussion by Keynes, 'West Saxon charters', pp. 1112–13, 1122.

The context of the 'Decimation' is crucial to under-standing its purpose. Æthelwulf in 854–855 was preparing for his pilgrimage to Rome. Unlike the royal pilgrims who preceded him, Æthelwulf intended to return and resume his kingship. Apparently, the king had divided a tenth of his private domain between his ecclesiastic and lay fol-lowers, hoping thereby to secure both the favour of God for his journey and the loyalty of his nobility during his absence, a wise precaution, if insufficient in light of sub-sequent events.

Before the king could begin his journey he needed to settle the realm politically. The death of Æthelstan some-time between 851 and 854 undoubtedly increased tensions at court. Æthelwulf's oldest surviving son, Æthelbald, appears with the title 'dux', the Latin equivalent for ealdorman, in charters from the early 850s, which suggests that he had been entrusted with administrative responsibilities. He presum-ably now aspired to succeed his late brother as underking of Kent, a position Æthelwulf had held under his father, Egbert. If so, his ambitions were frustrated. Given the uncertain-ties surrounding royal succession, Æthelbald could not have felt secure about his father's intentions, especially after his younger brother, Æthelberht, joined him in the rank of ealdorman in 854.[66] All knew the dangers that attended a pilgrimage to Rome and were aware of the possibility that Æthelwulf would not return. His departure to Rome all but invited the prowling of hungry *æthelings*.[67] Æthelwulf, how-ever, had no intention of joining Caedwalla as a permanent Roman tourist attraction. His immediate concern was to ensure the stability and security of his realm in his absence. The 'decimation' was undertaken with this in mind. Until he returned Æthelbald and Æthelberht would rule as kings in his place. To the former he entrusted the traditional

---

66. Æthelbald attests two charters of 850 as 'dux' (S 300: as 'dux filius regis' with Æthelbald witnessing as 'rex', but possibly spurious; 301). He and Æthelberht appear as 'duces' in S 302, 304, 305, 306, 307, 308, 309, 310. See Stafford, 'Charles the Bald, Judith and England', pp. 149–50, on Æthelbald's possible discontent.
67. The phrase is Kenneth Harrison's. *The Framework of Anglo-Saxon His-tory to AD 900* (Cambridge, 1976) p. 92.

shires of Wessex, and to the latter the southeastern shires of Sussex, Surrey, Kent, and Essex.[68]

The royal family suffered a second death about this time. The king's wife, Osburh, passed away within a year or two of Alfred's return from the Continent in 854.[69] Her death went unnoticed by the *Anglo-Saxon Chronicle*, which, given the low public profile of kings' wives in ninth-century Wessex, is not surprising. Asser's silence is more puzzling. We learn nothing about the young boy's response to the loss of his mother. One would expect him to have been affected by it. Outside of his journey to Rome, he had spent all his life in her company. Our one intimate glimpse of her in Asser's *Life*, holding out a book of poetry as a lure for her sons to pursue learning, provides a warm portrait of maternal affection and concern. While Asser's assurance that Alfred was her favourite may be exaggerated, we have no reason to doubt that she loved her youngest son and he her. But this is speculation. Osburh is a shadowy figure at best, invisible to the historical record outside Asser's brief comments about her ancestry and pious character. Whatever memories the adult Alfred had of his mother he seems to have kept to himself.

68. Æthelbald and Æthelberht bear the title 'dux', the Latin equivalent for 'ealdorman', in the attestation lists to the charters issued at the Easter assembly at Wilton in 854, which suggests that Æthelwulf had not yet raised them to underkingship. The latter appears as king in S 315 (*Charters of Rochester*, no. 23), a Rochester charter issued in 855, probably on the eve of Æthelwulf's departure for Rome, which is mentioned. Æthelbald's absence from the witness list may be explained by his assumption of duties in Wessex.

69. The *terminus post quam* is July 856, when Æthelwulf was betrothed to the Carolingian princess, Judith. Some historians have suggested that Æthelwulf repudiated Osburh in order to contract a more politically advantageous union, but this is highly unlikely. Æthelwulf's piety aside, the role played in the marriage and coronation ceremonies by Hincmar of Rheims, who two years later was to author a treatise on the indissolubility of marriage, is good evidence that Æthelwulf's first wife was no longer alive at the time of his second marriage. See P. Stafford, *Queens, Concubines, and Dowagers: The King's Wife in the Early Middle Ages* (Athens, GA, 1983) p. 85; Hincmar of Rheims, *De Divortione Lotharii Regis et Tetbergae Reginae*, ed. J.P. Migne, vol. 125, cols. 619–772 (Paris, 1857–1866); F. and J. Gies, *Marriage and the Family in the Middle Ages* (New York, 1987).

Surrounded by a large entourage and laden with magnificent gifts for the pope and St Peter, Æthelwulf departed for Rome in late spring 855.[70] Among those in his train was Alfred. Historians have often wondered why Æthelwulf would have exposed his youngest son to the hardships of a second arduous journey to the Eternal City. Some have even questioned – against the evidence – whether he did so at all and have asserted that the second trip was only a fiction created for propaganda purposes. But there is nothing implausible about Æthelwulf wishing to enter Rome with the 'spiritual son' of Pope Leo IV at his side. Alfred was the living link between the English king and the papacy and Æthelwulf undoubtedly wished to capitalize on the connection. As matters turned out, the spiritual affiliation proved more transitory than Æthelwulf had hoped. Leo IV died on 17 July 855, probably a month or so after the king departed from England and long before he arrived in Rome. Æthelwulf would not have learned about Leo's death until well into the journey, too late to send Alfred home. Not that Alfred would have wished to remain behind. Nothing in his brief years could have matched the exhilaration he experienced during his first visit to Rome. It had marked him as someone special and singled him out from his older brothers. In the competitive world of *æthelings* one was never too young to begin striving for prestige and dignities. A second pilgrimage to Rome would affirm Alfred's unique status as Roman consul and son of St Peter, as well as his special relationship with his father.[71] Osburh's death, if it occurred before the pilgrimage began, might also have made the boy eager to go. A pilgrimage to Rome meant that Alfred could offer prayers for his mother at the tomb of the Apostle. It also meant that he could cling to his surviving parent. Æthelwulf may have acted out of paternal concern as well as political considerations in bringing his youngest son with him to Rome.

As in 839, Æthelwulf sent ahead to the West Frankish court to advise Charles the Bald of his plans and to obtain

---

70. Asser, ch. 11; *ASC*, s.a. 855; *AB*, s.a. 855.
71. Asser, ch. 11, explains that Æthelwulf took Alfred with him because he 'loved him more than his other sons' (*eo quod illum plus ceteris filiis diligebat*).

from him safe passage through his kingdom. After landing at Quentovic and receiving Lupus's hospitality at St Judoc, Æthelwulf and his entourage were brought to the Frankish king's court. The *Annals of St-Bertin* noted the 'honourable reception' Charles accorded Æthelwulf. After feasts and the mandatory exchange of gifts, Charles gave Æthelwulf 'all the supplies a king might need and had him escorted right to the boundary of his realm with all the courtesies due to a king'.[72] The English pilgrims then entered the kingdom of the Emperor Lothar, Charles's older brother, whose illness and death in the autumn of that year were signalled by the appearance of two shooting stars.[73] The somewhat unsettled political conditions in Lower Burgundy, Provence, and Lombardy meant that the English pilgrims could not rely on the protection of a king for the remainder of their journey. However, they apparently acquired an expert guide during their sojourn with Charles the Bald. Markward, former abbot of Prüm and a veteran of the Roman pilgrimage, seems to have been with the company when they arrived in Pavia.[74]

As they neared the city, Alfred and his father first glimpsed the massive walls of the Leonine City, a suburb across the Tiber east of the ancient city which is now part of Vatican City.[75] Much of what they saw, and in particular the fortifications, was new in 855, the result of Pope Leo IV's ambitious building programme. The sight of this brand new city seems to have made a lasting impression on Alfred, for he alluded to it decades later in his translation of, or, more accurately, meditation upon, Augustine's *Soliloquies*.[76] Indeed, it would not be fanciful to discern a memory of Leo's great defensive works in Alfred's own later building programme. Anchored by the Castel S. Angelo, once Hadrian's mausoleum and now Rome's main fortress, the walls ran behind St Peter's,

---

72. *AB*, s.a. 855, trans. Nelson, p. 80.
73. *AB*, s.a. 855.
74. Becher, 'Das königliche Frauenkloster San Salvatore', pp. 379–80.
75. For the following, see R. Krautheimer, *Rome, Profile of a City, 312–1308* (Princeton, 1980) pp. 117–19, 263–4.
76. *Alfred's Soliloquies*, ed. Carnicelli, p. 97. The passage is based upon Augustine's *De Videndo Deo*, § 5 (Carnicelli, p. 107), but there is no counterpart in the Latin for Alfred's '*nat ic no ði hwa (Rome)burh timbrede þe ic self gesawe* (I know not who built Rome on account that I myself saw it)'.

embracing the convents, churches, and pilgrim communities that had grown up around it, and circled back east to the 'Saxon Gate' near the banks of the Tiber.[77]

As they entered the Leonine City through the Saxon Gate, the priests in Æthelwulf's entourage literate in Latin would have read to the others the words Leo ordered to be inscribed above each of the city's gates, calling upon the wayfarer (*viator*) to admire his work and to wonder at 'Rome, the head of the world, its splendour, its hope, golden Rome' (*Roma capud orbis splendor spes aurea Roma*).[78] Within the Leonine City, or *Borgo* as it was subsequently known, were found the *scholae* of the Greeks, Lombards, Franks, and Saxons, pilgrim communities that had sprung up in the shadow of the great basilica of St Peter. Arguably the oldest of these colonies, dating perhaps from Ine's pilgrimage of 726, was the *Schola Saxonum*, the Saxon compound or quarter, a cluster of wooden houses resembling an English village built alongside the Portico of St Peter's basilica, where the hospital of Sancto Spirito in Sassia now stands.[79] The *Schola Saxonum* had served generations of Anglo-Saxon pilgrims before Æthelwulf and his party arrived in summer 855 and was sufficiently well organized to have produced a military contingent which fought in defence of the city during the Saracen raid of 846. Yet what Alfred saw was virtually new. Fire was the great enemy of pre-modern cities. A fire caused by the 'carelessness of some of the Saxons' had destroyed all the houses in the compound and the Portico of St Peter's during the pontificate of Paschal I (817–824). The rebuilt compound was destroyed once again by fire in 847. This conflagration, the subject of Raphael's great painting 'Incendio del Borgo' now housed in the Vatican, reduced the Saxon and Lombard compounds and the basilica's Portico to ashes. Leo IV, as had Paschal before him, fed the destitute pilgrims and helped them repair and rebuild their houses. He also ordered the building (or rebuilding on a grander scale) of a church to serve the Saxon compound, 'Sancta Maria in Saxia', and in 854 issued a bull that organized the

77. Krautheimer, *Rome*, pp. 118–19, 264.
78. F. Gregorovius, *History of the City of Rome in the Middle Ages*, trans. G.W. Hamilton (London, 1903) III, p. 100; Krautheimer, *Rome*, p. 119. Cf. Lees, p. 81.
79. Moore, *Saxon Pilgrims*, p. 91; Krautheimer, *Rome*, p. 264.

Schola Saxonum into a 'pilgrim community with considerable property, unified by a centralized organization of a quasi-monastic character [centred upon] the church of S. Maria'.[80]

Possibly Æthelwulf contributed funds to the project even before he himself visited Rome. Alfred's first pilgrimage in 853 would have been a likely occasion for such largesse. Certainly, in 855 the king came bearing gifts. The *Liber Pontificalis* lovingly catalogues the wealth that Æthelwulf lavished on the Blessed Apostle Peter: a crown of pure gold weighing four pounds, an ornamental sword with gold inlay, a gilded silver candle holder in the Saxon style, a purple-dyed tunic embossed with golden keys, a golden goblet, and numerous valuable robes. The West Saxon king capped off his gift-giving with a public display of munificence, distributing gold and silver to the city's clergy and laity alike.[81]

Alfred and his father spent a full year in Rome, much of the time undoubtedly taken up by visiting the city's myriad churches and shrines.[82] To the historian of imperial Rome, the ninth-century city must seem a pathetic shadow of what it had once been. Until the mid-fourth century, Rome had boasted a population of nearly a million. Demographic catastrophe in the form of wars and plague struck Rome during the fifth and sixth centuries and it lost perhaps as much as ninety per cent of its inhabitants. Alfred saw a city of only about 30,000 people, its population concentrated around the forums and the Palatine, the Campus Martius, the Lateran palace, and the pilgrims' quarter near St Peter's. Whole sections of the city lay deserted or given over to agricultural production.[83] As bleak as this picture

80. Moore, *Saxon Pilgrims*, pp. 110–11.
81. *Le Liber Pontificalis*, ed. L. Duchesne, 2 vols (Paris, 1886–92) II, p. 148 (*Vita Benedicti III*); *The Lives of the Ninth-Century Popes (Liber Pontificalis): The Ancient Biographies of Ten Popes from AD 871 to 891*, trans. Raymond Davis (Liverpool, 1995) pp. 186–7.
82. Asser, ch. 11. The length of the stay may have been dictated by circumstances. Because of a violently contested papal election, Pope Leo IV's successor, Benedict III, was not ordained pope until late September or early October, and then only after having been incarcerated by his rival.
83. D. Whitehouse, 'Rome and Naples: survival and revival in central and southern Italy', in R. Hodges and B. Hobley, eds, *The Rebirth of Towns in the West AD 700–1050*, Council for British Archaeology Report 68 (London, 1988) pp. 29–30.

may seem to us, one cannot doubt that Rome remained
a great city to the pilgrims who visited it from the north.
What could they compare it against? Legend has it that in
860 the viking Hastein led a fleet into the Mediterranean
with the expressed intention of sacking Rome. He missed his
mark by 300 kilometres, pillaging Luni in the Val di Magra,
all the while believing it to be Rome. Nothing in northern
Europe could have prepared him, or the English pilgrims,
for the sheer size of Rome, even in decay. The great emporium of London (*Lundenwic*), located along what is now the
Strand, encompassed a settlement area of about sixty hectares
(about 148 acres) in which dwelled only perhaps 1,000 resid-
ents.[84] The greatest commercial town of Wessex, Saxon Southampton (*Hamwic*) covered at its height thirty-seven hectares
and would have fitted into the Baths of Caracalla in Rome.[85]
Even in its decline, Rome must have seemed unimaginably
large to the English pilgrims.

Even more impressive than Rome's sheer magnitude would
have been the monuments, basilicas, and public buildings
that greeted Alfred and Æthelwulf at every turn. Traces of
the Roman past could be seen in Britain. One could still
travel along Roman roads, visit the ruins of Roman towns,
and see the broken walls of great fortresses at places such as
Portchester in Hampshire, erected to defend the island's
shores against Alfred's forebears. But the remains of Rome
were profoundly alien to the Anglo-Saxons, seeming the work
of giants from some remote past.[86] Now they surrounded
Æthelwulf and Alfred, but this was not what Æthelwulf
and Alfred had come to see. They sought not the city of

84. R. Crowie and R. Whytehead, 'Lundenwic: the archaeological evidence for middle Saxon London', *Antiquity* 63 (1989) pp. 706–18,
   at 708; B. Hobley, 'Lundenwic and Lundenburh: two cities rediscovered', in Hodges and Hobley, eds, *Rebirth of Towns*, p. 73. Cf.
   W.J.H. Verwers, 'Dorestad: a Carolingian town?', in ibid., p. 55. See
   H. Clarke and B. Ambrosiani, *Towns in the Viking Age* (New York, 1991)
   pp. 28–9, 156–8.
85. P. Holdsworth, 'Saxon Southampton', *Anglo-Saxon Towns in Southern
   England*, ed. J. Haslam (Chichester, Sussex, 1984) pp. 331–43, at 335;
   Whitehouse, 'Rome and Naples', p. 29.
86. 'The Ruin', l.2, *The Anglo-Saxon Poetic Records, A Collective Edition: III,
   The Exeter Book*, ed. G.P. Krapp and E. Van Kirk Dobbie (New York
   and London, 1936) p. 227.

the Caesars but of the apostles. They found a city transformed by a series of able and energetic popes beginning with Gregory III (732–741) and Hadrian I (772–795), who had used the resources of St Peter, the gifts of pilgrims and kings, and the wealth of their own powerful families to repair aqueducts and public buildings, strengthen defences, refurbish ancient basilicas and monasteries, and build new ones.[87] The greatest of the papal builders, Hadrian I and Leo III (795–816), structurally restored between them seventy-four churches, largely through the pious contributions of Charlemagne, his son Louis, and, to a lesser extent, Offa of Mercia.[88] The remains of putative martyrs were removed by the cartload from decaying catacombs and churches outside the city and brought within the walls of Rome to be distributed among its many churches. There were over a hundred churches for Æthelwulf and Alfred to visit during their twelve-month stay. The great basilicas such as St Peter's were crammed with relics and priceless treasures of gold and silver; virtually every inch of their walls and floors was covered with frescoes and mosaics, reflecting the wealth and glory of the papacy.

Historians have puzzled over the sources of this wealth and the basis of the Roman economy. In the absence of evidence of any appreciable commercial activity, it seems that the prosperity of the papacy and the city was largely based on the generosity of the pious and pilgrims such as Æthelwulf.[89] William of Malmesbury, writing in the early twelfth century, preserved a tradition that Æthelwulf helped restore the Saxon compound during his stay, and the West Saxon king was doubtless no less generous to his countrymen residing in Rome than he had been to the local populace.[90] The ambitious public works programme of the late eighth- and ninth-century popes proved to be a wise investment.

---

87. Krautheimer, *Rome*, pp. 109–42.
88. P. Delogu, 'The rebirth of Rome in the 8th and 9th centuries', *Rebirth of Towns*, ed. Hodges and Hobley, pp. 32–42.
89. Delogu, 'Rebirth of Rome'.
90. *Willelmi Malmesbiriensis Monachi De Gestis Regum Anglorum*, 2 vols (London, 1887–9) I, p. 109.

. . .

'A DISGRACEFUL EPISODE'

The king and his company departed Rome around June 856. Alfred's homecoming, however, was to be delayed by months and, when he finally landed on Saxon shores, it was in the company of a twelve-year-old stepmother and to the threat of civil war. Alfred was to find himself a helpless spectator in a power struggle between his father and his oldest surviving brother, Æthelbald.

On their return, Æthelwulf and his company were entertained by Charles the Bald for several months, during which a marriage alliance uniting the two kings was negotiated. In July the West Saxon king was betrothed to Charles's daughter, Judith. Almost three months later, on 1 October, the marriage was celebrated in the royal palace of Verberie-sur-Oise.[91] That a fifty-year-old widower should take as his bride a twelve-year-old may seem odd to us. But the discrepancy in age was of little importance in a ninth-century marriage of state intended to link two dynasties. Judith was of age, if barely so.[92] Why the kings wanted this bond is less clear. There had been no previous conjugal unions between Continental and Insular royalty since the Frankish princess, Bertha, helped bring Christianity to Kent in the late sixth century. Charlemagne and Offa, to be sure, had engaged in unsuccessful marital negotiations a generation before, but there was neither recent precedent nor obvious purpose for the kings of Wessex and West Francia to seek this relationship.

The viking threat has been offered as an explanation, but a common enemy does not necessarily produce common purpose. The vikings were more likely to divide Charles and Æthelwulf than to draw them together. At the time of the marriage, the vikings were for Charles still more a nuisance than a real danger. True, Danish viking activity in the Loire, Seine, and Scheldt river basins increased in the early 850s,

91. *AB*, s.a. 856.
92. On ages of Carolingian brides, see Stafford, *Queens, Concubines, and Dowagers*, p. 55; J. Nelson, *Charles the Bald* (London and New York, 1992) p. 129. Medieval canonists regarded twelve to be the appropriate minimum age for a girl to marry. P. L'Hermite-Leclercq, 'The Feudal Order', *A History of Women in the West, II. Silences of the Middle Ages*, ed. C. Klapisch-Zuber (Cambridge, MA, and London, 1992) p. 217.

as political unrest within Denmark sent ambitious chieftains abroad in search of loot to further their domestic political ambitions. Yet, though churchmen such as Lupus and Ermentarius of St-Philibert spoke in the darkest terms of the devastation the raiders wrought,[93] the raiding was still local, limited, and sporadic. And in the summer of 856 Charles faced what must have seemed to him far more serious problems. 'It has been said that to Charles the Bald, fighting for his throne against his brothers, the attacks of the Danes were like the buzzing of a wasp in the hair of a man being strangled.'[94] For Charles the years 855-6 were taken up largely with political manoeuvring against his brother, Louis, over Aquitaine and the inheritance of their nephews, the sons of Lothar, and with attempts to extend his authority into Brittany. Prudentius of Troyes bitterly observed that the viking bands who pillaged Bordeaux and its environs in 855 and Orleans in the spring of 856 did so unopposed.[95] Only when a large Danish force sailed up the Seine in August 856 and established a base at Jeufosse, within easy striking distance of Paris and the royal palaces along the Oise, did Charles consider the provocation sufficient to warrant action. Æthelwulf and Alfred, as guests of the king, may have witnessed Charles's preparations for war and perhaps even accompanied him on the expedition. Though the Franks 'smote [the vikings] with great slaughter', they were unable to dislodge them from Jeufosse, where the Danes 'quietly passed the winter'.[96]

Even if Charles had been prepared to offer greater resistance to the Northmen who were pillaging his kingdom, a marriage alliance with the West Saxon king would not have helped the situation. In fact, when it came to the vikings, Frankish and West Saxon interests were in conflict. Strong Frankish defences, such as the fortified bridges that Charles

93. See, e.g., P.E. Dutton, ed., *Carolingian Civilization, A Reader* (Peterborough, Ontario, 1993) pp. 432, 434-7. The annals of St-Bertin, Fontanelle, Fulda, and Xanten are, of course, filled with notices of viking activity.
94. D. Hill, *An Atlas of Anglo-Saxon England* (Toronto, 1981) p. 38. Cf. Nelson, *Charles the Bald*, pp. 160-85.
95. *AB*, s.a. 855, 856.
96. *Annals of Fontanelle*, ed. J. Laporte, Société de l'histoire de Normande, 15 sér. (Rouen and Paris, 1951) s.a. 856, p. 91, cited by Nelson, *Charles the Bald*, p. 181; *AB*, s.a. 856.

built along the Seine and Loire in the 860s, meant problems for Wessex, and vice versa. Viking bands sought plunder, not war. Like water, they flowed to the points of least resistance. The Anglo-Saxon and Frankish chroniclers who followed their progress understood the relationship between peace on one side of the Channel and devastation on the other.[97] At most, Charles the Bald might have welcomed the prestige of a union with the hero of *Aclea*, given his own comparatively limited success against the vikings.

For his part, Æthelwulf had no need of more heirs or of a defensive alliance with the Franks. A more likely explanation for his marriage to Judith is that he needed her father's silver and support to weather a domestic crisis that threatened his very survival as king. Asser tells us that, 'while King Æthelwulf was lingering overseas, even for so short a time (*tantillo tempore*), a disgraceful episode – contrary to the practice of all Christian men – occurred in the western part of Selwood. For King Æthelbald and Ealhstan, bishop of Sherborne, along with Eanwulf, ealdorman of Somerset, are reported to have plotted that King Æthelwulf should never again be received in the kingdom on his return from Rome.'[98] Far from returning his father's gift of the underkingship with loyalty, Æthelbald had responded by plotting to seize the kingdom for himself. Asser was unsure whether the conspiracy was instigated by the bishop and ealdorman or was Æthelbald's plan from the start. Asser clearly preferred to believe the latter, since he admired his predecessor in the see of Sherborne and thought of him as an honourable man.[99] His assessment of Æthelbald's character was less favourable. In establishing responsibility for an action, one should ask: *Cui bono?* 'to whose benefit?' Despite having fought at his father's side at *Aclea*, Æthelbald could not count on succeeding his father as king of 'Greater' Wessex. His father had not selected him to be underking of Kent upon the death of Æthelstan. Worse yet, Æthelwulf had elevated Æthelberht to the underkingship of the southeastern shires rather than entrusting the entire kingdom to his eldest son. This may have suggested to Æthelbald that, at most,

97. Hill, *Atlas*, maps 54–7.
98. Asser, ch. 12, trans. Keynes and Lapidge, p. 70.
99. Asser, ch. 28.

he could hope to be king only of the western shires, of the old kingdom of Wessex. Would this have seemed sufficient to him, given his father's and grandfather's rule over a realm that stretched from sea to sea? Even Wessex was not guaranteed. Even young Alfred, his father's favourite, loomed as a possible threat given enough time. Insecurity, resentment, and ambition may have combined in Æthelbald's betrayal of his father. He had everything to gain and little to lose by a rebellion, especially if he could count upon the support of powerful royal officials and magnates such as Bishop Ealhstan and Ealdorman Eanwulf.

What Ealhstan and Eanwulf hoped to gain by undermining Æthelwulf is less clear. From the placement of their attestations in royal charters of the early 850s, it would seem that both men stood high in the king's favour. They were certainly two of Æthelwulf's most senior advisors. Ealhstan had been bishop of Sherborne for thirty-eight years at the time of the rebellion. His service to Æthelwulf went back at least to 825, when the bishop helped the young *ætheling* take control of Kent following Egbert's victory in the battle of Wroughton (*Ellendun*).[100] Eanwulf had been ealdorman of Somerset since the 830s, perhaps as early as 833.[101] The two men had distinguished themselves in battle by leading the western shires to victory in 845 against a Danish force seeking to force entry into the Parret. Given the length and quality of their royal service, they must have seemed suitable mentors for a young king. If this was how Æthelwulf regarded them, his confidence was severely misplaced.

Whether Bishop Ealhstan and Ealdorman Eanwulf instigated the rebellion, it is clear that they supported it and fostered Æthelbald's ambitions. Interest for the welfare of the realm could have played a role in their calculations. Æthelwulf was growing old and the kingdom faced renewed pressure from the vikings. Æthelbald, a proven warrior, was his father's natural successor. Or perhaps they had less selfless reasons. The *Beowulf*-poet advised an *ætheling* while young 'by his good deeds, by giving splendid gifts while still in his father's house, to make sure that later in life beloved companions will stand by him, that people will serve him when

100. *ASC*, s.a. 825, 867.
101. S 270, 280, 1438.

81

war comes'.[102] As underking, Æthelbald had the resources to seek and reward friends. Whether by promises or gifts, Æthelbald was able to obtain the support of some very powerful people for his succession to the throne of Wessex.

How much of this the child Alfred understood at the time we cannot say. His brother's betrayal, however, seems to have made a life-long impression upon him, to judge from Alfred's impassioned interpolation into his translation of Boethius:

> Very pleasant is it for a man to have wife and children, and yet many children are begotten to their parents' destruction, for many a woman dies in childbirth before she can bear the child; and moreover, we have learned that, long ago, there happened a most unwonted and unnatural evil, namely that sons conspired together and plotted against their father. Nay, worse still, we have heard an old story how in ancient times a certain son slew his father. I know not in what way, but we know that it was an inhuman deed.[103]

This may explain why Alfred, in later years, kept his own adult sons on a short leash, and why Asser in describing the king's court, made a point of telling his audience that Alfred's sons and daughters were always obedient to their father.[104]

Upon learning of his son's rebellion, Æthelwulf, like his father, Egbert, before him, went to the court of a Carolingian king as a supplicant, seeking aid for the recovery of his throne.[105] By becoming son-in-law of Charles the Bald,

102. *Beowulf and the Fight at Finnsburg*, ed. F. Klaeber, 3rd edn (Boston, 1950) l.20–4, pp. 1–2; trans. E. Talbot Donaldson (New York, 1966) p. 1.
103. *Alfred's Boethius*, trans. Sedgefield, ch. 31, pp. 76–77, ed. Sedgefield, p. 70. The ultimate source for this additon may be Statius's *Thebiad*, trans. D. Melville (Oxford, 1992) pp. 6–8, pertaining to the story of Oedipus and his sons. I owe this reference to D.R. Pratt.
104. Asser, ch. 75.
105. M.J. Enright, 'Charles the Bald and Æthelwulf of Wessex: the alliance of 856 and strategies of royal succession', *Journal of Medieval Studies* 5 (1979) pp. 291–302. Cf. Stafford, 'Charles the Bald, Judith and England', pp. 149–52, who sees the marriage as the cause for the rebellion. Asser's description of the rebellion as occurring '*tantillo tempore*' argues for Enright's position.

a much younger man, Æthelwulf achieved the support of a wealthy and powerful patron. Charles, for his part, enhanced his own prestige. As he had done earlier in the year by betrothing his eldest son, Louis, to the Breton leader, Erispoe, Charles was establishing himself as the senior 'in an extended family of kings', which was to include his two eldest sons.[106] Given the recent death of the Emperor Lothar and the leadership vacuum in the Carolingian political world, Charles's actions can be seen as an attempt to establish his claim to be his father's true successor, if not in the title 'emperor' at least in dignity, as *primus inter pares*, a king among kings.

Charles's dominant position in his relationship with Æthelwulf is brought home by the West Saxon king's willingness to permit the consecration of Judith as queen. As he informed his future father-in-law, the wives of West Saxon kings by tradition neither bore the title of queen nor sat on thrones beside their husbands. Asser explained, citing the authority of his 'lord the truthful Alfred' himself, that this 'perverse and detestable custom, contrary to the practice of all Germanic peoples' arose because of the wickedness of a particular West Saxon queen, Eadburh, the daughter of Offa and wife of King Beorhtric.[107] As the story went, Eadburh, a true daughter of the 'tyrant' Offa, enhanced her own position in court by eliminating her husband's favourites. If venomous slander did not suffice, there was always poison. Her royal career was cut short when Beorhtric inadvertently drank out of a poisoned cup she had prepared for one of his thegns. She absconded to Francia with 'countless treasures', muffed the opportunity to marry Charlemagne, became an abbess until ejected from her nunnery by order of Charlemagne because of her debauchery, and finally died in poverty in Pavia, begging for her food, accompanied only by a single slave boy. Asser, a Welshman who bore little love for the Mercians, obviously relished retelling the scandal. Historians are always suspicious of 'good stories', but there may be at least a kernel of truth in this one.[108]

---

106. Nelson, *Charles the Bald*, p. 182.
107. Asser, ch. 13–15, trans. Keynes and Lapidge, pp. 71–2.
108. But cf. P. Stafford, 'The king's wife in Wessex', *Past and Present* 91 (1981) pp. 5–27.

What evidence we have suggests that before Eadburh the wives of West Saxon kings enjoyed the same rank and honours accorded royal consorts in Mercia and other Anglo-Saxon kingdoms. The wives of Ine (688–726) and Æthelheard (726–740) attested their husbands' charters as queen (*regina*) and are even called called *cuen* in the *Anglo-Saxon Chronicle*.[109] The situation is very different in the ninth century. We do not even know the name of Egbert's wife, and Osburh's absence from the historical record is nearly as complete. Nor should one discount too cavalierly Asser's insistence that he had heard the story on a number of occasions from the lips of Alfred himself. It is not implausible that Alfred believed the story. The invisibility of Alfred's own spouse suggests that he approved of keeping the king's wife firmly in the political background. It also suggests that Alfred was not favourably impressed by the living example of the twelve-year-old his father caused to be anointed Queen of the West Saxons.

That Judith was to possess the title and dignity of a queen undoubtedly was a key issue negotiated during the summer and early autumn of 856. There was little honour for Charles the Bald in the match unless his daughter was a true queen. Charles also knew from personal experience the problems a young wife of an aging king might face; his own mother had endured scorn and vilification at the hands of her husband's adult sons. Charles did all he could to secure the safety and honour of his daughter and his future grandchildren in an alien land. The inviolability of God's anointed was a principle of Christian law familiar to English and Frank alike. The chrism would help protect Judith against potential enemies. Charles also believed that its spiritual magic would help ensure the fertility of the match. A decade later Charles, dissatisfied with the number and quality of his surviving sons, had his own wife anointed in the express hope that God would bless the aging couple with worthier offspring.[110] Æthelwulf, for his part, wanted the Frankish court to appreciate the great favour he was showing Judith by defying the custom of his people and permitting her to be his queen.

109. Keynes and Lapidge, p. 235, n. 28.
110. *Ordo* in *MGH, Capit.* II, no. 301, pp. 453–5, cited by Stafford, 'Charles the Bald, Judith and England', p. 146. See Stafford's discussion in ibid., pp. 145–8, and in *Queens, Concubines, and Dowagers*, pp. 46, 130–1.

That he was willing to do so and risk the anger of his sons and subjects, including the members of his entourage present at the ceremony, suggests how much he needed, or thought he needed, the Carolingian connection. Hincmar, archbishop of Rheims, an expert on inauguration rituals, anointed the child bride queen, using a royal *Ordo* perhaps borrowed from the West Saxons, and placed a diadem on her head. Æthelwulf then formally conferred on her the title of queen in the presence of the entire Frankish court and his own entourage.[111] The marriage was sealed with the obligatory exchange of gifts and Æthelwulf sailed for Wessex with his new queen and, presumably, with the treasure and men the marriage had brought him.

Æthelwulf's decision to brave a Channel crossing in October underscores the urgency of the political situation in Wessex. 'And afterwards he came home to his people, and they were glad of it', reports the *Anglo-Saxon Chronicle* in one of its most blatantly fallacious entries. Even the papal court heard the news that their benefactor, Æthelwulf, had lost his kingdom.[112] Whether Æthelberht and his advisors were gladdened by the old king's return is unknown, but at least the boy dutifully stepped aside for his father. Æthelbald did not. Playing Goneril to his brother's Cordelia, Æthelbald 'with all his counsellors – or rather co-conspirators' (as Asser editorializes), stood firm in refusing to allow Æthelwulf to reassume the reins of governance. With civil war or even anarchy on the horizon, the great nobles of the realm met in assembly. A compromise was hammered out and bloodshed avoided. The kingdom was to be divided, with the son to rule in the western shires and the father in the eastern.[113] Asser credits the reasonableness of the West Saxon nobility and, most of all, Æthelwulf's 'ineffable forbearance' for the peaceful outcome:

111. *AB*, s.a. 856, trans. Nelson, p. 83. J. Nelson, 'The earliest surviving royal *Ordo*: some liturgical and historical aspects', in *Authority and Power. Studies in Medieval Law and Government presented to Walter Ullmann*, ed. B. Tierney and P. Linehan (Cambridge, 1980) pp. 29–48, reprinted in Nelson, *Politics and Ritual in Early Medieval Europe* (London, 1986) pp. 341–60.
112. *Liber Pontificalis*, ed. Duchesne, II, p. 148; trans. Davis, p. 186 (and n. 84).
113. Asser, ch. 12, trans. Keynes and Lapidge, p. 70.

When, therefore, King Æthelwulf returned from Rome, the entire nation was so delighted (as was fitting) at the arrival of their lord that, had he allowed it, they would have been willing to eject his grasping son Æthelbald from his share of the whole kingdom, along with all his counsellors. But displaying great forbearance and wise counsel (as I have said), so that no danger should befall his kingdom, Æthelwulf did not wish this to happen.[114]

This seems more a face-saving sentiment than an accurate assessment, though Æthelwulf's 'decimation' of his realm before his departure for Rome ought to have secured him the loyalty of at least some of the many beneficiaries. Æthelbald remained in possession of Wessex. The great loser, if one wishes to tally such things, was Æthelberht, who emerged with his honour intact but without royal authority. As Asser admitted, Æthelbald got the better of the deal, since 'the western part of the Saxon land had always been more important than the eastern'. In reality, Æthelwulf had been deposed as king of the West Saxons. 'So that iniquitous and grasping son', Asser lamented, 'ruled where by rightful judgement the father should have done.'

We can say little with certainty about the final two years of Æthelwulf's 'reign' and nothing about Alfred's own movements and relationship with his father, stepmother, and brothers. No extant authentic charters can be dated securely to this period. Æthelwulf's first recorded act on resuming royal authority in Kent was to order 'that Judith, the daughter of Charles, whom he had received from her father, should sit beside him on the royal throne until the end of his life'. Asser's comment that Judith was enthroned 'without any disagreement or dissatisfaction on the part of his nobles' might, in fact, indicate quite the opposite.[115]

Æthelwulf's last recorded act was to issue his will. Asser provides only a brief synopsis emphasizing the king's political acuity and piety.[116] Æthelwulf seems to have regarded himself to the end as king of Wessex (as did the clerics responsible for keeping the regnal lists in Alfred's reign), for he had 'a testamentary – or rather advisory – document

114. Asser, ch. 13, trans. Keynes and Lapidge, p. 71.
115. Asser, ch. 13, trans. Keynes and Lapidge, p. 71.
116. Asser, ch. 16, trans. Keynes and Lapidge, pp. 72–3.

drawn up' detailing how his kingdom, including the western shires, and his property should be divided 'so that his sons should not quarrel unnecessarily among themselves after the death of their father'. Æthelbald was to remain king of Wessex, an acknowledgement of the practical reality of the situation, and Æthelberht was to resume rule over the southeast. Æthelwulf seems to have left his Kentish lands to Æthelberht and made a tontine from his personal estate in Wessex, bequeathing the latter lands jointly to Æthelbald, Æthelred, and Alfred under the stipulation that the property remain undivided with the final surviving brother succeeding to everything.[117] The old king seems to have intended to divide the kingdom permanently, with Æthelberht and his successors ruling forever more as kings of Kent, and his other three sons ruling Wessex in turn. If so, Æthelwulf's hopes were to be frustrated.

The testamentary bequests that most interested Asser were those intended for the benefit of Æthelwulf's soul. He enjoined on his successors to set aside one out of every ten hides of his hereditary land to feed and clothe the poor. He also ordered that each year 300 mancuses (9,000 pennies) be taken to Rome. One third was to go to the purchase of oil to light the lamps in St Peter's on Easter eve and morn; one third, for the lights of St Paul's; and one third for the use of 'the universal pope'. Despite what it had cost him politically and personally, Æthelwulf apparently never regretted his pilgrimage to Rome.

And what of Alfred? His love for Rome and St Peter continued unabated throughout his life. As king, he would more than match his father's generosity to the papacy and, in doing so, may have even laid the foundations for the tax that was later to be known as Peter's Pence.[118] But Æthelwulf's pilgrimage and its aftermath may have also taught the boy a hard lesson about the fragility of kingly rule. Perhaps this is why the adult Alfred resisted the siren call of Rome. Whatever childhood memories he retained of the splendour and glory of Rome, Alfred would never again venture to the 'thresholds of the Apostles'. He would not follow in the footsteps of Caedwalla and Ine – or his father.

---

117. *King Alfred's Will,* Harmer, ed., *SEHD,* no. 11, pp. 15–19 (trans. 49–53).
118. See pp. 190–1 below.

Chapter 3

SCOURGES OF GOD, 858–868

Æthelwulf's death ushered in an age of unprecedented threat to the survival of the West Saxon kingdom and the line of Egbert. For Alfred, who grew to manhood in the courts of his three brothers, adolescence proved a time of personal trial and domestic tragedy. He saw his brothers, one after another, mount the throne of Wessex, only to die after brief reigns. Not one lived to see his thirtieth birthday. Nor, many must have suspected, would Alfred, who, during these years, fell prey to a mysterious illness – a scourge of God, as he would later view it – that would plague him for the rest of his days.

The suffering and premature deaths that blighted the Ecgberhtings were mirrored in the 850s and 860s by the viking pestilence. The small scattered bands of viking marauders that had descended annually upon the coasts of Britain coalesced into cohesive armies bent on conquest. The victory Alfred's father had won at *Aclea* secured no more than a brief respite; new pirate fleets soon appeared in the estuaries of the West Saxon kingdom. In 853, the very year Æthelwulf helped King Burgred reduce the Welsh to submission and Alfred departed for Rome, a great Danish force defeated and killed Ealdormen Ealhhere of Kent and Huda of Surrey in a battle fought in Thanet. Two years later, within months of Æthelwulf's own pilgrimage to Rome, Danish raiders for the first time wintered over on Sheppey, awaiting spring to resume pillaging the eastern shires and East Anglia.[1] Then in 865 what the *Anglo-Saxon Chronicle* called the 'Great Heathen Army' appeared, and the game changed decisively.

---

1. *ASC,* s.a. 855–858.

The battles Alfred's brother, Æthelred I, and his contemporaries in Mercia, Northumbria, and East Anglia fought against viking armies in the 860s and 870s were to be ceaseless, heroic, and largely futile.

The vikings were to be Alfred's new tutors, and the subject they taught was war.

. . .

THE REIGNS OF ÆTHELBALD AND ÆTHELBERHT

King Æthelwulf died on 18 January 858 and, as befitted his status as king of eastern 'Wessex', was buried in the royal estate of Steyning in Sussex. Later, Alfred was to formally translate his father's body to the Old Minster in Winchester, interring him as a king of Wessex. Alfred, at the age of nine, had become an orphan. His father had seen to his and his brother, Æthelred's, futures by endowing them with property before his death. Royal power was transferred peacefully to the late king's two elder sons as Æthelwulf had stipulated in his will. In reality, the issue of succession had been settled by the events of 856, when the magnates of Wessex declared for Æthelbald and those of the southeast for Æthelwulf. The vikings undoubtedly also played a role in restoring harmony among the Ecgberhtings. With the Danes lurking in the background, civil war was too much of a luxury even for hungry *æthelings*. Better to rule securely in a truncated kingdom than to risk losing everything. Whatever Æthelbald's ambitions had been, he had since reconciled himself to the kingship of Wessex alone. When his father died, he stood aside as his younger brother, Æthelberht, was enthroned as king of Kent, Surrey, Sussex, and Essex. In practical terms, the old king's death changed little. Æthelbald continued to rule the western shires with the advice of ealdormen and bishops appointed by his father and grandfather, and, to judge by his two extant charters, those who now paid suit in Æthelbald's court had once done so in his father's.[2] Æthelberht similarly enjoyed the support of the magnates and thegns of the southeast who had saved his father from ignominious exile. He drew to his court some

2. S 1274. Cf. S 304, 307, 322.

new faces, but the power structure of the eastern kingdom remained largely intact.[3]

Relations between the brothers remained harmonious throughout Æthelbald's reign. As the older brother and as king of the greater realm, Æthelbald may have claimed a vague superiority; Æthelberht may even have been in attendance in the West Saxon court in 860, though the charter evidence upon which this is based does not inspire complete confidence.[4] A second questionable charter, Sawyer 1274, even presents Æthelbald negotiating from the bishop of Winchester a lease of an estate in western Surrey, within the boundaries of his brother's kingdom. Remarkably, Æthelbald confirms this charter as king, while Æthelberht is nowhere to be seen. This amity, of course, was predicated upon Æthelbald's acceptance of his brother's right to rule over the southeast. Whether Æthelbald was also willing to accept his father's plans for fraternal succession within Wessex is another matter. As a bachelor, Æthelbald had little choice but to regard one of his brothers as his heir. But the king had no intention of remaining a bachelor for long.

To Asser's disgust, Æthelbald compounded filial treachery with incest by marrying his stepmother. 'Once King Æthelwulf was dead, Æthelbald his son, against God's prohibition and Christian dignity, and also contrary to the practice of all pagans Æthelbald took over his father's marriage-bed . . . incurring great disgrace from all who heard of it.'[5] Æthelbald's flouting of canon law and Christian custom probably had less to do with love or lust than with political considerations. Judith's unique status as an enthroned queen of Wessex made her so desirable that to possess her Æthelbald was

3. S 328 (dated 858), the original of which survives, ought to be compared with Æthelwulf's Kentish charters of 855 (S 467, also in contemporary form, and S 315). Of the twenty-one thegns in the witness list fourteen never attested a charter of Æthelwulf. Among them is Eastmund the 'pedessecus' (attendant), who was chosen ealdorman of Kent 864–867.

4. S 326 (BCS 500). Cf. S 329. On these charters, see S.D. Keynes, 'The West Saxon charters of King Æthelwulf and his sons', *EHR* 109 (1994), pp. 1123–9.

5. Asser, ch. 17, trans. Keynes and Lapidge, p. 73. Stevenson, *Asser's Life*, pp. 214–15; P. Stafford, 'Charles the Bald, Judith and England', in M.T. Gibson and J.L. Nelson, eds, *Charles the Bald, Court and Kingdom*, 2nd rev. edn (Great Yarmouth, Norfolk, 1990) p. 151.

willing to risk clerical censure. The magic of the holy chrism had unalterably changed Judith. Though Æthelwulf had died, she still remained a consecrated queen.[6] Her sons – and fortunately for all concerned her brief marriage to Æthelwulf had proved barren – would be marked from birth for kingship. She was also attractive in other ways. Her marriage portion undoubtedly gave her power and wealth,[7] as did her parentage. Æthelbald would have appreciated no less than his father the advantages of being the son-in-law of Charles the Bald. And what of the fourteen-year-old widow? For Judith the choice was to marry Æthelbald or return home to her father's custody, to await his choice of another suitable spouse or to join so many other Carolingian princesses as a bride of Christ. Only in Wessex could she continue to enjoy the status and perquisites of a queen. Under such circumstances the resourceful and strong-willed Judith may have found her stepson irresistible.[8] With Judith at his side, Æthelbald went on to rule for another two and a half 'lawless' years, as Asser characterized them, before succumbing to disease.[9]

Where was Alfred while all this was going on? Since Æthelwulf's will specified that his personal property in Wessex was to be held jointly by Æthelbald, Æthelred, and Alfred,[10] it is likely that the young *ætheling*s took up residence in the court of their older brother, the custodian of their lands. But, given our lack of sources, we cannot be certain. Æthelbald's reign over Wessex and Æthelberht's over Kent

6. She attests Æthelbald's two charters as 'regina'. S 1274, 326.
7. Judith sold her English property before returning to Francia. *AB*, s.a. 862.
8. Stafford, 'Charles the Bald, Judith and England', pp. 150–2. After Æthelbald's death the twice-widowed teenager did return to Francia, where she was kept by her father 'at Senlis under his protection and royal and episcopal guardianship, with all the honour due to a queen'. She eloped with Count Baldwin of Flanders, circumventing her father's opposition by obtaining the permission of her brother in his stead. It took an appeal from the pope to get Charles to grant his belated consent to the match. *AB* s.a. 862, 863.
9. Asser, ch. 17. Cf. *ASC* s.a. 860. The twelfth-century chronicler, Henry of Huntingdon, presents a far more positive view of Æthelbald. *Historia Anglorum*, ed. T. Arnold (London, 1879) p. 142.
10. King Alfred's Will (S 1507), in Harmer, ed., *SEHD*, no. 11, pp. 15–19, trans. 49–53. Also trans. Keynes and Lapidge, pp. 174–8, and *EHD* I, no. 96.

are virtually blank in the historical record, as the *Chronicles* lapse into silence for these years and the numismatic and charter evidence is hardly more forthcoming. One would expect to be able at least to place Alfred at one of his brothers' courts by scrutinizing the witness lists of their formal diplomas. Unfortunately, for the period 858–860 we possess only one charter issued by King Æthelberht and two by King Æthelbald, and, oddly, neither Alfred's nor Æthelred's attestations appear on any of them.[11] Since the witness list for Æthelberht's charter is unusually lengthy one suspects that the absence of the *æthelings* is meaningful. The two charters purportedly issued by Æthelbald, on the other hand, survive in later medieval copies with truncated witness lists. The names of the *æthelings* may have been inadvertently omitted.

Æthelbald's reign proved brief. He died in 860 and was buried at Sherborne, the episcopal see of Bishop Ealhstan, his loyal supporter to the end. By King Æthelwulf's will Æthelred ought now to have succeeded to the throne of Wessex. Perhaps because of the *ætheling*'s youth and the omnipresent threat of Danish incursions, he was passed over in favour of his older brother, King Æthelberht. This appears to have been less a *coup d'état* than the result of negotiations among the three surviving brothers. Alfred, in his will, composed around 885, recalled how he and his brother, Æthelred, 'with the witness of all the counsellors of the West Saxons' agreed to entrust the inheritance their father had bequeathed to them and their brother, Æthelbald, to the care of Æthelberht, 'on condition that he restored it to us in the state in which it was when we entrusted it to him; and he did so, [leaving to us] the inheritance [belonging to us jointly], and what he had acquired by use of our share, and what he had himself acquired'.[12] The deal struck among the three brothers involved more than a lease of the young *æthelings*' property. The king agreed that after his death Æthelred should have custody not only of the lands his brothers lent him but also of those he himself had acquired. This suggests that Æthelberht's bookland in Kent was now added to the property that was to be held jointly and to pass by fraternal descent. Even more may have been involved.

11. Æthelberht: S 328 (an original); Æthelbald: 1274 and 326.
12. Harmer, ed., *SEHD*, no. 11, p. 49.

When King Æthelwulf bequeathed lands in Wessex jointly to Æthelbald, Æthelred, and Alfred, he probably intended that each in turn would hold the throne as well as the property. The idea was to provide the reigning king with as large a landed endowment as possible, so that he might sustain his court as befitted a king and reward his followers with suitable gifts and loans of land. Æthelbald's untimely death and Æthelberht's initiative spoiled that plan. A new one was needed and Æthelberht devised one acceptable to his kinsmen and their supporters. In return for accepting him as king of Wessex and entrusting him with their inheritances, Æthelred and Alfred obtained a promise that each would, if he lived long enough, succeed to the entire kingdom.[13]

Of course, the approval of the great magnates and local elites was necessary. Showing his good faith, King Æthelberht lobbied for the interests of his younger brothers in the tried and true method of exchanging land for loyalty. In a charter dated to 861, we find him granting land at Martin, Kent, to Abbot Drihtnoth and the community of St Augustine's in return for the abbot's continuing fidelity to the king and, most tellingly, to his brothers.[14] Æthelberht also sought reconciliation with his late brother's principal supporters, making a grant of privileges to the church of Sherborne in 864 for the benefit of Æthelbald's soul and that of their father.[15] There is some reason to believe that by 862 King Æthelberht had begun to associate his brother, Æthelred, in the kingship.[16]

The importance of King Æthelberht's accession and the brothers' agreement cannot be exaggerated. The political change was nothing short of revolutionary. As we have seen, Egbert and Æthelwulf had kept their administration of the western and eastern shires largely separate, taking counsel with West Saxon notables in Wessex and Kentish notables in Kent. Soon after his succession, King Æthelberht broke with this tradition and summoned to his court all the bishops (including, interestingly, Deorwulf, bishop of 'Mercian'

---

13. D.N. Dumville, 'The ætheling: a study in Anglo-Saxon constitutional history', *ASE* 8 (1979) pp. 21–4; Keynes and Lapidge, p. 314.
14. S 330, BCS 855; See S.D. Keynes, 'The Control of Kent in the Ninth Century', *Early Medieval Europe* 2 (1993) pp. 129–30.
15. S 333.
16. S 335 and 336, discussed by Keynes, 'West Saxon Charters', pp. 1129–31.

London) and ealdormen from both his realms. This unique assembly was meant to underscore Æthelberht's succession to the 'whole kingdom' (*to allum þam rice*, as the *Anglo-Saxon Chronicle* puts it).[17] Though King Æthelberht returned to the practice of local assemblies after this, 'West Saxon' and 'Kentish' thegns nevertheless mingle far more freely in the witness lists of his and Æthelred's royal diplomas than those issued in his father's name. In effect, King Æthelwulf's sons had rejected their father's intention to divide his realm into two separate kingdoms to be ruled by different branches of his lineage. From King Æthelberht's reign on, the western and eastern shires would form a single realm stretching from beyond the Tamar to Thanet. That Æthelberht and Æthelred continued to employ the royal style 'King of the West Saxons and also the Kentishmen' merely reflects the conservative character of diplomatic language. Alfred himself would issue charters for Kent as 'King of the Saxons' and, in the latter years of his reign, as 'King of the Anglo-Saxons' (*Angulsaxonum rex*). A new kingdom was coming into being.

Alfred grew to maturity during his brother, Æthelberht's, five-year reign. His literary education continued under the care of court tutors, and by the age of twelve, which he considered to be disgracefully late, he achieved literacy in the vernacular.[18] Though he was now able to read English poetry, his formal instruction continued to revolve around memorizing texts that his tutors read aloud to him. We can get some sense of what materials went into this education regimen from a commonplace book that Alfred began to keep about this time. According to Asser, Alfred's little handbook was crammed with 'the day-time offices and some Psalms and certain prayers, which he learned in his youth'. William of Malmesbury adds that it also contained genealogical tables for the West Saxon kings and anecdotes about the West Saxon abbot St Aldhelm.[19] The reference to the

17. S 327, ed. A. Campbell, *Anglo-Saxon Charters I: Charters of Rochester* (London, 1973) no. 24, pp. 27–8; *ASC* s.a. 860. See Keynes, 'Control of Kent', p. 129.
18. Asser, ch. 22.
19. Asser, ch. 88; William of Malmesbury, *De Gestis Pontificum Anglorum*, ed. W. Stubbs (London, 1870) bk. v, sect. 188, p. 333. See Stevenson, *Asser's Life of King Alfred*, pp. 153 n. 4, 326–7; Keynes and Lapidge, p. 268 n. 208.

Psalms and scriptural texts is to be expected; the Psalter, after all, was the primer of early medieval education and was what Alfred's own children later studied.[20] The genealogical table and regnal list in Alfred's handbook are more provocative. If they too were materials relating to his childhood education, Alfred's early studies included his family tree and the 'history' of the house of Cerdic. (Even Aldhelm would fit in here, since the saint was of West Saxon royal stock.) If so, Æthelwulf's sons were brought up to be conscious of their royal heritage. Their pedigree was not merely a reminder of the achievements of ancestors, but a challenge to future glory for the line of Egbert.

As Alfred himself ruefully admitted, his early formal education left much to be desired. To his father and his brothers the study of letters was undoubtedly less critical for an *ætheling* than learning the manly skills of hunting and fighting and mastering court etiquette. Hunting, as we have seen, was more than a noble pastime. Through it a youth became proficient in the handling of weapons and horses. Equally important, it inured him to the sight of blood and gore and cultivated the physical strength and endurance needed for war. Alfred probably received little in the way of theoretical instruction concerning the art of war. Though *De re militari*, a military manual by the fifth-century Roman author, Vegetius, was to become the 'bible' of medieval warfare, there is no compelling evidence in Alfred's own military career and writings of familiarity with it.[21] Given Alfred's laments about the state of learning in the Wessex of his youth, it would be remarkable if a late Roman military treatise had been translated into the vernacular for King Æthelwulf's use or the edification of his sons. What Alfred learned about the art of war came from his study of the history books of the Bible, from vernacular wisdom literature

20. Asser, ch. 75.
21. Cf. B. Bachrach, 'The Practical Use of Vegetius' *De re militari* during the early Middle Ages', *The Historian* 47 (1985) pp. 239–54. Charles the Bald possessed a copy of Vegetius. See R. McKitterick, 'Charles the Bald and his library: the patronage of learning', *EHR* 95 (1980) p. 31. Bede inserted brief passages from Vegetius into a number of his works. C.W. Jones, 'Bede and Vegetius', *The Classical Review* 46 (1932) pp. 248–9. The earliest extant Anglo-Saxon copy of the *De re militari* is in BL Cotton Cleopatra D I, an eleventh-century manuscript from St Augustine's, Canterbury.

and verse, and from the practical experience gained by his father, brothers, and the ealdormen from fighting the Danes and Welsh. Alfred's moral vision of what war was and what a warrior should be was shaped by his understanding of the Old Testament and by the heroic English poetry that we are told he so loved.

. . .

SCOURGES OF THE FLESH

In short, young Alfred was brought up to be a warrior and a prince. Asser fawningly describes the young *ætheling* as 'more comely in appearance than his other brothers, and more pleasing in manner, speech and behaviour'.[22] Disease, however, cast a shadow over this ideal portrait of a young hero. Alfred alludes to his poor health in his various writings, but Asser's description of his illness in chapter 74 is the fullest account.[23] Some historians have found Asser's presentation muddled and riddled with inconsistencies, a sure sign that the *Life* as it stands is an inexpert conflation of different accounts.[24] Others reject it altogether.[25] One can, however, recast Asser's narrative in a temporal sequence that makes sense not only in dramatic and moral terms but as a 'rational' medical account.[26] In essence, Asser tells us that Alfred suffered from haemorrhoids in his youth, and that this condition seemingly went away for a number of years only to be replaced by a mysterious affliction that caused him

22. Asser, ch. 22, trans. Keynes and Lapidge, p. 74.
23. Asser, ch. 74, trans. Keynes and Lapidge, pp. 88–90. For Alfred's allusions to his physical ailments see *Alfred's Boethius*, ed. Sedgefield, proem (p. xlvi), ch. 35 (p. 95); trans. Sedgefield, pp. lvi, 107–8; *Alfred's Soliloquies*, ed. Carnicelli, pp. 41, 71, 75; trans. Hargrove, pp. 3, 21, 25. For a comparison between the Old English and Latin versions, see *King Alfred's Old English Version of St Augustine's* Soliloquies, ed. H.L. Hargrove (New York, 1902) pp. 4, 33, 40–1.
24. See e.g., C. Plummer, *The Life and Times of Alfred the Great, Being the Ford Lectures for 1901* (New York, 1902) pp. 26–8; D.P. Kirby, 'Asser and his Life of King Alfred', *Studia Celtica* 6 (1971) pp. 14–15.
25. V.H. Galbraith, 'Who wrote Asser's Life of Alfred?', in his *An Introduction to the Study of History* (London, 1964) pp. 113, 127–8; A.P. Smyth, *King Alfred the Great* (Oxford, 1995) pp. 199–216. Their views of the authorship of the *Life* are discussed in the Appendix.
26. M. Schütt, 'The literary form of Asser's "*Vita Alfredi*"', *EHR* 62 (1957) pp. 209–20; Keynes and Lapidge, pp. 255–6.

excruciating pain and which persisted for more than two decades. Asser's explanation for both illnesses is the same: Alfred asked God for them, and his prayers were answered.

There is nothing incredible about the sequence of events as presented by Asser. His aetiology, on the other hand, depends upon the miraculous. According to Asser, Alfred contracted haemorrhoids soon after he first began to feel sexual urges. Wishing to obey God's commandments but finding himself unable to resist carnal temptation, the boy prayed for an illness that would temper his desires.[27] God responded with the 'ficus', so called because bleeding external haemorrhoids were thought by Roman and medieval medical authors to resemble burst figs. This most unromantic of ailments tormented Alfred through his early teens and has tormented the king's biographers ever since. (It was partly to save Alfred from the ignominy of piles that Vivien Galbraith undertook his ingenious and misguided attempt to prove 'Asser' a forgery.[28]) The haemorrhoids not only dampened Alfred's sexual ardour, but interfered with his training and activities as a prince. Hunting and martial exercises, the staples of a secular noble's life, became excruciating tests of endurance. Eventually, it became too much even for the pious Alfred. On his return from a hunting trip into Cornwall, he stopped at a local monastery, later made famous as the resting place of St Neot, to pray at the crypt of St Gueirir, an unidentified British holy man. He prostrated himself before the saint's tomb and prayed to God for relief from his infirmity. In its place he sought a more suitable and

27. Asser's language leaves little doubt that Alfred was sexually active before his marriage. J. Nelson has suggested that Osferth, who receives a bequest in Alfred's will and is called there the king's 'kinsman', was actually Alfred's bastard son. As Nelson points out, Osferth appears as 'king's brother' in the witness list of a charter purportedly from King Edward's reign. 'Reconstructing a royal family: reflections on Alfred from Asser, chapter 2', in I. Wood and N. Lund, eds, *People and Places in Northern Europe, 500–1600: Essays in Honour of Peter Hayes Sawyer* (Woodbridge, Suffolk, 1991) pp. 60–1. Cf. Keynes and Lapidge, *Alfred the Great*, p. 322 n. 79.

28. Galbraith, 'Who wrote Asser's Life of Alfred?', pp. 127–8. The suggestion that Alfred's haemorrhoids are a hagiographical invention is odd, since the disease does not figure in this way in any medieval saint's life of which I am aware. On the contrary, haemorrhoids figure in hagiograhical literature as an external manifestation of sin, and are particularly associated with pederasty.

bearable affliction, one that would not be outwardly visible and make him contemptible and useless, such as leprosy or blindness, but would still restrain his libido. God answered his prayers by curing him of the 'figs'.

In 868 Alfred, now around twenty, was suddenly struck with a mysterious pain during the feasting and festivities celebrating his marriage. Asser tells us that some thought he had fallen victim to witches, who were believed to cast spells upon new husbands to render them impotent. Some may even have suspected a political dimension to the bewitchment: King Æthelred I had sons who would look to succeed their uncle. Others attributed it to the envy of the devil. Some thought that it was caused by Alfred's childhood haemorrhoids. No one, especially the doctors, knew anything for sure.[29]

Historians have faced a similar quandary. Any attempt to diagnose Alfred's 'mysterious pain' eleven centuries after his death is admittedly a speculative exercise. Asser tells us only that the condition began suddenly when Alfred was about twenty, persisted sporadically for many years, was accompanied by intense pain, and gave rise to lassitude, which probably was as much an emotional response as physiological. 'If at any time through God's mercy, that illness abated for the space of a day or a night or even an hour', Asser says, 'his fear and horror of the accursed pain would never desert him.' The condition, whatever it was, did allow Alfred to lead Wessex in peace and war and to function sexually well enough to sire five children who survived infancy and a number of others who did not. Nevertheless, we ought to take seriously Asser's observation that Alfred feared his illness would render him useless 'for heavenly and worldly affairs'. In his translation of Boethius, Alfred added a telling passage about the difficulties of maintaining 'the righteousness of his mind' and of performing his duties when 'bodily sloth and infirmities [that] often vex the mind with a dullness . . . so that it cannot shine as brightly as it would'.[30]

29. Asser, ch. 74. For a contemporary Carolingian example, see J. Bishop, 'Bishops as marital advisors in the ninth century', in J. Kirshner and S. Wemple, eds, *Women of the Medieval World, Essays in Honor of John H. Mundy* (New York and Oxford, 1985) pp. 67–8.
30. *Alfred's Boethius*, trans. Sedgefield, ch. 35, p. 107; ed. Sedgefield, p. 95. Cf. Asser, ch. 74.

We may also perhaps infer from a record of remedies that Elias, patriarch of Jerusalem, sent to Alfred that the pain was abdominal, involving inward tenderness, and that the condition gave rise to both constipation and diarrhoea:

> A medicine: scammony for constipation of the inwards and 'gutamon' for pain in the spleen and stitch, and spikenard for diarrhoea, and tragacanth for corrupt phlegms in men, and aloes for infirmities, and galbanum for shortness of breath, and balsam anointing for all infirmities, and petroleum to drink alone for inward tenderness, and the white stone for all unknown afflictions.[31]

Alfred, according to Asser, exchanged letters and gifts with the patriarch and it is reasonable to think that the medical advice he sent was in response to a specific request from the king.[32]

Historians of the early middle ages are used to working with less than ideal evidence, and the game of medical diagnosis is nearly irresistible to those who bear the title of 'doctor' but are constantly reminded by friends and parents that they are not 'real doctors'. Nor need we fear malpractice with our patient safely dead for centuries. What, then, was Alfred's disease? From Elias's treatments and Asser's description, we should be looking for a chronic condition characterized by intense abdominal pain, digestive difficulties and, perhaps, shortness of breath. Gallstones, gastrointestinal tuberculosis, venereal disease, even epilepsy have been suggested.[33] The first is certainly a possibility, but in the light of Asser's emphasis on the bewilderment of the doctors it is likely that the condition was something more rare. The others each present problems. It is unlikely, for instance, that Alfred would have lived as long as he did with tubercular disease of the intestine.[34] Most recently a practising physician interested in Anglo-Saxon history diagnosed the

31. 'Bald's *Leechbook*', bk. II, ch. 64, in O. Cockayne, ed., *Leechdoms, Wortcunning, and Starcraft of Early England*, 3 vols (London, 1864–6) II, pp. 174, 290. See M.L. Cameron, *Anglo-Saxon Medicine* (Cambridge, 1993) pp. 72–3.
32. Asser, ch. 91.
33. E.g., Plummer, *Life and Times*, pp. 28, 214.
34. G. Craig, 'Alfred the Great: a diagnosis', *Journal of the Royal Society of Medicine*, 84 (1991) p. 304.

mystery ailment as Crohn's disease, the progression of which fits nicely with Asser's vague account.[35] Crohn's disease, which shares many of the symptoms of ulcerative colitis, often first occurs in the late teens and twenties. In many cases it is preceded by anorectal complications – fissures, perirectal abscesses, and haemorrhoidal-like extrusions – that may precede the incidence of the disease by years. Crohn's disease, moreover, is a chronic condition marked by sharp abdominal pains, loss of blood through the stool, fatigue and depression. Symptoms occur intermittently over decades. Some researchers have connected flare-ups to emotional stress. While laboured breathing as such is not a symptom of Crohn's disease, the panic often associated with the onset of attacks may in fact produce shortness of breath. The disease, moreover, is most pronounced among those in their twenties and thirties, which fits in well with Alfred's personal history. In short, Crohn's disease is an attractive possibility, though, given the state of the evidence, it can be no more.

Perhaps the only thing more questionable than attempting to diagnose the physical ailments of a man who died eleven centuries ago is to psychoanalyse him. Of course, historians have attempted both. Alfred's illness, some have concluded, was psychosomatic in origin, the result of pathological anxiety. Asser's account, which explicitly links Alfred's haemorrhoids with anxiety engendered by sexual desires and dates the onset of the mystery ailment to his wedding night, begs for a Freudian reading. The urge ought to be resisted. There is nothing to suggest that Alfred's symptoms were most virulent in times of crisis. On the contrary, Alfred proved himself capable over and over again of resolute, quick and decisive action at just such moments. Nor ought one make too much of the coincidence between the first acute attack and the wedding celebrations. Alfred was struck down not in his chamber, as one might expect if the condition were related to anxiety over the consummation of the marriage, but in public while surrounded by friends and well-wishers.

We need not doubt that the pain, whatever its cause, was real to Alfred. Its severity was so great as to distinguish it from the digestive disorders and abdominal discomfort caused by amoebic dysentery, sheep fluke, and various species

35. Craig, 'Diagnosis', pp. 303–5.

of intestinal worms, all of which were endemic in Alfred's Wessex.[36] (As Alfred himself pointed out, 'even little worms torment man within and without, and sometimes nearly kill him'.[37]) Perhaps as importantly, the pain was meaningful to him. While Asser's account may not enable us to reach a definitive diagnosis, it does yield additional insight into how Alfred and his biographer made sense of the king's life. For Asser, the haemorrhoids and the mysterious affliction that succeeded them were not due to contagion, poor hygiene, or even bad luck. They were, as odd as it may seem to us, God's gift in response to Alfred's prayers. Alfred's suffering was meant to scourge the sinful flesh, to help the king control his illicit passions. Though the pain could be excruciating, perhaps at times even debilitating, it was a rod of spiritual correction applied out of love. Was this also how Alfred viewed it? In his occasional comments about his ailments, Alfred speaks of them in the manner of Gregory the Great and Augustine, as a challenge to be overcome, as a burden to be borne patiently and, an occasion to reflect upon the Scriptural testimony that 'He scourgeth every son whom he receiveth' (Heb. 12:6).[38] Alfred's concern with the consequences of carnal sin, moreover, is evident from an interesting and original interpolation in his translation of Boethius's *Consolation of Philosophy*: 'The evil desire of unlawful lust disturbs the mind of well-nigh every man that lives. Even as the bee must die when she stings in her anger, so must every soul perish after unlawful lust, except a man return to virtue.'[39] Whether or not this reflects Alfred's personal experience – and the categorical character of the assertion makes it difficult to think otherwise – the sentiment fits

36. A. Hagen, *A Handbook of Anglo-Saxon Food Processing and Consumption* (Chippenham, Wilts, 1992) p. 113 (and references there); Cameron, *Anglo-Saxon Medicine*, pp. 5–18. 'Bald's *Leechbook*' devotes seven chapters (bk. 1, chs 46, 48–51, 53–4) to remedies for illnesses caused by various types of worms. Cockayne, ed., *Leechdoms*, II, pp. 115, 121–7.
37. *Alfred's Boethius*, trans. Sedgefield, ch. 16, p. 36.
38. Gregory the Great's *Letter to Leander*, which serves as a preface to his *Moralia in Iob*, ed. M. Adriaen (Turhout, 1979) p. 6. Bede quotes from the Letter in his short summary of Gregory's career in his *Ecclesiastical History. HE* I.2, ed. Colgrave and Mynors, p. 128. Cf. Asser, ch. 74. Scharer, 'The writing of history', p. 188; J. Bately, 'Old English prose before and during the reign of Alfred', *ASE* 17 (1988) pp. 120–3.
39. *Alfred's Boethius*, ed. Sedgefield, ch. 31 (p. 71); trans. Sedgefield, p. 77.

Asser's portrait of a sensitive youth who fought with mixed success against illicit desires and devoutly prayed for release from them. One hears resonances of this Alfred in the prayer with which the king concluded his Boethius: 'Lord God Almighty, confirm me against the devil's temptations; and keep far from me foul lust [*fulan galnysse*] and all iniquity . . . that I may inwardly love You before all things with pure thought and clean body [*clænu lichaman*].'[40] Alfred's law code, one might add, shows a greater interest in sexual crimes against women than any other Anglo-Saxon lawbook.[41] Of course, Alfred's observation about the ubiquity of sinful conduct and his legislation against molestation and rape may provide less of a window on the king's personal psychology than on general historical conditions. The reported sexual irregularities of the English form a veritable leitmotif in letters of spiritual correction dispatched by native-born and foreign ecclesiastics to Anglo-Saxon kings in the eighth and ninth centuries, and viking England undoubtedly was a dangerous place for women. Still, it is likely that Alfred approved of Asser's portrayal of him as a youth striving with God's help to avoid the sins of the flesh and helped promulgate the view that his illness was a divine blessing.

.   .   .

THE VIKING THREAT

The *Anglo-Saxon Chronicle*'s entry for the year 860 explains, rather misleadingly, that Æthelberht held the whole kingdom 'in good harmony and in great concord' (*on godre gethuænesse and on micelre sibsumnesse*). The Chronicler wished to emphasize the realm's internal harmony, the concord among the royal brothers (implied by *sibsumnesse,* a word used by Alfred in his translation of Gregory's *Pastoral Care* to mean 'brotherly love'), rather than peace from invaders.[42] King Æthelberht's reign, in fact, began and ended with viking raids. That these were the only two events the Chronicler

---

40. Trans. Keynes and Lapidge, p. 137; ed. Sedgefield, p. 149.
41. *Alfred* 8, 10, 11, 18, 25, 29.
42. ASC s.a. 860A, ed. Bately, p. 46. J. Bately has recently questioned Alfred's ownership of the prayer (personal communication).

thought significant enough to record for the years 860 to 865 probably tells us more about the preoccupations of the author in the early 890s than about their importance at the time. For Æthelberht's reign was to mark the end of an era in the history of the vikings in Britain. The age of viking raids was coming to an end. The next two kings of Wessex, Æthelred I and Alfred, were to confront viking armies intent upon conquest.

Viking activity along the coasts of Wessex was nothing new and the kings of Wessex had long since learned the importance of coastal watches. The Scyldings' guard who first sighted Beowulf's ship from his perch on the sea-cliffs was a figure of history as well as poetry:

> [He] saw bright shields borne over the gangway, armor ready for battle; strong desire stirred him in mind to learn what the men were. He went riding on his horse to the shore, thane of Hrothgar, forcefully brandished a great spear in his hands, with formal words questioned them: 'What are you, bearers of armor, dressed in mail-coats, who thus have come bringing a tall ship over the sea-road, over the water to this place? Lo, for a long time I have been guard of the coast, held watch by the sea so that no foe with a force of ships might work harm on the Danes' land.[43]

A wise West Saxon royal reeve exercised caution when welcoming those who came to his land by sea. They might be simple traders or friendly visitors seeking the hospitality of the king. Or they might be marauders. This lesson was learned the hard way by an unfortunate king's reeve in the days of King Beorhtric (786–802). Beaduheard, the reeve, was in Dorchester when news arrived that three ships were nearing the harbour at Portland. Like Hrothgar's guard, Beorhtric's reeve rode to greet the strangers. Presuming them to be traders, he took with him only a small number of men. This proved a fatal mistake. When Beaduheard attempted to force the seamen to accompany him to a nearby royal estate, they killed him and all his men. Thus came the first 'Danish men' to Wessex.[44]

---

43. *Beowulf, A New Prose Translation*, trans. E. Talbot Donaldson (New York, 1966) p. 5; *Beowulf and the Fight at Finn*, ed. F. Klaeber, 3rd edn (Boston, 1950) ll. 229–43.
44. *ASC* s.a. 789A; Æthelweard, *Chronicon*, Campbell, s.a. 789.

The vikings appeared suddenly and dramatically in the history of Western Europe at the end of the eighth century. The sack of the great monastery of Lindisfarne off the north-east coast of Northumberland in the summer of 793 made a lasting impression on contemporary observers. In one of its most famous entries, the *Anglo-Saxon Chronicle* recorded:

> In this year dire portents appeared over Northumbria and sorely frightened the people. They consisted of immense whirlwinds and flashes of lightning, and fiery dragons were seen flying in the air. A great famine immediately followed those signs, and a little after that in the same year, on 8 June, the ravages of heathen men miserably destroyed God's church on Lindisfarne, with plunder and slaughter.[45]

From his vantage point in Charlemagne's court, Alcuin viewed the marauders as a scourge of God visited upon the sinners in his native Northumbria. Like an English Amos or Isaiah, Alcuin lectured Æthelred, king of the Northumbrians: 'Behold, the church of St Cuthbert spattered with the blood of the priests of God, despoiled of all its ornaments; a place more venerable than all in Britain is given as a prey to pagan peoples.'[46] Nor did one need to look far for the reason for God's anger. Shameless fornications, adulteries, incest, avarice, robbery and violent judgements proliferated throughout Northumbria. Nobles and commoners alike had given themselves over to luxurious habits and fashions, even trimming their beards and hair after the manner of pagans. Kings who tolerate such sins among their people, Alcuin warned, lose their kingdoms. 'Behold, judgement has begun, with great terror, at the house of God.' Even the unfortunate bishop of Lindisfarne, Higbald, received a lecture. 'What assurance is there for the churches of Britain, if St Cuthbert, with so great a number of saints, defends not his own? Either this is the beginning of greater tribulation or else the sins of the inhabitants have called it upon them. . . . If anything ought to be corrected in your Grace's habits, correct it quickly.'[47]

The theme Alcuin sounded became a leitmotif of monastic writing for the next two centuries and helped shape

45. ASC s.a. 793A.
46. *EHD* I, no. 193, p. 842.
47. *EHD* I, no. 194, p. 845.

King Alfred's and his court-writers' vision of the vikings as 'pagan' hordes. For Lindisfarne was only the beginning. The ravages of these new Assyrians grew ever more frequent and ferocious, as churches, towns and villages in Britain, Ireland, and Francia fell prey to their lust for gold, silver, and slaves. Viking raids upon the coasts of Francia were serious enough to warrant Charlemagne establishing a coastal watch along the shores of his kingdom north of the Seine estuary and ordering a fleet to be built to patrol 'the Gallic sea' against the 'pirates that infested it'.[48] These defences proved effective until the rebellion of the sons of the Emperor Louis the Pious. The civil wars that wracked Francia after the death of Louis in 841 and the eclipse of Frisian naval power created conditions that allowed vikings to operate unimpeded along the coasts of the Frankish kingdoms from Frisia to Aquitaine and the great rivers that penetrated into the heart of west Francia. The increase in viking activity spilled across the Channel to England, as the coasts of Wessex and Kent increasingly suffered from viking raids. During the reigns of Alfred's father and grandfather, West Saxon armies fought viking raiders with mixed success at Carhampton, Hingston Down, Southampton, Portland, London, Rochester, Parret, Sandwich, Thanet and *Aclea.*

Though the raiding bands at this time were small, probably numbering in the dozens or hundreds rather than thousands, the devastation that marked their passage was considerable. Monasteries and towns were their favourite prey, since the plunder to be had there was especially plentiful. But settlements and estates in the countryside also suffered from their attention. When a Kentish noble woman, Ealhburg, made a pious grant of renders from her estate at Bradbourne, Kent, to the monks of St Augustine's sometime between 844 and 864, she promised the monks that if her estate at Bradbourne should be unable to pay the agreed-upon renders of meat, fowl, malt, bread, cheese, timber and

48. Royal Frankish Annals, s.a. 800, 811, ed. F. Kurze, *Annales regni Francorum 741–829 qui dicuntur Annales Laurissense maiores et Einhardi*, MGH, SRG (Hanover, 1895); B. Scholz with B. Rogers, trans. *Carolingian Chronicles* (Ann Arbor, Michigan, 1970) pp. 78, 94. For Charlemagne's naval strategy, see J. Haywood, *Dark Age Naval Power: A Reassessment of Frankish and Anglo-Saxon Seafaring Activity* (London and New York, 1991) pp. 118–35.

lard for three successive years because of the 'heathen army', the abbey would gain the right of reversion to the entire estate. That such a stipulation should have been deemed necessary is eloquent testimony to the local destructive power of the raiders.[49] Like other armies living off the land, viking bands foraged for their supplies. This entailed seizing whatever was valuable or edible from the estates and villages along their route and killing or destroying what was not. Some of the most valuable 'livestock' to be had was human. As in Ireland and Francia, the vikings in Britain rounded up healthy young peasants to be sold in distant slave markets. Captives of the better sort also faced slavery unless fortunate enough to be ransomed by kinsmen or lords. Only in this sense did vikings appreciate the 'value of human life'. Even allowing for the bias and hostility of monastic chroniclers, there can be little doubt that vikings were capable of acts of stunning brutality. At Donnybrook in Ireland, the excavation of a burial mound in 1879 revealed the remains of a viking warrior, adorned in death with a magnificent sword and by the bodies of two females, presumably ritually murdered slave girls. Heaped around the warrior were the bones of hundreds of men, women, and children, many of whom showed signs of violent death, 'suggestive of a massacre'.[50]

Just as Charlemagne responded to the early viking raids by reorganizing his coastal defences, so Offa of Mercia and his son-in-law, Beorhtric of Wessex, answered the threat with military innovations that were to be critical for Alfred's own defence of his kingdom. Even before Lindisfarne was sacked, Northmen had launched coastal raids that prompted Offa in the late summer or autumn of 792 to impose upon the churches of Kent the military burdens of the construction and repair of bridges and fortifications and expeditions to defend 'against pagan seafarers' (*contra paganos marinos*).[51] By the end of the eighth century these three 'common

---

49. S 1198; Harmer, ed., *SEHD*, no. 6, pp. 9–10. See N. Brooks, *The Early History of the Church of Canterbury: Christ Church from 597 to 1066* (Leicester, 1984) pp. 150–1.
50. H.B. Clarke, 'The bloodied eagle: the vikings and the development of Dublin, 841–1041', *The Irish Sword* 18 (1991) p. 99. See also R.A. Hall, 'A viking-age grave at Donnybrook, Co. Dublin', *Medieval Archaeology* 22 (1978) pp. 64–83.
51. S 134. Cf. S 1264.

burdens' had been imposed upon bookland in Mercia and Wessex as well. The result was a revolution in the idea of military obligation, as secular and religious landholders acknowledged the king's right to demand new services from them. The obligations Offa and Beorhtric imposed in the late eighth century were to form the basis of the military resources that Alfred would inherit when he became king in 871. And Alfred, as we shall see, would creatively exploit the possibilities presented by the 'common burdens' to preserve his kingdom and lay down the foundations for a new state, the tenth-century kingdom of England.[52]

The vikings who sacked Winchester soon after Æthelberht's accession in 860 were typical of the larger raiding bands that preyed upon Francia and England before 865. The *Anglo-Saxon Chronicle*'s account of their activities and defeat is brief. After landing in Hampshire and sacking Winchester, the raiders ravaged further north, pushing perhaps as far as the Berkshire Downs. The West Saxon military response fell to Ealdorman Osric of Hampshire, an experienced war leader, who as ealdorman of Dorset fifteen years before had helped defeat a Danish army in Somerset, and to the Mercian-born ealdorman of Berkshire, Æthelwulf. The combined military forces of the two shires intercepted the marauders as, laden with booty, they slowly made their way back to their ships. The West Saxons won a great victory. Asser related that, 'the battle having been joined in earnest, the heathens were cut to pieces everywhere. When they could not resist any longer, they took to flight like women, and the Christians had mastery over the field of death'.[53]

Who were these viking raiders and what prompted them to raid Wessex in 860? Contemporary Frankish chronicles, in particular the *Annals of St-Bertin*, permit us to track in unique detail the movements of these vikings before and after they undertook their ill-fated expedition to Wessex and to glimpse the complex political reality underlying contemporary sermons. The tale that emerges from the pens of Bishop Prudentius

52. R. Abels, *Lordship and Military Obligation in Anglo-Saxon England* (Los Angeles and London, 1988) pp. 53–7. Cf. N. Brooks, 'The Development of Military Obligations in Eighth- and Ninth-Century England', *England before the Norman Conquest*, ed. P. Clemoes and K. Hughes (Cambridge, 1971) pp. 69–84.
53. Asser, ch. 18.

and Archbishop Hincmar is far more complicated than a simple story of heathen predators and Christian prey. It tells, rather, of Frankish princes, predators themselves, who were not above hiring vikings to fight other vikings or even Christian rivals. In Anglo-Saxon kingdoms, too, the raiders sometimes found allies among the local nobility; Alfred's nephew, Æthelwold, for example, sought the support of the vikings of East Anglia in his revolt against Alfred's son, Edward.[54]

According to the *Annals of St-Bertin*, these same vikings had established themselves the previous year near the River Somme. There they had come to an agreement with King Charles the Bald to drive off or kill a different band of vikings, who had built a fortress on the island of Oissel in the Seine, from which they had conducted raids deep into the countryside. Charles the Bald, to the consternation of clerical chroniclers, was far more interested in securing his throne against the threats of his brothers, nephews, and counts than in dealing with viking depredations. But Oissel was too near Paris and the heartland of his domain to be ignored. Charles agreed to pay the Somme vikings 3,000 lbs (1,360 kg) of silver, weighed out under their watchful eyes – these would-be mercenaries no more trusted Charles than he them – and they undertook to drive out the Seine vikings. While Charles raised the cash by taxing the treasures of churches and the houses and moveable wealth of landholders and merchants, the Somme vikings took hostages from the Franks and struck out across the Channel. Their rough reception at the hands of the West Saxons persuaded them to return to Francia where, under the leadership of a chieftain named Weland, they finally fulfilled their bargain with Charles by besieging the Oissel stronghold of the Seine vikings, who in the meanwhile had sacked Paris in January 861.

While Weland and his men, their numbers swelled by the addition of forces from a newly arrived fleet of sixty ships, settled down for a siege, Charles raised silver and gathered livestock and corn for his viking allies so that the realm would not be looted.[55] Finally, the besieged Seine vikings, 'forced by starvation, filth and general misery', surrendered. They agreed to pay Weland 6,000 lbs (2,721 kg) of gold and

---

54. *ASC* s.a. 900, 902, 903.
55. *AB* s.a. 861.

silver, and then joined up with him. With winter coming on, Weland's forces chose not to brave the hazards of the North Sea and wintered over in Francia. Splitting up into smaller bands (*sodalitates*), they scattered among the ports and abbeys of the Seine basin as far upstream as St-Maur-des-Fossés, southeast of Paris. Eventually they left Charles's kingdom, but only after Weland's son led the former Oissel vikings from their base in the deserted monastery of Fossés in an attack upon Meaux. For Bishop Hildegar of Meaux, Charles's forbearance in allowing the vikings to ravage the Seine basin was a disgrace and his permission for them to winter upstream from Paris nothing short of treachery. The raid upon Meaux may, in fact, have had Charles's tacit approval, as a warning to his rebellious son, Louis the Stammerer, and Louis's powerful guardian, the queen's uncle, Adalard. As one historian commented, 'if Charles did not actually let the Fossés vikings loose on Meaux, their activities there would not wholly have displeased him. In the ashes of Meaux's buildings, late in 862, Louis the Stammerer and Hildegar would have seen daily reminders of the wages of sin.'[56]

Whether or not Charles turned a blind eye to the Danish attack on Meaux, it gave him an opportunity to enhance his prestige through decisive action. The Frankish nobility's failure to respond effectively to the viking threat had already provoked a near rebellion among the peasantry of the Seine–Loire region, who in 859 had attempted to take matters into their own hands by forming a sworn association to resist the Danes by force of arms.[57] Though the local magnates (*potentiores*) had quickly and forcefully put an end to such presumption, by 862 they must have come to share their dependants' frustration. Charles responded by raising an army and stationing troops along both banks of the Oise, Marne and Seine, threatening to cut off viking escape to the open sea. By spring 862 Weland, who had done fealty to Charles, and the leaders of the other viking bands agreed to return the captives they had seized and to depart the kingdom. The great fleet broke up into smaller bands, many of which sailed to Brittany to take service with the Breton chieftain,

56. Nelson, *Charles the Bald*, p. 206.
57. *AB* s.a. 859. See E.J. Goldberg, 'Popular revolt, dynastic politics, and aristocratic factionalism in the early middle ages: the Saxon *Stellinga* reconsidered', *Speculum* 70 (1995) p. 500.

Salomon. Others signed on with Salomon's rival, Robert the Strong of Anjou. Weland himself returned to Charles's court within the year, having apparently lost command of his fleet. He, his wife, and their entourage accepted baptism, presumably in order to secure the Frankish king's favour. But in an odd turn of events, the viking chieftain was accused by one of his own men of 'bad faith' and of having sought baptism 'as a trick'. He proved his accusation by killing Weland in single combat in the presence of Charles and his court.

The story of the viking Weland sheds a great deal of light upon the viking menace that King Alfred faced. The vikings who ravaged Francia and Britain in the mid- and late ninth century were not a 'people' and their war bands were not well regulated 'armies'. Though the chronicle sources often label viking fleets as 'Danish' or 'Norse', these terms better describe the leaders rather than their crews, who probably were a heterogeneous and variable lot. The viking 'army' of the Somme quite clearly was a composite force made up of various warbands. Like flocks of migrating geese that join together under one leader, only to break up and re-form under another, the viking 'armies', or *heres* as they were termed in the English sources, represented fluid and shifting combinations of small fleets.

Some viking raiders undoubtedly were men like the *Orkneyinga Saga*'s Svein Asleifarson, who went a-viking in the Hebrides every spring after he had overseen the sowing of his fields, and every autumn after the harvest. But the ship crews that crossed the Channel in search of loot seem to have been a different sort. By the 850s these vikings practised piracy as a profession. In many respects their lives and exploits resembled those of the buccaneers who plundered merchantmen and sacked towns throughout the Caribbean in the late seventeenth century. Exquemelin's observations about his shipmates might serve equally well for the vikings: 'They live in no particular country; their home is wherever there is hope of spoils, and their only patrimony is their bravery.'[58] A viking was as much at home in his longship as he was in Jutland, Vestfold, Skane, or any of the Danish islands of the Kattegat. Many were young *bondi*, the sons and

58. Quoted by K. Eldjárn, 'The Viking Myth', *The Vikings*, ed. R.T. Farrell (London and Chichester, 1982) p. 267.

110

brothers of lesser landowners. Population growth, spurred in part by pagan polygamy, combined with inheritance custom to threaten this class of middling farmers with eventual impoverishment, leading the more adventurous to renounce their share of the patrimony and seek fortunes abroad. Piracy was a time-honoured way to acquire resources to establish oneself as a man of substance. By joining a *lith*, a ship or fleet under the command of a chieftain, a viking bound himself to his captain by ties of fellowship and lordship, becoming in essence a member of a seaborne household of warriors. Unsurprisingly, their leaders often came from the class of jarls. Some even claimed royal blood and styled themselves 'king' (though Alfred would more readily have recognized them as *ætheling*s). Given the internecine warfare that marked the consolidation of power by royal dynasties in ninth-century Denmark and Norway, there was never a lack of noble exiles to lead expeditions. A few, such as Godrum, nephew of King Horic I of Denmark, practised piracy in order to obtain the wealth and followers necessary to renew their pursuit of royal power at home.[59] Most probably did not. Certainly by the second half of the ninth century, viking chieftains were in search of new lords to serve and lands to rule. Though some of the sea-captains may have had royal or noble blood, or at least claimed the right to be called 'king' or 'jarl', leadership of these bands was precarious in the extreme. Weland appears to have been raised up by the captains of the various *liths* or *sodalites* and cast out by them when he ceased to be successful. What held the fleets together was little more than the prospect of plunder. Perhaps most crucially, the history of the raiders who sacked Winchester in 860 reminds us that the viking raids on England were part of a larger story of viking depredations in western Francia (as well as in Ireland and Wales). The bands that raided the shores of Britain were the same vikings who looted and pillaged along the rivers of Charles the Bald's kingdom.

Æthelberht's reign not only began with a viking raid, but ended with one. In the autumn of 864, a viking host made camp on the isle of Thanet. Rather than attempting to oust the raiders, the chief men of Kent, presumably

59. K.L. Mund, '"A turmoil of warring princes": political leadership in ninth-century Denmark', *The Haskins Society Journal* 6 (1994) p. 41.

111

led by Archbishop Ceolnoth and Ealdormen Dryhtwald and Æthelred (or Eastmund), negotiated a peace treaty and promised to pay the viking band cash. The vikings, however, broke the peace, 'stole away by night' and ravaged eastern Kent. How this crisis was finally resolved is unknown, but the example of Christ Church, Canterbury, which by the 870s no longer possessed scribes with a basic command of Latin, suggests the severity of the damage.[60]

King Æthelberht died in 865/866; his brother Æthelred I succeeded to the entire kingdom. Alfred, having now outlived three of his brothers, emerged at the age of seventeen or eighteen as the 'second man' in the realm, heir apparent to the new young king.[61] The two were to face a viking threat far greater than any experienced by their predecessors. The two raids that Wessex had suffered during the five-year reign of Æthelberht were merely a prelude to what was to come. For in the autumn of 865, what the *Anglo-Saxon Chronicle* describes as 'a great heathen army' arrived in East Anglia. Led by the sons of the semi-legendary viking hero, Ragnarr Lodbrok (Leather-Breeches), as well as other less celebrated 'kings' and jarls, this new army came to conquer and settle rather than merely raid.[62] Its arrival struck the death-knell for the ancient kingdoms of Northumbria, East Anglia, and Mercia, and very nearly for Wessex as well.

. . .

THE GREAT HEATHEN ARMY

Though the *Anglo-Saxon Chronicle* provides a basic outline of the movements of the Great Heathen Army, the West Saxon Chronicler supplies few details about its leadership and composition before 871, when Alfred ascended the throne and the Danish invaders finally turned their attention to the conquest of Wessex. Surprisingly, he does not even give an estimate of the number of ships that landed in East Anglia in 865. That the combined fleets were formidable, fully justifying the Chronicler's description of the Army as 'large', is

60. Brooks, *Early History of the Church of Canterbury*, pp. 171–4.
61. The term that Asser uses is *secundarius*. Asser, chs 29, 38, 42.
62. For Ragnarr Lodbrok and his sons, see A.P. Smyth's stimulating and controversial *Scandinavian Kings in the British Isles, 850–880* (Oxford, 1977) pp. 22–9, 169–213.

indicated by the forces its individual chieftains were able to command. In 878 one of Ragnarr's sons led a fleet of twenty-three ships into Devon, where he lost in battle some 840 men (if we are to trust the *Chronicle*).[63] Given this, and in light of the linguistic and institutional evidence for a considerable Scandinavian settlement in Northumbria and East Anglia in the tenth century, the total forces that gathered in East Anglia between the autumn of 865 and the summer of 866 may well have been in excess of 5,000 combatants.[64] We cannot even begin to guess at the number of non-combatants who accompanied the Army. Nearly a fifth of the 249 bodies unearthed from a mass grave near the viking winter camp at Repton, which can be dated to 873/874 on the basis of coins, proved to be female. The skeletons, at least those of the males, are of 'non-local physical type', and given the lack of evidence for violent death, appear to be the bodies of vikings who fell victim to disease in Repton. The presence of females among them suggests that the invaders brought women with them to England or attracted native camp followers once they arrived.[65]

The origins of the Great Heathen Army are obscure. Though the army was to operate in tandem in its campaigns between 866 and 871, it may have formed much like Weland's army in 861/862, through a combination of separate and formerly independent *liths*. Asser, in one of his odder mistakes, asserts that these Northmen came from the 'Danube', which may mean nothing more than that he believed this force originated in the Danish homeland, through which, obviously, the 'Danubia' flowed.[66] Some vikings may have

63. *ASC* s.a. 878. Cf. Asser, ch. 54: twenty-three ships and 1,200 viking casualties; Æthelweard, *Chronicon*, s.a. 878, Campbell, ed., p. 43: thirty ships and 800 casualties.
64. N. Lund, 'The settlers: where do we get them from – and do we need them?', *Proceedings of the Eighth Viking Congress*, ed. H. Bekker-Nielsen, P. Foote, O. Olsen (Arhus, 1981) pp. 145–71. On the military threat posed by the vikings, see N. Brooks, 'England in the ninth century: the crucible of defeat', *Transactions of the Royal Historical Society*, 5th series, 29 (1979) pp. 1–20. Cf. P.H. Sawyer, *The Age of the Vikings* (London, 1962) pp. 117–28.
65. J. Graham-Campbell, ed., *Cultural Atlas of the Viking World* (Abingdon, Oxfordshire, 1994) pp. 128–9.
66. Stevenson, *Asser's Life*, pp. 217–18. Cf. A. Smyth, *King Alfred the Great* (Oxford, 1995) pp. 304–6, for a different and less plausible explanation.

sailed directly from Scandinavia, but others came from areas much closer to hand. The vikings who had wintered on Thanet and ravaged eastern Kent in the previous year may well have formed one strand of this army. Francia apparently supplied another. West Francia in recent years had become decidedly less attractive to viking raiders. Beginning with the construction of Pont-de-l'Arche on the Seine downstream from the royal palace at Pîtres in 862, Charles the Bald oversaw the creation of a series of fortified bridges along the Rivers Seine, Loire, and Oise designed to prevent the vikings from sailing upriver, a strategy that may have later influenced Alfred. While the fortifications were under construction, Charles resorted to the tried and true policy of purchasing peace. In June 866 he promised to pay the Northmen 4,000 lbs (1,814 kg) in silver, according to their scales, and wine, to depart his realm. He even agreed to round up and return, or ransom at a price set by the Northmen, any slaves who escaped after the peace had been ratified. The vikings then left their island stronghold near the monastery of St Denis and sailed to the mouth of the Seine, where, as they awaited payment, they repaired their ships and built new ones. Charles, meanwhile, raised the cash by levying taxes on the peasants, traders and clerics of his realm. He also marched to Pîtres with workmen and carts to complete his fortifications on the Seine to ensure that if the peace failed, the vikings could never again force their way up the river.[67] In July the vikings, their ships loaded with cash, wine and slaves, departed Charles's realm. Some sailed to Frisia to plunder and seek the patronage of King Lothar; others crossed the Channel to join the great army massing in East Anglia.

Even more astounding than the sheer size of the Great Heathen Army was its leaders' ability to coordinate its actions in order to accomplish strategic goals. The movements of the various contingents of the Army between 866 and 878 reflected a well-thought-out strategy of conquest that involved diplomacy as well as brute force. Upon landing in East Anglia, the Army's leaders negotiated a peace with King Edmund, later to be their most famous victim, and arranged for winter provisions. At this point, East Anglia was a staging ground, rather than a strategic target. From the first, the vikings

67. *AB*, s.a. 866.

probably had their sights set on the Northumbrian city of York, which may have been familiar to them because of its commercial connections with Scandinavia.[68] York was attractive for a number of reasons. Control of York meant military access to the entire north country, and in military matters, as in real estate, location is everything. At the confluence of the Foss and the Ouse, then navigable to the Humber, the town was easily accessible to the North Sea. From York, one could reach south to Nottingham in Mercia by following the Ouse to the Humber to the Trent. As the former headquarters for the Romans' northern command, the city was also a hub for Roman roads leading in all directions, including the main routes to East Anglia and to the northern reaches of Northumbria, the ancient kingdom of Bernicia. York was also probably the most prosperous town in Northumbria. Well sited for commerce and dominating rich agricultural lands, it boasted a vital economy that included markets, a mint, and even a local glass-making industry.[69] And as the site of a diocesan church, library, and monastery, it offered the vikings their favourite prey and plunder: clerics and ecclesiastical riches. Even York's Roman walls were an attraction to the vikings, who routinely fortified their bases.

The Great Heathen Army sojourned in East Anglia for a full year, building up strength. Their numbers probably swelled as news of the enterprise spread to viking bands on the Continent. The 'peace' purchased by the East Anglians protected their lands and monasteries from being ravaged, but at considerable cost. The vikings demanded from their hosts not only food, drink and 'gifts', but horses as well, and it may well have taken the East Anglians a year to round up enough horses to satisfy their guests. In the autumn of 866 preparations were finally complete. Supplied with mounts and provisions, they swept across the Humber estuary and

---

68. Altfrid in his *Life of St Liudger*, ch. 11, mentions a community of Frisian merchants settled in York in the late eighth century. *EHD* I, no. 160, p. 788. R. Hodges, *The Anglo-Saxon Achievement: Archaeology and the Beginnings of English Society* (Ithaca, N.Y., 1989) pp. 102–4; N.J. Higham, *The Kingdom of Northumbria AD 350–1100* (Frome, Somerset, 1993) pp. 167–70. For the archaeological evidence, see R.A. Hall, *Jorvik, Viking Age York*, York Archaeological Trust (York, 1987) p. 14.
69. R. Hall, *The Viking Dig* (London, 1984) pp. 43–8.

descended upon York, some 300 kilometres distant. The well-timed attack took place on 1 November, during the celebration of All Saints. Even if the Northumbrians had been keeping an eye upon the Danes massing to their south, few would have expected a raid this late in the campaigning season. The vikings had learned from their long interaction with Christians to put the Christian calendar to good strategic use. All Saints' Day, as Ivarr undoubtedly knew, was one of the principal feasts in ninth-century Northumbria. The vikings anticipated not only the accumulated wealth of the monastery and church of St Peter's, but a rich harvest of plunder and slaves from the faithful who flocked into the town to worship and celebrate.[70]

The Danish attack on York was aided, perhaps even inspired, by a bitter civil war then raging between the expelled King Osberht and the man who had ousted him, King Ælle, whom the *Anglo-Saxon Chronicle* says lacked royal blood.[71] The viking seizure of York persuaded the rivals to put aside their differences 'for the common good', at least long enough to deal with the foreign threat. On either Palm Sunday, 23 March 867, or the Friday before that – the sources differ – Osberht's and Ælle's combined forces arrived before York. On their approach, the Danes retreated within York, preferring, as was their wont, to defend fortifications rather than engage a formidable enemy in the open. The Northumbrians managed to breach the decaying Roman walls and force their way into the city, but, 'driven on by grief and necessity, the pagans attacked them fiercely, cut them to pieces, put them to flight, and overthrew them inside and outside'.[72] By day's end both Northumbrian kings, eight

70. Smyth, *Scandinavian Kings*, pp. 148, 155–6, 178–82.
71. *ASC* s.a. 867. The accusation that Ælle lacked royal blood is not substantiated by northern sources. For these events, see D.P. Kirby, 'Northumbria in the ninth century', *Coinage in Ninth-Century Northumbria: The Tenth Oxford Symposium on Coinage and Monetary History*, ed. D.M. Metcalf, British Archaeological Reports British Series 180 (Oxford, 1987) pp. 11–25.
72. Asser, ch. 27; trans. Keynes and Lapidge, p. 76. J. Radley, 'Excavations in the defences of the city of York: an early medieval stone tower and the successive earth ramparts', *Yorkshire Archaeological Journal* 44 (1972) pp. 38–64; R.A. Hall, 'York 700–1050', *The Rebirth of Towns in the West, AD 700–1050*, ed. R. Hodges and B. Hobley, Council for British Archaeology Research Report 68 (London, 1988) p. 126.

ealdormen, and large numbers of their troops lay dead in the streets. The vikings followed up their victory by ravaging the entire kingdom as far north as the mouth of the Tyne. The remaining Northumbrian leaders, led perhaps by Wulfhere, archbishop of York, whose close association with the Danes would lead to his expulsion in a popular uprising five years later, sought peace. As they would also later do in Mercia, the Danes found a compliant native *ætheling*, named Egbert, to rule the region north of the River Tyne, the ancient kingdom of Bernicia, under their power.[73] The invaders retained possession of York as their military base in the north, and probably assumed direct control over southern Northumbria, Deira.

Northumbria was the first English kingdom to fall to the Great Heathen Army. There, more than anywhere else in the British Isles, Scandinavian settlement and culture would take root, culminating in the establishment of the great tenth-century Norse kingdom of York which would resist West Saxon rule until the death of its last viking king, Eric Bloodaxe, at the battle of Stainmore in 954. Perhaps because of this, the viking conquest of Northumbria became woven into the sagas. The death of King Ælle was remembered in medieval prose and verse as an act of revenge by the viking leader, Ivarr the Boneless, against the man who reputedly had had his father, Ragnarr Loþbrok, killed in a snake-pit. According to these thirteenth-century sagas, Ælle did not fall in battle, as suggested by the *Anglo-Saxon Chronicle*, but was captured and tortured to death through the rite of the 'blood-eagle'. This purportedly involved either carving the figure of an eagle on a captive's back or, in its most elaborate literary form, hacking the ribs away from the backbone, then ripping out the lungs of the still-living victim and draping them over his spread ribs, so as to form the 'wings' of an eagle.[74] Though the sagas' personalized explanation for Ivarr's expedition has been shown to be without historical basis, some historians, following the lead of

73. *Symeonis Monachi Opera Omnia*, ed. T. Arnold, 2 vols (London, 1882–5) I, pp. 55, 225; II, pp. 106, 377, 391; Roger of Wendover, *Flores Historiarum*, s.a. 867, in *EHD* I, no. 4, p. 282; *ASC* s.a. 867A; Asser, ch. 27.
74. Smyth, *Scandinavian Kings*, p. 190, quoting the *Thattr af Ragnars sonum*, in *Fornaldarsrögur Nordurlanda*, ed. G. Jónsson and B. Vilhjálmsson, 3 vols (Reykjavík, 1943–4) I, p. 158

Professor Alfred Smyth, have accepted the reality of the 'blood-eagle'. In their view, the sagas accurately preserve the memory of a brutal pagan ritual in which captured kings or chieftains were sacrificed to the god Odin as an offering for victory. The gruesome fate awaiting defeated kings, it has been further suggested, lent special urgency to Alfred's flight into the Somerset fens in 878 to evade capture by King Guthrum and the fate of Ælle and St Edmund.[75]

Did Alfred and his brothers face a sadistic heathen enemy intent upon cruelly sacrificing them to their gods? Was the penalty for defeat really the 'blood-eagle'? Probably not. That vikings were capable of butchery is not in doubt, though we ought not to think of them as being substantially more brutal than other Dark Age warrior societies. Nor should we dismiss the possibility that pagan vikings practised human sacrifice.[76] There is, however, no contemporary ninth-century evidence for the ritual sacrifice of captured kings or princes, and this despite the unremitting hostility of Christian chroniclers, who revelled in painting their pagan oppressors in the darkest colours possible. Archbishop Wulfhere's collaboration with Ivarr would have been particularly cynical if the viking chieftain had recently publicly sacrificed King Ælle to his pagan gods. Rather, the tale seems to have originated centuries later, based perhaps on a literal-minded misreading of some extraordinarily convoluted eleventh-century skaldic verses, in which the eagle is presented as a poetic symbol for battle. As Professor Roberta Frank concluded, 'The ultimate begetter of the blood-eagle was not a sadistic bird-fancier but an antiquarian revival . . . sweeping northwestern Europe in the twelfth and thirteenth centuries when tales about the savagery and ferocity of the Northmen were all the rage.'[77]

75. Ibid., pp. 52, 189–94, 211–23, 248, 250; Smyth, *King Alfred the Great*, p. 77.
76. P.H. Sawyer, *Kings and Vikings* (London and New York, 1982) pp. 27–8, 40; E. Roesdahl, *The Vikings* (London, 1992) pp. 153, 156–7. Ibn Fadhlan, an Arab envoy who visited a camp of *Rus* vikings at Bulghar on the Volga River in 922, described the sacrifice of a slave-girl during the funeral of a viking chieftain. M. Canard, 'La relation du voyage d'Ibn Fadlan chez les Bulgares de la Volga', *Annales de l'institut d'études orientales*, Alger 16 (1958) pp. 41–145, at 131–2.
77. R. Frank, 'Viking atrocity and Skaldic verse: the rite of the blood-eagle', *ASE Review* 99 (1984) pp. 332–43, at 340–1. See also Sawyer, *Kings and Vikings*, p. 95.

Most of what we 'know' about Scandinavian pagan religion comes from twelfth- and thirteenth-century Christian sources that tell us as much about the preoccupations and myths of the vikings' descendants as about the beliefs and culture of the vikings themselves. But what little evidence we do have suggests that the heathen vikings of the ninth and tenth centuries practised a syncretistic and eclectic paganism that allowed them to tolerate and accommodate missionaries such as St Anskar and even to accept Christian rituals of conversion when the situation demanded it, though they were just as likely to 'lapse' when the crisis or opportunity for gifts had passed.[78] The aggressive paganism of the 'blood-eagle' simply does not ring true.

. . .

MERCIAN MILITARY AND MARRIAGE ALLIANCES

In autumn 867 the vikings rode south from York into the heart of Mercia and took up winter quarters at Nottingham, a royal vill on the River Trent attractive to the vikings for its ready-made defences and its accessibility to York by both land and river. This viking incursion into Mercia was to have a profound effect upon Alfred's life, providing his first, frustrating taste of war against the Great Heathen Army. It also provided the context for his marriage to a Mercian noblewoman, Ealhswith. King Burgred of Mercia had himself taken Alfred's sister, Æthelswith, as his bride in the spring of 853 under analogous circumstances. Then the Mercians had sought West Saxon help against the Welsh. Now it was the vikings who threatened Mercia. As we have seen, viking assaults had transformed relations between these traditional enemies and had facilitated the peaceful transference of power over Berkshire to Wessex at the time of Alfred's birth. As viking activity intensified in the mid-860s, the old rivals drew even closer. One of Æthelred I's first actions upon becoming king was to adopt the Mercian Lunette type penny as his standard issue, establishing a common currency in

---

78. I.N. Wood, 'Christians and pagans in ninth-century Scandinavia', B. Sawyer, P. Sawyer and I. Woods, eds, *The Christianization of Scandinavia* (Alingsås, 1987) pp. 36–67, esp. 49–58. Cf. Smyth, *King Alfred the Great*, pp. 77–81. For the tendency of baptized Northmen to relapse into paganism, see *AB*, s.a. 876.

the two kingdoms that was to persist into Alfred's reign.[79] It is little wonder that the Mercians now turned to their allies to the south. On the advice of his counsellors, King Burgred sent messengers to his West Saxon kinsmen asking for military aid to oust the invaders. Despite the recent deaths of two of the kingdom's most experienced military leaders, Bishop Ealhstan of Sherborne and Ealdorman Eanwulf of Somerset, Æthelred readily agreed to help his brother-in-law. He and Alfred raised 'an immense' West Saxon army from every part of the kingdom and marched to Nottingham, 'single-mindedly seeking battle'.[80]

If Alfred had expectations of winning glory to rival that of his father and grandfather, they were soon dashed by the prudence of an enemy who preferred the safety of the town's defences to the risks of battle. The ditch and earthen ramparts that defended Nottingham might as well have been the walls of Rome, given the inexperience of the English in siege warfare. All the combined Mercian and West Saxon armies could do was surround Nottingham and hope that their supplies would last longer than those of the besieged. Faced with a stalemate, King Burgred decided to negotiate a peace. As in Francia, this probably entailed some sort of payment and exchange of hostages in return for a promise that the vikings would leave the kingdom. Burgred may also have pledged 'friendship' with the vikings. Four years later when the Northumbrians rose against the Danes and their native allies, Burgred honourably received the exiled King Egbert and Archbishop Wulfhere.[81] Nor did the Mercian king make any effort to prevent the Great Heathen Army from crossing his territories when they invaded East Anglia in 869 or even Wessex in 870. The Danish army departed for York, where it resided for much of the following year. Alfred and Æthelred returned to Wessex.

Alfred married Ealhswith in 868, presumably soon after the siege of Nottingham. The marriage apparently took place at a royal estate in Sutton Courtenay, Berkshire, on

79. P. Grierson and M.A.S. Blackburn, eds, *Medieval European Coinage, I: The Early Middle Ages (5th–10th Centuries)* (Cambridge, 1986) pp. 307–8, 310–12.
80. Asser, ch. 30, trans. Keynes and Lapidge, p. 77.
81. Roger of Wendover, *Flores Historiarum*, s.a. 872, trans. *EHD* I, no. 4, p. 282.

the Thames border between Wessex and Mercia, from which King Æthelred I issued a charter in 868 that was attested by a Mercian *ætheling*, Beorhtferth.[82] It was perhaps also the occasion for a rather odd charter issued by Alfred's sister, Æthelswith, as queen of Mercia, in which she granted land at Lockinge, Berkshire, near Wantage, to a thegn named Cuthwulf.[83] Among the witnesses to the grant were her brothers, King Æthelred (given pride of place in the list), Alfred, Oswald 'son of the king' (possibly an illegitimate son of Æthelred), a number of West Saxon clerics, ealdormen, and thegns, her husband, and an ealdorman named Mucel, who witnessed immediately before Alfred. This Mucel was apparently Alfred's new father-in-law. Ealhswith's father, Æthelred, 'who was known as Mucel', was ealdorman of the *Gaini*, and her mother, Eadburh, whose virtues Asser praises at length, was descended from the great Mercian king, Cenwulf.[84] Oddly, Asser devoted far more space in his *Life* to Alfred's new mother-in-law than to his hero's 'excellent wife from the stock of noble Mercians'.[85]

Asser's reticence may well have reflected Alfred's own attitude. Alfred's wife was not to be his queen. Unlike his brother Æthelred's wife, Wulfthryth,[86] Ealhswith did not even attest her husband's charters. Why, we cannot say. Alfred's reported fondness for the story of the wicked Mercian Queen Eadburh, like the unusual emphasis in his law code and writings upon avoidance of sexual temptation, is certainly suggestive. So is his preference, expressed in his will, that his property remain in the male line ('spear side'). This may reflect more than the desire, manifested by the tontine arrangement with his brothers,[87] to provide the reigning king with as large a landed endowment as possible, and

---

82. S 539, discussed by Keynes, 'West Saxon charters', pp. 1130–1.

83. S 1201.

84. Asser, ch. 29, trans. Keynes and Lapidge, p. 77 (p. 241 n. 58). S 1442 (read in conjunction with *ASC* s.a. 901) establishes Ealhswith's descent from King Cenwulf.

85. Asser, ch. 73, trans. Keynes and Lapidge, p. 88. Smyth cites Asser's failure to name Ealhswith as evidence that the *Life* is a late forgery: *King Alfred the Great*, pp. 24, 196, 359. But, to put this in perspective, Alfred's will does not give the names of his younger son or his three daughters, whereas Asser does (ch. 75).

86. S 340.

87. See pp. 92–3 above.

may express Alfred's own beliefs about the proper role of women.

The union proved fruitful. By 886 Ealhswith had borne Alfred five children: a daughter, Æthelflæd, a son, Edward, two additional daughters, Æthelgifu and Ælfthryth, and a second son, Æthelweard. She had also lost an unknown number of children to the hardships of childbirth and infancy.[88] Otherwise, the life and activities of Alfred's wife are poorly attested. Alfred names her in his will as his successor in three estates, Lambourn and Wantage in Berkshire and Edington in Wiltshire. Though Alfred was far more generous to his sons, there may be some sentimental significance to his decision to leave to her Wantage, his birthplace, and Edington, the scene of his greatest military triumph.[89] That Ealhswith was pious is suggested by her own bequest of land to the Nunnaminster in Winchester, a record of which was inscribed into a prayerbook of private devotion that may once have belonged to her.[90] She outlived her husband by three years, dying on 5 December 902, and was buried alongside him in the New Minster their son, King Edward, had founded in Winchester. Her commemoration as 'the true and beloved Lady of the English (*uera domina Anglorum Ealhswythe cara*)' in an early tenth-century metrical calendar suggests not only the affection she inspired but, perhaps, the political importance she assumed as Alfred's Mercian widow during the turbulent early years of her son's reign.[91]

88. Asser, ch. 75. Cf. Alfred's Will, in Harmer, ed., *SEHD*, no. 11, pp. 17–18 (*EHD* I, no. 96; Keynes and Lapidge, pp. 173–8).
89. Ibid.
90. The Book of Nunnaminster, B. Library, Harley 2965, f. 40v. B. Raw, 'Alfredian Piety: the Book of Nunnaminster', in J. Roberts, J.L. Nelson, and M. Godden, eds, *Alfred the Wise: Studies in Honour of Janet Bately on the Occasion of her Sixty-Fifth Birthday* (Woodbridge, Suffolk, 1997) p. 145.
91. *ASC* s.a. 903. S.D. Keynes, ed., *The Liber Vitae of the New Minster and Hyde Abbey Winchester* (Copenhagen, 1996) pp. 18 (n. 24), 81, 114 (n. 40). Ealhswith's death notice appears along with that of her husband in two tenth-century manuscripts, 'Hampson's Metrical Martyrology' and 'Junius 27 Kalendar', the latter probably composed at Canterbury in the 920s. See S.D. Keynes, 'King Alfred and the Mercians', in *Kings, Currency, and Alliances: The History and Coinage of Southern England AD 840–900*, ed. M.A.S. Blackburn and D.N. Dumville (Woodbridge, forthcoming); P. McGurk, 'The Metrical Calendar of Hampson: a new edition', *Analecta Bollandiana* 10 (1986) pp. 76–125, at p. 110; D.N. Dumville, *Wessex and England* (Woodbridge, 1992) pp. 105–6, 155.

There is little more that one can say about Ealhswith. Whatever she was in life, historically she is a near cipher. A biographer of Alfred cannot help but have a sneaking sympathy for the screenplay writers of the dreadful 1969 film *Alfred the Great*, who overcame the lack of source material for Ealhswith by simply fabricating a character, complete with a courting scene involving hunting dogs (a nice touch given Alfred's fondness for hunting) and a torrid adulterous love affair with the dashing viking king, Guthrum!

With marriage, Alfred ceased to be a 'youth' and became a 'man'. This entailed the establishment of his own household, an entourage that included warrior retainers as well as domestics. Henceforth, Alfred would divide his time between the royal household and his own estates, lands that, at least technically, he held on loan from King Æthelred. Because of the deaths of his other brothers and the youth of his nephews, Alfred was now the most important lay person in Wessex after the king. The next few years would prove momentous for Alfred. The viking invasion of Wessex in 871 would provide the young *ætheling* with his first taste of military victory – and defeat. By the end of the year, he would be king.

Chapter 4

'A VERY GREAT WARRIOR', 869–879

At Alfred's birth, four great English kingdoms still remained of the dozens of petty tribal states that had dotted the landscape of seventh-century Britain. Wessex was the strongest of the kingdoms south of the Humber, but there was no reason to believe that it would remain so. Egbert's 'Greater Wessex' might well have proved as transitory as the Mercian hegemony of the previous century if not for the advent of the Great Heathen Army.

Between 869 and 879, viking armies conquered East Anglia, Northumbria, and Mercia and extinguished their royal houses. By Alfred's death in 899, only one native kingdom and royal lineage remained. Wessex survived the onslaught because of Alfred's military and political genius. He would leave his son, Edward, and daughter, Æthelflæd, the military, financial, and administrative resources not only to defend their patrimonies but to expand their rule over the Scandinavian-controlled territories and kingdoms to the north and east. This, along with the cultural and spiritual renaissance he sponsored, was to be Alfred's legacy and claim to historical greatness. In 869 few could have predicted what lay in store for the frail young *ætheling*. A decade later, they may have had an inkling. For it was in his response to the viking invasions of Wessex between 870 and 878 that Alfred revealed the pragmatism, resolution, and innovative spirit that were to make him a great warlord and king.

. . .

INVASION OF WESSEX

After a year's sojourn at York, the Great Heathen Army returned to East Anglia in the autumn of 869. Riding across

Mercian territory, they crossed the fens by way of a Roman road and marched south upon the Icknield Way until they arrived at Thetford, where they made their winter camp. The peaceful dealings that had marked their stay in 865/866 gave way to fire and the sword: 'and they destroyed all the monasteries they came to. In this same time they came to *Medeshamstede* (Peterborough), burnt and destroyed it, killed the abbot and the monks and all they found there, and brought it to pass that it became nought that had been very mighty.'[1] Caught by surprise, King Edmund was slain and the kingdom subdued. Whether Edmund died in battle, as implied by the *Anglo-Saxon Chronicle*, or as a martyred captive is unclear, though the rapid spread of his saint's cult within Danish-ruled East Anglia supports the latter.[2] It is possible that Edmund was offered and rejected the same client status that Egbert accepted in Northumbria and that Ceolwulf II was to obtain in Mercia in 874. The conquest of East Anglia was to be Ivarr's last victory in England. Within a year, he disappeared from the English scene, possibly returning to Ireland to resume his rule among the vikings of Dublin.[3]

Wessex was next. In the winter of 870, the Great Heathen Army, now under the command of two other viking kings, Bagsecg and Ivarr's brother, Halfdan, crossed the Thames into Berkshire and set up camp at Reading.[4] Again, the viking leaders showed good strategic sense. Straddling the Thames and the Kennet, Reading was within easy striking

---

1. *ASC* s.a. 870E, trans. *EHD* I, no. 1, p. 192.
2. *ASC* s.a. 870; Abbo of Fleury, 'Life of St. Edmund', in *Three Lives of English Saints*, ed. M. Winterbottom (Toronto, 1972) pp. 67–87. See D. Whitelock, 'Fact and fiction in the legend of St. Edmund', *Proceedings of the Suffolk Institute of Archaeology* 31 (1967–9) pp. 217–33; S.J. Ridyard, *The Royal Saints of Anglo-Saxon England: A Study of West Saxon and East Anglian Cults* (Cambridge, 1988) pp. 61–9.
3. Æthelweard, *Chronicon*, ed. Campbell, s.a. 870, p. 36. See A.P. Smyth, *Scandinavian Kings in the British Isles 850–880* (Oxford, 1977) pp. 224–39, but cf. review of Smyth, *Scandinavian Kings* by R.W. McTurk in the *Saga-book of the Viking Society* 20 (1978–81) pp. 231–4, and D. Ó Corráin, 'High kings, vikings and other kings', *Irish Historical Studies* 22 (1979) pp. 284–96.
4. For possible routes taken by the army and fleet from East Anglia, see J. Peddie, *Alfred the Good Soldier: His Life and Campaigns* (Bath, 1989) pp. 76–7.

distance of Wallingford, an important royal estate at a major ford over the Thames, and the rich lands of Abingdon monastery. It offered easy access to the major lines of communication in the middle Thames valley, the river itself, Icknield Way along the crest of the Berkshire Downs, and the complex of Roman roads that met at the ruins of Silchester lying about thirteen kilometres to the southwest. As a royal *tun*, Reading was the administrative centre for the surrounding region, which meant that the invaders could expect to find food supplies, the king's 'food rent' (*feorm*), stored there.[5] This was especially important since the campaign began in winter, probably around Christmas. Such unseasonal warfare ensured surprise, but created logistical problems of the first order. The immediate objective of an army campaigning so late in the year had to be acquisition of supplies. As the viking leaders undoubtedly knew, the cellars and storehouses of royal and monastic estates would be especially well stocked in the autumn. In the ninth-century agricultural calendar, late October and November were devoted to threshing and to slaughtering and salting the meat of excess livestock in preparation for the winter months. Indeed, Martinmas, 11 November, was when peasants paid 'churchscot', which in the ninth century may have been rendered in kind.[6] In short, Reading was well chosen to serve as the base camp for the Viking conquest of Wessex.

Three days after occupying Reading, while the Army was busily fortifying its southern boundaries between the Rivers Thames and Kennet with ditch and rampart defences, Halfdan and Bagsecg sent out a large detachment under the command of two jarls to forage for provisions and reconnoitre. Æthelwulf, the veteran ealdorman of Berkshire, and King Æthelred both reacted swiftly to the seizure of Reading. While the king raised forces and marched toward Reading, Æthelwulf, in command of the local levies that made

5. P. Sawyer, 'The royal *tun* in pre-Conquest England', in *Ideal and Reality in Frankish and Anglo-Saxon Society. Studies Presented to J.M. Wallace-Hadrill*, ed. P. Wormald with D. Bullough and R. Collins (Oxford, 1983) pp. 280–1, 283–4.
6. *Ine* 4, 61; S 359 (record of services and dues rendered at Hurstborne, Hants, AD 900); H.P.R. Finberg, 'Anglo-Saxon England to 1042', *The Agrarian History of England and Wales* AD *43–1042*, vol. 1, part 2 (Cambridge, 1972) pp. 453, 457–8.

up the Berkshire *fyrd*, intercepted the raiding party at Englefield, near the River Kennet some nine or ten kilometres west of Reading. The West Saxons enjoyed victory in this first engagement. After one of their jarls was killed 'and a great part of the army overthrown', the Danes broke and ran.[7] Ealdorman Æthelwulf wisely chose to await the arrival of his lords King Æthelred and Alfred rather than pursue the fleeing enemy. Four days after the skirmish at Englefield, the full West Saxon *fyrd*, including the victorious forces under Ealdorman Æthelwulf, engaged the main Danish army at Reading. The West Saxons fought their way to the gate of the vill, slaughtering all the Danes they found outside. But when they reached the vill's defences, the Danes suddenly 'like wolves burst out of all the gates and joined battle with all their might'.[8] This time the vikings had the better of it, as the Christian forces fled in the face of the determined Danish counter-attack. Among the dead was the victor of Englefield, Ealdorman Æthelwulf, whose body was secretly taken from the battlefield and carried back north to be buried at *Northworthig* (Derby) in his native Mercia. Alfred and his brother, according to a late source, eluded capture only through their knowledge of the local terrain. They lost their pursuers by fording the River Loddon at Twyford and escaping into territory unfamiliar to the Danes. What was left of their forces regrouped at Windsor.[9]

Morale and discipline, rather than technology or even tactics, determined the outcome of this and most of Alfred's other battles against the vikings. The viking and the West Saxon forces were, very likely, nearly evenly matched in terms of numbers and equipment, so a sudden counter-attack, such as that launched by the Danes at Reading, could well prove decisive. The ordinary warrior on both sides was armed with an ash wood spear, perhaps 1.8 to 2.4 metres in length, surmounted with a leaf-shaped, iron spearhead, suitable for either thrusting or hurling. He bore on his left arm a round shield, either flat or slightly concave, that protected him from his shoulder to his thigh. His shield, which constituted

---

7. Asser, ch. 35, trans. Keynes and Lapidge, p. 78.
8. Asser, ch. 36, trans. Keynes and Lapidge, p. 78.
9. Gaimar, *L'estorie des Engleis*, ed. A. Bell, Anglo-Norman Text Soc., 14–15 (1960) ll. 2963–72.

his main defence, was made of wood perhaps faced with leather and reinforced with a band of iron around the rim. A central iron boss protected the hand-grip that lay under it. Warriors of higher status and wealth, whether West Saxon or Viking, were distinguished by their splendid pattern-welded swords, the aristocratic weapon par excellence. 'I am a wondrous creature', an Old English riddle has the sword boast, 'shaped in strife, loved by my lord, fairly adorned.'[10] Several of these 'wondrous creatures' survive from Alfred's time, double-edged blades, seventy to ninety centimetres long, made out of hardened carbonized iron and graced with elaborately decorated guards and pommels.[11] The wealthiest may also have worn chain-mail byrnies and simple conical helmets with nose guards, though there is little trace of either in the archaeological record of the period. It is unlikely that the vikings, at this time, used battle-axes, the weapon that would characterize them in the eleventh century, or that either side made extensive use of archers.[12] Given the weapons at their disposal, it is not surprising that battles between West Saxon and viking armies were in large measure pushing and thrusting matches, not unlike the hoplite warfare of Classical Greece. The standard battle formation was the 'shield-wall', in which the warriors closed rank in preparation for rushing or receiving the enemy's attack. Battle tactics were rudimentary at best. In a typical engagement the armies would approach in open order. At about twenty-five

10. R.K. Gordon, trans., *Anglo-Saxon Poetry* (London, 1970) p. 295; *The Exeter Book. The Anglo-Saxon Poetic Records III*, ed. G.P. Krapp and E.V.K. Dobbie (New York and London, 1936) p. 190.
11. See, e.g., L. Webster and J. Blackhouse, eds, *The Making of England: Anglo-Saxon Art and Culture AD 600–900* (London, 1992) pp. 276–7.
12. D.M. Wilson, ed., *The Archaeology of Anglo-Saxon England* (London, 1976) pp. 14–20; H.R. Ellis Davidson, *The Sword in Anglo-Saxon England* (Oxford, 1962); H. Clarke, 'Society, kingship and warfare', in J. Graham-Campbell et al., eds, *Cultural Atlas of the Viking World* (Abingdon, 1994) pp. 52–5. On the minor role of bowmen in Anglo-Saxon armies, see J. Manley, 'The archer and the army in the late Saxon period', *Anglo-Saxon Studies in Archaeology and History* 4 (1985) pp. 223–35. Cf. J. Bradbury, *The Medieval Archer* (New York, 1985) pp. 12–19. Archers may have played a more prominent role in siege warfare of the period. B. Bachrach and R. Aris, 'Military Technology and Garrison Organization: Some Observations on Anglo-Saxon Military Thinking in Light of the Burghal Hidage', *Technology and Culture* 31 (1990) pp. 1–17.

metres, each side would let loose a volley of spears, then close ranks and engage. In the battle itself 'winged' spears, used like poleaxes, swords, and shields became the main weapons, as warriors pushed and struck at one another in an attempt to disrupt the enemy's lines. As death depleted the front ranks, the solid formations would again open, providing enough space to permit warriors to throw spears, slash with long swords and parry blows with their shields. A battle was won when one side broke ranks and fled, leaving their opponents in possession of the field and of anything of value that could be looted from the dead and dying. As the *Judith*-poet observed in describing the Assyrian conquest of the Hebrews, victory brought wealth: 'The dwellers in the land had a chance to spoil the most hateful ones, their ancient foes now lifeless, of bloody booty, beautiful ornaments, shields and broad swords, brown helmets, precious treasures.'[13]

Four days later the two armies clashed again, this time in the open at Ashdown. The name 'Ashdown' was used in pre-Conquest times for various stretches along the Berkshire Downs, and definite identification of the site may be impossible.[14] However, the recent suggestion that it was at Kingstanding Hill on the Icknield Way just west of Streatley is attractive on military and common-sense grounds.[15] It not only takes into account the possible approaches of the two armies in relation to the waterways and roads of the Downs, but places the battle within marching distance of Reading, which seems to me most probable. The West Saxons who, according to Asser, were 'aroused by grief and shame', had reason to seek a return engagement.[16] The motivation of Bacgsecg and Halfdan for risking a battle in the open is less clear, though their victory at Reading and the need to replenish supplies, in particular fodder for their mounts, may have emboldened them. The seizure of Reading was intended as the opening shot in a campaign of conquest,

13. *Judith*, trans. Gordon, *Anglo-Saxon Poetry*, p. 325.
14. Stevenson, *Asser's Life of King Alfred*, pp. 234–8; M. Gelling, *The Place-Names of Berkshire*, 3 vols, English Place-Name Society 49–51 (Cambridge, 1973–6) II, pp. 495, 499; Keynes and Lapidge, p. 242 n. 67.
15. Peddie, *Alfred the Good Soldier*, pp. 81–8. Peddie's is by far the most detailed military account of Alfred's reign.
16. Asser, ch. 36, trans. Keynes and Lapidge, p. 78.

and the Danes now may have felt that they could destroy the demoralized West Saxon army as easily as they had the Northumbrians and East Anglians.

Bacgsecg and Halfdan arrived first and deployed along the ridge, giving them a decided advantage in fighting that emphasized shock. They also divided their forces into two large contingents to provide greater tactical control, themselves taking charge of one while placing the other under the command of the jarls. When West Saxon scouts reported this, King Æthelred and Alfred decided to divide their forces to match the enemy's. The king, they agreed, would engage Bacgsecg and Halfdan, while Alfred would face the jarls. King Æthelred then retired to his tent to hear mass and to pray for victory. Some years earlier Prudentius of Troyes had explained Frankish failures against the heathens with the observation, 'God in his goodness and justice, so much offended by our sins, had thus worn down the lands and kingdoms of the Christians.'[17] No doubt similar thoughts now ran through Æthelred's and Alfred's minds. Alfred seems to have been quicker in his prayers. While his brother lingered at his devotions, Alfred led his division to the battlefield, fully expecting that his brother would quickly follow. Alfred found himself and his men alone on the battlefield facing the entire Danish army.[18] The enemy had drawn up their forces into a shield-wall, and Alfred responded by ordering his men to close ranks. The problem he faced had no solution. If he stayed, he ran a risk of being outflanked and overwhelmed by the larger Danish forces, but turning his back on the enemy all but invited pursuit, and retreat could easily turn into rout. Alfred probably also realized that withdrawal would place his brother's forces in jeopardy when they finally did arrive. He made his decision:

> He finally deployed the Christian forces against the hostile armies, as he had previously intended (even though the king had not yet come), and acting courageously, like a wild boar, supported by divine counsel and strengthened by divine help, when he had closed up the shield-wall in proper order, he moved his army without delay against the enemy.[19]

17. *AB* s.a. 845, trans. Nelson, p. 61.
18. Asser, chs 37–8.
19. Asser, ch. 38, trans. Keynes and Lapidge, p. 79.

Shouting, Alfred's troops rushed up the slope and charged into the Danish line. The battle now raged around a small solitary thorn tree on the hill. Though Asser and the *Anglo-Saxon Chronicle* focus on Alfred's audacious action, it was the sudden appearance of King Æthelred's forces that proved decisive. The late arrival transformed the king's troop into a tactical reserve (which may have been Æthelred's intention all along).[20] There is no reason to believe that the Danes knew of the West Saxon division of their forces or of Æthelred's delay. This new attack from an unexpected quarter must have proved a nasty shock to the Danes, especially if Æthelred took advantage of the situation to fall on the enemy's flank or rear. The viking shield-wall collapsed, and what had been an army degenerated into a panic-stricken mob. Asser rejoiced:

> the pagans (by divine judgement) were unable to withstand the Christians' onslaught any longer; and when a great part of their forces had fallen, they took to ignominious flight. One of the two pagan kings and five earls were cut down in that place, and many thousands on the pagan side were slain there too – or rather, over the whole expanse of Ashdown, scattered everywhere, far and wide: so King Bagsecg was killed, and Earl Sidroc the Old, Earl Sidroc the Younger, Earl Osbern, Earl Fræna, and Earl Harold; and the entire pagan army was put to flight, right on till nightfall and into the following day, until such time as they reached the stronghold from which they had come. The Christians followed them till nightfall, cutting them down on all sides.[21]

The jubilant tone of Asser's account may reflect Alfred's own pride in his first military success. No doubt the death of a king and five earls was a severe blow to the Great Heathen Army, as were the losses among the rank and file, but it was far from fatal. A mere two weeks later King Æthelred and Alfred were fighting the vikings at Basing, a royal vill about twenty-five kilometres south of Reading. This time the vikings won. It was now deep winter. The season and the mauling both armies had suffered dictated a respite. King Æthelred

20. Asser's intention was to highlight Alfred's courage. As an encomiast, he was quite capable of recasting events so as to deprive Æthelred of credit for the victory.
21. Asser, ch. 39, trans. Keynes and Lapidge, p. 80.

and Alfred, unable to dislodge Halfdan from his strongholds in eastern Berkshire, withdrew to plan their spring campaign.

After four battles in quick succession, the war ground to a near halt. What fighting there was in late January and February was small-scale and sporadic, as local thegns tried to protect their lands and those of their neighbours from being despoiled by viking foragers. Overwintering in Reading no doubt created serious logistical difficulties for the vikings. Even if we place their numbers in the upper hundreds rather than thousands, Halfdan's troops still would have required at least a ton of grain a day and their horses seven times as much fodder.[22] Within weeks, they would have depleted the stocks of corn and salted meat stored in Reading. A constant stream of foragers must have poured out of the viking camp scouring the frozen countryside for provisions. Larger estates, whether royal, noble or monastic, were particularly attractive for their promise of rich stores and supplies of seed corn. The vikings stripped them of anything edible and portable, as eagerly as if they were looting silver and gold plate from churches. The West Saxons responded with their own small bands of mounted warriors, composed of king's thegns and their personal retainers, who rode after the raiders, hoping to intercept and destroy them before they made their way back to the safety of their fortress. Alfred himself led many such expeditions in the months before he became king, and with each successful foray his reputation as a warrior grew among those whose support he would need for succession to the throne.[23] Alfred's experience combatting the hit-and-run tactics of Viking marauders would prove invaluable seven years later when the young king found his world turned upside down and himself in the uncomfortable position of outlaw raider.

It was probably during this period that Alfred and his brother met in assembly at *Swinbeorg* with the king's *witan*, the ecclesiastical and lay magnates who counselled Æthelred, to renegotiate the terms of their father's will. Though Æthelred and Alfred were still young men, they probably had little expectation of long life. Their three brothers had died when

22. See D. Engels, *Alexander the Great and the Logistics of the Macedonian Army* (Berkeley, 1978) pp. 123–30, 144–5.
23. *ASC* s.a. 871.

little older than they. Alfred was suffering from a mysterious disease that defied diagnosis, and his brother had survived a series of hard-fought battles. Deep winter had brought respite from large-scale fighting but not peace, and the warfare that loomed before them threatened the untimely death of one if not both of the royal brothers. King Æthelred had two young sons, and Ealhswith may have already borne Alfred a daughter, Æthelflæd, and perhaps even a son, Edward. Now that they were 'all afflicted by the heathen army', Alfred and his brother felt it wise to resolve any question about the succession. Their children would also need property to maintain themselves, come what might to their fathers during this time of troubles.[24] The new agreement affirmed Æthelwulf's and Æthelberht's intention to preserve the unity of the bulk of the Ecgberhting inheritance, to be passed from brother to brother along with the kingship. The brothers agreed that the personal property that their father had left jointly to them and Æthelbald would pass to whichever of them lived longer. To guarantee that the king should have the necessary wealth and resources to rule effectively, the longer-lived brother was to 'succeed both to lands and to valuables and to all his estate, with the exception of that portion which either had bequeathed to his children'. The deceased's children, however, were to receive in addition to whatever property and riches their father had settled upon them, 'the lands which we ourselves had acquired, and the lands which King Æthelwulf gave us in the lifetime of Æthelbald, excepting those which he settled on us three brothers jointly'.[25] In effect, Æthelred had confirmed Alfred's status as his heir apparent. But the agreement had done more than this. It had tacitly decided the descent of the throne as it passed to a new generation of Ecgberhtings, since the last surviving brother would have sole possession of the joint property that their father had bestowed upon them and the right to dispose of it as he saw fit. In effect, the *Swinbeorg* agreement meant that Alfred's son, Edward, would one day rule, rather than Æthelred's sons, Æthelhelm and Æthelwold, a decision that at least the latter would be unwilling to accept without a fight.

24. *Alfred's Will* [S 1507], in *SEHD*, no. 11, pp. 16, 49.
25. *SEHD*, no. 11, pp. 16, 49–50.

In late March or early April the war resumed. The armies met at *Meretun*, probably the same royal estate that had witnessed the murder of King Cynewulf eighty-five years before, and once again the Danes split their forces into two divisions. The West Saxons had the better of the going for much of the day, putting both divisions to flight. But the Danes managed to regroup, and by the end of the day, it was they who enjoyed possession of the battlefield. The defeat proved costly to the West Saxons; their dead numbered many 'important men', including Bishop Heahmund of Sherborne.[26] To make matters worse, a 'great summer fleet' (*micel sumorlida*), freshly arrived from overseas and probably under the command of three new viking 'kings', Guthrum, Oscetel and Anwend, unexpectedly sailed up the Thames to join Halfdan at Reading.[27] Reports of the Great Heathen Army's victories in Britain had spread to the Continent, where the scent of fresh, vulnerable lands to plunder proved all but irresistible to marauders facing Charles the Bald's new fortified bridges. England now replaced the rich but well-defended fields of the Loire and the Seine as the favourite stomping ground for viking adventurers. Whether invited or not, the newcomers were welcomed by Halfdan. By the spring of 871 the Great Heathen Army operating from its base at Reading probably did not look quite so *micel*, given the detachments Halfdan had undoubtedly left behind in East Anglia and York and the casualties the Army had suffered not only at Ashdown but in its victories over the West Saxons. If successful, there would be enough plunder to satisfy all.

Soon after Easter, 15 April, King Æthelred died, perhaps from wounds suffered in battle at *Meretun*, and was buried at Wimborne Minster in Dorset. The intimations of mortality that had led the brothers to reconsider the disposition of their joint inheritance at *Swinbeorg* just a month or two before had proved tragically well founded. Alfred had little leisure to mourn the passing of his last brother. On the very day Alfred attended Æthelred's funeral, the West Saxons

---

26. *ASC* s.a. 871. Asser omits this battle.
27. *ASC* s.a. 871A; Asser, ch. 40; Æthelweard, *Chronicon* s.a. 871, ed. Campbell, p. 40. See discussion by Smyth, *Scandinavian Kings*, pp. 240–54.

suffered defeat at the hands of the combined Danish forces at Reading, after which the victors 'dispersed, carried off plunder, and ravaged places'.[28]

Given the military crisis facing the kingdom, Alfred's succession was probably not contested by his young nephews or their supporters. King Æthelred's sons, Æthelhelm and Æthelwold, were much too young to provide military leadership. While Alfred could presumably have led the armies of Wessex as regent for one of his nephews, he had no intention of playing the self-effacing Beowulf to Æthelhelm's or Æthelwold's Heardred.[29] Asser insists that Alfred 'took over the government of the whole kingdom as soon as his brother had died, with the approval of divine will and according to the unanimous wish of all the inhabitants of the kingdom'.[30] That Alfred enjoyed the support of his brother's *witan* is confirmed by the continuity in attestations between Æthelred I's and Alfred's early charters (c. 871–877). Though some new ealdormen and king's thegns appear, especially in charters from Kent, reflecting perhaps the greater devastation wrought there by the vikings, the royal establishment remained largely unchanged. Wulfhere, the veteran ealdorman of Wiltshire, Ælfstan, ealdorman of Dorset, Oswald the 'king's son' (possibly a royal bastard), and the king's thegn Milred, a longtime retainer of the Ecgberhtings whose service went back to Æthelwulf, retained the same prominence in Alfred's court that they had enjoyed in his brother's.[31] Yet Asser goes further, insisting upon Alfred's unanimous popularity as well as the workings of divine providence, and the reader may be excused for thinking that he doth protest too much. The explanation is surely to be sought in the politics of the late 880s and early 890s. By the time Asser wrote, King Æthelred's sons had grown to manhood. They had already unsuccessfully challenged their uncle on the disposition of their father's property. If they or their supporters had also whispered criticism of Alfred's rectitude at the time of his

28. Æthelweard, *Chronicon* s.a. 871, ed. Campbell, p. 40.
29. *Beowulf*, ll. 2369–79. Tellingly, there is no analogue in the history of Wessex to the regency described in *Beowulf*.
30. Asser, ch. 42, trans. Keynes and Lapidge, p. 80.
31. *S* 1203, 1275, 1605. Cf. S 290, 294, 303, 304, 307–11, 317, 327, 331, 333–5, 337–8, 340, 342, 539, 1201.

succession, Asser has suppressed it. His implicit response was to praise his hero's great forbearance in allowing his brother to remain king until his death:

> Indeed, he could easily have taken the kingdom over with the consent of all while his brother Æthelred was alive, had he considered himself worthy to do so, for he surpassed all his brothers both in wisdom and in all good habits; and in particular because he was a very great warrior [*nimium bellicosus*] and victorious in virtually all battles.[32]

Asser's uncritical enthusiasm has taken him too far. Though Alfred must have been the odds-on favourite for succession in 871, it would have been remarkable indeed if anyone had entertained the thought of replacing Æthelred during his lifetime with his younger brother. Far from being victorious in 'virtually all battles', Alfred the 'great warrior' had led troops to victory only once in a general engagement, at Ashdown, and had suffered defeat on at least three occasions. But Asser wrote with the knowledge that Alfred would be successful in war and would save his kingdom from the viking invaders. Perhaps even more importantly, Asser wished to demonstrate Alfred's moral fitness for kingship by establishing that he began his reign 'almost unwillingly' (*prope quasi invitus*). The model here is the good 'rector' of Gregory the Great's *Pastoral Care*, which Alfred, with Asser's help, would later translate into English. A good king, like a good bishop, ought to be filled with Christian humility and accept the duties and cares of governance with a proper show of reluctance. Accordingly, Asser emphasized that Alfred had become king in the proper manner, through the will of God and the full consent of his subjects.

Alfred was now king. As improbable as it must have seemed to his contemporaries, the youngest and most frail of King Æthelwulf's five sons had outlived all his brothers to succeed to the throne of Wessex. The challenge now was to keep it.

· · ·

ALFRED THE KING

The diffidence with which Alfred assumed the throne in Asser's account may be no more than a Gregorian topos,

32. Asser, ch. 42, trans. Keynes and Lapidge, pp. 80–1.

and yet, as the Welsh monk points out, there were very real reasons for Alfred to have evinced concern in the spring of 871: 'for indeed he did not think that he alone could ever withstand such great harshness from the pagans, unless strengthened by divine help, since he had already sustained great losses of many men while his brothers were alive'.[33] Despite King Æthelred's and Alfred's own best efforts to dislodge them, the Danes remained firmly planted in their fortress at Reading. If anything, they were stronger now than when they had first arrived. The advent of the 'summer fleet' had made good the losses the Great Heathen Army had suffered at Ashdown and in their other engagements with West Saxon forces. King Alfred, on the other hand, was hard-pressed to find the forces needed to continue the war against the Danes. Within a month of his accession, Alfred, greatly outnumbered, fought the whole viking army on a hillside near the royal vill of Wilton, about seventy-five kilometres southwest of Reading. That the field of combat had now moved to Wiltshire, in the very heart of ancient Wessex, indicates how much the military situation had deteriorated in the few weeks since the death of Æthelred.

The battle was a see-saw affair, with the West Saxons dominating early on only to lose in the end. 'When both sides had been fighting violently and resolutely on all fronts for much of the day', Asser relates, 'the pagans realized of their own accord the complete danger they were in, and, unable to bear the onslaught of their enemies any longer, they turned tail and fled. But alas, scorning the small number of pursuers, they advanced again into battle, and seizing victory they were masters of the battlefield.'[34] As would happen to another English army in the Battle of Hastings two centuries later, the West Saxons at Wilton, sensing victory and booty, abandoned the safety of their shield-wall to pursue an apparently routed foe, and paid for their rashness when the enemy reformed and rounded upon them.

To judge by Asser's account, Alfred had not distinguished himself in his first sole battlefield command. No ninth-century general could have been expected to control the movements of his troops during the chaos and confusion of

33. Asser, ch. 42, trans. Keynes and Lapidge, p. 81.
34. Asser, ch. 42, trans. Keynes and Lapidge, p. 81.

battle. The heroic model of leadership dictated that a commander fight in the front lines, risking his life with the same abandon he expected from his followers, and even if he had the technical means to convey orders during battle and men trained to respond to them, a commander would have had little leisure to do so once the thrusting and parrying began. A good commander, however, needed to be aware of his men's morale and take steps to maintain battle discipline in the face of sudden panic or elation. Alfred was apparently unable or unwilling to restrain his men from breaking ranks to chase the enemy. A similar charge had proved decisive at Ashdown, and the memory of viking corpses scattered over the whole broad expanse of the downs may have spurred him on. If so, Alfred miscalculated. The vikings may have been withdrawing but they were not yet in disarray.

In the final analysis, however, numbers rather than tactics decided the battle of Wilton. Alfred did not have sufficient troops to exploit his early success or to recover from the reversal he suffered late in the battle. 'Nor should it seem extraordinary to anyone that the Christians had a small number of men in the battle', Asser explains, 'for the Saxons were virtually annihilated to a man in this single year.'[35] It is clear from both Asser and the more laconic account of the battle of Wilton in the *Anglo-Saxon Chronicle* that Alfred was losing a war of attrition. The forces that King Alfred had at his disposal had been all but exhausted by the hard fighting of the winter and spring months. Casualties had been heavy (the truth underlying Asser's hyperbole about the Saxons having been 'virtually annihilated to a man') and Alfred was unable to fill the ranks with replacements pulled from the fields and halls of Wessex. Like a shipwrecked man dying of thirst in the midst of an ocean, Alfred could not refresh his drained military strength by drawing upon the considerable manpower resources of his kingdom.[36]

---

35. Asser, ch. 42, trans. Keynes and Lapidge, p. 81.
36. Unsurprisingly, the total population south of the Thames in the late ninth century cannot be ascertained. An order of magnitude, however, is suggested by the Domesday Book, William the Conqueror's great land register, which records over 90,000 heads of free, rural households for these shires in the year 1086. By the end of his reign, Alfred would have 27,071 men stationed as garrisons in the thirty boroughs he had built south of the Thames.

The armies of Wessex, the so-called *fyrds*, were not levies en masse but select forces of king's men and their retainers.[37] In conception and practice, a *fyrd* was the king's following arrayed for battle. At its core was the complement of royal household thegns, perhaps fifty to a hundred men, who repaid their royal lord's gifts of rings, robes, and feasts with loyalty and service.[38] This 'standing' force, however, was too small to conduct full-scale campaigns or engage in battles on its own. For that, Alfred needed to call upon the shire *fyrds*. These territorial forces, consisting mainly of landowners and their personal followings, were led by ealdormen, royal reeves, and local king's thegns, either as battalions within the king's army or, in many instances, as independent armies defending localities against raiders. Because they were raised on an ad hoc basis, in response to an ealdorman's summons, shire *fyrds* were ill-suited to meet the challenge presented by viking raiders. By the time an ealdormen had gathered his army from the various vills and estates scattered throughout a sparsely populated countryside, a highly mobile raiding party might well have already devastated a region and moved on. This led individual ealdormen and thegns to mount small-scale actions against the invaders in 871, presumably attacking bands of foragers as they scattered to plunder the countryside. We are assured by the Chronicler that Alfred himself often rode on such expeditions before he became king.[39]

But problems of time and space told only part of the story. The lack of effective royal administrative institutions meant that the actual turnout for an expedition depended a great deal upon moral and political persuasion. Landed thegns would respond more eagerly and quickly to a call to arms from a successful ruler, with whom they had previously shared victory and booty, than from an unproved one, and

37. R. Abels, *Lordship and Military Obligation in Anglo-Saxon England* (Los Angeles and London, 1988) pp. 1–6, 11–25, 58–78, 175–9.
38. The size of a royal military household may be gauged by the eighty-four men who fell at the side of the *ætheling* Cyneheard in his unsuccessful attempt to seize the throne of Wessex. *ASC* s.a. 786. The late seventh-century Laws of Ine (13, § 1), a copy of which Alfred appended to his own legislation, defined an 'army' (*here*) as a band totalling more than thirty-five men.
39. *ASC* s.a. 871.

the newly elevated Alfred had not yet proved himself to be a king who could command the 'love' and loyalty of the West Saxon elite. Given such systemic problems, Alfred and his ealdormen may well have found themselves in the late spring and summer of 871 leading shire forces that consisted largely of their own retainers and familiars.

Alfred's defeat at Wilton smashed any hope he might have harboured of driving the invaders from his kingdom. He was forced instead to make peace with them.[40] The sources do not tell us the terms of the peace. Asser, putting the best face on the situation, trumpets that the pagans agreed to vacate the realm and made good their promise, and, indeed, the viking army did withdraw from Reading in the autumn of 871 to take up winter quarters in Mercian London. The *quid* that Alfred paid for this *quo* was undoubtedly cash, much as the Mercians were to do in the following year.[41] How Alfred raised the money is suggested by an interesting and unusual charter issued by Alfred after 879. It describes in some detail the fate of two large estates, fifty hides at Chisledon in Wiltshire and sixty hides at Hurstborne Priors in Hampshire, which the church of Winchester had received from King Æthelwulf. Bishop Ealhferth of Winchester (871–877), it seems, was forced by circumstances to sell the monks' reversionary rights to these lands to Alfred, who previously had had only a life interest in them. When bishop and the community were unable 'to pay the great tribute that the whole people were accustomed to render to the pagans', they turned to Alfred, who agreed to pay the church's share in return for title to the estates.[42] Hoards dating to the viking occupation of London in 871–2 have been excavated at Croydon, Surrey, about fifteen kilometres south of London; at

---

40. Asser, ch. 43; *ASC* s.a. 871.
41. Æthelweard, *Chronicon*, ed. Campbell, s.a. 872, p. 40: '*Myrcii confirmant cum eis faederis pactum stipendiaque statuunt.*' The *Anglo-Saxon Chronicle* and Asser simply say that the Mercians made peace with the army, but a charter, S 1278, issued in 872 by Wærfeth, bishop of Worcester, explains that the bishop leased the Warwickshire estate in question 'chiefly because of the very pressing affliction and immense tribute of the barbarians, in that same year when the pagans stayed in London'. *EHD* I, no. 94, p. 532; Keynes and Lapidge, p. 244, n. 80. See also *ASC* s.a. 865, 866, 868, 872, 873.
42. S 354. See the discussion by S.D. Keynes, 'The West Saxon charters of King Æthelwulf and his sons', *EHR* 109 (1994) pp. 1137–8.

Gravesend, on the mouth of the Thames; and under the south end of Waterloo Bridge.[43] These finds also hint at the costs involved in making peace with the vikings. Cash and plunder, after all, were what the vikings traditionally sought, and when one was dealing from a position of weakness, as were Alfred in 871 and King Burgred of Mercia in 873, cash was what one offered and hoped would be accepted.[44]

Here Alfred followed Frankish precedent. Tribute was the primary way in which Charles the Bald and other Frankish princes dealt with the vikings throughout the second half of the ninth century.[45] Since the composition and leadership of the viking companies that ravaged Francia and England often overlapped, it is not surprising that Scandinavian raiders in the mid-860s would carry the practice with them across the Channel and extort tribute from their English hosts.

Monetary 'appeasement' has gained a bad odour among historians and literati, both because of the disastrous failures of Alfred's great-great-grandson, Æthelred II, 'the Unready', and because it seems so unheroic. Nineteenth- and early twentieth-century Romantics idealized the Middle Ages as an Age of Chivalry and Faith, when knights were willing to fight to the death for their ideals. As President Theodore Roosevelt lectured the American people from a bully-pulpit at Harvard University in 1907, 'A really great people, proud and high-spirited, would face all the disasters of war rather than purchase that base prosperity which is bought at the price of national honor.' Of course, such sentiments are most confidently enunciated when the necessity of choosing between national honour and survival is safely remote.

---

43. N.P. Brooks and J.A. Graham-Campbell, 'Reflections on the Viking-age silver hoard from Croydon, Surrey', in M.A.S. Blackburn, ed., *Anglo-Saxon Monetary History. Essays in Memory of Michael Dolley* (Leicester, 1986) pp. 91–110. The Croydon hoard, with its hack silver and its handful of Arabic and Carolingian coins, is thought to be a viking deposit. Croydon belonged at the time to the archbishop of Canterbury and the monks of Christ Church, who subsequently leased it to Ealdorman Ælfred in exchange for Chartham, Kent. S 1202. The other hoards are likely to have belonged to panicked locals. The viking occupation of London may also explain the less well-preserved coin deposits found at Barking and Westminster Bridge.
44. Cf. *ASC* s.a. 865, and Asser, ch. 20, trans. Keynes and Lapidge, p. 74.
45. See E. Joranson, *The Danegeld in France* (Rock Island, Illinois, 1923) pp. 26–38, passim.

Alfred and his contemporaries on both sides of the Channel had no such luxury. Purchasing peace was often an eminently sensible solution to an immediate viking problem. In the summer of 871 Alfred chose to be pragmatic. He had tried war, and that route had failed. He now either 'made peace' or faced the distinct possibility that Wessex would go the way of Northumbria and East Anglia. It is perhaps more surprising that Halfdan and his soldiers were willing to settle for cash than that Alfred would offer it. Perhaps, the Great Heathen Army, bloodied by its victories as well as its defeats at Englefield and Ashdown, had also had its fill of fighting for the time being. For all the odes to glory in the sagas, real vikings were closer in temperament to pirates than to heroic warriors. Their favourite targets were defenceless monasteries crammed with wealth. When confronted by a superior enemy army, vikings were more likely to retreat to the safety of a fortified camp than risk their lives and booty in battle.[46] Æthelred and Alfred had forced them to pay in blood for every silver plate and cartload of corn. The certainty of tribute must have seemed more appealing than fighting another battle against such a stubborn foe. The West Saxons' dogged resistance had accomplished at least that much.

'If once you have paid him the Dane-Geld / You never get rid of the Dane', Kipling wryly observed.[47] Perhaps not permanently, but Alfred's peace-making with the vikings in 871 did buy him a five-year respite, as the Great Heathen Army turned its attention once more to Northumbria and Mercia. The conquest of East Anglia and attempted subjugation of Wessex almost cost the vikings their gains in the north. In 872 the Northumbrians took advantage of the extended absence of the Great Heathen Army to drive out the vikings' client king, Egbert, and his ally, Archbishop Wulfhere. The Army responded to these events by moving its operations in the autumn of 872 to Torksey, Lindsey, a town on the River Trent in the northeasternmost reaches

---

46. On the viking way of war, see K. Leyser, 'Early Medieval Warfare', in J. Cooper, ed., *The Battle of Maldon, Fiction and Fact* (London, 1993) pp. 106–7. See also P. Griffith, *The Viking Art of War* (London, 1995).
47. Rudyard Kipling, 'Paying the Dane-Geld', *A Choice of Kipling's Verse*, selected by T.S. Eliot (London, 1941) p. 288.

of Mercia. From here the Danes could strike in virtually any direction. Just as vikings on the Continent relied upon rivers such as the Seine and Loire for their raiding, so the Great Heathen Army used the Trent for quick movements between Northumbria and Mercia. Moreover, a Roman-cut canal connected Torksey with Lincoln, and from Lincoln the vikings could sail down the River Witham into East Anglia, and from there to the Wash and the sea beyond.[48] The occupation of Torksey presented King Burgred with a dilemma: should he fight or attempt to cut another deal? Despite the cash he had paid them the year before while they sojourned in London, the Army had not vacated his kingdom, and Burgred must have wondered whether additional payments would bring about any better results. But something had to be done. From Torksey, as the king well knew, the way lay open for the vikings to reoccupy Nottingham and plunder the Mercian heartland.

In similar circumstances four years before, Burgred had turned to his West Saxon brothers-in-law for military aid. This time he did not, perhaps because Alfred was in no position to give it. The Mercian king decided to appease his unwanted guests. He made a good-will gesture by offering their Northumbrian clients, the deposed King Egbert and Archbishop Wulfhere, the hospitality of his court, and proceeded to negotiate another peace treaty with the Danes in Torksey. By doing so he hoped, perhaps, to persuade them that it was in their best interests to recover Northumbria rather than continue to ravage Mercia. If so, he miscalculated badly. No sooner had peace been confirmed with the standard oaths and exchange of hostages then the vikings treacherously violated it. A detachment of the Army rowed down the Trent past Nottingham, seized Repton, Derbyshire, an important Mercian royal centre, the burial place of kings, and proceeded to fortify about 1.5 hectares of it with ditches and earthworks.[49] Though the force in Repton may

---

48. Peddie, *Alfred the Good Soldier*, p. 100.
49. Excavations directed by Martin Biddle have revealed a camp defended on one side by the River Trent and on the other three by about 150 metres of ditch and earthwork defences, anchored by St Wynstan's Church. Biddle's team also uncovered the skeletal remains of a viking chieftain of high rank surrounded by the remains of 250 other people, presumably also vikings. M. Biddle and B. Kjolbye-Biddle, 'Repton

have numbered fewer than 1,000, given the small size of the camp and the mere 100 metres of enclosed strand available to beach ships, the suddenness of the viking incursion proved decisive.[50] Taken completely by surprise and faced with the defection of a number of powerful nobles, King Burgred fled the kingdom. Rather than take refuge with Alfred, he and his wife, Æthelswith, chose instead to exchange the sceptre of secular authority for the pilgrim's staff. The royal exiles made their way to Rome and took up permanent residence in the 'Saxon quarter', the English village within the Leonine City where Alfred and his father had stayed under happier circumstances two decades before.[51]

The history of Mercia between 874 and 877 graphically illustrates what would have happened to Wessex if Alfred had not been able to fight the Danes to a stalemate in 871. The vikings, perhaps themselves still uncertain whether they were raiders or conquerors, did not immediately refashion Mercia into an Anglo-Scandinavian kingdom. Following the pattern they had established in Northumbria, the Danes set up a compliant Mercian *ætheling*, named Ceolwulf, as their client king. Though dismissed in the *Anglo-Saxon Chronicle* as a 'foolish thegn', Ceolwulf may well have traced his descent to King Ceolwulf I (821–823) or his brother King Cenwulf (798–821). He certainly exercised the usual perquisites of an Anglo-Saxon king during his five-year reign, granting land by charter and issuing coins. His charters indicate, moreover, that he enjoyed support among the Mercian nobility and

---

and the Vikings', *Antiquity* 66 (1992) pp. 36–51. See R. Hodges, *The Anglo-Saxon Achievement: Archaeology and the Beginnings of English Society* (Ithaca, N. Y., 1989) p. 153. See also C. Batey, H. Clarke, R.I. Page, N.S. Price, *Cultural Atlas of the Viking World*, ed. J. Graham-Campbell (Abingdon, Oxfordshire, 1994) pp. 128, 129.

50. Peddie, *Alfred the Good Soldier*, p. 75, estimates a requirement of about seven yards per boat, which applied to Repton would give a maximum of thirty to thirty-five ships. The average crew size was probably around thirty. See *ASC* s.a. 896.

51. Burgred's and Æthelswith's names ('Burgureth rex Adelsuith regina') are recorded in the 'Liber Vitae' of Brescia, fol. 31v. S.D. Keynes, 'Anglo-Saxon Entries in the "Liber Vitae" of Brescia', in J. Roberts and J.L. Nelson with M. Godden, eds, *Alfred the Wise: Studies in Honour of Janet Bately on the Occasion of her Sixty-Fifth Birthday* (Cambridge, 1997) pp. 109–10, 115–16. Burgred was buried in the Church of St Mary's in the borgo; Æthelswith died in Pavia in 888. *ASC* s.a. 874, 888.

ecclesiastical establishment. At least two of Burgred's ealdor-men continued in office under Ceolwulf and frequented his court. Burgred's bishops apparently found nothing incongru-ous about serving a king who had betrayed his – and their – royal lord and who owed his office to the good graces of pagan invaders.[52]

Surprisingly, Mercia's relations with Wessex, at least con-cerning fiscal matters, remained largely undisturbed by the change in administration. Whatever his private thoughts about the deposition and disgrace of his brother-in-law, Alfred was willing to negotiate with Mercia's new king a con-tinuation of the monetary convention that had joined the two kingdoms since the 860s. Indeed, Alfred's and Ceolwulf's joint issues of the new 'Cross-and-Lozenge' penny and the (much rarer) 'Two Emperors' penny signalled a signific-ant restoration of the silver content of both the West Saxon and Mercian currency, from less than 20 per cent fine in Alfred's first and Burgred's last issues to better than 90 per cent. If the numismatists are correct in their dating of the sequence of these issues, Ceolwulf followed Alfred's lead in this major currency reform.[53] Interestingly, the two kings shared not only coin types but also London mints, indicat-ing either that Alfred in the mid-870s enjoyed authority in this formerly Mercian town or that London had become

52. S 215 and 216 (with the attestations of ealdormen Beornoth and Æthelhun, both of whom also attest charters of Burgred). A regnal list preserved in a Worcester manuscript, ca. 1000, London, British Library, MS Cotton Tiberius A. Xiii, fo. 114v, accords Ceolwulf a five-year reign. T. Hearne, ed., *Hemingi Chartularium Ecclesiae Wigoriensis*, 2 vols (Oxford, 1723) I, p. 242.

53. On the coinage of Ceolwulf II, see P. Grierson and M.A.S. Blackburn, *Medieval European Coinage with a Catalogue of the Coins in the Fitzwilliam Museum, Cambridge. I The Early Middle Ages (5th–10th Centuries)* (Cam-bridge, 1986) pp. 312–13. For the restoration of the debased coinage, see ibid, pp. 307–8, 311–12, 598–605 (citing researches of Metcalf and Northover). For an interesting interpretation of Alfred's and Ceolwulf II's coinage, which involves a redating of the issues back to c. 875 from the usually accepted c. 878/9, see M.A.S. Blackburn, 'Alfred's vision for the coinage', paper read to the Institute for Histor-ical Research, November 1988, and M.A.S. Blackburn, 'The London Mint during the Reign of King Alfred', and S.D. Keynes, 'King Alfred and the Mercians', both in M.A.S. Blackburn and D.N. Dumville, eds, *Kings, Currency, and Alliances: The History and Coinage of Southern England, AD 840–900* (Woodbridge, forthcoming).

something of an 'open city'. At least two Mercian moneyers accorded Alfred royal styles that pronounced him king of 'Angles' and 'Mercians' as well as West Saxons, and it is not inconceivable that Alfred had taken advantage of Burgred's deposition to extend his control over London and parts of eastern Mercia, or even that Ceolwulf had allowed this as the price for Alfred's 'friendship'.[54]

Alfred's acceptance of Ceolwulf's kingship left no trace in the *Anglo-Saxon Chronicle*, which remembered the Mercian only as a 'foolish king's thegn'.[55] By the time this annal was written in the early 890s, Alfred ruled western Mercia, which was administered in his name by his Mercian son-in-law, Ealdorman Æthelred. These new political realities entailed a reassessment of Mercia's last native king. He was to be remembered with scorn as one who chose to submit rather than fight. The *Chronicle*, thus, implicitly contrasted Ceolwulf, the lap dog of the Danes, with Alfred, their conqueror. This judgement, as biased as it is, is not entirely without merit. Ceolwulf II was not his own man. He ruled Mercia on the sufferance of his Danish masters. In return for their support he had sworn oaths and given hostages that the kingdom 'should be ready for them on whatever day they wished to have it, and he would be ready, himself to serve them along with all who would follow him'.[56] That day came in August 877, when Guthrum, Oscetel, and Anwend led their part of the army 'into Mercia and shared out some of it, and gave some to Ceolwulf'.[57] The army assumed direct control over eastern Mercia, while allowing Ceolwulf to continue to rule, for a time, in the west. The vikings retained Gloucester, however, as a base for future military actions

---

54. R.H.M. Dolley and C.E. Blunt, 'The chronology of the coins of Ælfred the Great', *Anglo-Saxon Coins: Studies Presented to F.M. Stenton on the Occasion of his 80th Birthday, 17 May 1960*, ed. R.H.M. Dolley (London, 1961) pp. 80–1. Two of Alfred's earliest surviving 'Cross-and-Lozenge' pennies, both struck by the Mercian moneyer, Liafwald, bear the title *rex sm*, quite possibly an abbreviation for *rex Saxonum et Merciorum*, king of the Saxons and Mercians. Alfred's 'Two Emperors' style penny awards him the title *rex Anglo*, standing either for 'king of the Angles' or, possibly, for 'king of the Anglo-Saxons'. The moneyer who struck it, like Liafwald, had also worked for Burgred.
55. *ASC* s.a. 874.
56. *ASC* s.a. 875.
57. *ASC* s.a. 877.

against western Wessex and perhaps to ensure Ceolwulf's continued cooperation.[58]

Ceolwulf's accommodation with the vikings meant that the Danes had virtually free use of the Thames and could use bases located within Mercian territory to launch attacks upon Wessex. Fortunately for Alfred, the viking conquest of Mercia in 874 was the last unified action taken by the combined viking armies. At Repton the Danish leaders decided to dissolve their joint enterprise. Halfdan led part of the army north into Northumbria intent upon conquest and settlement. By the end of 876 he had brought the region south of the Tyne under his direct rule and had begun parcelling out territory to his jarls and their followers. Guthrum, Oscetel, and Anwend, meanwhile, led the forces under their command to Cambridge, on the border between Mercia and East Anglia. They encamped in Cambridge for a year, during which time they tightened their control over eastern Mercia and East Anglia and began to prepare for a second invasion of Wessex.

Alfred's activities during this period are obscure. He appears to have turned his attention to the West Saxon economy, restoring the silver content of the West Saxon coinage perhaps in an effort to increase the value of the monetary exactions that he extracted from his subjects. He may also have begun the far-reaching military reforms that were to revolutionize Anglo-Saxon warfare, but, given the ease with which the Danes would penetrate the kingdom in 875/6, this is less likely. Two surviving contemporary charters, one from 873 and the other from 875, give some indication as to Alfred's itinerary and concerns. Having preserved the kingdom from the vikings, Alfred apparently sought to shore up his support among the elites of Wessex and, especially, Kent. Soon after his accession, for example, he made a gift of bookland at *Hamme* (?Ham in Romney Marsh) in Kent to a thegn named Eardwulf. Eardwulf, in turn, sold this land, in Alfred's presence and with his consent, in 875 to his friend, Wighelm.[59] By a single grant, Alfred secured the support of two local Kentish thegns. Significantly, the assembly at which this transaction took place was

58. Æthelweard, *Chronicon*, ed. Campbell, s.a. 877, p. 42.
59. S 1203.

well attended. Among those who witnessed the grant were Archbishop Æthelred and Ealdormen Ælfstan and Beorhtwulf and more than a dozen king's thegns, including Sigewulf and Sigehelm, members of an important Kentish noble family whom Alfred took into his court and, eventually, made ealdormen of Kent.

Except for a naval skirmish in the summer of 875 against a fleet of seven ships, one of which he captured, Alfred remained at peace with the vikings. Some months later, however, King Guthrum and his two colleagues led their army from Cambridge into Wessex. Alfred appears to have been taken completely by surprise. The viking army slipped past the West Saxon forces, which, given the length of their march through West Saxon territory does not say much for Alfred's precautions or preparations, and seized the convent and royal burh of Wareham, Dorset, an eminently defensible site bounded by the Rivers Fromme and Tarrant. From this secure base they began to raid the surrounding countryside.[60]

Alfred promptly laid siege to Wareham, but could achieve only the same stalemate he and his brother had confronted in Nottingham in 868: the vikings could not escape, and he could not force his way in. Alfred's essential pragmatism is revealed by the negotiations that followed.[61] Unable to achieve military victory over the Danes, he attempted to find common ground with them, some ceremony or ritual of peace-making that the vikings would recognize as binding. He thought he found it by combining a payment of money with an exchange of hostages and the swearing of oaths.[62] As the *Anglo-Saxon Chronicle* relates:

> and then the king made peace with the enemy and they gave him hostages, who were the most important men next to their king in the army, and swore oaths to him on the holy ring – a

---

60. *ASC* s.a. 876; Æthelweard, *Chronicon*, ed. Campbell, s.a. 876, pp. 41–2; Asser, ch. 49, trans. Keynes and Lapidge, pp. 82–3.

61. R. Abels, 'King Alfred's peace-making strategies with the Danes', *Haskins Society Journal* 3 (1992) pp. 23–34.

62. Æthelweard, *Chronicon*, ed. Campbell, p. 41, says that Alfred gave them money at the same time that he made a pact of peace (*rex pactum cum eis pacis confirmat, simulque pecuniam dando*). Neither Asser nor *ASC* mentions a cash payment.

thing which they would not do before for any nation – that they would speedily leave his kingdom.[63]

Sacred oaths played a critical role in resolving disputes in ninth-century England. Sworn on holy relics, they drew upon a force more powerful than any wielded by an earthly king, the shared Christian belief that divine retribution would visit oathbreakers. A supernatural sanction was needed to secure a man's promise in a period when the coercive power of government was so weak.[64]

Because of their disregard for the wrath of the Christian God, the pagan vikings must have appeared untrustworthy in the extreme to the English. How could one deal with a foe to whom oaths were only words? An exchange of hostages and promise of good behaviour, Alfred realized, was insufficient warranty for the withdrawal of Guthrum and his army. An oath was necessary to bind the enemy with supernatural fetters, but oaths upon relics constrained only Christian foes. To bind heathens one needed something that they believed sacred, hence the 'holy ring,' an arm-ring associated with the worship of Thor.[65] Asser was embarrassed enough by it to change the holy ring into 'relics in which the king placed the greatest trust after God' when he translated his text of the *Anglo-Saxon Chronicle* into Latin. (He did, however, retain the Chronicler's boast, made meaningless by the alteration, that the vikings 'had never been willing before to [swear such an oath] to any race').[66] His Christian hero had been willing to engage in a pagan ritual, in fact had insisted upon a pagan ritual, to resolve a conflict.

As clever as Alfred's stratagem may have been, it failed. 'But one night, practising their usual treachery, after their

---

63. *EHD* I, 194. The 'A' recension omits the reference to hostages, but both Asser and Æthelweard mention them.
64. Alfred's emphasis upon oaths in his laws and his successors' insistence on oaths of fidelity from their subjects underscore just how important the oath was to maintaining the Anglo-Saxon political and social order. Abels, *Lordship and Military Obligation*, pp. 83–90, esp. pp. 85–87. Patrick Wormald emphasizes this point in his forthcoming *The Making of English Law: King Alfred to the Norman Conquest.*
65. That the Danes in 876 swore upon an *arm*-ring is confirmed by Æthelweard, who describes it as *armilla sacra. Chronicon*, ed. Campbell, p. 41.
66. Asser, ch. 49, trans. Keynes and Lapidge, p. 83. Cf. the explanation offered by Keynes and Lapidge, pp. 245–6.

149

own manner, and paying no heed to the hostages, the oath and the promise of faith, they broke the treaty, killed all the hostages they had, and turning away they went unexpectedly to another place, called Exeter . . . There they spent the winter.'[67] The oath and exchange of hostages had provided the Danes with the cover they needed to escape Wareham. It is difficult to say why the ring of Thor had proved so inefficacious. Guthrum's Danes may simply have been a slippery crew, even by viking standards. Perhaps these pagan vikings did not regard an oath to a Christian as binding, even if taken on the ring of Thor. Or, possibly, Alfred was wrong in believing that vikings could, like Christians, be bound by a sworn oath. We know very little about pagan practices in viking-age Denmark. Most of the evidence comes from twelfth- and thirteenth-century Icelandic and Norse sagas. In a number of these, notably *Eyrbyggja Saga* and *Landnamabok*, we read about a holy ring of Thor upon which oaths were taken, and in others about peace-oaths taken before the formal handshakes or hand slaps that ended conflicts.[68] While this evidence is late, the *Annals of St-Bertin* twice relate that viking chieftains swore oaths of fealty to Charles the Bald 'in their own fashion' [*suatim*].[69] It is possible, however, that oaths did not play as critical a part in resolving disputes in ninth-century Denmark as in Anglo-Saxon England.[70] In any event, Alfred's attempt to find common ground failed. The betrayal of the oath explains Asser's bitter comment that the heathens were by nature perfidious.

Alfred pursued the Danes with his own mounted forces, but they reached Exeter before he could catch up with them. Guthrum and the other Danish leaders, however, had little

67. Asser, ch. 49, trans. Keynes and Lapidge, pp. 82–3.
68. A number of twelfth- and thirteenth-century sagas, most notably *Eyrbyggja saga*, chs 4 and 16, and *Landanamabok*, iv, ch. 7, refer to a silver altar ring consecrated by being dipped into the blood of a sacrificial ox that was to be kept in the inner sanctuary of pagan temples and worn by chieftains during the meeting of the Thing. According to *Eyrbyggja saga*, ch. 4, all oaths in matters relating to ordeals were to be sworn on such a ring.
69. *AB*, s.a. 858, 862, ed. Grat et al., pp. 77, 88. Cf. Alfred Smyth, *King Alfred the Great* (Oxford, 1995) pp. 78–9.
70. It is striking how little a role oaths play in the reconciliation of disputes in the Icelandic saga. They are virtually absent from J. Byock's *Feud in the Icelandic Saga* (Berkeley, 1982).

reason to rejoice. Just as an 'English wind' would save England from invasion seven centuries later, the unpredictable winds and uncertain seas of the Channel did what Alfred alone could not. A sudden squall off Swanage wrecked a large viking fleet as it sailed west along the coast to join the Danish land forces in Exeter.[71] The Danes had counted on these reinforcements; the loss of men and ships changed the military situation drastically. Alfred's army sat outside Exeter, and the Danes, lacking the forces to challenge him, could do little more than crouch down behind its walls. Alfred had no need now to purchase peace. The besieged invaders agreed to give Alfred as many hostages as he desired and swore 'great oaths' that they would leave the kingdom. This time they did. In the month of August, during harvest season, the Danes left Exeter and retired to Mercia, where they established a base at Gloucester. They now called upon Ceolwulf to make good his pledge to them. The Mercian king, whether out of loyalty or fear, surrendered part of his kingdom into the hands of his viking lords. The viking armies in Northumbria and eastern Mercia had abandoned the role of raider for that of colonist.

Guthrum was now in sole command of the viking forces south of the River Humber. The other two sea-kings, Anwend and Oscetel, with whom he had shared command of the 'summer fleet' of 871 and of the Danish army in Cambridge, are last mentioned in the *Anglo-Saxon Chronicle* entry for 875. Whether they had died or merely left the army is unknown. Even with the failed invasion of Wessex in 877, Guthrum had surpassed all but a handful of his contemporaries, acquiring rule over all of East Anglia as well as the western half of Mercia. But he was still not satisfied. Like a wolf prowling for his next meal, Guthrum looked hungrily south to the one kingdom that he and his comrades had not yet been able to subdue or despoil. The treasures and rich farmlands of Wessex were irresistible to the viking adventurer. Despite the hard fighting he had experienced there in 871 and the setbacks he had recently suffered at Wareham and Exeter, Guthrum judged Wessex to be a prize ripe for the taking.

---

71. *ASC* s.a. 877A. The *Chronicle* says that 120 ships were lost, but this looks suspiciously like an estimate and an exaggerated one at that.

. . .

ATHELNEY AND THE BATTLE OF EDINGTON

The decisive moment came early in the following year. If Alfred believed that he had cowed Guthrum into abiding by his word, he was mistaken. Soon after the celebration of Twelfth Night (6 January) 878, Guthrum at the head of a large force 'stealthily' descended upon the important royal estate of Chippenham on the River Avon in north-western Wiltshire, catching Alfred completely unawares. Before Alfred could react, the Danes pressed their advantage by ravaging the surrounding countryside of Wiltshire, Somerset, and Hampshire. Bent upon conquest, they sought submission rather than loot. Like the viking occupation of Repton in 878, the seizure of Chippenham was meant to expose the weakness of the king. Guthrum's unopposed ravaging revealed King Alfred, the 'lord and protector' of the West Saxons, to be unable to defend his lands or his people. Landowners throughout the region confronted painful choices: bow to the Danes and by doing so preserve their tenures and lives, flee across the sea to safety, or loyally resist and die. As in Mercia and Northumbria, many chose to submit, possibly among them Ealdorman Wulfhere, a leading member of Alfred's court who had held the office of ealdorman (probably of Wiltshire) since the days of King Æthelwulf. A charter of Edward the Elder (dated 901) refers to Wulfhere having forfeited his office and inheritance because he had 'deserted without permission both his lord King Alfred and his country in spite of the oath that he had sworn to the king and all his leading men'.[72] That the crisis of 878 was the occasion of Wulfhere's treason is suggested by the ealdorman's conspicuous absence from charters Alfred issued in the 880s and 890s.[73] Wulfhere was undoubtedly not alone. The Chronicler tells us that 'the enemy army . . . drove a great part of the people across the sea, and

---

72. S 362 (BCS 595), trans. *EHD* I, no. 100, p. 542.
73. Wulfhere attests as ealdorman from 854 until ca. 877/8. See S 290, 303–7, 309–11, 313, 318, 327, 335–6, 337, 1201, 339–41, 1275, 1605, 343, 357. Cf. S 345. He seems to have been replaced by Æthelhelm (S 348, 356).

conquered and subjected to them most of the others, except King Alfred'.[74]

Guthrum's subjugation of Wessex was, however, less complete than the language of the *Chronicle* would suggest. How much of Wessex the Danes actually occupied is unknown, as is the proportion of landowners and nobles who took Guthrum as their lord. Because of the *Chronicle*'s focus upon Alfred and the western shires, nothing is related concerning events in eastern Hampshire, Kent and the other shires of the southeast. If Ealdorman Wulfhere had indeed defected, Guthrum could claim rule over Wiltshire, and from the flight of Ealdorman Æthelnoth into the marshes, it would seem that Guthrum also dominated much of Somerset east of the Levels. In any event, Guthrum did not have the manpower to directly occupy much more than Chippenham and its immediate environs. Asser himself implies as much. By force of arms, he informs us, the vikings compelled 'very nearly all the inhabitants of *that region* [*illius regionis*] to submit to their rule'. The 'region' in question from context seems to have been northern Wiltshire.[75] Guthrum understood that final victory depended upon negating Alfred, by capturing and killing him or by forcing him to abandon the kingdom. Then he could set up a cooperative native noble on the throne, or perhaps even assume direct rule over Wessex.

That Guthrum's authority was geographically limited is revealed by an unsuccessful viking attack upon Devonshire. While Alfred was 'journeying in difficulties through the woods and fen-fastness with a small force' and Guthrum was establishing control of the lands around Chippenham, a brother of Halfdan and Ivarr, whom later sources identify as Ubbe, suddenly appeared off the northern coast of Devonshire with a fleet of twenty-three ships.[76] He had come from Dyfed in southeastern Wales, Asser's native homeland, where he had spent the winter. Sailing up the Bristol Channel, he

---

74. *ASC* s.a. 878A. It is unclear whether the 'sea' in question was the Channel (as thought by the late tenth-century chronicler, Ealdorman Æthelweard (*Chronicon*, ed. Campbell, s.a. 878, p. 42) or the Bristol Channel.

75. Asser, ch. 40, ed. Stevenson, p. 40; trans. Keynes and Lapidge, p. 83.

76. *ASC* s.a. 878. Asser, ch. 54, and Æthelweard, *Chronicon*, ed. Campbell, s.a. 878, p. 43, provide additional valuable information.

landed with his forces at *Cynuit* (Countisbury Hill) on the northern coast of Devonshire, where he was met by the men of the shire under the command of their ealdorman, Odda. Ubbe's attack may have been in support of Guthrum's, as part of a strategic pincer action by land and sea meant to cut off Alfred's retreat and capture the king; it is equally likely that Ubbe was an opportunist trying to profit from the West Saxon preoccupation with Guthrum. In either case, he met with disaster. Ironically, in the battle fought at *Cynuit* the West Saxons and the vikings reversed roles. Odda retreated with the king's thegns and their followers behind the meagre defences of the stronghold (described by Asser as 'unprepared and altogether unfortified, except for ramparts thrown up in our [Welsh] fashion'). Though *Cynuit's* man-made defences were weak, it was strongly sited. Ubbe, calculating that the West Saxons would be forced to surrender due to hunger and thirst, decided upon siege rather than assault. Apparently, the West Saxons feared the same thing. Rather than face inevitable starvation and surrender, they decided to burst out unexpectedly at dawn, 'and by virtue of their aggressiveness, from the very outset they overwhelmed the enemy in large part, together with their king, a few escaping by flight to the ships'.[77] Ubbe died in the fray, along with 840 of his men. Later sources relate that the West Saxons captured there the famous 'Raven' banner woven, according to legend, by the daughters of Ragnarr Loþbrok, who had endowed it with the magical quality of fluttering before victory and drooping before defeat.[78]

Unable to raise an army, Alfred was thrown back on the resources of his household and loyal ealdormen. His hearth troop was loyal and experienced in war, but, as he well knew, it alone was too small to offer effective resistance against Guthrum's army. The only other forces he could count on were those of the newly appointed ealdorman of Somerset, Æthelnoth, who 'was tarrying in a certain wood with a small troop'.[79]

77. Asser, ch. 54, trans. Keynes and Lapidge, p. 84.
78. See p. 112, n. 62, above.
79. Æthelweard, *Chronicon*, ed. Campbell, s.a. 878, p. 42. Æthelnoth first attests as ealdorman around 878. S 352 and 345. A thegn with this name attests S 1275, a charter from 871–877. We do not know who served as ealdorman of Somerset between the death of Eanwulf in 867 and the accession of Æthelnoth.

At Wilton Alfred had fought despite being outnumbered and had lost. With the very survival of the last independent Anglo-Saxon kingdom at stake, he could not risk another engagement. In short, Alfred faced the same dilemma as King Edmund and King Burgred. Alfred's response was neither to seek the spiritual haven of Rome nor court martyrdom at the hands of the pagans. Rather, he chose to resist as best he could with what he had. His one advantage was his knowledge of the land, especially of the 'woods and fenfastness' of the Somerset Levels. Fleeing from Guthrum, he sought refuge among the hidden trackways of these marshlands, so familiar to him from his days of hunting stag and water fowl.

In later years, Alfred and his court would remember the king's flight as a glorious epic of a courageous Christian king who refused to submit to the enemies of God, choosing instead to hide in woods and wastelands, abandoned by all except a handful of his most faithful thegns, until he could gather the strength to win back his kingdom and convert the heathen foe to Christ. Even the account in the usually laconic *Anglo-Saxon Chronicle* emphasizes the drama of the situation – and rightly so. Asser and the Chronicler may have played up Alfred's difficulties in order to make his ultimate victory all the more impressive, but they did not invent the tale.[80] Alfred in the winter of 878 was reduced to the ignoble expedient of hiding from Guthrum. In the words of the chronicler, Ealdorman Æthelweard, 'King Alfred, indeed, was then in greater straits than was befitting.'[81] Accompanied only by his wife, children, and a handful of nobles and retainers, mainly members of his household, 'he led a restless life in great distress amid the woody and marshy places of Somerset'.[82]

The military challenge was to survive long enough to reestablish communications with loyal ealdormen and thegns. The method he chose was pragmatic and tough-minded. If

80. R.H.C. Davis, 'Alfred the Great: propaganda and truth', *History* 56 (1971) pp. 169–82, questions the gravity of Alfred's situation. Cf. the rejoinder by D. Whitelock, 'The importance of the Battle of Edington AD 878', in *From Bede to Alfred: Studies in Early Anglo-Saxon Literature and History* (London, 1980) no. 13.
81. Æthelweard, *Chronicon*, ed. Campbell, s.a. 878, p. 42.
82. Asser, ch. 53, trans. Keynes and Lapidge, p. 83.

he could not fight like a king, he would survive as a raider. Since Guthrum sat in Chippenham like a West Saxon king, Alfred would become the viking marauder, waging guerilla war against the entrenched invaders and their native allies. Alfred's flight into the Somerset marshes was a strategic withdrawal that revealed his keen appreciation of the military situation. Rather than retreat into Devon to join Ealdorman Odda, Alfred chose instead to contest Guthrum's control over the West Saxon heartland by maintaining a military presence in Somerset and Wiltshire. With the Danes in possession of his estates and food-rents, Alfred raided in order to feed his men. But by harrying the lands of his foreign enemies and the traitors who supported them, Alfred also reminded his subjects that their king had not abdicated and still had power to punish the disloyal. Guthrum, on the other hand, lacked the manpower to protect the lands and people he now claimed to rule. In a sense, Alfred and Guthrum were waging a war for hearts and minds; the former knew that he could not regain his kingdom, and the latter that he could not maintain even the pretence of rule, without the active support of the local elites.

After Easter (23 March), Alfred regularized his existence by establishing a base on the natural fortress of the isle of Athelney, a stretch of high ground arising out of the Somerset marshes and bounded on its north side by the River Tone. Athelney could only be reached by punt and found by those who knew where to look. Fens and marshes were wild, inhospitable places, the secret haunts of saints, Grendel-like monsters, and desperate exiles. Felix's description of the Cambridgeshire fenlands in his eighth-century *Life of St Felix* serves equally well for Alfred's refuge: 'a most dismal fen . . . now consisting of bogs, now of marshes, sometimes of pools, concealed by black mists, sometimes studded with wooded islands and traversed by the windings of tortuous streams'.[83] Athelney was one such 'wooded' island. It offered scarcely two acres of dry ground, fringed with a dense wood of alders harbouring game such as stags, wild goat, and

83. *Felix's Life of St Guthlac*, ed. and trans. B. Colgrave (Cambridge, 1956) ch. 24, p. 87; P. Stafford, *The East Midlands in the Early Middle Ages* (Leicester, 1985) p. 16.

water fowl.[84] The name Athelney, 'isle of nobles (or princes)', associated it with royalty, and it may well have been a favoured hunting ground for Æthelwulf and his sons.[85] If so, Alfred came now as the hunted rather than the hunter. The fugitive king probably established a watch on Burrow Mump about 800 metres northeast of Athelney near the confluence of the Tone and the Parrett. The Mump, a seventy-five-metre high hillock reminiscent of the famous Tor at Glastonbury, looms over the A361, providing a commanding view of the surrounding countryside. Though archaeologists have yet to uncover ninth-century remains there, it is only reasonable to assume that Alfred would have taken advantage of this natural lookout.

Today there is little to see at Athelney. Even the name 'Athelney' itself is preserved only in a private farm. It is difficult for a modern visitor to envision Athelney as an 'island' rising out of the marshes; erosion and tractors have considerably lowered the hill even over the last fifty years, and the Somerset fens have long since been drained. What does impress one, though, is how small the site is: about 365 paces long and 50 paces across. By walking the field at Athelney one can begin to appreciate Alfred's situation; it would be surprising if he had as many as a hundred followers with him in his marshland stronghold.

Though Athelney lay hidden in the heart of the Somerset Levels, a nearby network of Roman roads and trackways, which skirted the marshes, allowed Alfred and his followers easy access to the surrounding countryside.[86] In short, Athelney proved not only the perfect refuge for the king and his family but an ideal camp for a guerilla band. From his 'fen-fastness' Alfred 'struck out relentlessly and tirelessly against the pagans', leading his household troops and the loyal men from nearby Somerset villages and estates on a series of raids intended not only to supply his troops but to

---

84. William of Malmesbury, *Gesta Pontificum Anglorum*, ed. W. Hamilton, Rolls Series (London, 1870) ch. 92.
85. Alternately, the isle may have gained its name from Alfred's sojourn there with his wife and children, or from an unknown early Somerset settler whose name began with 'Æthel'. Stevenson, *Asser's Life of King Alfred*, pp. 259–60 n. 4.
86. Asser, ch. 92, trans. Keynes and Lapidge, pp. 102–3; Peddie, *Alfred the Good Soldier*, pp. 108–9.

demoralize his enemies.[87] In later centuries, Alfred's 'restless' life in the Somerset marshes gave rise to a series of picturesque stories meant to illustrate the king's moral virtues and to connect him with St Neot and St Cuthbert, a reflection of the desire of Alfred's descendants to extend their patronage and political control over the churches of Wales and Northumbria.[88] The most famous is the tale of the burnt cakes, which has become to Alfred what the spider is to Robert Bruce. The story as first recounted in the eleventh-century *Vita S. Neoti* relates how the desperate king, travelling incognito and alone, was reduced to taking refuge in a swineherd's hut. He was too distracted by thoughts of his plight to mind some loaves of bread baking in the oven, and, as a result, they burnt. When the swineherd's wife shrewishly scolded him, the Job-like Alfred, remembering St Neot's admonition that 'Whom the Lord loves, He chastises; He scourges every son whom He adopts' [Hebrews xii, 6], patiently bore her reproofs, thereby winning the approval and miraculous aid of St Neot.[89] A second story, this one from the early eleventh-century *Historia de Sancto Cuthberto*, has Alfred sharing his meagre rations of fish with a stranger, who turns out to be St Cuthbert. Like St Neot, Cuthbert subsequently appears to Alfred in a dream, promising him help against the Danes and revealing to him that God has chosen him to be king of all Britain.[90] A third tale, as apocryphal as the others but lacking their miraculous elements, has Alfred, disguised as a mime and juggler and accompanied by a single faithful attendant, sneaking into the Danish camp in order to spy upon them. He completely fools the Danes with his consummate art, and in the matter of a few days learns all their plans. He then returns to

87. Asser, ch. 55, trans. Keynes and Lapidge, p. 84; *ASC* s.a. 878; Æthelweard, *Chronicon*, ed. Campbell, s.a. 878, p. 42.
88. E. Johnson-South, 'Competition for King Alfred's aura in the last century of Anglo-Saxon England', *Albion* 23 (1991) pp. 613–26. E. Conybeare, *Alfred in the Chroniclers* (London, 1900), translates excerpts dealing with Alfred's life from various medieval chronicles.
89. 'Vita Prima Sancti Neoti et Translatio', ed. M. Lapidge, *The Anglo-Saxon Chronicle, A Collaborative Edition*, vol. 17 (Cambridge, 1985) ch. 12. For the development of this story over the ages, see Keynes and Lapidge, pp. 197–202.
90. 'Historia de Sancto Cuthberto', chs 14–18, ed. T. Arnold, *Symeonis Monachi Opera Omnia*, 2 vols, Rolls Series (London, 1882–5) I, pp. 204–6.

Athelney, assures his men of an easy victory over an indolent enemy, and makes good his promise by winning the battle of Edington.[91]

All these stories emphasize not only Alfred's piety and Christian humility, but the desperate straits to which he had been reduced. Each in its own way attempts to explain how a fugitive king holed up in a marshland refuge could suddenly gather together a large army from enemy-occupied territory and win a decisive victory over a superior enemy. The explanation lies not in recourse to the miraculous but in Alfred's careful planning, mastery of logistics, and qualities of leadership. The *Anglo-Saxon Chronicle* reports that in the seventh week after Easter [4–10 May 878], around Whitsuntide, Alfred rode to 'Egbert's Stone' east of Selwood, where he was met by 'all the people of Somerset and of Wiltshire and of that part of Hampshire which is on this side of the sea [that is, west of Southampton Water], and they rejoiced to see him'.[92] Evidently, Alfred's emergence from his marshland stronghold was part of a carefully planned offensive that entailed raising the *fyrds* of three shires. This meant not only that the king had retained the loyalty of ealdormen, royal reeves and king's thegns, those charged with levying and leading these forces, but that they had maintained their positions of authority in these localities well enough to answer Alfred's summons to war. Alfred's actions also suggest a finely honed system of scouts and messengers. The story of the minstrel king spying on the enemy camp may be pure fantasy, but one can well imagine that Alfred kept close tabs both on Guthrum's movements and on the sentiments of the landed nobility who had not fled 'overseas'. How many of these local landowners and their dependants responded to Alfred's call and convened at 'Egbert's Stone' is uncertain, though it must have been a large force, perhaps a few thousand strong. Alfred in later years wished it to be remembered that he had been greeted

91. William of Malmesbury, *Gesta Regum*, bk. 2, ch. 4, ed. W. Stubbs, *Willelmi Malmesbiriensis Monachi De Gestis Regum Anglorum Libri Quinque*, 2 vols, Rolls Series (London, 1887–9) I, p. 126.
92. *ASC* s.a. 878. Asser, ch. 55, took the reference to the 'people of Hampshire this side of the sea' to mean those had not fled abroad. It is more likely that the Chronicler intended it as a geographical reference point.

with unbridled enthusiasm 'as if one restored to life after suffering such great tribulations' – a particularly apt sentiment for Whitsuntide.[93]

At the head of his household troop and accompanied by the Somerset *fyrd* under the command of Ealdorman Æthelnoth, Alfred had ridden about fifty kilometres to reach the agreed meeting place on the other side of Selwood. Though the site of 'Egbert's Stone' has defied certain identification, most think it lay immediately east of Selwood, around where the Hardway clears the forest, in the vicinity of Wiltshire's southern border with Somerset. The most attractive suggestions locate it between Penselwood and the Brixtons, and there is much to be said for the claims of both Kingsettle Hill in Stourhead, where a well-to-do local gentleman and antiquarian, Mr Henry Hoare, erected the scenic fifty-metre. Alfred's Tower in 1772, and Kingston Deverill about another ten kilometres to the northeast. Both would have offered Alfred easy access to a network of roads and trackways leading to Chippenham, an adequate supply of fresh water, and a well-drained, open field suitable for encampment.[94]

Alfred's movements, first to 'Egbert's Stone' and then to Iley Oak, leave little doubt as to his strategic goal: to drive the Danes from Chippenham or force Guthrum into accepting battle by threatening his camp. This, however, was more easily said than done. The immediate task confronting Alfred was to raise an army large enough to meet Guthrum in battle. To do so, he needed to call upon the military resources of three shires and meld them into a single force. And he had to do so before Guthrum got wind of his intentions. This may explain Alfred's choice of the Whitsuntide season for

93. Asser, ch. 55, trans. Keynes and Lapidge, p. 84. The Chronicler's characterization of the joy with which Alfred was received (*ASC* s.a. 878: '*and his gefægene wærun*') finds echoes in Alfred's own introduction to Psalm XXIII: '*And eac he witgode be him sylfum, hu his ealdormenn sceoldon fægnian his cymes of his wræcswiðe*' ('And likewise he [David] prophesied about himself, how his ealdormen were destined to rejoice in his return from exile'). *Liber Psalmorum. The West-Saxon Psalms, being the Prose Portion, or the 'First Fifty,' of the so-called Paris Psalter*, ed. J.W. Bright and R.L. Ramsay (Boston and London, 1907) p. 48.

94. The identifications of Egbert's Stone, Iley Oak, and *Ethandun* are fully discussed by Peddie, *Alfred the Good Soldier*, pp. 120–34, and J. Peddie and P. Dillon, *Alfred's Defeat of the Vikings* (Downwriter Publications: Devizes, Wilts, 1981), and references therein.

the campaign. The week of Whitsuntide provided a clear and easily remembered meeting time for the forces streaming from all directions toward 'Egbert's Stone'. Nor could the symbolism and spiritual power of the holy season have escaped the pious Alfred. Alfred had emerged from Athelney 'as if one restored to life', to lead a Christian people in a holy war against the enemies of God. If Guthrum's confidence stemmed from his recent successes, Alfred's came from his faith that God would not desert him any more than He had abandoned David in his time of tribulation.

'Egbert's Stone' was simply an assembly point. Alfred had no intention of lingering there and chancing a surprise attack upon his army in what was almost certainly an open and undefended site. Rather than await stragglers, Alfred made camp there for only a single night. At the break of dawn he marched north and encamped at *Iglea*, persuasively identified as 'Iley Oak' (the present Eastleigh Wood in Sutton Veney, on the outskirts of Warminster), the meeting place for the courts of the Hundreds of Warminster and Heytesbury into the fifteenth century. Alfred's decision to encamp at Iley, within ten kilometres of the battlefield, makes a good deal of military sense, especially if he knew that Guthrum's army had deployed around the nearby Iron Age hillfort at Bratton near the village of Edington, in the hope of intercepting Alfred's forces before they advanced upon Chippenham. Alfred had, once again, chosen his camp site well. The River Wylye provided both fresh water and security from sudden attack, while the surrounding dense forest shielded Alfred's army from discovery by Guthrum's patrols. At dawn Alfred advanced upon the enemy.

Bratton Camp offered Guthrum a strong defensive position guarded on three sides by a steep escarpment and surrounded by ancient ditches cut into the chalk. The only approach is along a ridgeway from the south. After crossing the River Wylye, Alfred ordered his men up Battlesbury Hill, and, after driving back any Danish sentinels found there, marched six kilometres or so along the ridge until he came into sight of the enemy. Guthrum's army, drawn up in battle array, awaited him in front of the Camp. When he had approached within a hundred metres or so, Alfred ordered his men to close ranks, shield brushing against shield, and attack. Asser describes what happened next:

Fighting fiercely with a dense shield-wall against the whole pagan army, and persevering resolutely for a long time, at length he gained the victory through God's will. He overthrew the pagans with very great slaughter, and chased those who fled as far as the stronghold, hacking them down.[95]

Alfred pursued the remnants of Guthrum's army to its stronghold, probably Chippenham, which lay about twenty kilometres north of the battlefield, and laid siege to it. He seized all the horses and cattle and summarily killed all the men he found outside the burh. Alfred had been in this position before. At Ashdown he and his brother had won nearly as great a victory, only to see it come to nought because of irresolution. He would not repeat the mistakes of Wareham and Exeter; this time the prey would not be allowed to slip away. The only conclusion now acceptable to Alfred was Guthrum's surrender. For a fortnight he and his army camped outside Chippenham, until

the pagans, thoroughly terrified by hunger, cold and fear, and in the end by despair, sought peace on this condition: the king should take as many chosen hostages as he wanted from them, and give none to them; never before, indeed, had they made peace with anyone on such terms. When he had heard their embassy, the king (as is his wont) was moved to compassion and took as many chosen hostages from them as he wanted. When they had been handed over, the pagans swore in addition that they would leave his kingdom immediately, and Guthrum, their king, promised to accept Christianity and to receive baptism at King Alfred's hand; all of which he and his men fulfilled as they had promised.[96]

Three weeks later Guthrum, along with thirty of his most noble followers, was baptized at Alfred's court at Aller, near Athelney. Alfred himself raised Guthrum from the font and received him as his spiritual son. For eight days Guthrum and his men wore the white robes of the newly baptized, their heads wrapped with white cloths where they had been an-ointed with the holy oil. The 'unbinding of the chrism' took place with great ceremony at the royal estate of Wedmore

95. Asser, ch. 56, ed. Stevenson, pp. 45–6; trans. Keynes and Lapidge, p. 84.
96. Asser, ch. 56, trans. Keynes and Lapidge, p. 85.

in Somerset. There Alfred hosted Guthrum for twelve days and nights, and 'freely bestowed many excellent treasures on him and all his men'.[97]

After the festivities, Guthrum fulfilled his promise to Alfred to leave Wessex. In the autumn of 878, he and his army withdrew from Chippenham to Cirencester, across the border in territory belonging to his client, King Ceolwulf II. There Guthrum resided for a full year, during which a newly arrived viking fleet sailed up the Thames past London and encamped at Fulham, on the 'Mercian' north banks of the river. Though Asser implies that these newcomers joined Guthrum, the silence of the *Chronicle* suggests that they were independent players, perhaps remnants of the viking band that Louis III and Carloman II had defeated on the Loire in November 879. Indeed, their presence on the Thames may have persuaded Guthrum to look to his interests in East Anglia. In 880 he evacuated Cirencester and returned to East Anglia, where he 'settled and shared out the land'.[98] The Fulham vikings, perhaps in response, sailed for Ghent soon after Guthrum's return.

The arrival of this new fleet and the death or deposition of Ceolwulf II sometime around 879 or 880 may have formed the context for the famous treaty between Alfred and Guthrum that divided between them what had once been Mercia. By the terms of this treaty the boundary between Alfred's and Guthrum's kingdoms was to run up the Thames to the Lea; follow the Lea to its source near Luton; extend from there to Bedford, and from Bedford follow the River Ouse to Watling Street.[99] In other words, Alfred was to succeed to Ceolwulf's kingdom of western Mercia and Guthrum was to incorporate the eastern part of Mercia into an enlarged kingdom of East Anglia.[100] Alfred, moreover, was to have

97. Asser, ch. 56, trans. Keynes and Lapidge, pp. 84–85.
98. *ASC* s.a. 880.
99. Keynes and Lapidge, trans., pp. 171–2.
100. See R.H.C. Davis, 'Alfred and Guthrum's frontier', *EHR* 97 (1982) pp. 803–10, reprinted in Davis, *From Alfred the Great to Stephen* (London, 1991) pp. 47–54. David Dumville makes a bold, but ultimately unpersuasive, attempt to redraw the frontier by having it run eastward from the source of the Thames. This would place western Mercia under Guthrum's rule and Essex under Alfred's. D.N. Dumville, 'The treaty of Alfred and Guthrum', in *Wessex and England from Alfred to Edgar* (Woodbridge, 1992) pp. 1–28.

control over London and its mints, at least for the time being. The disposition of Essex, held by West Saxon kings since the days of Egbert, is unclear from the treaty, though, given Alfred's political and military superiority, it would have been surprising if he had conceded any disputed territory to his godson.

Alfred's dealings with Guthrum after Edington, like his payment of danegeld after Wilton, find an echo in ninth-century Francia. Carolingian rulers ordinarily required conversion before they would ally themselves with viking chieftains.[101] When in 826 the exiled Danish king, Harald Klak, sought aid from Louis the Pious in the recovery of his kingdom, the emperor agreed only on condition that his pagan suppliant convert, because (in the words of St Anskar's biographer, Rimbert): 'there would then be a more intimate friendship between them, and a Christian people would more readily come to his aid and the aid of his friends if both peoples were worshippers of the same God'.[102] Harald was baptized with his wife in Louis's palace at Ingelheim. 'Then', according to Louis's biographer, Thegan, 'the Emperor gave him a large part of Frisia, and having honoured him with many gifts, he sent him and his messengers away in peace.' Similarly, in 862 Charles the Bald required the viking chieftain, Weland, to accept baptism, along with his family, before accepting his oath of fealty.[103] And in 873, five years before Edington, Charles required conversion from a group of vikings whom he had defeated at Angers who expressed a desire to remain in his territories.[104]

Though Alfred's peace-making strategy in 878 may not have been as innovative as his attempt in 876, it was far more successful. He was now dealing from strength. Alfred had decided to remake his enemy after his own image. With

---

101. Eleanor Searle has some interesting comments about two apparent exceptions to this practice, Lothar I's grant of Walchern to Harald in 841–842, and Charles the Simple's negotiations with the still-pagan Seine vikings in the mid-890s. *Predatory Kinship and the Creation of Norman Power, 840–1066* (Berkeley, 1988) pp. 16, 41–42.

102. Rimbert, *Vita Anscharii*, MGH, SRG, ch. 7; C.H. Robinson, trans., *Anskar the Apostle of the North* (London, 1921) p. 38.

103. *AB* s.a. 862; see discussion at p. 110 above.

104. *AB* s.a. 873. Cf. the conversion of Gotfrid, 'king of the Norsemen', as described by Regino of Prum. *Reginonis abbatis Prumiensis Chronicon*, ed. F. Kurze, MGH, SRG Hannover, 1870) s.a. 882 (pp. 119–120).

his baptism the Danish sea-king, Guthrum, had been reborn; renamed 'Æthelstan', he was now Alfred's adoptive son, much as Alfred had been the spiritual son of Pope Leo IV. The ceremonies at Aller and Wedmore were intended to impress Guthrum and enmesh him in webs of obligation and dependency. By standing sponsor at the baptism, Alfred was asserting his political as well as spiritual superiority over his new adoptive son.[105] The rich gifts that he showered upon Guthrum and his followers were freely given and freely accepted, in pointed contrast to the previous payments of tribute. Alfred was now the ring-giver, the open-handed lord, and Guthrum the grateful – and subordinate – recipient of largesse.

Alfred had not only received Guthrum to God but had welcomed him into the political community of English rulers. This is clearly reflected in the treaty between the two kings. Although the frontiers established by this treaty may have collapsed within a decade,[106] the document is nonetheless interesting for the light it sheds on Alfred's relationship with Guthrum after Wedmore. Its prologue establishes the tone: 'This is the peace which King Alfred and King Guthrum and the councillors of all the English race and all the people who are in East Anglia have all agreed on and confirmed with oaths, for themselves and for their subjects, both for the living and for the unborn, who care to have God's favour or ours.' The language is that of traditional Anglo-Saxon law, emphasizing oaths and the favour of God. The agreement that follows defines the social classes of Danish East Anglia in terms equivalent to those of Wessex, so that redress and compensation for crimes could be offered. It also attempts to minimize opportunities for conflict by regulating movement and commerce between the two kingdoms. The Guthrum of this treaty is no longer the sea-raider of the summer army of 871.

The numismatic evidence underscores Alfred's success in acculturating his enemy to the Anglo-Saxon political culture. The Danes lacked a tradition of minting coins, and the vikings who settled in Britain and Ireland seem to have been unfamiliar with the use of coin *per se*. The large,

105. Keynes and Lapidge, *Alfred the Great*, p. 249.
106. R.H.C. Davis, 'Alfred and Guthrum's Frontier'.

well-regulated coinages of pennies and halfpennies struck in the Danelaw at the end of the ninth century suggest that the new Anglo-Danish rulers quickly learned the value of a monetary system. Guthrum was the earliest to adopt this attribute of kingship. Between 880 and 890 he issued a series of Two-line coins under his baptismal name, Æthelstan. The coin type was not only based on a West Saxon issue, but some of Guthrum's coins were minted by moneyers who also struck for Alfred. There is even evidence that the two kings shared a mint.[107]

One cannot assess how seriously Guthrum regarded his conversion. Pope Formosus, for one, had his doubts. In a letter to the bishops of England sometime between 891 and 896, he excoriated the English clergy, even threatening them with 'the sword of anathema', for their dismal failure to combat 'the rites of the abominable pagans' (*nefandorum ritus paganorum*) that were again flourishing on their island.[108] Whatever 'abominable rites' he may still have practised, Guthrum's use of his baptismal name on his coinage implies that he at least wished to be thought of as a Christian king. By the mid-890s the most popular coinage in the southern Danelaw was the St Edmund's penny, commemorating a king martyred by the fathers of those who proclaimed his sanctity upon their coins. The power of the Anglo-Saxon

---

107. Grierson and Blackburn, *Medieval European Coinage*, I, p. 318. See further M.A.S. Blackburn, 'The Ashdon (Essex) Hoard and the currency of the southern Danelaw in the late ninth century', *The British Numismatic Journal* 59 (1990 for 1989) pp. 13–38, and his 'The earliest Anglo-Viking coinage of the southern Danelaw (late 9th century)', *Proceedings of the 10th International Congress of Numismatics*, ed. I.A. Carradice (London, 1990 for 1986) pp. 341–8.

108. *EHD* I, no. 227 (pp. 890–2). The Danish settlement of East Anglia and Northumbria profoundly and permanently disrupted the pre-Viking ecclesiastical organization of these regions. F.M. Stenton, *Anglo-Saxon England*, 3rd edn (Oxford, 1971) pp. 433–8. But cf. D.M. Hadley, ' "And they proceeded to plough and to support themselves": the Scandinavian settlement of England', *Anglo-Norman England* 19 (1997) pp. 76–80, 89–92. The churches of East Anglia preserved their landed endowment far better than did those of Northumbria or eastern Mercia. In 1066 the Church held between a fifth and a third of all land in East Anglia and what had been Greater Wessex and western Mercia, and less than a tenth in the rest of the Danelaw. R. Fleming, 'Monastic lands and England's defence in the Viking Age', *EHR* 100 (1985) p. 249.

model of kingship is demonstrated in the widespread minting of 'Alfred' coins throughout the Danelaw at the beginning of the tenth century.[109] This does not mean that the vikings of Northumbria accepted even the theoretical overlordship of West Saxon kings, any more than Offa's imitation Arabic coins meant that he recognized the superiority of the Caliph. But it does indicate the integration of the victorious viking chieftains into an Anglo-Saxon Christian culture and an adoption of the conquered people's concept of rulership. Guthrum and other Danish chieftains in Britain did not abandon their Scandinavian identity, any more than Kublai Khan did his Mongol heritage when he adopted a Chinese dynastic name and assumed the trappings of his Chin and Sung predecessors. Nonetheless, for their own purposes, viking 'sea-kings' aspired to possess the powers and authority of Anglo-Saxon rulers. The acculturation of the vikings to the political culture of their erstwhile English enemies is far from historically unique. The Romans, after all, created 'German' political tribes with which they could deal,[110] and European colonial powers reshaped traditional African chieftainship and redefined traditional concepts of property in the late nineteenth century in order to have kings with which a 'civilized' power could deal and contract treaties.[111] 'Civilizing' entailed not only the creation of stable political units, but the Christianization of the native populace, to provide a common cultural ground upon which to deal.

In retrospect, Alfred's victory at Edington is one of the few truly decisive battle of the English Middle Ages. But in 879/880 Alfred must have appreciated how near he had come to having lost his kingdom and life. He had won a

109. Grierson and Blackburn, *Medieval European Coinage*, I, pp. 315–20.
110. P.J. Geary, *Before France and Germany: The Creation and Transformation of the Merovingian World* (New York, 1988) pp. vi–viii, 39–75. See also E. James, *The Franks* (Oxford, 1988) p. 163.
111. T. Ranger, 'European attitudes and African realities: the rise and fall of the Matola chiefs of south-east Tanzania', *Journal of African History* 20 (1979) pp. 63–8; A.E. Afigbo, 'The Establishment of Colonial Rule, 1900–1918', in J.F. Ade Ajayi and M. Crowder, eds, *History of West Africa*, 2 vols. (New York, 1976) II, pp. 424–83; T. Ranger, 'The Invention of Tradition in Colonial Africa', in E. Hobsbawm and T. Ranger, eds, *The Invention of Tradition* (London, 1983) pp. 211–62, esp. 220–36.

respite, but this did not wipe out the memory of his desperate flight into the Somerset marshes. He could not rely upon the existing military system of Wessex to counter the continuing threat offered by the Danes. Nor could he rest content with the impoverished spiritual and cultural condition of his kingdom, which, to his mind, had brought down God's wrath upon it. If he and his kingdom were to survive – and be worthy of survival – Alfred would have to innovate. And over the next two decades innovate he did.

Chapter 5

KING OF THE ANGLO-SAXONS, 880–891

Simply to defend Wessex against its enemies did not satisfy Alfred's ambitions. Whatever the image he chose to project in his writings and translations, Alfred in practice was a traditional West Saxon king, motivated by thoughts of earthly glory as much as hope of heaven. Like his grandfather and father before him, Alfred sought to enhance the prestige of his house by extending his power and influence over his neighbours. In the 880s he had the opportunity to do so. In a decade of war and mayhem, the Great Heathen Army had permanently altered the political world of the Anglo-Saxons by extinguishing and replacing all but one of the native English royal lines south of the Tyne. Alfred took advantage of the power vacuum created by King Burgred's flight to Rome and Ceolwulf II's death to bring the magnates of western Mercia under his lordship. To underscore the significance of their submission, he assumed a new and unheard-of royal style: king of the 'Anglo-Saxons'. Alfred secured his dominion over the Mercians by marrying his daughter to their most powerful ealdorman, Æthelred, to whom he entrusted the governance of Mercia.

Alfred's hard-won *rapprochement* with Guthrum raised almost as many political questions as it answered. Would the Danes be content with East Anglia? Could Alfred trust Guthrum/Æthelstan to remain loyal to his godfather or to curb the ambitions of his viking followers? Who would rule in western Mercia now that Ceolwulf II had lost his patron and throne? And closer to home, how could Alfred secure the loyalty of his own subjects and prevent a recurrence of the events of the winter of 877/878? In finding answers to these questions, Alfred reshaped the political order of Wessex and its neighbours.

. . .

AN IMPERFECT PEACE

Despite the formal ceremonies of Aller and Wedmore, Alfred's peace with Guthrum was, at best, imperfect. What Alfred, and perhaps Guthrum, hoped to achieve was a stable political situation in which West Saxons and East Anglian Danes might be able to trade with one another and co-operate in the apprehension and punishment of criminals.[1] Alfred undoubtedly also hoped to exercise authority over the man whom he had defeated in battle and accepted as godson. If he ever did, it was only briefly. Edington had preserved Wessex and, to a large extent, tamed Guthrum by absorbing him within the political community, but it did not preclude raiding by foreign vikings, abetted, on occasion, by opportunistic East Anglian Danes. To some the distinction between this 'peace' of the 880s and the era of war that had preceded it was a fine one. The anonymous translator of Orosius may have had such faint-hearted souls in mind when he declared it 'exceedingly disgraceful to us that we complain about what we now call war, when strangers and foreigners come upon us, despoil us a little and then, soon after, leave again; and we are unwilling to think upon what it was like when no one could even purchase his life from another'.[2]

Throughout the 880s, foreign raiders occasionally descended upon the shores of Wessex, Sussex, Kent and Essex, though the damage they inflicted was generally local and minor. To the Chronicler, writing around 892, they were little more than an irritant, hardly worthy of attention. His eyes were fixed, rather, on vikings abroad, whose rampages through northern and northeastern Francia he obsessively followed. *He* knew the difference between war and peace. Still, his relative silence should not mislead us. Though Alfred's and his ealdormen's forays against viking marauders

1. The concerns most evident in Alfred's treaty with Guthrum. F.L. Attenborough, ed., *The Laws of the Earliest English Kings* (Cambridge, 1922) pp. 98–101; *EHD* I, no. 34.
2. *Old English Orosius*, ed. Bately, III.11, p. 83 (and comment on p. xcii).

170

went largely unrecorded, this does not mean that raiding had ceased or that Alfred suffered his kingdom to be despoiled, even 'a little', without taking action. If not for a casual remark in the dating element of a charter, we would not know, for instance, that Alfred campaigned near Epsom in Surrey in 882.[3] Even major military events of the period are shrouded in uncertainty. A number of the recensions of the *Chronicle* mention in passing a successful siege of London conducted by Alfred in 883,[4] but do not explain who Alfred was besieging in London or what provoked him to take military action. One cannot even be certain that such a siege really did occur in 883, since the annal itself might be a misplaced and garbled allusion to events that took place three years later. The 880s were probably filled with many small-scale actions against elusive raiders, but we will never know for certain.

The Chronicler's reporting of military actions in Wessex in the 880s is not only patchy but idiosyncratic. What he chose to include or omit may have had less to do with historical significance than with his personal knowledge of the event or Alfred's interest in it. Though Alfred's expedition to Surrey in 882 went unnoticed, another minor military action in that year drew his rapt attention:

> King Alfred went out with ships to sea and fought against four crews of Danish men, and captured two of the ships – and the men were killed who were on them, and two crews surrendered to him. And they had great losses in killed or wounded before they surrendered.[5]

What made the skirmish worthy of note was that Alfred presided over the slaughter in person. What made it even more remarkable was that it took place at sea. A naval battle, even a small one, was rare enough to warrant comment, especially given Alfred's own demonstrated interest in such matters. The *Chronicle* records only four sea battles for the entire ninth century, and three of these involved Alfred. Late in his reign, Alfred would even try his hand at ship design – with, one might add, decidedly mixed results.[6] To

---

3. S 345 (which, however, survives only in a corrupt twelfth-century copy).
4. *ASC* s.a. 883 B,C,D,E (but not A). See below, p. 175.
5. *ASC* s.a. 882A; *EHD* I, p. 197.
6. See pp. 304–6 below.

judge by the few examples we have, the battle of 882 was typical of the naval warfare of the day. Alfred's eldest brother, Æthelstan, and Ealdorman Ealhhere of Kent commanded a fleet in 851 that 'slew a great army . . . and captured nine ships' off the coast of Sandwich.[7] Alfred himself had fought the Danes once before at sea. In the summer of 875, he had engaged a fleet of seven ships, capturing one and driving off the rest. His victory in 882 was more decisive; not only did he capture all four enemy vessels but his men slaughtered most of their crews.

The blood-letting through which Alfred achieved victory was a consequence of the nature of naval warfare during this period. Ninth-century warships were troop transports that differed from merchant vessels only in their speed and handling. Unlike Greek triremes or modern battleships, they were not weapon systems designed to disable or sink other vessels. As a result, a battle at sea differed little from one on land; in both a premium was placed on hand-to-hand combat. As the enemy fleets approached one another, the crews would exchange volleys of arrows and other missiles. This was the prelude to the real work, which began when the ships drew side by side and were lashed together so that the warriors could board and kill at will. A battle was won when the enemy surrendered or had too few men left to row away.[8] Fighting of this sort could only take place in calm waters, and the site of Alfred's naval victories of 875 and 882, though not located by the Chronicler, must have been in the coastal waters of Wessex, perhaps even in an estuary.

The four ships that Alfred intercepted and captured in 882 hardly constituted a major threat. The army of seasoned viking warriors which descended upon Rochester in 885 was a different matter. Since 880 such men had been wreaking devastation over much of northern Francia in what is now Belgium and the Netherlands. After wintering in Amiens in 884, the main viking army divided into two bands. One headed east to Louvain; the other chose to try their fortunes on the English side of the Channel. Entering the Medway, they attacked Rochester, but were unable to take the town by storm because of the stubborn resistance of its

7. *ASC* s.a. 851.
8. See P. Griffith, *The Viking Art of War* (London, 1995) pp. 196–202.

citizenry. In what was almost a dry run for the celebrated siege of Paris in the following year, the vikings encamped opposite the entrance to the town and fortified their own position with ramparts and ditches.

Alfred reacted quickly to the threat, hurriedly marching east with a large force gathered from Wessex in relief of the town. The suddenness of Alfred's approach caught the Danes by surprise. Alfred seized their fortifications and even captured their horses and prisoners. Some of the vikings made it back to their ships and set sail for Francia. Others, however, stayed behind and came to terms with Alfred. As in the past, hostages and oaths failed to bind the vikings, who twice that year raided the region bordering the southern banks of the Thames.[9] For the Danes settled in East Anglia this was too good an opportunity to pass up. Blatantly violating their peace with Alfred, an army from East Anglia marched south into Essex. At Benfleet, just north of the Thames estuary, the two viking forces met and made camp. The situation was potentially disastrous, as Alfred was forced to contemplate the possibility of an invasion up the Thames and into the West Saxon heartland. Fortunately for Alfred, the allies could not agree among themselves. The invasion force dissolved as a 'ghastly commotion' (*lurido motu*) broke out between the factions.[10] The East Anglians returned home. The others sailed back to Francia to rejoin their comrades.

The reaction of the East Anglians underscored the fragility of the peace between Alfred and Guthrum. He had hoped to bind the viking leader through personal affiliation and spiritual bonds. Now he decided to remind the Danes of East Anglia that he could deliver blows as well as gifts. Alfred sent a naval force from Kent to harry and plunder East Anglia.[11] As soon as it entered the mouth of the Stour, Alfred's fleet encountered sixteen viking ships. In the savage fighting that ensued, the Kentishmen captured all the enemy ships, killed their crews and seized their booty. The victory proved transitory. On that same day, a large Danish fleet, hastily assembled 'from everywhere', intercepted and

---

9. Æthelweard's copy of the *Chronicle* includes information left out of the surviving recensions. See *Chronicon*, ed. A. Campbell pp. 44–5. Cf. *ASC* s.a. 885; Asser, ch. 66.

10. Æthelweard, *Chronicon*, ed. Campbell, p. 45.

11. Asser, ch. 67; *ASC* s.a. 885.

defeated the English fleet as it turned homeward with its plunder.

The sudden appearance of a viking army in Kent in 885 and the equally unforeseen support they received from their East Anglian compatriots underscored the continuing military vulnerability of Wessex. By 885 Alfred had probably already initiated a massive military building programme designed to refurbish existing defences and construct new ones along the kingdom's major arteries. Rochester could not have so successfully resisted such a determined siege unless its defences had been previously put into order. Still, the events of 885, especially the defeat of his fleet, must have heightened Alfred's concerns about the security of his kingdom.

Strategic considerations may explain Alfred's decision in 886 to take possession of London. Alfred undoubtedly appreciated that a fortified London, especially one with defences on both banks of the river, could prevent viking fleets from using the Thames to gain access to Wessex and discourage raiding expeditions across the southeastern frontier with East Anglia. Alfred's interest in the Mercian city was long-standing. Given London's later prominence, it is surprising how little we know about its history in the 870s and early 880s. What evidence we have suggests that the city changed hands a number of times, beginning in 871/872 when the Danes wintered there after their withdrawal from Wessex. The army stayed in London long enough to intimidate the Mercians into paying them an immense ransom. Their sojourn may have been less disruptive than one might otherwise think, since the city's population at the time was concentrated along the Strand in the 'Aldwych' (the 'old settlement'), while the vikings probably made their base within the walled Roman city immediately to the east. They did, however, make at least two locals nervous enough to bury their cash near the present-day Waterloo Bridge and Westminster Bridge.[12] The viking army marched back north in

12. R. Cowie and R. Whytehead, 'Lundenwic: the archaeological evidence for middle Saxon London', *Antiquity* 63 (1989) pp. 706–18; A. Vince, *Saxon London: An Archaeological Investigation* (London, 1990) pp. 13–22, 81–5; N.P. Brooks and J.A. Graham-Campbell, 'Reflections on the Viking-age silver hoard from Croydon, Surrey', in M.A.S. Blackburn, ed., *Anglo-Saxon Monetary History. Essays in Memory of Michael Dolley* (Leicester, 1986) p. 106.

the following year, but whether they evacuated their strong-hold in London is unclear. Ceolwulf II presumably retained control over London even after the partition of Mercia in 877. Unsurprisingly, London moneyers issued coins in Ceolwulf's name. Some of the same men, however, also struck for Alfred in the late 870s and, perhaps, 880s, a confusing situation that led two prominent numismatists to conclude that London was a sort of 'open city' before 886.[13] This might explain how, as we have already seen, a viking band from the continent managed in 879 to establish a base on the Thames in an episcopal palace at Fulham, a few kilometres upriver from London, until driven off by the return of Guthrum to claim his kingdom of East Anglia in the following year. If the B recension of the *Anglo-Saxon Chronicle* is to be believed, Alfred successfully besieged the city in 883, and it is quite possible that Alfred took the city on more than one occasion.

How Alfred came into possession of the city in 886 is not at all certain. The *Anglo-Saxon Chronicle* simply reports that he occupied (*gesette*) the city. Asser, on the other hand, says that it was 'after the burning of cities and the massacre of peoples', implying that it represented the culmination of a larger military campaign.[14] The evidence is inconclusive. In 886, however, Alfred came to stay. For once, Asser did not exaggerate when he declared that 'Alfred, king of the Anglo-Saxons, restored the city of London splendidly . . . and made it habitable again.'[15] The most significant aspect of Alfred's 'restoration' now appears to have been the removal of London's population from the 'Aldwych' on the Strand to the deserted Roman walled city, previously the haunt of viking

13. R.H.M. Dolley and C.E. Blunt, 'The chronology of the coins of Ælfred the Great', *Anglo-Saxon Coins: Studies Presented to F.M. Stenton on the Occasion of his 80th Birthday, 17 May 1960*, ed. R.H.M. Dolley (London, 1961) p. 81. For Alfred's possible authority in London before 886, see S.D. Keynes, 'King Alfred and the Mercians', and M.A.S. Blackburn, 'The London mint during the reign of Alfred the Great', in M.A.S. Blackburn and D.N. Dumville, eds, *Kings, Currency and Alliances: The History and Coinage of Southern England, AD 840–900* (Woodbridge, forthcoming).
14. *ASC* s.a. 886; Asser, ch. 83.
15. Asser, ch. 83, trans. Keynes and Lapidge, pp. 97–8. I would like to thank John Clark, Curator, Early London History and Collection, Museum of London, for his guidance and insights.

raiders. The reoccupation of Roman London entailed what amounted to the creation of a new planned town (see Fig. 1, p. 358). The Alfredian burh lay between Cheapside and the Thames. The settlement area, much of it still unoccupied at Alfred's death, was defined by an ambitious grid of streets that extended a thousand metres from east to west and three hundred from south to north.[16]

What made the events of 886 so significant was not only that Alfred took control of London but that he used the occasion to redefine the nature of his kingship and relationship with the Mercians. Alfred's entry into London, a city which had long been under Mercian rule, was followed by a formal submission of 'all the English people who were not under subjection to the Danes' to his lordship. The king of the West Saxons had become king of the Angles and Saxons.

Guthrum, for his part, was to live only four more years. He died in 890, two years before the arrival of a second Great Army revived unpleasant memories of his past exploits. His death was recorded in the *Anglo-Saxon Chronicle* in language that reminded its reader not only of what Guthrum had been but of what he had become because of Alfred: 'And the northern king, Guthrum, whose baptismal name was Æthelstan, died. He was King Alfred's godson, and he lived in East Anglia and was the first [of the Danes] to settle that land.'[17] Though Alfred's dealings with his viking godson had at times been stormy, overall he could take satisfaction in having achieved the transformation of a heathen viking raider into what could pass for a Christian king.

. . .

DOMESTIC AND FOREIGN RELATIONS

Even an unquiet peace had its dividends. No longer engaged in a desperate fight for survival, Alfred could turn his attention toward pressing matters at home and abroad. The *Chronicle*, with its narrow focus upon Alfred's holy war against the

16. See A. Vince, *Saxon London.* See further pp. 215–16 below.
17. *ASC* s.a. 890.

heathen vikings, pays remarkably little attention to Alfred's consolidation of power within Wessex and his moves to extend his authority over the magnates of 'English' Mercia and the kings of Wales. Fortunately, Asser and the few surviving charters of the period provide some insight into Alfred's concerns and activities during these years. Between 880 and 892, Alfred would regain through persuasion much of what his grandfather, Egbert, had seized by force of arms. But Alfred, creative as always, would not look to the past to describe his accomplishments. Rather, he and the international coterie of scholars he gathered for his court would devise a new conception of kingship that transcended the narrow tribal identifications of earlier days, a sort of political analogue to Bede's vision of an 'English' race united in Christ.

Alfred's most pressing concern in the early 880s was to re-establish his authority within the kingdom. Given our meagre sources for this period, how he accomplished this must remain conjecture. One might reasonably assume that he undertook a triumphant progress through the realm, especially in the southeast. (The sources are conspicuously silent about what transpired in Essex, Kent, Surrey and Sussex while Alfred was fighting for his life and throne in the west.) Justice, good lordship and self-preservation also dictated that he make close inquiry into the behaviour of his nobles during the crisis, in order to reward the faithful and punish the disloyal. Guthrum's success in the winter of 877 had led to the defection of a number of West Saxon noblemen. Even though Alfred prided himself on his Christian mercy, his forbearance did not extend to traitors. (Christ Himself, he would later write, refused pardon to those who had betrayed Him.[18]) But who fell and who rose to replace them is impossible to ascertain. The *Anglo-Saxon Chronicle*, unlike the Frankish chronicles of the period, is discreetly silent about court intrigues, and Asser was committed to a portrayal of his hero that would admit no disaffection amongst his subjects.

The witness lists of the surviving charters indicate that the composition of Alfred's court changed greatly during this period, though the charters themselves shed little light on

18. *Alfred* Preface. 49.7; 4; 4§2. See discussion pp. 249–50 below.

the whys and wherefores.[19] Ealdorman Wulfhere, as we have seen, was among those who paid for their treason with the loss of office and land. The sources name no others, but the changes in personnel in the office of ealdorman around 877/878 are striking. Seven of the twelve ealdormen who attested Alfred's charters before 879 cease to appear in witness lists thereafter. The most prominent were Cuthred of Hampshire, Ælfstan of Dorset, Eadwulf, Mucel and Wulfhere, all of whom had been leading members of King Æthelred's entourage. Another familiar name that vanishes is that of the king's thegn, Milred, a fixture in the West Saxon court since the 840s. Eight new ealdormen appear in West Saxon charters issued in the decade after Edington. We are less well informed about the West Saxon episcopacy. The only see that we can be sure changed hands around 877 was that of Winchester. Whether by reason of disgrace, death in battle, or the natural ravages of time, the composition of Alfred's *witan* changed dramatically after 878. This development represented a shift in moral authority from counsellors to king. The old guard had been great men even before Alfred had achieved the throne. Indeed, they had helped make him king. Matters stood differently with the new men; he had made *them*.

The loyalty of the great was the foundation of a ninth-century king's power. Even though Alfred's victory brought him prestige and wealth, it did not alter the fundamental character of West Saxon politics. Every *ætheling* was throne-worthy. The greatest domestic threat to the peace of the realm was likely to come from the king's own kinsmen, as they jostled for supporters and followers in what passed for ninth-century electioneering. Alfred had been fortunate that his nephews were young children when their father, King Æthelred, died in 871, or matters might have turned out

19. Only eight credible 'Alfredian' charters survive for the period 879–889, all in later medieval copies: S 352, 321, 345, 346, 217, 218, 219, 220 (the last four are Mercian issues). Some of these may be forged, while others contain scribal errors or 'improvements'. The only charter that may shed direct light on Alfred's meting out of justice to the disloyal is, oddly, a charter of Edward the Elder, dated 901, S 362 (*EHD* I, no. 100, p. 542), which refers to Ealdorman Wulfhere's 'desertion of both his lord King Alfred and his country'. See p. 152 above.

quite differently for him. Not everyone rejoiced in Alfred's good fortune. Æthelred's two sons, in particular, had reason to be resentful. In the mid-880s and 890s the *æthelings* and their supporters were complaining sufficiently loudly about what they perceived to be Alfred's high-handed disregard of his nephews' rights to their inheritance to provoke Alfred into responding. He summoned a meeting of the West Saxon *witan* at *Langandene* (perhaps in Devonshire) to answer his nephews' charges and prove his right to the disputed property.

What we know of the meeting comes from Alfred's will, a rather tendentious document that was intended not only to record Alfred's wishes concerning the disposition of his personal property but to demonstrate to the world that he had dealt with his nephews in a fair and proper manner.[20] At the time of the assembly, most probably in the mid-880s, Æthelhelm and Æthelwold were at least adolescents.[21] Though they posed little immediate threat to Alfred's continued rule, their accusations had a political dimension. What was at stake was not only the king's reputation for probity, but his and his sons' control over wealth and land. The *æthelings* and their supporters undoubtedly looked forward to the inevitable contest for succession that would break out upon Alfred's death. By shaming Alfred into handing over the lands they claimed, Æthelhelm and Æthelwold thought to obtain resources to reward followers, while depriving their cousins of the same. The assembly at *Langandene* was Alfred's response, a publicly staged display of the king's rectitude and of the love and loyalty borne him by his subjects. After King Æthelwulf's will had been read to the assembly, Alfred asked his councillors to judge the dispute, pledging that he would bear no ill will against any one of them for speaking the truth. 'None should hesitate', he told them, 'for love or fear of me, to declare what is right by custom [*folcriht*] in such a case, lest any man should say that I had wronged my young kinsmen, whether the older or the younger. Then they all

20. S 1507, in *SEHD* no. 11, pp. 17, 50, trans. Keynes and Lapidge, pp. 174–8.
21. The possible dates are established by the references to Bishop Wærferth, who became bishop of Worcester around 872, and Archbishop Æthelred, who died on 30 June 888. Alfred's bequest to Ealdorman Æthelred implies a date in the 880s. Keynes and Lapidge, p. 313.

duly declared and stated that they could not devise a more just title, nor find one in the will [of King Æthelwulf].'[22] His title to the lands thus established, Alfred then publicly declared his own will. The modesty of Alfred's bequests to his nephews was a clear indication of how they stood with him. The landed wealth he provided for his elder son, Edward – thirteen estates in the western half of the kingdom, two in Surrey, and all Alfred's bookland in Kent – meant that he would have the wherewithal to contend for the throne. Alfred's younger son, Æthelweard, was also provided for generously. Whether motivated by fear or love or simply a sense of justice, the magnates had stood firmly behind their king. For the time being, the crisis had passed.

The one ealdorman singled out for special attention in Alfred's will was a Mercian, Æthelred, to whom the king bequeathed a sword worth 100 mancuses. Though he only bore the title ealdorman, Æthelred was the effective ruler of what was left of Mercia. As such, he was central to Alfred's plans to bring western Mercia under his authority. It would be surprising if Alfred did not aspire to rule the Mercians. Alfred was, in some ways, a very traditional ninth-century nobleman, brought up to believe that the measure of a good king was success in war, generosity in gift-giving and the extension of rule over neighbouring folk. His grandfather and father had transformed Wessex into a great power at the expense of the Mercians. Alfred had the opportunity to enhance his prestige and that of his house by completing their work. The recent history of friendship between the kingdoms and the marriage ties that united his house to the Mercian nobility dictated the approach. There would be no second *Ellendun*. As Æthelwulf had obtained Berkshire for Wessex by offering friendship, aid and his daughter's hand in marriage to King Burgred, so Alfred would win for himself that part of Mercia that still remained in English hands.

That the Danes' client king, Ceolwulf II, turned out to be Mercia's last native ruler may have been due, at least in part, to Alfred. When Ceolwulf died or was deposed around 879/880, the ealdormen and bishops of 'English' (that is, western) Mercia failed to elect a successor. Instead, they entrusted the power, though not the title, of king to one of their number,

22. Ibid, pp. 174–8.

Ealdorman Æthelred. Æthelred is somewhat of a mysterious character. If he was the king's thegn of that name who attested charters of King Burgred and Bishop Wærferth between 866 and 872 (though not Ceolwulf's two surviving charters),[23] his rise to power was nothing short of meteoric. To judge by the first element of his name, he may have claimed royal blood and kinship to several other Mercian ealdormen, including perhaps Alfred's father-in-law, Æthelred 'Mucel', and his brother-in-law, Æthelwulf, the latter apparently one of the new men in Æthelred's court in the mid-880s.[24] Æthelred's *witan* was a mixture of old and new. Not only did he share bishops with Ceolwulf but at least two ealdormen.[25] The greatest change came at the lower levels of court society, among the king's thegns. Ceolwulf's men simply disappear from attestation lists along with their master.

The anomalous, quasi-regal status enjoyed by Ealdorman Æthelred presented a challenge to the Mercian clerics who drew up his charters in 883 and 884. They were forced into impressive circumlocutions in order to define his authority. For one he was 'Ealdorman Æthelred, by the inspiration of God's grace endowed and enriched with a portion of the realm of the Mercians'; for another, he was 'by the gift of divine grace raised to the rule and lordship [*principatu & dominio*] of the Mercian people'.[26] This is the language of regality; only the title 'rex' is lacking. It is understandable why some later writers, notably the late tenth-century chronicler, Ealdorman Æthelweard, would have supplied what was so obviously missing from their sources.[27] Yet Æthelred had not been chosen king. Why the Mercians opted for an interregnum is a matter for speculation, but Alfred in 879/880 was certainly in a good position to meddle. As the conqueror of their conquerors, he was a feared and respected

---

23. S 212, 214, 1278. Keynes, 'King Alfred and the Mercians'.
24. S 219, 220, 1442.
25. Beorhtnoth and Æthelwold: S 215 and 216 (Ceolwulf); cf. 218 and 219 (Æthelred).
26. S 218, 219. Keynes, 'King Alfred and the Mercians'.
27. Æthelweard, *Chronicon*, ed. Campbell p. 49. Æthelred is the last 'king' in a late tenth-century or eleventh-century Mercian regnal list; *Hemingi Chartularium ecclesiae Wigorniensis*, ed. Thomas Hearne, 2 vols (London, 1723) I, p. 242. Keynes, 'King Alfred and the Mercians', suggests that Æthelred may have been briefly regarded as king before his submission to Alfred.

neighbour. As grateful or fearful as they may have been, the Mercian nobility were not yet ready to renounce their ancient freedom and entrust what remained of their kingdom to a West Saxon. But if Alfred lacked the support necessary to take the Mercian throne for himself, his power was sufficient to discourage others from doing so against his wishes. Alfred had reason to believe that the Mercians, weakened by the loss of their eastern territories, would eventually turn to him for patronage and protection, especially if there was no sitting king to complicate matters. In short, Alfred had an interest in keeping the Mercians kingless. If we cannot prove that he was responsible for the interregnum, it is clear that he profited from it.

Alfred gradually imposed his lordship over Mercia during the 880s. The pivotal moment came with the submission of Ealdorman Æthelred in or before 883.[28] Æthelred may have sought Alfred's lordship even earlier. In 881 the western Mercians were dramatically reminded of their reduced circumstances by the sons of Rhodri Mawr of Gwynedd. The battle of Conwy cost them control over northern Wales and threatened their dominance over the southern Welsh kingdoms.[29] The Mercians had turned to the West Saxons for aid in subduing the Welsh almost thirty years before, and the pact had been sealed by the marriage of King Burgred to King Æthelwulf's daughter. Ealdorman Æthelred, confronted with the pragmatic reality of Mercian weakness and West Saxon strength, came to terms with Alfred, accepting him as his lord. What this entailed is made clear by Asser in a passage describing how the king of Gwynedd, Anarawd ap Rhodri, submitted to Alfred's lordship. There Asser remarked that the Welsh king 'subjected himself with all his people to King Alfred's lordship on the same condition as Æthelred and the Mercians, namely that in every respect he would be obedient to the royal will'.[30] The ritual was formal and solemn, with Æthelred bowing his head to his lord and Alfred placing his hands upon it. To underscore his superiority, Alfred bestowed lavish gifts upon his newly created

28. S 218: 'Ic do mid Æfredes cyninges leafe'.
29. *Annals Cambriæ*, s.a. 877, 880, ed. and trans. J. Morris, *Nennius: British History and the Welsh Annals* (London, 1980) p. 90. W. Davies, *Wales in the Early Middle Ages* (Leicester, 1982) p. 106.
30. Asser, ch. 80, trans. Keynes and Lapidge, p. 96.

dependants, as much to impress onlookers with his generosity and greatness as to enrich the recipients of the largesse. Both parties gained from the transaction. In the technical language of lordship, Æthelred received his lord's 'love, protection and defence' (*amorem, tutelam ac defensionem*). He could now rely upon Alfred's support against domestic rivals who might challenge his primacy.[31] For the Mercians in general, it meant the protection of the most powerful king in the region. In return, Alfred's prestige was enhanced. Perhaps more importantly, he gained control over Mercian foreign policy, obtained an ally for his own military endeavours and secured the northern flank of his kingdom against possible viking incursions along the Thames.

The oath that Æthelred swore to Alfred was much the same as the one Ceolwulf had given to Guthrum. In theory, Æthelred had surrendered himself and his people to his lord's will, promising to regard Alfred's enemies and friends as his own. In practice, Alfred demanded little from Æthelred other than suit in his court and support for his military campaigns. Though Æthelred had formally acknowledged Alfred's superiority, the West Saxon king keenly appreciated how much he needed and relied upon the ealdorman. Æthelred, after all, ruled Mercia in fact if not in name. In an age of personal governance, marriage was among the most powerful tools of diplomacy. Alfred's own marriage had helped secure the friendship between his brother and the Mercian King Burgred. Now Alfred arranged to bind Æthelred to him by bonds of kinship as well as oaths of loyalty. Sometime before 888, Æthelred wedded Alfred's eldest daughter, the teenaged Æthelflæd, who, as Lady of the Mercians, was to prove as formidable a ruler as her brother or father.[32] The marriage honoured Æthelred; it also indebted him even further to his father-in-law.

31. Asser, ch. 81, ed. Stevenson, p. 67. A disaffected Mercian *ætheling*, Brihtsige, son of Beornoth, died in 903 fighting for Alfred's rebellious nephew, Æthelwold, and the Danes against Alfred's son and successor, Edward the Elder. *ASC* s.a. 903.

32. She first attests a charter alongside her husband in 888 (S 220). Since Alfred married Ealhswith in 868, Æthelflæd could not have wedded before 882/883. The best study of Æthelflæd remains F.T. Wainwright, 'Æthelflæd, Lady of the Mercians', *Scandinavian England*, ed. H.P.R. Finberg (Chichester, 1975) pp. 305–24.

As befitted one 'by the inspiration of God's grace endowed and enriched with a portion of the realm of the Mercians', Æthelred enjoyed some of the perquisites of a king. He could grant land or immunities from royal exaction on his own authority without recourse to Alfred.[33] In Alfred's presence, however, Æthelred showed proper respect by seeking his lord's permission.[34] Alfred, without taking the title of king, had in effect obtained control over western Mercia. Whatever the clerics might claim for Æthelred in his charters, the fact was that he answered to and served Alfred. Alfred's understanding of their relationship and of his status within Mercia may be gauged from the combined *witan*s of Wessex and Mercia over which he presided for matters of consequence. When Ealdorman Wulfhere's treason was exposed, Alfred sought judgement from 'all the councillors of the Gewisse [i.e. West Saxons] and of the Mercians'.[35] On such occasions, Alfred came closer to playing the role of king of Mercia than even Æthelred.

Alfred would not take the final step until 886, when he occupied and 'splendidly restored' Mercian London. Alfred apparently regarded it as a turning point in his reign. As we have seen, he celebrated his acquisition of London by receiving the submission of 'all the English people that were not under subjection to the Danes'.[36] The festivities presumably involved a formal, public ceremony of subordination, complete with oaths. Finally, in a grand gesture, Alfred entrusted the city to its natural lord, Ealdorman Æthelred, thus preserving its 'Mercian' identity.

Whatever else the submission at London may have meant, it did not signal the absorption of 'English' Mercia into 'Greater Wessex'. Alfred's political aspirations took him in a different direction, one which owed perhaps more to the influence of Bede than the legacy of Egbert.

Distinguishing himself from his father and brothers, he assumed a new and unheard-of royal style: 'king of the Angles and Saxons' or 'king of the Anglo-Saxons'.[37] On the one

33. S 219.
34. S 218. Cf. 217, 220.
35. S 362; *EHD* I, no. 101 (p. 543). Cf. S 223; *EHD* I, no. 99 (pp. 540–1).
36. *ASC* s.a. 886.
37. Asser, chs 1, 7, 9, 14, 30, 68 (for Ine's, Beorhtric's, Æthelwulf's and Æthelred's styles: 'king of the West Saxons/Saxons'). Cf. chs 1,

hand, it claimed what was obviously true, for Alfred now ruled Anglian Mercians as well as Saxons. On the other hand, it seemed to be groping toward something new and radical, a political expression of Bede's 'English people' united spiritually in Christ. The connection was perhaps not lost upon the late ninth-century Mercian cleric who translated Bede's history into English. Nor upon Alfred himself, who used in his writings the terms *Angelkynn* and *Englisc*, 'England' and 'English', to denote the land and language of a people, and who negotiated a treaty with Guthrum with the advice and consent of the 'councillors of all the English race' (*ealles Angelcynnes witan*).[38] The scholars in Alfred's court, many of them Mercians, shared the king's vision. By focusing on the person of Alfred, Asser and, to a lesser extent, the authors of the *Anglo-Saxon Chronicle* transcended a narrow West Saxon perspective on events. Their characterization of the vikings as 'heathens' had the effect of transforming the West Saxon victory over the Danes into a Christian and 'English' triumph over enemies of God. Asser rammed home the point by dedicating the *Life* to 'Alfred, ruler of all the Christians of the island of Britain, king of the Angles and Saxons'. Whether or not one wishes to call

13, 21, 64, 67, 71, 73, 83 and 87 (where Alfred is described as *rex Angul-Saxonum*). Discussed by Stevenson, *Asser's Life*, pp. 147–52, and Keynes and Lapidge, pp. 227–8. S 346 (AD 889), 347 (AD 891), 348 (AD 892), 354, 355, 356 (the last three undated). Though these charters survive only in late copies, their preservation in the archives of six different monasteries strongly suggests that the royal style is authentically Alfredian. D. Whitelock, 'Some charters in the name of King Alfred', in *Saints, Scholars and Heroes: Studies in Medieval Culture in Honour of Charles W. Jones*, ed. M.H. King and W.M. Stevens, 2 vols (Collegeville, MN, 1979) I, pp. 89–90. Cf. A.P. Smyth, *King Alfred the Great* (Oxford, 1995) pp. 384–91.

38. Preface to *Alfred's Pastoral Care*, ed. Sweet, pp. 2–7 (also in *Sweet's Anglo-Saxon Reader in Prose and Verse*, ed. D. Whitelock (Oxford, 1967) pp. 4–7; trans. *EHD* I, no. 226 (pp. 88–9). *Laws of the Earliest English Kings*, ed. Attenborough, p. 98. See P. Wormald, 'Bede, the *Bretwaldas* and the origins of the *Gens Anglorum*', in P. Wormald, D. Bullough, and R. Collins, eds, *Ideal and Reality in Frankish and Anglo-Saxon Society: Studies Presented to J.M. Wallace-Hadrill* (Oxford, 1983) pp. 103–4, 121; P. Wormald, '*Engla Lond*: the making of an allegiance', *The Journal of Historical Sociology* 7 (1994) pp. 10–15; S. Foot, 'The making of *Angelcynn*: English Identity before the Norman Conquest', *Transactions of the Royal Historical Society*, Sixth Series, 6 (1996) pp. 25–49.

this 'propaganda', it served the contemporary political purpose of justifying Alfred's dominion over 'English' Mercia. As Alfred's obituary in the *Anglo-Saxon Chronicle* put it, he had been 'king over the whole English people except for that part which was under Danish rule'.[39] It is tempting to see this as the birth-announcement for 'England'. But it was not that. Alfred's accomplishment was to lay the groundwork for the *idea* of an English nation. The ancient kingdoms of Wessex and Mercia outlived him into the tenth century, and while Alfred experimented with grander titles, he never completely abandoned the older royal style: king of the West Saxons. Nonetheless, the title 'king of the Anglo-Saxons' was the royal style favoured by Alfred's son and successor, Edward the Elder, whose military successes added the Danes to the kingdom of Angles and Saxons created by his father.[40]

When Asser called his patron 'ruler of all the Christians of the island of Britain' he wrote as one who appreciated that Alfred's dominion extended over Wales as well as Mercia.[41] Politics in ninth-century Wales was as rugged as the terrain. Overcoming the challenge of mountain and dense forest, half a dozen or so petty kings competed bloodily with one another for control over land and resources, while simultaneously trying to fend off the attacks of Irish-based vikings and Mercians.[42] The most powerful and aggressive of the native predators was Anarawd ap Rhodri, ruler of Gwynedd in the extreme northeast. In 881 he and his brothers avenged the death of their father, Rhodri Mawr (the Great), by defeating the Mercians at Conwy. Having secured their

39. *ASC* s.a. 900.
40. S.D. Keynes, 'The West Saxon charters of King Æthelwulf and his sons', *EHR* 109 (1994) pp. 1147–9; Keynes, 'King Alfred and the Mercians'. Ealhswith's commemoration as 'Lady of the English' (*domina Anglorum*) in an early tenth-century metrical calendar may be related to Edward's claim to be king of the Anglo-Saxons. See p. 122 above.
41. Asser, ch. 80; Stevenson, *Asser's Life*, pp. 316–18; D.P. Kirby, 'Northumbria in the reign of Alfred the Great', *Transactions of the Architectural and Archaeological Society of Durham and Northumberland* 11 (1965) pp. 341–2; D.P. Kirby, 'Asser and his Life of King Alfred', *Studia Celtica* 6 (1971) pp. 17–19.
42. J.E. Lloyd, *A History of Wales from the Earliest Times to the Edwardian Conquest*, 2 vols, 3rd edn (London, 1939) I, pp. 324–30; W. Davies, *Wales in the Early Middle Ages*, pp. 90–114.

western frontier, they turned their hungry eyes toward their neighbours to the south. Their intended prey, King Hyfaidd of Dyfed and King Eliseg ap Tewdwr of Brycheiniog, sought the protection of King Alfred. It was a measure of Alfred's prestige that they did so. Wessex was distant, separated from Wales by sea and mountains. The West Saxons had not been directly involved in Welsh affairs since 853, five years after Alfred's birth, when King Æthelwulf had harried Wales on behalf of his allies, the Mercians.[43] But Alfred's warlike reputation (and perhaps the memory of his grandfather's hegemony over southern Wales[44]) drew Hyfaidd and Eliseg to him nonetheless. The same was true for Hywel ap Rhys, king of Glywysing, and Ffernfæl and Brochmæl ap Meurig, the kings of Gwent, though the bogey that drove them to Alfred was Ealdorman Æthelred. All these kings 'petitioned King Alfred of their own accord, in order to obtain lordship and protection from him in the face of their enemies'.[45] This turn of events left Gwynedd isolated and its king apprehensive. Around 885, Anarawd formed an alliance with the Northumbrian Danes but received from it (in Asser's words) 'no good, just injury'. Finally, sometime before 893, he and his brothers submitted to Alfred. They came to Alfred in person and were received with honour. As in his dealings with Guthrum, Alfred used the bonds of spiritual kinship as well as secular lordship to tie Anarawd to him. He accepted the king of Gwynedd as his son from the hands of the bishop who confirmed him, and showered gifts upon him and his entourage. Then Anarawd with all of his followers bowed to Alfred and, like their old enemy, Æthelred, pledged their obedience to him in all things.

Alfred's court, as Asser knew it in the late 880s and early 890s, was swarming with non-West Saxons, Welshmen, Mercians, Franks, Frisians, Irishmen, Bretons and even Scandinavians, all drawn by the king's reputation for generosity.[46] Alfred was sufficiently traditional to desire such a reputation – his friend Bishop Wulfsige knew enough to

43. *ASC* s.a. 853.
44. *ASC* s.a. 830. Egbert, however, has left no trace in the Welsh annals, and it is possible that the Chronicler's account of his reduction of the Welsh 'to humble submission' was influenced by Alfred's activities.
45. Asser, ch. 80, trans. Keynes and Lapidge, p. 96.
46. Asser, ch. 76.

flatter him as 'the greatest treasure-giver of all the kings' he had ever heard of[47] – and to believe that the splendour of a court reflected the majesty of its lord. He lured distinguished scholars from their monasteries and churches in Mercia, Wales and the Continent with lavish gifts and promises of ecclesiastical preferment, and gave employment to Frisian sailors and craftsmen of all races. Merchants and other travellers with good stories to tell found welcome with a king who prided himself on his inquiring mind. The Norwegian, Ohthere, enriched both Alfred and himself with stories of his travels to Hedeby and England, and of his adventures with the exotic Lapps of the distant far north, while a fellow merchant, Wulfstan, an Englishman or perhaps a Frisian, regaled the court with an account of a journey into the Baltic and of the odd customs of the Ests who lived there.[48] Others came to the king by chance. When three Irish holy men, seeking the 'white martyrdom' of exile from their beloved Ireland, washed up on the shores of Cornwall after seven days at sea in an oarless, animal-hide boat, they were immediately taken to see King Alfred, who learned from them of the death of a great Irish scholar, 'Suibhne, son of Máelhumai, anchorite and excellent scribe of Clonmacnoise'.[49] The strange, even providential, appearance of these Irish pilgrims in Alfred's court attracted the notice of the Chronicler, but it was how they arrived, not that they were visitors from distant lands, that was remarkable.

To maintain such a court was expensive. When Alfred, characteristically, systematized his finances by allocating monies for recurring expenditures, he reserved one-sixth of his annual revenues to receive and reward foreigners into

47. Preface by Wulfsige, bishop of Sherborne, to Bishop Wærferth's translation of Gregory's *Dialogues*, trans. Keynes and Lapidge, p. 187.
48. *Old English Orosius*, ed. Bately, I.i, pp. 13–18 (commentary pp. lxxi–lxxii, 179–200); N. Lund, ed., *Two Voyagers at the Court of King Alfred* (New York, 1984). Ohthere calls Alfred 'my lord'. Wulfstan's failure to mention Alfred led Bately to express doubt as to whether he, too, should be connected with Alfred, but most commentators have accepted that he did.
49. *ASC* s.a. 891. *Annals of Ulster* s.a. 890 (for 891). See Keynes and Lapidge, pp. 282–3, nn. 11–14, and Smyth, *King Alfred the Great*, pp. 495–8. Smyth points out that the *Chronicle*'s *Swifneh* is a correct phonetic rendering of Suibhne, suggesting that the author of this annal was present when the Irishmen informed King Alfred of the scholar's death.

his entourage. What Alfred received in return for his lavish spending was a reputation for magnificence and the dignity that it conferred, a transaction that Thorstein Veblen would have well appreciated. And, after Edington, Alfred could afford to play the role of the open-handed lord to the full. As Alfred himself observed, success in war meant prosperity to a king. Alfred's gift-giving, as munificent as it may have been, was more than matched by the fruits of victory, tribute and taxes.

As the composition of his court suggests, Alfred's political horizons reached beyond the shores of Britain. Piety, prestige and pragmatic politics dictated that he, like his father before him, should maintain friendly relations with Rome and Francia. Asser, influenced by Einhard's *Life of Charlemagne*, emphasized Alfred's dealings with distant notables. Alfred, he explained, was in constant communication with kings and prelates 'from the Mediterranean to the farthest limit of Ireland'.[50] Asser himself had seen the letters and gifts Elias, the patriarch of Jerusalem (ca. 879–907), had sent to Alfred. As we have seen, 'Bald's *Leechbook*' contains a set of medical remedies that Elias is said to have sent to King Alfred, perhaps in response to the king's request.[51] Given Alfred's familial connection with Charles the Bald and the interest shown by the Chronicler in Frankish affairs, there is surprisingly little evidence concerning Alfred's dealings with Francia. Of the letters Alfred exchanged with Frankish laymen and prelates, only one has survived, the response of Fulk, archbishop of Reims and abbot of St-Bertin, to Alfred's plea for help in his plans to revive learning and religion within his kingdom.[52] One suspects that the monk chosen, Grimbald, maintained connections with his brethren in St-Bertin, but this cannot be proved. Alfred was certainly in contact with others on the Continent, as evidenced by his recruitment of the Old Saxon scholar, John, and the marriage of his youngest daughter, Ælfthryth, to Count Baldwin II of Flanders sometime between 893 and 899.[53]

50. Asser, ch. 91, trans. Keynes and Lapidge, p. 101.
51. Stevenson, *Asser's Life*, pp. 328–9. See above, p. 99. Elias corresponded with a number of western princes. In 881 he wrote to Charles the Fat for monetary aid to rebuild churches, which may have been the occasion of his correspondence with Alfred.
52. *EHD* I, no. 223. See below, p. 224.
53. Asser, chs 78, 94; Æthelweard, *Chronicon*, p. 2.

Alfred's best-documented embassies were to the Holy See.
The Chronicler records that Alfred in 887, 888, and 890 dispatched legations to Rome bearing 'the alms of the West
Saxons and of King Alfred'.[54] The king's failure to mount an
expedition in 889 warranted comment from the Chronicler,
who, almost apologetically, observed that the king sent two
couriers with letters instead. It seems that Alfred intended to
pay 'Rome-scot' annually. If so, we may see here the origin
(or at least the ancestor) of the famous medieval tax peculiar
to England known as 'Peter's Pence', a render of one penny
from each free household collected by the Church each
year on Peter's Mass Day (1 August) and sent to Rome to be
divided between the pope's personal use and the upkeep of
the 'English quarter' (*schola Anglorum*).[55] It is not surprising
that Alfred, given his childhood experiences, should have
demonstrated his devotion to the papacy with such gifts.
When and why he began the practice, however, is a matter
of debate. Much depends on what one makes of the entry
for 883 in the B,C,D,E recensions of the *Anglo-Saxon Chronicle*:

> Pope Marinus sent some wood of the Cross to King Alfred. And in
> that year Sigehelm and Æthelstan took to Rome the alms which
> King Alfred had promised thither, and also to India[56] to St Thomas
> and St Bartholomew, when the English were encamped against
> the enemy army at London; and there, by the grace of God, their
> prayers were well answered after that promise.

54. *ASC* s.a. 883, 887, 888, 889, 890. The two extant Alfred coins with the
    reverse legend ELIMO[*sina*], 'alms', may be associated with these
    offerings to Rome. R.H.M. Dolley and C.E. Blunt, 'The chronology of
    the coins of Ælfred the Great, 871–899', in R.H.M. Dolley, ed., *Anglo-
    Saxon Coin: Studies Presented to F.M. Stenton on the Occasion of his 80th
    Birthday, 17 May 1960* (London, 1961) pp. 77–8.
55. F. Stenton, *Anglo-Saxon England*, 3rd edn (Oxford, 1971) p. 217 n. 1.
    Attempts have also been made to trace 'Peter's Pence' to Offa and
    Æthelwulf (see Asser, ch. 16), both of whom left personal legacies to
    purchase oil for lamps in St Peter and St Paul. Unlike them, Alfred
    offered the payments on behalf 'of the West Saxons' as well as him-
    self. See Stevenson, *Asser's Life*, pp. 211 n. 2, 243–7. Edmund or Edgar
    may have been responsible for regularizing the Romescot into a penny
    hearth-tax and for making the dioceses responsible for its collection.
    I *Edmund* 2; II *Edgar* 4. See H.R. Loyn, 'Peter's Pence', *Friends of Lam-
    beth Palace Library Annual Report* 1984, pp. 10–29; reprinted in idem,
    *Society and Peoples: Studies in the History of England and Wales ca. 600–
    1200* (London 1992) pp. 241–58.
56. 'Iudea' in B and C.

Unfortunately, these events are missing from MS A, the earliest surviving manuscript of the *Chronicle*, as well as from the accounts given by Asser and Æthelweard. It is therefore unlikely that they were in the lost original. On the other hand, their presence in all the other surviving recensions implies that the additions were made at an early stage in the redaction of the *Chronicle*. Some have concluded from its reference to a siege of London that the events described here originally formed part of the entry for 886, perhaps as marginalia, and were simply inserted in the wrong place. This solution, however, creates problems of its own. Pope Marinus died on 15 May 884. His death notice appears in all versions of the *Chronicle* under 885, where he is credited with having sent Alfred a fragment of the True Cross and other gifts, and with having exempted the English quarter from taxation 'at the request of Alfred, king of the West Saxons'. Whatever else is true, Alfred could not have exchanged letters and gifts with Marinus in 886. Nor is it likely, given the 885 entry, that the Chronicler thought he had.[57] On balance, it is preferable to accept the B, C, D, E texts as they stand and conclude simply that their author, whether a cleric who composed the original *Chronicle* or an early tenth-century scribe improving upon his exemplar, believed that all these events occurred in 883. If he was right, then Alfred's alms-giving to Rome began in 883 as a classic *quid pro quo*. On this view, Pope Marinus granted the English quarter exemption from taxation in return for Alfred's pledge to send alms to Rome on an annual basis. (The promise of alms may have done double duty, acquitting an oath Alfred made while besieging London.) To confirm this agreement, Marinus sent emissaries to England, bearing great gifts, including a fragment of the True Cross. Alfred responded by dispatching Sigehelm, the future ealdorman of Kent, and Æthelstan, presumably one of his court priests, to carry the promised alms to Rome (and beyond).[58]

---

57. Keynes, 'King Alfred and the Mercians'.
58. Ealdorman Sigehelm is the beneficiary of S 350 (AD 898), a Kentish charter that survives in a late ninth- or early tenth-century copy. He became the father-in-law of Edward the Elder. S 1211. Æthelstan may be the Mercian priest of that name mentioned by Asser in ch. 77. An Æthelstan *sacerdos* attests S 350 and a number of Alfred's and Edward's other charters.

The mention of 'India' also requires explanation. The story of a ninth-century delegation to India was popular among nineteenth-century English writers for obvious reasons, inspiring (if that word is not too strong) Wordsworth to announce,

> Though small his kingdom as a spark or gem
> Of Alfred boasts remote Jerusalem,
> And Christian India, through her widespread clime,
> In sacred converse gifts with Alfred shares.[59]

But, as the better Victorian scholars realized, Alfred as a prefigurement of Clive was too good to be true. Though SS Thomas and Bartholomew were indeed associated with India in the early Middle Ages, the term 'India' did not then necessarily mean the subcontinent. Alcuin used it as a synonym for Asia, and there is no reason to believe that the author of the entry for 883 had any better idea where India was. To complicate matters further, the B and C manuscripts of the Chronicle have 'Iudea' instead of 'Indea'. If Sigehelm and Æthelstan did make this trek, the object of their pilgrimage was as likely to have been the church of St Thomas in Edessa as a Christian shrine on the Indian peninsula.[60]

The earliest version of the *Anglo-Saxon Chronicle* probably ended with the annal for 890. That annal's report of the death of Alfred's godson and former viking enemy, Guthrum, made a fitting conclusion to what had been intended as a celebration of the rise of Wessex and of the triumph of King Alfred over the heathen vikings. The Chronicler had established Alfred as lord of 'all the English people that were not under subjection to the Danes'. But the annal of 890 does not end with Guthrum's death but rather with a notice of a Breton victory over a viking army at St-Lô. This is in keeping with the character of the *Chronicle*'s entries for the 880s, with their close attention to the movement and military activities of viking armies on the Continent. The events of 885 had proved, if proof was necessary, that the viking shadow had not yet been lifted from Wessex. The threat remained.

59. William Wordsworth, 'Ecclesiastical Sonnets, no. xxvi: Alfred' (1821–22).
60. Stevenson, *Asser's Life*, pp. 288–9.

It was only a matter of time before the vikings operating on the Continent would tire of throwing themselves against the fortified bridges and defences that Charles the Bald had had built on the Seine and the Loire and rediscover the riches across the Channel. The challenge was to be ready for them.

Chapter 6

THE DEFENCE OF THE REALM

Over the last two decades of his reign, Alfred undertook a radical reorganization of the military institutions of his kingdom, strengthened the West Saxon economy through a policy of monetary reform and urban planning, and strove to win divine favour by resurrecting the literary glories of earlier generations of Anglo-Saxons. Alfred pursued these ambitious programmes to fulfil, as he saw it, his responsibility as king. This justified the heavy demands he made upon his subjects' labour and finances. It even excused the expropriation of strategically located Church lands. Recreating the *fyrd* into a standing army and ringing Wessex with some thirty garrisoned fortified towns were costly endeavours that provoked resistance from noble and peasant alike. Alfred, lacking the institutions of bureaucratic coercion, was forced to persuade and cajole the magnates of his realm to fulfil his vision. It is a testament to his greatness that they did.

.　.　.

MILITARY REFORMS: THE BURGHAL SYSTEM

Alfred had won no more than a respite with his victory at Edington. If the battle highlighted Alfred's ability to inspire and lead troops, the events preceding the engagement illustrated just as dramatically the limitations of the military system Alfred had inherited. It had been shaped by the kind of warfare that prevailed among the kingdoms of early England. Though vikings' objectives were familiar to equally predatory Anglo-Saxon kings, the manner in which they waged war was new and disconcerting. While Anglo-Saxon commanders sought battle, vikings avoided it. As we have seen, their *modus operandi* involved seizing a defensible site, often a royal estate, and fortifying it further with ditches, ramparts and palisades. From that base they would ride through the countryside, plundering as they went. If confronted by a superior military force, they would retreat to their camp. As slight as were its makeshift defences, they nonetheless proved effective against an enemy unfamiliar with siege warfare and saddled with a logistical system designed only for short, decisive campaigns. A besieged viking army would try to outwait the enemy, knowing that once the besieging force exhausted its supplies, it would either have to leave or offer a profitable peace. Or, if the besiegers grew careless, the vikings might burst out suddenly from behind their defences in a furious counter-attack or sneak away under cover of night. Anglo-Saxon commanders often found themselves outmanoeuvred or stalemated. The logistical inadequacies of the existing West Saxon military system were further exacerbated by the manner in which armies were raised. Assembling levies of local landowners and their followers was time-consuming; viking raiders could ravage an entire region before the king's army appeared in the field.

Alfred's flight into the Somerset marshes impressed upon him the need to reorganize the military resources of his kingdom. And this he did. Thirteen years later when the vikings returned in force they found the kingdom defended by a standing, mobile field army and a network of garrisoned fortresses that commanded its navigable rivers and Roman roads. Alfred had analysed the problem and found a solution. If under the existing system he could not assemble forces quickly enough to intercept mobile viking raiders, the obvious answer was to have a standing field force. If this necessitated transforming the West Saxon *fyrd* from a sporadic levy of king's men and their retinues into a mounted standing army, so be it. If his kingdom lacked strong points to impede the progress of an enemy army, he would build them. Characteristically, Alfred's innovations were firmly rooted in traditional West Saxon practice, drawing as they did upon the so-called 'common burdens' of bridge work, fortress repair and service on the king's campaigns that all holders of bookland and royal loanland owed the Crown. Where Alfred revealed his genius was in designing the field force and 'burhs', as these fortified sites were called, to be parts of a coherent military system. Neither Alfred's reformed *fyrd* nor his burhs alone would have afforded a sufficient defence against the vikings. Together, however, they robbed the vikings of their major strategic advantages: surprise and mobility. In the parlance of modern strategic studies, Alfred created a 'defence-in-depth' system.[1]

The transformation of the *fyrd* was an enormous challenge in itself. The king's household had always been, in a sense, a standing army, though its numbers were insufficient for major military actions. Alfred intended to make the rank and file of his army, the landowners and their followers, equally battle-ready. It was one thing to call upon landowners to fight battles as needed, quite another to command them to leave home and family for extended tours of duty upon a regular basis. Only a threat as severe as the viking invasions could have persuaded the nobility of the realm to submit to such radically increased demands. The *Chronicle* describes Alfred's reorganization of the *fyrd* in its entry for 893, and it may not have been until after the vikings returned in the autumn of 892 that Alfred fully imposed the change.

To ensure that the localities continued to be defended and to moderate the demands a standing army made upon the *fyrd*-worthy, Alfred split 'his army into two, so that always half of its men were at home, half on service'.[2] Dividing the *fyrd* into rotating contingents was the only way of guaranteeing continuity of military action. Rather than responding to viking incursions with ad hoc levies which would disband once the crisis had passed, the West Saxons would now always have a force in the field. The *fyrd*-men who waited their turn at home also performed a necessary defensive function. It was essential that some king's thegns and their retainers remain behind to guard their lands and those of their neighbours, if for no other reason than the obvious one that landholders would have been reluctant to leave their estates and families totally undefended. The division of the *fyrd* preserved local administration even in wartime.

1. For this (and for much of what follows) see R. Abels, *Lordship and Military Obligation in Anglo-Saxon England* (Los Angeles and Berkeley, 1988) pp. 58–78.
2. *ASC* s.a. 893.

Since the same men who fought in the king's armies maintained law and order, would-be miscreants were particularly pleased to see them march off. Even with half of the *fyrd*-worthy remaining behind, Alfred still found it prudent to double the fines for housebreaking while the army was on campaign.[3]

The reform of the *fyrd* was revolutionary, and it is well to emphasize that Alfred could find no contemporary model for what he wished to do. Typically, he sought guidance from books. One was the Bible. Asser explicitly compared Alfred to King Solomon, and many of Alfred's innovations and reforms parallel the activities of that king. Some of this may be Asser's doing, but we should not dismiss the possibility that Alfred himself looked to Solomon for inspiration. Alfred learned from Scripture how Solomon in his wisdom had divided his own army into three cohorts, which he sent against the enemy in monthly relays, so that the troops spent two months at home for every month in the field.[4] Alfred followed precisely the same arrangements in managing the court attendance of his landed thegns. 'The king's followers', Asser asserts, 'were sensibly divided into three groups, so that the first group lived at the royal court for one month, performing its duties by day and night; when the month was up and the next group had arrived, the first returned home and spent two months there, each man seeing to his own private affairs.'[5] To apply what worked so well in his household to the *fyrd* would have been eminently practical. Since Alfred divided the army into halves rather than thirds, it is possible that he was influenced by a second ancient book, Orosius's *Seven Books of History against the Pagans*. This early fifth-century Christian history was extraordinarily popular throughout the Middle Ages. Alfred was long credited with having translated the work, but this attribution has been recently disproved through painstaking comparison of the vocabulary and syntax of the *Old English Orosius* with Alfred's authentic translations.[6] Still, the author of the *Orosius* clearly had access to Alfred's court, and it is not unlikely that Alfred

---

3. *Alfred* 40 § 1.
4. I Kings 5:13–14. I owe this suggestion to David Howlett.
5. Asser, ch. 100, trans. Keynes and Lapidge, p. 106.
6. *Old English Orosius*, ed. Bately, pp. lv–lvi, lxxiii–lxxxvi.

himself commissioned the translation. Alfred would have been familiar with Orosius's description of Amazonian military organization. As Orosius explained, the Amazons split their forces into two parts, one of which remained at home to guard their land while the other waged war. The similarity to the 893 annal is striking.[7] Alfred and his advisors may have drawn upon both these precedents when they went about redesigning his army.

Alfred's innovations did not affect the basic make up of the *fyrd*, which remained composed of nobles and their lesser-born followers. He did, however, make greater demands upon the resources of those called to fight. They had always been responsible for arming themselves, though the king's personal followers did so with weapons received as gifts from their royal lord. Now they were also asked to supply horses and sixty days' worth of provisions as well. The latter was a consequence of fighting a defensive war which precluded living off the land. The precedent for the former was anything but biblical. In horsing the *fyrd* Alfred emulated the Danes. As a result his army became as mobile as the enemy they pursued. The *Chronicle* consistently describes Alfred's armies during the 890s as 'riding after the Danes' and at one point reports that the English *fyrd* besieging a viking army in Chester used the crops in the field as fodder for their horses.[8] The 'great horse' of the Middle Ages was unknown to the Anglo-Saxons, and even in the eleventh century the heriot of thegns called for 'palfreys' (in the Domesday Book scribes' terminology) rather than destriers.[9] Nonetheless, horses were valuable animals in ninth-century England, and the warriors who were required to supply them would have found this a novel and expensive demand.

Alfred's mobile field army was designed to act in concert with permanent garrisons that the king had settled in newly constructed or refurbished fortresses. The creation of the burghal system as outlined in the early tenth-century document known as the 'Burghal Hidage' marks a watershed in

7. *Old English Orosius*, ed. Bately, p. 220; C. Plummer, *Two of the Saxon Chronicles Parallel*, 2 vols (Oxford, 1892–9; repr. 1952) II p. 109.
8. *ASC* s.a. 893. On the vikings' use of horses, see J.H. Clapham, 'The horsing of the Danes', *EHD* 25 (1910) pp. 287–93.
9. E.g., *Domesday Book* i. 189 (Cambridge).

the history of Anglo-Saxon governance.[10] Despite formidable obstacles, including noble recalcitrance, Alfred managed
to oversee the construction and maintenance of a network
of some thirty burhs, many of which were designed to be
permanent urban settlements rather than temporary refuges.
The defensive system that Alfred sponsored, and its extension to Mercia under Ealdorman Æthelred and the Lady
Æthelflæd, enabled his kingdom to survive and formed the
basis for the conquest of the Danelaw by his son, Edward,
and grandson, Æthelstan. Alfred's burhs, moreover, were not
merely fortresses. They were designed as centres of trade and
royal administration, islands of royal power through which
the king and his agents, ealdormen, bishops and reeves, were
able to dominate the countryside. In short, Alfred's burghal
system was the most impressive administrative achievement
of his reign and the single most important factor in the survival and future success of his dynasty.

The concept of fortresses was not original to Alfred, though
his burhs were among the first fortified centres established
in Wessex. As we have seen, Charles the Bald in the 860s
had created an analogous system of fortified bridges over
the Loire and the Seine,[11] and the Danes themselves routinely fortified their camps. Nor could Alfred have forgotten
childhood memories of the great walled city that Pope Leo
IV had ordered built to defend St Peter's and the pilgrim
communities of Rome against other raiders from the sea.
Nearer to home were the examples of Mercia and Kent.
Offa of Mercia had imposed the burden of fortress-work
upon those who held bookland and the physical remains of

10. D. Hill, 'The Burghal Hidage: the establishment of a text', *Medieval Archaeology* 13 (1969) pp. 84–92; D. Hill and A.R. Rumble, eds,
The Defence of Wessex: The Burghal Hidage and Anglo-Saxon Fortifications
(Manchester, 1996).
11. In terms of physical characteristics and methods of construction, the
closest Continental analogues are the Carolingian and Ottonian *Burgen*
of the German marches, though these tended to be quite a bit smaller
than Alfred's burhs. The similarities, however, may be due less to
cultural transmission and conscious imitation than a shared environ-
ment and similar threats. See E.J. Schoenfeld, 'Anglo-Saxon *Burhs*
and Continental *Burgen*: Early Medieval Fortifications in Constitutional Perspective', *The Haskins Society Journal* 6 (1995) pp. 49–66, at
pp. 59–60, 65–6.

the building efforts of Offa and his successors suggest that they exacted these dues with rigour. The construction of Offa's Dyke must have consumed millions of hours of conscripted peasant labour,[12] and the ditch and rampart defences at the Mercian royal vills of Hereford and Tamworth thousands more. Not all Mercian administrative centres, however, were fortified. Repton, for instance, was an undefended site until the Danes captured it in 874 and enclosed it with ditches and ramparts. Still, the Mercian kings are to be credited with developing the idea of the three military 'common burdens' and introducing it into neighbouring Kent[13] and Wessex. Offa's son-in-law and ally, King Beorhtric (786–802), was the first West Saxon king to define military services as an obligation of landholding, but it was not until after 850 that reservation of 'fortress-work' became a regular feature of West Saxon charters.[14]

This accords well with the archaeological evidence. Excavators have not, as yet, identified any fortifications that can be safely dated to before Alfred's reign. Middle Saxon Southampton, *Hamwic*, the kingdom's major royal trading centre and largest 'city' throughout the eighth and early ninth centuries, was an undefended site, which may have been one reason for its abandonment in the mid- to late ninth century. Of the Alfredian burhs, Wareham has the best claim to pre-existing defences. Asser's account of the Danish occupation of Wareham in 876 characterizes the place as a *castellum*, 'fort', which may imply that it had acquired its impressive

12. R. Abels, 'English logistics and military administration, 871–1066: the impact of the Viking wars', in A.N. Jørgensen and B.L. Clausen, eds, *Military Aspects of Scandinavian Society in a European Perspective, AD 1–1300. Papers from an International Research Seminar at the Danish National Museum, Copenhagen, 2–4 May 1996*, Publications from the National Museum Studies in Archaeology & History, 2 (Copenhagen, 1997) p. 258, n. 6.

13. Offa imposed 'fortress work and service on campaigns' upon the lands of Kentish churches at the Synod of *Clofesho*. S 134, 1264. N. Brooks, 'The development of military obligations in eighth- and ninth-century England', in P. Clemoes and K. Hughes, eds, *England Before the Conquest: Studies in Primary Sources Presented to Dorothy Whitelock* (Cambridge, 1971) pp. 78–80, 84; Abels, *Lordship and Military Obligation*, pp. 53–7.

14. Alfred's father and brothers reserved 'fortress-work' in their charters. S 267, 467, 496, 507.

ditch and rampart defences by then.[15] Though there were apparently few, if any, fortified towns in Wessex, estates were a different matter. That timber palisades and gates protected the main halls and outlying buildings of major royal centres is clear from the *Chronicle*'s vivid account of the murder of King Cynewulf at *Meretun* in 786. When confronted by the murdered king's thegns, the rebels locked the gates of the royal estate they had seized; the besiegers had to break their way in.[16] Fenced-in dwellings may not have been uncommon in eighth- and ninth-century Wessex. Ine's late seventh- or early eighth-century law-code assesses penalties for the crime of *burgbryce*, literally, breaking into fortified premises, not only of the king, but also bishops, ealdormen and even king's thegns and other landed nobles.[17]

Alfred's scheme was unique in its sheer scale, the strategic disposition and purpose of the burhs, and the administration through which he manned and maintained them. Alfred's intention was not merely to fortify a few towns. He planned the construction of a *network* of burhs, and for this he could find no model in Britain, except perhaps for the ancient Roman forts of the 'Saxon Shore'. Asser, again drawing upon Einhard (and perhaps biblical accounts of Solomon's reign), boasted of the cities and towns that Alfred refurbished and 'of others constructed where previously there were none'.[18] Here, for once, Alfred's accomplishments match, if not exceed, the praise lavished upon him by his faithful servant. Under his direction, some thirty fortified centres of varying sizes were either built or refurbished.[19] In many cases, Alfred restored the defences of Roman cities or reused the sites of Iron Age hill-forts.

15. Asser, ch. 49. Cf. ch. 91 (Stevenson, pp. 78, 331–2). C.A.R. Radford is unpersuaded by the evidence for defences at Wareham in 876. 'The pre-Conquest boroughs of England, ninth to eleventh centuries', *Proceedings of the British Academy* 64 (1978) p. 140. Cf. N. Brooks, 'England in the ninth century: the crucible of defeat', *Transactions of the Royal Historical Society*, 5th ser., 29 (1979) pp. 9, 17.
16. *ASC* s.a. 757.
17. *Ine* 45. Cf. *Alfred* 40 (which modifies the fines and adds a reference to the fenced enclosures of commoners).
18. Asser, ch. 91, trans. Keynes and Lapidge, p. 101.
19. D. Hill, 'Gazetteer of Burghal Hidage sites', in Hill and Rumble, 'Defence of Wessex', pp. 189–228, provides an excellent overview.

Alfred's restoration of Roman London is a prime example. As we have seen, after Alfred's occupation of London in 886, the main London settlement, a trading port extending 'from the Fleet to Whitehall with its axis on the Strand', was abandoned in favour of the walled Roman City.[20] At about the same time, Southwark was built on the southern bank of the Thames opposite the City. Perhaps similar events transpired on a smaller scale on the Southampton peninsula, where the once-thriving, but now virtually abandoned, commercial settlement of *Hamwic* was passed over and the small Roman fort of *Clausentum* at Bitterne, half a kilometre to its northeast, reoccupied.[21] Some of the smaller burhs, notably Hastings, Chichester and Portchester along the southern coast, were also Roman in origin, while others, such as Chisbury, Halwell and Bredy, were reoccupied Iron Age hill-forts.

Alfred also built upon virgin soil. This was the case at Twyneham (now Christchurch), Lyng and Lydford. The regular layout of Wallingford (Berkshire), with its grid of streets, suggests that it too may have been a new foundation (see Fig. 2, p. 359). If so, it reveals the magnitude of Alfred's endeavour, since the burh's forty-one hectares made it the second-largest town in Wessex.[22] Most of the new forts were located near royal estates, evidently to permit the king better control over his strongholds and to consolidate royal administration within a single area. Though some of these royal residences were themselves fortified, many were not. In such cases the new burghal forts protected their commercial and/ or administrative counterparts. Sashes, in Berkshire, on an island in the Thames where the St Albans–Silchester road crossed the river, was a mere half a kilometre east of Cookham, a rich estate and important monastic foundation coveted by

20. B. Hobley, 'Lundenwic and Lundenburh: two cities rediscovered', in R. Hodges and B. Hobley, *The Rebirth of Towns in the West, AD 700–1050* (London, 1988) pp. 73–6. See also A. Vince, *Saxon London: An Archaeological Investigation* (London, 1990) pp. 18–25.
21. J.F. Cherry and R. Hodges, 'The dating of Hamwic: Saxon Southampton reconsidered', *Antiquaries Journal* 58 (1979) pp. 299–309; P. Holdsworth, 'Saxon Southampton', in J. Haslam, ed., *Anglo-Saxon Towns in Southern England* (Chichester, Sussex, 1984) pp. 336–9; A. Morton, *Excavations in Hamwic: Volume 1*, CBA 84 (1992) pp. 70–7.
22. M. Biddle, 'Towns', in D. Wilson, ed., *The Archaeology of Anglo-Saxon England* (1976) pp. 124–34; G. Astill, 'The Towns of Berkshire', in Haslam, *Anglo-Saxon Towns*, pp. 63–4.

Mercian and West Saxon kings.[23] Similarly, Langport defended nearby Somerton (Somerset); Axbridge, the royal palace at Cheddar (Somerset); Pilton, the harbour of Barnstaple (Devon); and Chisbury, Great Bedwyn (Wiltshire), an extensive royal estate within whose boundaries the fort lay.

The burhs listed in the Burghal Hidage were distributed widely throughout the shires of ancient Wessex, Surrey and Sussex, and situated in such a way that no place was more than thirty-two kilometres, a day's march, from a burh.[24] The desire to protect existing centres of royal administration explains the siting of some of the burhs. But Alfred's overriding concern was strategic. It was not by chance that his burhs commanded all the major navigable rivers, estuaries, Roman roads, and trackways crossing or leading into his kingdom (see Map 5, p. 354). A viking fleet rowing up the Thames would encounter no fewer than five burhs in succession: Southwark, Sashes, Wallingford, Oxford and Cricklade.[25] Raiders sailing along the southern coastline of Wessex or the northern shores of Devonshire or Somerset would find few places where they could beach their ships without a fight. The burhs and the *fyrd* formed in practice an integrated system, and it is difficult to believe that Alfred had not intended that from the start. An extensive network of roads

23. N. Brooks, 'The unidentified forts of the Burghal Hidage', *Journal of the Society of Medieval Archaeology* 8 (1964) pp. 74–90 (at 79–81); Astill, 'The Towns of Berkshire', pp. 63–4. See also B. Yorke, *Wessex in the Early Middle Ages* (London, 1995) p. 118.

24. Abels, *Lordship and Military Obligation*, pp. 68–71, 236 nn. 67, 68; idem, 'English logistics', pp. 260–1. On the siting of the burhs and their archaeology, see D. Hinton, *Alfred's Kingdom: Wessex and the South, 800–1500* (London, 1977) pp. 29–58. There are puzzling omissions in the document, notably London and all of Kent. London may have been omitted as a 'Mercian' burh, but why Canterbury and Rochester were not included is difficult to understand.

25. Assuming, of course, that Oxford was one of Alfred's burhs. Oxford lay within Mercia and belonged to Ealdorman Æthelred until his death in 911, when Edward the Elder assumed control over both it and London (*ASC* s.a.). Coins were struck in Alfred's name at Oxford, perhaps as early as the 880s. See M.A.S. Blackburn, 'The London mint during the reign of King Alfred', and S.D. Keynes, 'King Alfred and the Mercians', in M.A.S. Blackburn and D.N. Dumville, eds, *Kings, Currency, and Alliances: The History and Coinage of Southern England, AD 840–900* (Woodbridge, forthcoming). Cf. C.S.S. Lyon, 'Historical problems of Anglo-Saxon coinage (4), the Viking Age', *British Numismatic Journal* 39 (1970) pp. 196–7.

and trackways connected the burhs to one another, making it possible for the garrisons to support one another and to work in tandem with the field force. From Exeter, for example, one could follow Roman roads north to Bath, Malmesbury, Cricklade, or Axbridge, and east to Bridport, Wilton, Winchester and London. Complementing the major thoroughfares were *herepaths*, 'army paths'. Running along the boundaries of estates, the *herepaths* facilitated the assembly of local contingents.[26] If, as seems likely, Alfred used the burhs to store his food rent, his field forces would never be more than a day's march from food and supplies.[27]

Alfred's strategic plan required that the burhs be garrisoned. Not only did this protect them against seizure by enemy forces, but it provided them with an offensive dimension that is too often ignored. Tactically the burhs supplemented the field forces, allowing the latter to pursue the main body of the enemy without exposing the various localities to a secondary attack. The presence of well-garrisoned burhs along the primary travel routes presented a major obstacle for viking invaders. Even if a viking force avoided the English field army and successfully raided the interior, the booty-laden marauders would face borough garrisons as they attempted to return to their ships or strongholds. The viking armies that invaded Kent in 892 discovered just how effective these garrisoned fortresses were in opposing raiders.[28]

To man and maintain thirty burhs, however, was a formidable task that required Alfred to develop a sophisticated and effective administrative system, which is outlined in the text known as the 'Burghal Hidage'.[29] Though in its present form the Burghal Hidage probably postdates 914, it is generally believed that it represents Alfred's original conception for the maintenance of his burhs.[30] The text names

26. E.g., S 229, 255, 272, 334, 345.
27. Yorke, *Wessex*, p. 121.
28. See pp. 294–5 below.
29. Hill, 'Burghal Hidage', pp. 84–92.
30. R.H.C. Davis, 'Alfred and Guthrum's frontier', *EHR* 97 (1982) pp. 807–9, dates it to early 886, immediately before Alfred's occupation of London (through which he explains its omission), but the presence of Buckingham in the list, a double-burh raised by order of Edward the Elder in 914, is damaging to his argument. See discussion by D.N. Dumville, *Wessex and England: From Alfred to Edgar* (Woodbridge, Suffolk, 1992) pp. 24–7.

twenty-nine West Saxon and two Mercian burhs and quotes
the number of hides 'belonging' to each. The meaning of
the latter is made clear in an appendix that relates hidage allotments to the burhs' defensive requirements: 'For
the maintenance and defence of an acre's breadth of wall
[4 poles or 22 yards (20.1 metres)], sixteen hides are required. If every hide is represented by one man, then every
pole [5½ yards (5 metres)] of wall can be manned by four
men.'[31] This equation permits one to calculate on the basis
of its allotted hidage the length of wall belonging to each
burh and the number of men required to man and maintain it. In some cases the correspondence between the actual length of walls and its hidage allocation in the text is
nothing short of remarkable. For Winchester it is almost
exact: the text's 2,400 hides allow 3,017 metres of wall, while
the city's actual Roman walls extend for 3,033 metres. In the
case of some burhs, historians have perhaps made the fit
more exact than it really was.[32] Wareham's 1,600 hides, for
example, allowed for 2,012 metres of wall, which tallies well
against the ramparts that surround the landward sides of
the town, to the north, west and east. It made no provision,
however, for defence along the River Frome, a natural route
for a viking raid, and archaeologists have uncovered no traces
of a rampart or ditch there. The logical inference is that
the assessment of the Burghal Hidage was supplemented by
another, unrecorded obligation. Perhaps the town's two
minsters were to provide the men to guard the river side.[33]
Though there are other exceptions, notably the woefully
inadequate provisions made for Exeter, generally the stated
hidages accord fairly well with actual measurements upon

31. A.J. Robertson, ed., *Anglo-Saxon Charters* (Cambridge, 1956) Appendix II,
   no. 1, pp. 246, 247. For what this meant in practical military terms,
   see B. Bachrach and R. Aris, 'Military technology and garrison organization: some observations on Anglo-Saxon military thinking in light
   of the Burghal Hidage', *Technology and Culture* 31 (1990) pp. 1–17.
32. D. Hill, *An Atlas of Anglo-Saxon England* (Toronto, 1981) fig. 149
   (p. 85); idem, 'The nature of the figures', in Hill and Rumble, eds,
   Defence of Wessex, pp. 82–6. Cf. N. Brooks, 'The administrative background to the Burghal Hidage', in Hill and Rumble, eds, *Defence of
   Wessex*, pp. 129–32.
33. Hinton, *Alfred's Kingdom*, pp. 34–5. As Brooks observes, the bank of
   the River Frome is 'where ship-borne Viking attacks might most be
   expected' ('Administrative background', p. 131).

the ground. Whoever put together the Burghal Hidage had at hand a great deal of factual information about the individual burhs. One cannot help but believe that this document was prepared by royal agents, who based it upon other now lost official administrative records.[34]

The cost of building, maintaining, and garrisoning thirty fortresses while simultaneously keeping a standing army in the field year round drained the resources of the West Saxon landholding class, already suffering from the devastation wrought by Danish incursions and the tribute paid to the enemy during the previous decade. Alfred's new burhs and those that lacked Roman stone walls were defended by outer and inner ditches and earthen ramparts. These ramparts, on the average, were about three metres high and nine to ten metres wide.[35] Even burhs with stone Roman walls required work. Not only did the walls need patching, but the ditches outside the walls had to be recut or replaced. At Winchester an impressive new double ditch was dug and traces of its 8.2 metres wide by 1.7 metres deep outer trench survive. As with Offa's Dyke, dump construction was the rule, though the earthen walls were often reinforced with turf and timber revetments, and, in some cases, crowned with wooden palisades. Construction of Wallingford's 2,800 metres of bank would alone have absorbed more than 120,000 man-hours of labour.

Obviously, Alfred's burhs were major public works. As Asser makes clear, many nobles were reluctant to comply with what must have seemed to them outrageous and unheard-of demands – even if they were for 'the common needs of the kingdom'.[36] In effect, Alfred had regularized and vastly expanded the existing and relatively recent obligation of landowners to provide 'fortress work' on the basis of the hidage

34. Keynes and Lapidge, p. 341; Yorke, *Wessex*, pp. 116–18. Hill suggests that the Burghal Hidage was drawn up some time after 919 to aid King Edward's officials to calculate hidage assessments for the newly created shires of Mercia. 'The calculation and the purpose of the Burghal Hidage', in Hill and Rumble, eds, *Defence of Wessex*, pp. 92–7.
35. C.A.R. Radford, 'The later pre-Conquest boroughs and their defences', *Medieval Archaeology* 14 (1970) pp. 83–103; Biddle, 'Towns', pp. 126–34. Interestingly, to the *Beowulf*-poet a stronghold was an *eorðweall* (earth-wall), ll. 2957, 3090, or an *eorðweard* (earth-guard), l. 2334.
36. Asser, ch. 91, trans. Keynes and Lapidge, pp. 101–2.

assessed upon their lands. The hidage allotments of the Burghal Hidage represent the creation of administrative districts for the support of the burhs. The landowners attached to Wallingford, for example, were responsible for producing and feeding 2,400 men, the number sufficient to maintain 3,017 metres of wall. The larger burhs became centres of territorial districts of considerable size, carved out of the neighbouring countryside to support the towns. In one sense, Alfred conceived nothing truly new. The shires of Wessex went back at least to the reign of Ine, who probably also imposed a hidage assessment upon each for food rents and other services owed the Crown. But it is equally clear that Alfred did not allow the past to bind him. With the advice of his *witan*, he freely reorganized and modified what he had inherited. The result was nothing short of an administrative revolution, a reorganization of the West Saxon shire system to accommodate Alfred's military needs.

On paper, to man and maintain Alfred's thirty burhs would have required 27,071 men. Since the total population of 'Greater' Wessex in 890 could not have much exceeded 450,000, this meant 6 per cent of the kingdom's total population.[37] By comparison, the Prussian military at the height of the Napoleonic Wars absorbed only 4 per cent of that nation's population. To fully man the burhs would have required one out of every four free adult males in Wessex to serve in a garrison – and this does not include Alfred's field army. And since Devonshire was significantly under-assessed in the Burghal Hidage, the burden on the other shires may even have been greater. At a seed grain ratio of 1:2, the true surplus produced by three peasant farmers working nineteen hectares of arable land was needed to feed just one non-agricultural labourer.[38] What Alfred was demanding of his subjects was an extraordinary war effort. That effort, however, ultimately made possible both an expanded civilian economy and a strengthened royal administration.

37. The Domesday Book records 85,963 heads of households and 15,058 (individual) slaves in these shires. My total is based on a generous multiplier of five for each free man. Cf. Brooks, 'England in the ninth century', pp. 18–19.
38. B. Bachrach, 'The cost of castle building: the case of the tower at Lageais, 992–994', in K. Reyerson and F. Powe, eds, *The Medieval Castle: Romance and Reality* (Dubuque, IA, 1984) pp. 51–3, 61.

. . .

BURHS, COINS AND THE ECONOMY

Though created to protect Wessex from viking depredation, the burghal system's most lasting consequence may have been the enhancement of the institutional power of the West Saxon monarchy over its subjects. The maintenance of the burhs reinforced the traditional connection between landowning and military obligation to the Crown. It also regularized these demands. The landed nobility not only formed the backbone of the armies of Alfred, his children, and grandchildren, but were responsible for producing the workforce to maintain burhs, bridges, and probably roads as well. Long after the burhs ceased to be garrisoned, the obligation of landowners to secure labour to refurbish their defences remained. Æthelstan's second law code, issued at Grately, Hampshire, around 930, ordered that every fortress be repaired by a fortnight after Rogation Days (§ 13).[39]

From the beginning, Alfred's burhs had civil as well as purely military functions, and with the successful defence of Wessex and the conquest of the Danelaw by Alfred's son and grandsons, their commercial and governmental aspects came to the fore. The law codes of Edward the Elder and his sons show how central the burhs were to Anglo-Saxon administration and economy in the tenth century, serving as seats of royal justice, sites of royal mints during a period of profound currency reform, sources of royal rent and revenues, and as market towns where trade could be supervised by reeves and milked for profit. Edward the Elder decreed that no man was to buy and sell except in a market town and in the witness of the 'port-reeve or other men of credit who can be trusted'. His son, Æthelstan, made the law more realistic and enforceable by altering the provision to apply only to transactions of goods worth more than twenty pennies.[40] In short, Alfred's towns became in the tenth century islands of royal power through which the king and his agents, ealdormen, bishops and reeves dominated the surrounding countryside. Edward recognized their importance to his regime by placing the image of an elaborate burh

---

39. V *Æthelred* 26 § 1, 27; VI *Æthelred* 32, § 3, 33.
40. *I Edward* 1 § 1; *II Æthelstan* 12.

gate on the reverse of his coins. Alfred left to his successors what he himself had lacked when he ascended the throne: a means of projecting the royal presence throughout the kingdom and an instrument of coercion that could be used to bend, if need be, the nobility to his will.

Related to Alfred's building programme, and in the long run perhaps as significant, were the king's monetary reforms. Almost a thousand of Alfred's coins survive, excavated from various hoards deposited during his reign. They tell a story of increasingly effective central government, especially in the regulation of commerce. King Alfred inherited a strong tradition of royal control over currency. Coins in eighth- and ninth-century England had both symbolic and economic purposes. Like the coins of the early barbarian kingdoms, they were symbolic manifestations of regality. By Alfred's time they also served as true measures of value and a medium of exchange. England was part of a vigorous cross-Channel commercial network in the eighth and in the early ninth century. Since money was needed to facilitate the exchange of prestige goods, royal mints were established at the main ports of entry, London and Canterbury, where foreign currency could be melted down and restruck as local coinage. Coins were also important for domestic transactions. The archaeological investigations of Richard Hodges, among others, suggest that the main activities in royal middle Saxon emporia such as *Hamwic* involved agricultural and craft production for local exchange, which undoubtedly helped to monetarize regional economies.[41] Though viking attacks upon *Hamwic*, London, Dorestad, and other great North Sea emporia in the 840s significantly reduced the volume of cross-Channel trade, the Danish raids paradoxically increased the need for coins, as kings, including Alfred, raised cash to buy off the invaders. This cash, of course, came from the king's subjects, some of whom we know were forced to sell land in order to meet the king's demands.[42]

---

41. R. Hodges, *The Anglo-Saxon Achievement. Archaeology and the beginning of English society* (Ithaca, New York, 1989) pp. 80–92, 136–42, 161–6.
42. *EHD* I, no. 94, p. 532, which relates how Bishop Wærferth was forced to lease an estate belonging to the Church of Worcester in order to raise cash, 'chiefly because of the very pressing affliction and immense tribute of the barbarians, in that same year [872] when pagans stayed in London'.

Numismatists estimate that upwards of fifty million pennies were struck in the name of King Burgred of Mercia (852–874), a mediocre ruler in all other respects, and Alfred himself is said to have produced tens of millions of pennies. Such figures may seem inflated, and some of the assumptions upon which they are based are indeed questionable.[43] Nonetheless, millions of pennies were likely circulating in Alfred's Wessex. The monetary tariffs for injuries in Alfred's law code suggest the importance of cash, though compensation may have often been paid in kind. The same cannot be said for the bequests detailed in Alfred's will. Altogether Alfred distributed 486,000 pennies (nominally valued at £2,000) among various beneficiaries, an astonishing amount of money in terms of its bulk alone, weighing fully a ton,[44] and apparently more cash than Alfred and his treasurers could accurately estimate. After listing all of his monetary legacies, Alfred paused to observe, 'I do not know for certain whether there is so much money, nor do I know whether there is more, though I suspect so.'[45]

Though the 'Grately Code' issued by Alfred's grandson, Æthelstan, contains the earliest English legislation regulating currency, its concern with royal control over moneyers and mints echoes Alfred's monetary policies.[46] Moneyers in the late ninth century were highly esteemed craftsmen, not unlike jewellers. The same London-based moneyers struck coins in the late 870s for Ceolwulf II of Mercia and for King Alfred, and it is questionable whether one should yet classify them as royal servants or even agents. Though the skill

---

43. The sum is based on the maximum production of the known dies, the assumption being that a die would have been used until it was no longer functional. See D. Metcalf, 'The prosperity of North-Western Europe in the Eighth and Ninth Centuries', *Economic History Review*, 2nd series, 20 (1967) p. 355. But, as J.R. Maddicott observes, changes in dies and moneyers associated with an issue of coinage may be explained by 'the frequent disruption of the mint rather than its high productivity' ('Trade, industry and the wealth of King Alfred', *Past and Present* 123 (1989) p. 13).

44. Calculated on the basis of 1.56 grams per penny.

45. Alfred's Will, S. 1507, trans. Keynes and Lapidge, pp. 177, 324.

46. *II Æthelstan* ch. 14, 14.1–2, discussed by M.A.S. Blackburn, 'Mints, burhs, and the Grately Code ch. 14.2', in D. Hill and A.R. Rumble, eds, *The Defence of Wessex: The Burghal Hidage and Anglo-Saxon Fortifications* (Manchester, 1996) pp. 160–75.

and art were theirs, the king and his councillors determined the coins' metallic composition and design. This permitted the circulation of standard issues throughout Wessex and Mercia in the 860s and 870s. More than any English king since Offa, Alfred displayed a keen interest in and willingness to experiment with coinage.[47] When he ascended the throne there were only two mints operating south of the Humber, one in Canterbury and the other in London. They had churned out for his brother, Æthelred I, and for King Burgred of Mercia a severely debased currency with a silver content of just over 20 per cent. At Alfred's death there were eight or nine mints operating in the burhs of Wessex and English Mercia.[48] The pennies they produced were almost pure silver and weighed 1.56 grams as opposed to the 1.3 grams of earlier West Saxon issues. Somehow Alfred had managed to withdraw from circulation the debased coinage and replace it with fine. That he was able to do so is impressive testimony to the authority he enjoyed over his subjects. Without a substantial increase in the availability of silver, Alfred's restoration of the West Saxon penny to fine silver in ca. 875–6 must have entailed a severe contraction of the money supply; it took the silver content of four of Alfred's early *Lunette* type pennies to match the silver content of just one new *Cross-and-Lozenge* type penny.[49]

Central control over the coinage is also reflected in the standardization of its iconography. At least in the first half of his reign, Alfred, like his father, followed the Carolingian practice of 'monetary renovation', periodically withdrawing and replacing old coinage with new. Because the designs were consciously selected and the images upon the coins represented the public 'face' of the king, they have often been regarded as expressions of royal ideology. Issuing laws and minting coins were traditional demonstrations of regality. If Alfred looked to Moses and Christ for his laws, he

---

47. R.H.M. Dolley and C.E. Blunt, 'The chronology of the coins of Ælfred the Great 871–99', in R.H.M. Dolley, ed., *Anglo-Saxon Coins* (London, 1961) pp. 77–95. See also Blackburn, 'The London mint in the reign of Alfred'.

48. Blackburn, 'Mints, burhs', pp. 161–4.

49. See D.M. Metcalf and J.P. Northover, 'Debasement of the coinage in southern England in the age of King Alfred', *Numismatic Chronicle* 145 (1985) pp. 150–76, and the discussion above, pp. 145–6.

turned to the Roman imperial past of Britain for his coins. Roman models underlie the great majority of English coin issues of the eighth and ninth centuries. The coins struck for Alfred's father and brothers and their Mercian contemporaries, however, bore highly stylized (and crude) portraits on the obverse; Alfred's moneyers, in contrast, struck at least three separate types in the late 870s and mid-880s that adhered closely to fourth- and fifth-century Roman prototypes.[50] The transformation of the coinage, the close adherence to Roman originals and improvement in quality of craftsmanship and silver content, is dramatic and perhaps significant. But we need to be careful about reading too much into the Roman iconography of his earlier coins, for Alfred's main issues in the last decade of his reign, when one would expect the iconography of the currency to be at its most 'imperial', abandoned portraiture entirely in favour of text. *Romanitas* was indeed associated with the royal activity of coining, but the image of king as Roman emperor apparently was not essential to Alfred's own understanding of his regality.

Alfred understood the relationship between wealth and effective rule. As a king he could not afford to repudiate wealth as unreservedly as an imprisoned Boethius or a saint such as Augustine, and he consistently changed their pronouncements on the vanities of material possession to reflect the practical necessities of royal governance.[51] For Alfred earthly rule was a divine charge laid upon a ruler, and to fulfil that duty a ruler needed wealth. 'I never greatly delighted in covetousness and the possession of earthly power, nor longed for this authority, but I desired tools and materials to carry out the work I was set to do, which was that I should virtuously and fittingly administer the authority committed to me.'[52] For Alfred the 'tools' and 'materials'

---

50. M.A.S. Blackburn, 'Alfred's vision for the coinage', paper read to the Institute for Historical Research, November 1988, p. 15: 'Presumably one person at Alfred's court was responsible for this, and it may have been he who also supplied the author of the *Chronicle* with the information about the Romans hiding their treasure in the ground recorded in the annal for 418'.

51. See below, pp. 251–2.

52. *Alfred's Boethius*, ed. Sedgefield, ch. 17, pp. 40–1; trans. Sedgefield, p. 41.

of kingship were a land well-peopled with praying men, fighting men and working men, and the land, gifts, weapons, food, ale, clothing and other necessities to support them. Alfred obtained these 'necessities' by war and by managing the economic resources of the Crown. The main sources of his wealth were the profits of the commercial activity and the mints in his burhs, the dues of justice, the tribute he received from client rulers, and, above all, the revenues generated by his private estates and the 'public' lands that belonged to the fisc.

The importance of land to a ninth-century king or noble cannot be exaggerated. Land was power; its possession gave a noble the right to exploit and rule those who dwelled upon it. All royal followers hoped to earn land in the king's service. Above all, a thegn desired bookland to pass on to his heirs. The pressures on a king to enrich his followers with land were immense, especially in times of war when loyalty was at a premium. Though Alfred was by far the wealthiest landowner in Wessex, as is attested by the bequests in his will, it was still not enough. His need to acquire more land to attract and reward warriors drove him to appropriate monastic estates recovered from the vikings, even at the risk of alienating the despoiled churchmen.[53]

Whether Alfred or any ninth-century king was conscious of 'economic trends' or thought in terms of 'economic policy' is doubtful.[54] But Alfred, for practical reasons, took an active role in managing the economic resources of his kingdom. There was nothing new about this. Two centuries before, Ine had issued legislation, that Alfred appended to his own, forbidding landowners to abandon their holdings without first sowing 60 per cent of that land, evincing his concern with production and, in particular, his determination 'that the landscape should be carefully divided between what was cultivated and what was under pasture'.[55] Early English kings also concerned themselves with the activities

---

53. See pp. 244–6 below.
54. R. Balzaretti, 'Debate: trade, industry and the wealth of King Alfred, I', *Past & Present* 135 (1992) pp. 142–3, in response to J.R. Maddicott, 'Trade, industry and the wealth of King Alfred', *Past & Present* 123 (1989) pp. 3–51.
55. *Ine* 64–6; R. Hodges, *Dark Age Economics: The Origins of Towns and Trade AD 600–1000* (New York, 1982) p. 136.

of traders. If a trader planned to travel into the West Saxon interior, we are told in Ine's laws, he was to buy and sell only in the presence of witnesses. Alfred went further, decreeing that would-be traders were to bring before a king's reeve at a public meeting all the men whom they planned to take with them up-country. The point, as the law makes clear, was to establish accountability. A trader was to be responsible for bringing to justice any of his men who committed a crime.[56] This had less to do with regulating commerce than with royal concerns about justice and good order. It was often difficult to distinguish between a company of traders and a band of marauders, a lesson that the unfortunate West Saxon royal reeve who first encountered vikings learned firsthand.[57] Traders, almost by definition, were rootless men lacking kinsmen and lords to vouch for their good character. As such they presented problems for a justice system that depended upon local reputation and personal affiliations. Like gypsies of a later age, they were welcomed for the exotic wares they plied, but regarded with suspicion and mistrust by the locals, who probably counted their livestock and children when they heard that merchants had arrived in the neighbourhood. Nor was this simply xenophobia. Foreign traders were in an ideal position to rustle cattle and dispose of the goods before anyone was the wiser.[58] But if traders were to be watched carefully by the king's agents, they were also to be protected. This was done not only to foster commerce but as a matter of royal dignity. Foreigners were guests of the king and under his protection.[59]

Ine's impact upon the commercial development of Wessex went far beyond supervising and protecting foreign merchants. By establishing the emporium of *Hamwic*, he revolutionized the economy of Wessex.[60] Archaeologists and

---

56. *Ine* 25; *Alfred* 34.
57. See above p. 103. The final clause of the treaty that Alfred made with Guthrum specified that if either a Dane or an Englishman wished to cross the border to trade in cattle and other goods, he was to give hostages as security that no treachery was intended. *Alfred and Guthrum* 5.
58. *Ine* 25 § 1.
59. *Ine* 23. Cf. *Alfred* 30, which stipulates that the king is to receive half the wergeld if a man without kinsmen is slain. The other half is to go to his 'associates' (*gegildan*).
60. R. Hodges, *The Anglo-Saxon Achievement: Archaeology & the Beginnings of English Society* (Ithaca, N.Y., 1989) pp. 85–6, 192–3.

historians agree that *Hamwic* was a carefully planned royal foundation, with a population that had been deliberately resettled there from the countryside. The expenses that Ine incurred in moving gravel and people were more than repaid by the foreign prestige goods that *Hamwic*'s markets attracted, and by the link that Ine now had to the Continent. Ine and his successors also profited financially from the economic activity that went on in *Hamwic*. As Barbara Yorke observes, 'there is little sign of personal wealth amongst the inhabitants of Hamwic, which could suggest that much of the profits was going into other (royal) coffers'.[61] Alfred's town-building proved to be another watershed in the economic development of southern England. By the time Alfred came to the throne, viking activity had all but destroyed the vigorous cross-Channel trade of the late eighth and the early ninth century, and even Alfred's military victories could not reverse the decline of *Hamwic* and its trading partners in northern Francia. Rather, Alfred's burh-building, whether he intended it or not, resulted in the creation of a domestic commercial network based on a ranked hierarchy of markets.[62]

The excavations of archaeologists have transformed our understanding of the Alfredian burhs. The organization of internal space within Alfred's burhs was as carefully planned out as their defences. The grid-like street plans of the larger towns show a remarkable consistency. The pattern Martin Biddle discovered at Winchester – a principal thoroughfare, the High Street, sometimes paralleled by back streets on either side, with regularly spaced side streets at right angles to the High Street, and a 'wall street' running along the defences – is found not only in 'Roman' burhs but in Alfred's new foundations at Wareham, Wallingford, Cricklade, and Oxford.[63]

The same is true of London. Over the last decade, the researches of archaeologists, numismatists, and historians have deepened our understanding of Alfred's London and

61. B. Yorke, *Wessex in the Early Middle Ages*, Studies in the Early History of Britain Series, N. Brooks, gen. ed. (London, 1995) p. 307.
62. Hodges, *Anglo-Saxon Achievement*, p. 156.
63. M. Biddle, 'Towns,' in D.M. Wilson, ed., *The Archaeology of Anglo-Saxon England* (London, 1976) pp. 129–30. The essays in J. Haslam, ed., *Anglo-Saxon Towns in Southern England* (Chichester, Sussex, 1984) provide an excellent overview of the archaeology of Alfred's burhs.

of the king's own contribution to its development.[64] Alfred's 'refurbished' London was a planned town laid out within the walls of the old, deserted Roman city (see Fig. 1, p. 358). Two charters are of critical importance for understanding the economic development of the burh. Both concern an estate in the vicinity of Queenhithe, then known as *Æthelredes hid* (wharf), after Alfred's son-in-law, the ealdorman to whom Alfred had entrusted the care of the city. The earlier charter, dated 889, records a grant made jointly by Alfred, 'king of the Anglo-Saxons', and Æthelred, 'under-ruler (*subregulus*) and patrician of the Mercians', to Bishop Wærferth of Worcester of an enclosure in an stone building called *Hwætmundes stan*, along with the privilege of holding a market there with full rights to the profits. The later is the abstract of a lost memorandum from a council held at Chelsea in 898/899, at which Alfred and his *witan* discussed measures for the restoration (*instauratio*) of London. One of the decisions was to confirm Bishop Wærferth in his holding and to allocate a neighbouring plot along the Thames to Archbishop Plegmund. Both prelates were accorded the privilege of mooring boats along their property.[65]

That Alfred promoted commerce in his burhs is not surprising. To survive, these towns had to be economically viable. Alfred was also aware of the profits that he and his ealdormen could derive from urban markets and mints, and of the patronage that they could distribute in the form of privileges and exemptions from taxes and tolls.[66] Alfred's economic pragmatism even led him to abandon the practice of periodic recoinage in the late 880s, at a time when his power to control his coinage was at its height. As the numismatist Michael Dolley suggests, this was a 'characteristically imaginative response to changing circumstances', namely

---

64. G. Milne, 'King Alfred's plan for London?', *London Archaeologist* 6 (1990) pp. 206–7. I would like to thank John Clark, Curator (Medieval) Early London History and Collection, Museum of London, for his guidance and his insights about early London.

65. S 346 and S 1628. See T. Dyson, 'Two Saxon grants for Queenhithe', in J. Bird, H. Chapman and J. Clark, eds, *Collectanea Londiniensia*, London & Middlesex Archaeological Society Special Paper 2 (1978) pp. 200–15; idem, 'King Alfred and the restoration of London', *The London Journal* 15 (1990) pp. 99–110; A. Vince, *Saxon London: An Archaeological Investigation* (London, 1990) pp. 20–2.

66. See, e.g., S 223 (*EHD* I, no. 99, pp. 540–1).

the establishment of Scandinavian kingdoms in East Anglia and Northumbria. By abandoning the policy of renewal of the currency, Alfred encouraged the acceptance of viking-struck imitations of his various coin types. This, in turn, facilitated trade across Watling Street.[67] It may be stretching the point to credit Alfred with initiating the 'First English Industrial Revolution' – even if, archaeologically, 'the pre-eminent feature of the large burhs is the great range of craft production' found in them.[68] What is certain is that he was instrumental in creating the preconditions for the emergence of an English market economy in the follow-ing century. Alfred's burhs became centres of industry and commerce because he planned that they should be. Alfred appreciated, as a practical matter, the importance of redu-cing the risks and costs of commercial transactions.[69] Behind the safety of ramparts and walls, craftsmen and merchants could go about their business under the watchful eyes of a 'port-reeve', creating wealth for themselves and for their king. Burhs and coins testify to Alfred's achievements as king no less than his military and political accomplishments. All these were consequences of Alfred's ability to govern effectively and of his skill at binding his subjects to his will.

Whether Alfred intended it or not, he had begun a pro-cess that was to result in a unified kingdom of England ruled by an effective, if demanding, central authority. Before the end of Alfred's reign, his daughter, Æthelflæd, and her husband, Ealdorman Æthelred, had begun to build burhs on Mercian soil. One interesting charter explains that the Ealdorman and his Lady, at the urging of 'Bishop Wærferth their friend', ordered fortifications to be built at Worcester 'for the protection of all the people, and also to exalt the praise of God therein'. At a meeting of the Mercian witan over which King Alfred presided, Æthelred and Æthelflæd came to an agreement with the church of St Peter whereby

---

67. M. Dolley, 'Ælfred the Great's abandonment of the concept of peri-odic recoinage', in C.N.L. Brooke, B.H.I.H. Steward, J.G. Pollard and T.R. Volk, eds, *Studies in Numismatic Method Presented to Philip Grierson* (Cambridge, 1983) pp. 153–60.
68. Hodges, *The Anglo-Saxon Achievement*, p. 160.
69. S.R.H. Jones, 'Transaction costs, institutional change, and the emer-gence of a market economy in later Anglo-Saxon England', *Economic History Review* 41 (1993) pp. 658–71, at p. 670

the couple would receive the monks' prayers and the church would get 'half of all the rights which belong to their lordship, whether in the market or in the street, both within the fortification and outside', except for payments on the carting of salt, which were to remain with the king. The bishop and church undoubtedly earned these privileges by bearing much of the financial burden for construction of the ramparts.

The system that Alfred had created for the defence of Wessex became a tool for conquest and territorial consolidation after his death. Each stage of the conquest of the Danelaw by Edward the Elder, Ealdorman Æthelred and the Lady Æthelflæd was marked by the construction and manning of burhs. And like the burhs of Wessex, these new towns became centres for royal administration and commerce in the Midland shires. By the mid-tenth century, a burh was defined more by its mint and its market than by its ramparts. The burhs, in some ways, became the armature for the new kingdom that emerged in the tenth century. Though the specific military demands that Alfred and his children made upon their subjects were allowed to lapse either during the halcyon reign of Alfred's great-grandson, Edgar the Peaceable (959–975), or the troubled years that followed it, the habit of bureaucracy that he, his son and grandsons fostered was to shape royal governance to 1066 and beyond.

Chapter 7

THE REIGN OF SOLOMON

The hard-won victory of Edington secured an imperfect peace. While intermittent small-scale viking raids continued for years to come, Alfred enjoyed for the first time a breathing space in which to implement necessary reforms. Alfred undertook not only an ambitious programme of construction and conscription, but a systemic overhaul of religious and educational life. The latter, to his mind, supported the military defence of the kingdom as directly as did the system of fortified towns he created. The initial success of the Great Heathen Army, he was certain, had been punishment for the moral failings of the English people.[1] Repentance and reform were as urgent priorities to Alfred as a stronger standing army.

The images of Alfred as the dutiful, pious and thoughtful Christian ruler and the victorious warrior king extending his rule over neighbouring peoples are not incompatible. Alfred aspired to be both. In 877/878 Alfred had been forced into the role of the fugitive David, emerging from his wasteland refuge to defeat the enemies of Israel and God. Now he had the opportunity to emulate Solomon, 'who', as Asser observed, 'once upon a time, having come to despise all renown and wealth of this world, sought wisdom from God, and thereby achieved both (namely, wisdom and renown in this world)'.[2] Alfred's programme, as he enunciated it in the Preface to his translation of Pope Gregory the Great's *Pastoral Care*, was to restore to 'the English race' (*Angelcynn*)

---

1. As implied in his Prose Preface to his translation of Gregory the Great's *Pastoral Care*. ed. Sweet, pp. 2–5. Cf. *AB*, s.a. 839.
2. Asser, ch. 76, trans. Keynes and Lapidge, p. 92.

the happy times when God-fearing kings not only maintained peace, morality and rule at home but extended their territory abroad, prospering in both 'warfare and wisdom'.[3]

. . .

THE ALFREDIAN RENAISSANCE

In the 880s, at the same time as he was 'cajoling and threatening' his nobles to build and man the burhs, Alfred undertook an equally ambitious effort to revive learning. It entailed the recruitment of clerical scholars from Mercia, Wales and abroad to enhance the tenor of the court and of the episcopacy; the establishment of a court school to educate his own children and those of his nobles; an attempt to require literacy in those who held offices of authority; a series of translations into the vernacular of Latin works the king deemed 'most necessary for all men to know'; the compilation of a chronicle detailing the rise of Alfred's kingdom and house; and the issuance of a law code that presented the West Saxons as a new people of Israel and their king as a just and divinely inspired law-giver.

This enterprise was to Alfred's mind as essential for the defence of his realm as the building of the burhs. As Alfred observed in the preface to his translation of Gregory the Great's *Pastoral Care*, kings who fail to obey their divine duty to promote learning can expect earthly punishments to befall their people. The pursuit of wisdom, he assured the readers of his *Boethius*, was the surest path to power: 'Study Wisdom, then, and, when you have learned it, condemn it not, for I tell you that by its means you may without fail attain to power, yea, even though not desiring it.'[4] The portrayal of the West Saxon resistance to the vikings by Asser and the Chronicler as a Christian holy war was more than mere rhetoric or 'propaganda'. It reflected Alfred's own belief in a doctrine of divine rewards and punishments rooted in a vision of a hierarchical Christian world-order in which God is the Lord to whom kings owe obedience and through

---

3. *Alfred's Pastoral Care*, ed. Sweet, Preface, pp. 2, 3.
4. *Alfred's Boethius*, ed. Sedgefield, ch. 16, p. 35; Sedgefield, trans. p. 35. The sentiment expressed is 'Solomonic'. Cf. I Kings 3:10–14; Prov. 8:21; Wisdom 7:11–14).

whom they derive their authority over their followers.[5] The need to persuade his nobles to undertake work for the 'common good' led Alfred and his court scholars to strengthen and deepen the conception of Christian kingship that he had inherited by building upon the legacy of earlier kings such as Offa as well as clerical writers such as Bede, Alcuin and the other luminaries of the Carolingian renaissance. This was not a cynical use of religion to manipulate his subjects into obedience, but an intrinsic element in Alfred's world-view. He believed, as did other kings in ninth-century England and Francia, that God had entrusted him with the spiritual as well as physical welfare of his people. If the Christian faith fell into ruin in his kingdom, if the clergy were too ignorant to understand the Latin words they butchered in their offices and liturgies, if the ancient monasteries and collegiate churches lay deserted out of indifference, he was answerable before God, as Josiah had been. Alfred's ultimate responsibility was the pastoral care of his people.

These were the practical concerns that spurred Alfred to devote time, energy and resources to his project. But there was also a more private and personal reason. Alfred loved learning. He possessed an inquiring intellect that found solace and enjoyment in wrestling with philosophical and theological questions. 'I can not find anything better in man', he declared, 'than that he know, and nothing worse than that he be ignorant.'[6] Perfect wisdom, Alfred acknowledged, was an impossibility in this life. But to yearn for and strive after wisdom brought rewards in this life and the next. 'It is not to be supposed', Alfred declared, 'that all men have like wisdom in Heaven. For everyone has it in the measure which he here merited. As he toils better here and better yearns after wisdom and righteousness, so has he more of it there, and likewise more honour, and more glory.'[7] Although Alfred found refuge from the toils and pains of this world in study, he was far too much the king to hide from his responsibilities

---

5. The view was shared by the Carolingians, and was ultimately derived from the Old Testament. See, e.g., 2 Kings 22–23, on the reign of Josiah. See discussion below, pp. 250–2.
6. *Alfred's Soliloquies*, ed. Carnicelli, p. 84; trans. Hargrove, p. 36. Smyth's discussion of Alfred's intellectual temperament is sensitive and insightful: A.P. Smyth, *King Alfred the Great* (Oxford, 1995) pp. 567–602.
7. *Alfred's Soliloquies*, ed. Carnicelli, p. 96; trans. Hargrove, p. 43.

in some ivory tower of ideas. Like Plato's philosopher-king, Alfred believed that it was his duty to share his wisdom with his subjects. 'When I rise aloft with these my servants', he has Wisdom say to Mind in his *Boethius*,

> we look down upon the storms of this world, even as the eagle does when he soars in stormy weather above the clouds where no storms can harm him. So would I have you, Mind, come up with us if you so desire, on condition that you return again with us to help good men.[8]

Alfred took to heart Pope Gregory the Great's ideal that a ruler (*rector*) must be a teacher of virtue, and, perhaps influenced by Alcuin's teachings, added that it was the duty of those to whom a king delegated authority to learn and practise wisdom.[9] Alfred's ultimate goal was nothing short of a religious revival.

We do not know just when Alfred began to contemplate a programme of educational renewal, but it was probably sometime in the early 880s when he began to assemble in his court a coterie of scholars gathered from neighbouring kingdoms in Britain and from the Continent. Dissatisfied with the condition of learning in his kingdom and with his own early education, Alfred avidly sought scholars from neighbouring Mercia, holding out promises of 'honours and offices of authority'. Among those who accepted his patronage were Wærferth, bishop of Worcester; Plegmund, whom Alfred would later appoint archbishop of Canterbury; and the mass-priests Æthelstan and Wærwulf.[10] Whether or not by conscious design, Alfred's enlistment of the aid of prominent Mercian clerics for his programme of religious reform and his appointment of them to ecclesiastical office in Wessex complemented his cultivation of Ealdorman Æthelred and the Mercian lay establishment in furthering his political aspirations north of the Thames. The very notion of a kingdom of the 'Anglo-Saxons' may have originated with the Mercian clerics of Alfred's court, to whom the king was more than merely the hereditary ruler of the West Saxons.

---

8. *Alfred's Boethius*, ed. Sedgefield, ch. 7, p. 18; trans. Sedgefield, p. 15.
9. Asser, ch. 106. For Alcuin's conception of a Christian king as a *doctor* of the faith, see J.M. Wallace-Hadrill, *Early Germanic Kingship* (Oxford, 1971) pp. 100–08.
10. Asser, ch. 77.

Alfred turned to the Celtic west as well, summoning Asser to his court from the community of St David's in the kingdom of Dyfed. How the king had come to hear of Asser's scholarly accomplishments is unknown, though it is possible that Asser was a member of the embassy King Hyfaidd sent to Alfred to seek his lordship and protection. Asser explains in detail how Alfred wooed him, and how he insisted upon obtaining the permission of his community before accepting the king's offers.[11] As we have seen, the story shares the same general outlines as that told about Alcuin's entry into Charlemagne's service in the anonymous ninth-century Frankish *Life of Alcuin*, and perhaps intentionally so.[12] What comes through clearly are Alfred's methods of persuasion. The courtship ritual entailed commands, flattery, cajoling letters, and a stream of material rewards – not only gifts of monasteries with their lands and people, but 'worldly riches of all kinds'. (Asser mentions 'an extremely valuable silk cloak and a quantity of incense weighing as much as a stout man', which clearly impressed him, even if Alfred pooh-poohed them as mere 'trifles'.[13]) Much like a modern corporate head hunter, Alfred was willing to spend for talent.

Charlemagne, a century before, had looked overseas to the educational traditions of Britain, in particular, to the Church of York, to restore religion and learning in his kingdom. The efforts of Alcuin and his lesser-known countryman, Cathwulf, helped shape not only the Carolingian renaissance but the conception of kingship that runs through Charlemagne's and his successors' capitularies. Alfred, perhaps in emulation, also reached across the Channel for scholars and clerics to adorn his court and help him fulfil his spiritual and educational endeavours. He filled his new monastic foundation at Athelney with men 'of the Gaulish race' and placed over them a German priest and monk, John the Old Saxon, whose 'habitually sharp mind' and 'experience in the military arts' proved invaluable when the abbot was forced to fight off two would-be assassins hired by a disaffected priest and a deacon.[14] Around 886, Alfred negotiated with Archbishop Fulk of Rheims and abbot of St-Bertin in Flanders for the

11. Asser, chs 79, 81.
12. See above pp. 10–12.
13. Asser, ch. 81, trans. Keynes and Lapidge, p. 97.
14. Asser, chs 94–7.

services of Grimbald, a priest and monk of St-Bertin whose scholarly reputation had reached the king's ears. Only Archbishop Fulk's response survives, but the tenor of Alfred's appeal is clear from the prelate's letter.[15] Alfred, it appears, had requested Grimbald by name 'to superintend the administration of pastoral care' and sent an embassy of noblemen and distinguished clerics to fetch him. The petition emphasized the military success that Alfred had enjoyed in their common struggle against the pagans. Having safeguarded the peace of his kingdom 'with warlike weapons and divine support', Alfred now sought 'to increase the dignity of the ecclesiastical order with spiritual weapons'. As he was to do in the preface to the *Pastoral Care,* Alfred lamented that the Christian faith had fallen into near-ruin in his kingdom due to the onslaught of pagans and the lassitude of the native English. In a clever metaphoric gesture, he sent to Fulk hunting dogs to guard the flock of St Remigius against wolves, and asked from the archbishop in return a spiritual dog to drive away 'the savage wolves of the impure spirits who threaten and devour our souls'. The purpose of the archbishop's letter was to remind Alfred how great a favour he had done for him by parting with so beloved and valuable an assistant 'in every ecclesiastical concern', and to encourage the king to fulfil his promise to elevate Grimbald to the episcopacy, a rank he surely would have achieved in his own homeland. As it happened, Grimbald did not become a bishop, supposedly declining the see of Canterbury in favour of Plegmund when it fell vacant in 888, and instead contenting himself with a small monastery of his own in Winchester.[16] Grimbald took his place at court as the king's mass-priest and exercised an enormous influence on the course of the Alfredian renaissance. Grimbald's hand may

15. J. Nelson, '". . . *sicut olim gens Francorum . . . nunc gens Anglorum*": Fulk's letter to Alfred revisited', in J. Roberts and J.L. Nelson with M. Godden, eds, *Alfred the Wise. Studies in Honour of Janet Bately on the Occasion of her Sixty-Fifth Birthday* (Cambridge, 1997) pp. 135–44. Cf. Smyth, *King Alfred the Great,* pp. 257–9. The letter is translated and discussed by Keynes and Lapidge, pp. 182–6, 331–3.
16. P. Grierson, 'Grimbald of St-Bertin', *EHR* 55 (1940) pp. 529–61. For the possibility that Alfred planned to make Grimbald abbot of what was to be the New Minster, see S.D. Keynes, *The Liber Vitae of the New Minster and Hyde Abbey Winchester* (Copenhagen, 1996) pp. 16–17.

perhaps be seen in the Frankish material inserted in the *Anglo-Saxon Chronicle*'s entries for the 880s. Most definitely, he and his Frankish colleagues in court were responsible for replenishing the ransacked ecclesiastical libraries of England with manuscripts brought from the Continent.[17]

Alfred's purpose in recruiting so distinguished a circle of court scholars was in part personal; he had sought them out for spiritual and intellectual companionship. Among their main duties was to read aloud to the king from books, which Alfred demanded of them both day and night. Alfred, according to Asser, carried around on his person a sort of commonplace book, filled with a miscellany of writings he thought important: the ecclesiastical daytime offices, selected Psalms, his favourite prayers from childhood, and interesting passages from the readings he had heard.[18] In short, Grimbald, Asser and the others served as the king's tutors, encouraging him in his pursuit of wisdom. Alfred gradually became discontented with so passive an approach to learning. His early education had trained his memory and given him familiarity with letters. He could, perhaps, recite the Psalter from memory as well as the vernacular poetry that he so loved. What he could not do – and what he desperately desired – was to engage the books more directly, to be able to read the Latin words himself, comprehend their meaning, and render them into his own language. Until 887 he was unable to do this. Then, on St Martin's Day, 11 November, he began (in Asser's words) 'through divine inspiration to read and to translate at the same time, all on one and the same day'.[19] It was fitting that Alfred should have resolved to undertake this religious obligation on Martinmas, the traditional day for the collection of church-scot and other ecclesiastical dues.[20] This is not to say that he was 'illiterate' before this. Alfred may well have been able to read the vernacular, and was perhaps sufficiently versed in Latin to be able to grasp the basic meaning of what was read to him. What had

17. D.N. Dumville, 'King Alfred and the tenth-century reform of the English Church', in his *Wessex and England from Alfred to Edgar: Six Essays on Political, Cultural and Ecclesiastical Revival* (Woodbridge, Suffolk, 1992) pp. 196–7.
18. Asser, chs 77, 88–9.
19. Asser, ch. 87, trans. Keynes and Lapidge, p. 99.
20. *Ine* 4; *II Edgar* 3. Cf. Smyth, *King Alfred the Great*, p. 227.

changed was that Alfred now set himself the task of mastering the written word, beginning with 'the rudiments of Holy Scripture'. Typically, his goal in reading and translating was not simply to entertain and inform himself, but to acquire the skills needed to instruct others and engage them in the pursuit of wisdom.[21]

What Alfred hoped to gain by educating his people is expressed most fully in his preface to his first translation, the *Pastoral Care* of Pope Gregory the Great.[22] 'I would have you informed', Alfred wrote to his bishops,

> that it has often come into my mind what wise men there were in former times throughout England, both of spiritual and lay orders; and how happy times there were throughout England; and how the kings who had ruled over the people were obedient to God and his messengers; and how they both upheld peace and authority at home, and also extended their territory abroad; and how they prospered in warfare and wisdom; and also how zealous the spiritual orders were both about teaching and learning and all the services which they should do for God.

But that golden age of wisdom and prosperity had long passed. Learning had decayed so thoroughly, Alfred lamented, that few men south of the Humber, and probably north of it as well, could understand the meaning of the divine services they recited or even translate a letter from Latin into English. So few, he declared, 'that I cannot even recollect a single one south of the Thames when I came to the throne'. Alfred did not blame the vikings for the decay of learning. On the contrary, the vikings were the consequence of its

---

21. Asser, ch. 89; cf. ch. 75.
22. The translation (with a few changes) is Whitelock's in *EHD* I, no. 226, pp. 887–90. For further discussion of the preface, see D.A. Bullough, 'The educational tradition in England from Alfred to Ælfric: teaching *utriusque linguae*', in his *Carolingian Renewal: Sources and Heritage* (Manchester and New York, 1991) pp. 297–334, at pp. 298–301; J. Morrish, 'King Alfred's Letter as a source on learning in England in the ninth century', in P.E. Szarmach, ed., *Studies in Earlier Old English Prose* (Albany, N.Y., 1986) pp. 87–107; Keynes and Lapidge, pp. 125, 294–5; H. Gneuss, 'King Alfred and the history of Anglo-Saxon libraries', in P.R. Brown, ed., *Modes of Interpretation in Old English Literature: Essays in Honour of Stanley B. Greenfield* (Toronto, 1986) pp. 29–49, esp. 29–32; Dumville, *Wessex and England* pp. 185–205.

neglect.[23] They were God's scourge sent to remind those who were only 'Christians in name' where true wealth was really stored. Even before 'everything was ravaged and burnt', when there were still churches throughout England filled with books, there were few who could understand anything in them. They were, in a characteristic hunting metaphor, like tracks that could not be followed. Now, the English people had lost both the wealth and the wisdom through their neglect. The solution, Alfred announced, was to render in the vernacular 'certain books which are most necessary for all men to know', that he would then distribute to all his bishops so that they could be studied throughout the kingdom. Finally, he would 'bring it to pass, as we can very easily do with God's help, if we have the peace, that all the youth now in England, born of free men who have the where-withal (*speda*) may be devoted to learning as long as they cannot be of use in any other employment, until such time as they can read well what is written in English'. Everyone would have access to the translations and profit from the wisdom contained in them. Those who were to be advanced to holy orders, of course, would continue their study, receiving instruction in Latin. If all this were done, Alfred believed, wisdom would flourish throughout the kingdom and the peace and prosperity of the old days would return.

Alfred undoubtedly exaggerated for dramatic effect the abysmal condition of learning in southern England, as he did the decay of ecclesiastical institutions in his letter to Archbishop Fulk. Nor was Alfred completely consistent in his Preface to the *Pastoral Care*. Alfred boasted that he was surrounded by learned bishops, and one wonders where they had been educated if not in monastic or episcopal schools. The presence of Plegmund, Wærferth and the other Mercians in Alfred's court gives proof of the persistence of a tradition of learning north of the Thames. Bishop Wulfsige of Sherborne, presumably a West Saxon, possessed the literary skill to write a verse preface to Wærferth's Old English translation of Gregory's *Dialogues*. Nor was Æthelwulf's court as uncultured a backwater as his son's diatribe implies.

23. Cf. Bede, *HE* ii.15, where Bede characterizes the ravaging of Britain by the Angles, Saxons and Jutes as 'God's just vengeance for the crimes of the people' and compares it to Nebuchadnezzar's burning of Jerusalem (II Kings 24:18, 25:8–10).

Alfred had tutors and a mother who encouraged him to read as a child, and Æthelwulf had in his employ a Frankish secretary who was able to frame letters to men like Abbot Lupus. The Preface, in short, must be read as a polemic rather than as ninth-century journalism. Its account of 'happy times' past is itself a literary motif based on Bede's description of the episcopate of Theodore of Canterbury in the late seventh century.[24]

Having said all that, one cannot entirely discount Alfred's account of the times before 'everything was ravaged and burnt'. The vikings did have a devastating effect upon the institutional practice of religion in England and upon the state of learning. Manuscript production declined precipitously around 860, not to be restored until after 890.[25] Many of the literary treasures of the past went up in flames with the churches that had housed them. A few were spared because their colourful illumination and rich decorations suggested to some canny vikings that they might be marketable. One such, an eighth-century manuscript now known as the Golden Gospels of Stockholm, was sold by enterprising vikings to Ealdorman Alfred (probably of Surrey) and his wife, who then donated it to Christ Church, Canterbury. In this case, at least, the misfortune of one church enriched another, but most manuscripts must have seemed to illiterate vikings more suitable as tinder than loot.[26] Alfred may also have been right in thinking that the decline in standards of literacy pre-dated the coming of the Great Heathen Army. Based on the surviving charter evidence from Christ Church, command of the Latin language had been on the wane since the early ninth century. By the early 870s the situation had reached crisis proportions. A Canterbury diploma dated 873 is little more than a string of formulas, some clearly inappropriate for the nature of the grant, padded out with ungrammatical Latin transitional phrases. The scribe, a man who had been drawing up charters for Christ Church for eighteen years, compounded his poor Latinity

---

24. *HE* iv.2. See Keynes and Lapidge, p. 294, n. 2; cf. Smyth, *Alfred the Great*, p. 576.
25. Dumville, *Wessex and England*, p. 190.
26. *EHD* I, no. 98, pp. 539–40, discussed by N. Brooks, *The Early History of the Church of Canterbury: Christ Church from 597 to 1066* (Leicester, 1984) p. 151.

with the egregious blunder of appending to this diploma a witness list that was some twenty or thirty years out of date, presumably copying it from the original 'book' of that estate. As the historian Nicholas Brooks observes, 'When solemn Latin diplomas had to be written either by a man who could no longer see to write or by a man who knew little or no Latin, then it is clear that the metropolitan church must have been quite unable to provide any effective training in the scriptures or in Christian worship.'[27]

There is no educational equivalent to the 'Burghal Hidage' to tell us how Alfred intended to implement his educational programme. All that we know is that he set his ealdormen and reeves, most illiterate from childhood, the task of learning to read, on pain of forfeiting their 'offices of worldly power'.[28] If parish and monastic schools were established to teach the local free laity to read in the vernacular, they have left no trace. We are better informed, however, about Alfred's court school in the early 890s. Asser, in a description of Alfred's domestic arrangements modelled on a similar chapter in Einhard's *Life of Charlemagne*, explains in broad outline the education offered there.[29] Alfred's younger son, Æthelweard, along with children of the nobility and 'a good many of lesser birth as well' – probably a group whose composition changed whenever the court relocated – received instruction in the liberal arts. They were taught to read books 'in both languages', Latin and English. This went beyond the education that Alfred envisaged for 'all free-born boys with the wherewithal', who would have to be content with pursuing wisdom in their native tongue. In both cases, however, the goal was to inculcate basic literacy and a habit of learning that was to last through life, and this was to be achieved before (in Alfred's words) 'they could be of use in any other employment'.[30] At that time, when they were in their early teens, the young noblemen would turn to mastering horsemanship and the arts of war and the hunt. Alfred's hope was that by then they would have obtained both the tools and the desire to seek wisdom.

27. Brooks, *Early History*, pp. 172–3, citing S 344 (dated 873).
28. Asser, ch. 110. See further, pp. 283–4 below.
29. Asser, ch. 75; cf. Einhard, *Life of Charlemagne*, ch. 19.
30. Preface to the *Pastoral Care*, trans. *EHD* I, no. 226, p. 889.

Alfred's other children were apparently already too old for this schooling. The eldest, Æthelflæd, was by then married to Ealdorman Æthelred, and her younger sister, Æthelgifu, was serving God in the new convent her father had established in Shaftesbury. Edward and Ælfthryth, though, were still in attendance upon their father in court. At the time that Asser wrote, Edward was already a proved warrior and trusted commander, and Ælfthryth was only a few years away from marriage. They, like their father, had been 'fostered at the royal court under the solicitous care of tutors and nurses'.[31] Lest anyone think that Alfred was derelict in his paternal responsibilities, Asser assures his audience that the king saw to it that his older children would also engage in the pursuit of wisdom. Edward and Ælfthryth[32] may not have been as intensively educated as their younger brother, but this did not mean that they were 'permitted to live idly and indifferently, with no liberal education'. Rather, they attentively learned the Psalms and to read English books, especially those of poetry, and, Asser assures us, 'very frequently make use of books'.[33] Asser's portrayal of the education of Alfred's children is idyllic. It may have less to do with the actual activities of the youth that thronged Alfred's court than with the cleric's desire to convey an image of domestic propriety pleasing to his patron.

We do not know whether the court school survived Alfred, or whether any of his bishops and abbots carried out his wishes that they educate the laity in their dioceses. His dream of educating all the free-born was just that, a dream. Alfred's educational legacy was not universal literacy, but it was considerable and original, nonetheless. The parallels between Alfred's desire to educate the free-born and Charlemagne's educational programme as revealed in his capitularies are perhaps too close to be mere coincidence. Most striking, perhaps, is the commonality of goal: the renewal of religion

31. Asser, ch. 75, trans. Keynes and Lapidge, p. 90.
32. Ælfthryth's sex rather than her age may have been at issue. Charlemagne's palace school was coeducational; Alfred's may not have been. Asser says that Alfred personally instructed the *sons* of his ealdormen and thegns, whom he 'loved no less than his own children'. Asser, ch. 76, trans. Keynes and Lapidge, p. 91. Cf. Einhard, *Life of Charlemagne*, ch. 19.
33. Asser, ch. 75.

through the revival of literacy. Following a tradition that stemmed from Augustine's great treatise on Christian education, *De doctrina Christiana*, Charlemagne and Alfred both understood that the ultimate purpose of studying the liberal arts was to master the intellectual tools necessary to comprehend the subtleties of Scripture.[34] Their court scholars, moreover, went well beyond Augustine's grudging acceptance of the study of the liberal arts as a necessary evil, celebrating it instead as a sacred pursuit in itself.[35] But there were differences that, again, show Alfred to have been more than simply a 'minor league' Charlemagne. Characteristically, Alfred analysed the problem as he saw it and came up with a solution that was practical and flexible. Whereas Charlemagne strove to improve the quality of Latin learning and writing, and to extend it beyond a narrow circle of ecclesiastical scholars, Alfred and his advisors chose to foster literacy in the vernacular among both the clergy and the laity.[36]

They built upon a pre-existing foundation. English had increasingly come into use for secular administrative documents, in particular charters and wills, during the course of the ninth century. In Alfred's day, the use of sealed letters, or writs, in the vernacular by kings and other lords to make their will known to their followers and agents was already so well established that Alfred felt free to use it as the basis for a metaphor arguing the authority of sacred writings in his translation of St Augustine's *Soliloquies*.[37] As the Preface to the *Pastoral Care* implies, there was a ready-made reading

34. J. Bately, 'The literary prose of King Alfred's reign: translation or transformation?', *Old English Newsletter Subsidia*, vol. 10 (Binghamton, NY, 1984) p. 10.

35. J.J. Contreni, 'The Carolingian Renaissance: Education, Literacy and Culture', in R. McKitterick, ed., *New Cambridge Medieval History, Vol. 2: c. 700–c. 900* (Cambridge, 1995) pp. 709–57, esp. at 709–12.

36. Bullough, 'Educational tradition', p. 299. For Charlemagne's educational goals, see P. Riché, *Les Écoles et l'enseignement dans l'Occident chrétien de la fin du Ve siècle au milieu du Xi^e siècle* (Paris, 1979) pp. 287–313.

37. *Alfred's Soliloquies*, ed. Carnicelli, p. 62 (l. 23): '*ðines hlafordes ærendgewrit and hys insegel*'. For discussion of the uses of vernacular literacy in ninth-century England, see S. Kelly, 'Anglo-Saxon lay society and the written word', and S.D. Keynes, 'Royal government and the written word in late Anglo-Saxon England', both in R. McKitterick, ed., *The Uses of Literacy in Early Medieval Europe* (Cambridge, 1990) pp. 246–62, 228–34, 244–5.

audience for books in the vernacular. Alfred undoubtedly hoped to restore the lost treasures of learning by reviving Latin literacy among the clerical elite; but his programme for the laity was one in which the wisdom contained in these books would be made available through translation into English.

For the most part, we can only make an educated guess concerning when Alfred composed his law code and translated the *Pastoral Care*, the *Boethius*, the *Soliloquies*, and the first fifty Psalms, or even the order in which he undertook these tasks.[38] William of Malmesbury in the first quarter of the twelfth century preserved a tradition that Alfred had been engaged in translating the Psalms at the time of his death, and since he rendered only the first fifty, there may be some truth in this. If we assume that the earliest translations would have been the most literal, Alfred's first full translation was Gregory's *Pastoral Care*.[39] There is some uncertainty about whether the *Boethius* or the *Soliloquies* came next. The question is complicated by what appears to be mutual borrowing of language.[40] Most critics, however, consider the *Soliloquies* the later of the two. If Alfred did begin with the *Pastoral Care*, as seems likely from the tenor of its Preface, then he must have waited until the early 890s to begin his programme of translation. From references to Archbishop Plegmund and Bishop Swithwulf in the preface we can date the *Pastoral Care* to sometime between 890, when Plegmund succeeded to Canterbury, and 895, when Swithwulf died. Some historians have opted for a date of 890 or soon after, simply to provide Alfred with sufficient time to have translated all the works before his death in 899. Alfred's comment that he began to translate Gregory 'amidst the various and multifarious afflictions of this kingdom,' however, might

38. The best general introduction to Alfred's writings is A.J. Frantzen, *King Alfred* (Boston 1986). D. Whitelock, 'The prose of Alfred's reign', in E.G. Stanley, ed., *Continuations and Beginnings: Studies in Old English Literature* (London, 1966) pp. 67–103, though still fundamental reading, is corrected by J. Bately, 'Old English prose before and during the reign of Alfred', *ASE* 17 (1988) pp. 93–139.

39. That Alfred's translation of the Psalms only rarely strays from the Vulgate should not be regarded as evidence for an early date of composition, but rather as testimony to the great authority of the Psalter.

40. See Carnicelli's discussion in the introduction to his edition of the *Soliloquies*, pp. 29–40.

suggest that he began after the return of the vikings in 892, as does Asser's failure to mention the project.

Alfred explained the process of translation in his Preface to the *Pastoral Care*. There he says that he translated Gregory's Latin

> sometimes word for word, sometimes sense for sense, as I had learnt it from my Archbishop Plegmund, and my Bishop Asser, and my mass-priest Grimbald and my mass-priest John. When I had learnt it, I turned it into English according as I understood it and as I could most meaningfully render it; and I will send one (copy) to every see in my kingdom; and in each will be an *æstel* [book-marker or pointer] worth fifty mancuses.[41]

One imagines Alfred surrounded by his ecclesiastical helpers working out together the meaning of the text. One would read the Latin aloud, and then all would join in a discussion of its meaning. When Alfred had heard enough, he would put the passage into his own words, dictating them to a secretary who carefully copied down what the king said.[42] Alfred's was the 'authorial voice'; the lexical and syntactical analyses of the canon make this much clear. But the effort was fundamentally collegial.

The translations represented the combined learning of the court, which included knowledge of a wide range of classical sources. As Janet Bately has demonstrated, the treatment of the story of Orpheus in Alfred's *Boethius*, for example, draws upon Ovid's *Metamorphoses*, Virgil's *Aeneid* and Fourth Georgic, and a commentary on Virgil such as that written by Servius.[43] Even more to the point, Alfred

41. *EHD* I, no. 226, pp. 889–90; *Sweet's Anglo-Saxon Reader*, ed. Onions, p. 6. Cf. the preface to Alfred's *Boethius*, ed. Sedgefield, p. 1. '*Hwilum word be worde, hwilum andgit of andgiete*' echoes Asser's characterization of Bishop Wærferth's translation of Gregory's *Dialogues* as '*aliquando sensum ex sensu ponens*'. Asser, ch. 77. The phrase was used by both Gregory the Great and Jerome. Keynes and Lapidge, p. 259, n. 164.

42. K. Sisam, *Studies in the History of Old English Literature* (Oxford, 1953) pp. 140–7; R.W. Klement, 'The production of the *Pastoral Care*: King Alfred and his helpers', in P.E. Szarmach, ed., *Studies in Earlier Old English Prose: Sixteen Original Contributions* (Albany, NY, 1986) pp. 129–52.

43. J. Bately, 'Those books that are most necessary for all men to know: the Classics and late ninth-century England: a reappraisal', in A.S. Bernardo and S. Levin, eds, *The Classics in the Middle Ages* (Binghamton, NY, 1990) pp. 56–7.

makes discriminating and sophisticated use of the Classics; his additions and expansions are always to the point, never merely there to demonstrate his erudition. An example of Alfred's confident handling of his materials is his rendering of Boethius's question, 'Where now are the bones of faithful Fabricius?'[44] Alfred, apparently, did not think that his audience would understand the allusion to the Roman hero, and so replaced the consul Fabricius with a hero possessing greater name recognition, 'Where now are the bones of the famous and wise goldsmith Weland?' The substitution is in some ways almost comic. *Faber* and *fabricus* meant 'smith' in medieval Latin, and on first glance it seems that Alfred simply mistook the name for a noun. But Alfred goes on to add, 'I call him wise, for the man of skill can never lose his cunning, and can no more be deprived of it than the sun may be moved from his station.' This is not in Boethius, at least not in any version that has come down to us. Rather, the source is another classical work, *De Viris Illustribus*, where Fabricius is characterized in a virtually identical manner.[45] Alfred, it would seem, not only knew who Fabricius was – and even had additional information about him – but chose to use the figure of Weland instead because it made his point more clearly. It is always possible that Alfred and his team used a pre-existing gloss on Boethius, though if they did, it is one that has since been lost, or had a text that included commentary in it.[46] Nonetheless, it is hard to escape the conclusion that Alfred and his helpers were surprisingly well versed in classical learning.[47]

Alfred's debt to his helpers is acknowledged in his translation of Augustine's *Soliloquies*. Alfred rendered Augustine's Latin particularly freely, so often supplementing or replacing its text with passages and thoughts culled from other

44. *Alfred's Boethius*, ch. 19, ed. Sedgefield, p. 46; trans. Sedgefield, p. 48.
45. Bately, 'Those books', p. 52.
46. See J. Wittig, 'King Alfred's *Boethius* and its Latin sources: a reconsideration', *ASE* 11 (1983) pp. 157–98.
47. Despite Alfred's late start as a Latin reader, one ought not to entirely discount the possibility that he himself contributed to the scholarly discussions. The king, after all, was an apt and enthusiastic student. Asser tells us that he carried around with him a handbook crammed with favourite passages copied from works of various authors. Such a collection would have made a useful reference book for the translators.

writers that the book is less a 'translation' of a single work than a 'florilegium', 'blossoms' plucked from various sources and arranged as the compiler saw fit.[48] One of the most dramatic changes was to Augustine's discussion of friendship. For Augustine, who wrote the book while on retreat, solitude was the only state truly conducive to learning and friendship was merely another attractive worldly distraction. For Alfred, on the other hand, it was inconceivable to pursue knowledge without the aid of 'a few intimate and skillful' friends.[49] 'Above all others', Alfred wrote, 'I love those who most help me to understand and to know reason and wisdom, most of all about God and about our souls; for I know that I can more easily seek after him with their help than I can without.'[50]

While the translation sessions were fundamentally a continuation of the king's education, he took an active role, both in seeking the meaning of the Latin words read aloud to him, and in selecting books which would advance his personal search for wisdom and his broader educational programme. The preface to the *Pastoral Care* explains in a straightforward manner why Alfred undertook to translate 'the books that are most necessary for all men to know': to restore wisdom to the kingdom, and with it, peace and prosperity. Another of his prefaces, that written for the *Soliloquies*, provides additional insight into what Alfred meant by wisdom. The preface begins with a wonderful extended metaphor. Alfred portrays himself as going into a wood to gather 'staves, and stud-shafts, and cross-beams, and handles for each of the tools that I could work with', and the finest timber he could find with which to build a house.[51] The 'timber', we discover, is the writings of the holy fathers – St Augustine, St Gregory and St Jerome are mentioned by name – and the 'houses' are the translations that Alfred and his helpers made. These 'houses' are both comfortable temporary dwellings – the wisdom to live well in this world – and prefigure the eternal home that God has promised us

---

48. Alfred himself characterized the book as *blostman*, 'blossoms'. *King Alfred's Soliloquies*, ed. Carnicelli, pp. 83, 92.
49. Ibid, p. 49; trans. Hargrove, p. 3.
50. Ibid, p. 74; trans. Hargrove, p. 25.
51. *Alfred's Soliloquies*, ed. Carnicelli, pp. 47–8; trans. Hargrove, p. 1; Keynes and Lapidge, pp. 138–9.

in these very books. Alfred drives home his point by comparing this life to a lease granted to a man by his lord, and salvation to the bookland that he hopes to earn through his good service and his lord's kindness. 'May He who created both', Alfred prays, 'and rules over both grant that I be fit for both: both to be useful here and likewise to arrive there.' Alfred also made it clear that he expected others to share in his labours. Everyone who is 'strong and has many wagons' (a characteristically concrete metaphor) ought to follow him into the forest and fetch out as much wood as he can carry. Bishop Wærferth answered the call by translating Gregory's *Dialogues*. Other anonymous helpers lent a hand in turning into English Orosius's popular early fifth-century Christian history, *The Seven Books of History against the Pagans*, and Bede's masterpiece of Christian historiography, *The Ecclesiastical History of the English People*.

Alfred chose his 'timber' carefully. Gregory's *Pastoral Care*, Boethius's *Consolation of Philosophy*, and the Psalms were obvious choices. Virtually any ninth-century cleric or educated layman would have included them in his shortlist of books necessary for all men to know. Gregory's *Pastoral Care* was essential reading for every medieval bishop. It addressed such questions as what sort of people ought to be chosen to rule the Church, how these prelates ought to live, how they ought to instruct and correct different types of listeners, and how earnestly they ought to reflect daily upon their own frailty.[52] Bede had taught the English to revere St Gregory the Great, pope from 590 to 604, as their very own 'Apostle', and they, in turn, through Alcuin, had passed their enthusiasm to the Franks.[53] Archbishop Hincmar of Rheims, the dominant religious personality in mid-ninth-century Francia, thought so much of *Pastoral Care* that he made holding it a part of the consecration ritual for bishops.

Alfred probably chose the *Pastoral Care* for both personal and practical reasons. Gregory's handbook for pastors was precisely the tonic needed, in his view, to restore the episcopate

52. This description is based on Bede's excellent synopsis. *HE* ii.1.
53. *HE* i. 23–32, ii. 1. S. Allott, *Alcuin of York, c. AD 732 to 804: His Life and Letters* (York, 1974) p. 11; *EHD* I, no. 170. See H. Davis, *St Gregory the Great: Pastoral Care*, Ancient Christian Writers 11 (Westminster, MD, 1950) pp. 9–11; Keynes and Lapidge, p. 215, n. 30; Smyth, *King Alfred the Great*, p. 531; Frantzen, *King Alfred*, p. 25.

of his kingdom to spiritual health. Alfred also undoubtedly identified with Gregory, an intellectual who had accepted authority reluctantly as a duty and strove, as best he could, to maintain the joys of the contemplative life while fulfilling the obligations of his office. He was also drawn to the saint by the more personal and private bond of shared illness. 'Almost continually throughout his early manhood', Bede explained, 'he had been, in his own words, tortured with frequent pains in the bowels and every moment of the day he was exhausted by a weakness of the internal organs.'[54] For Alfred, the *Pastoral Care* was as much a handbook for princes as it was for bishops. Alfred, indeed, did not see much difference between the two. For Alfred all authority, whether secular or spiritual, derived from God, and kings, ealdormen and reeves were as responsible as bishops and priests for upholding God's laws among their subjects.

In different ways, Boethius's *The Consolation of Philosophy* and the Psalms of King David offered Alfred and his subjects much the same thing, a message of comfort in times of tribulation and an alternative to despair. Amicius Manlius Severinus Boethius, born around 480 into an old aristocratic Roman family, and executed in 524 on suspicion of treason by King Theodoric the Great, was the source of much of what early medieval Europe knew about classical philosophy. The *De Consolatione Philosophiae* was, and is, by far his most famous work, and enjoyed extraordinary popularity throughout the Middle Ages. Written in prison while Boethius awaited execution, the *Consolation* was an examination of the comforts of philosophical study and detachment from the vicissitudes of this world. Oppressed by vikings and illness, Alfred was drawn to Boethius's meditations, but the philosopher's late antique Neo-Platonism was foreign to him. Boethius lacked, in Alfred's mind, the 'authority' of St Gregory, and the king felt free to revise the Latin text to reflect more closely his own ideas. Alfred recast the dialogue between the imprisoned Boethius and 'Lady Philosophy' as a conversation between 'mind' (*mod*) and 'Wisdom'. As a result, what had been the consolations of philosophy became, in Alfred's hands, the comforts of Christian Wisdom. Alfred's 'authorial voice' also differed from Boethius's.

---

54. *HE* ii. 1, trans. Colgrave and Mynors, p. 129.

Rather than an unjustly condemned philosopher, Alfred's protagonist is 'a high-born chieftain, cherishing his lord . . . a giver of treasure, glorious ever, wise toward this world, wishful of honour, learned in booklore'.[55] In short, the speaker became King Alfred himself.

Alfred had undoubtedly memorized the Psalms as a child, and it was natural that he should turn them into English. His personal affection for the Psalms was such that he was 'in the invariable habit of listening daily to divine services and Mass, and of participating in certain Psalms and prayers, and in the day-time and night-time offices' (which consisted of chanted Psalms).[56] Alfred's purpose was educational, and his intended audience were laymen with little or no prospect of pursuing their studies beyond the vernacular. Alfred knew from personal experience how much richer the experience of reading was if one was guided by those who truly understood the texts. Consequently, he undertook not only to translate the words of the Vulgate, but to explain what they *really* meant as clearly as he could by writing brief introductions that explained three separate levels of meaning in each Psalm: the historical (what the Psalm meant for David), the moral (what it means for each of our lives), and the analogical (how it prefigures events in the life of Christ). The expositions given in Alfred's introductions are highly derivative; the material is taken largely from a seventh-century Irish exegesis of the Psalms that had been attributed (wrongly) to Bede.[57]

Nevertheless, the tone of the introductions is personal, and one cannot help but suspect that Alfred was writing about himself when he explained that the second Psalm is

55. 'The Lays of Boethius', in *Alfred's Boethius*, trans. Sedgefield, p. 179.
56. Asser, ch. 76, trans. Keynes and Lapidge, p. 91, 153. Alfred's prose Psalms are preserved in the Paris Psalter. *Liber Psalmorum, The West Saxon Psalms, being the Prose Portion, or the 'First Fifty,' of the So-Called Paris Psalter*, ed. J.W. Bright and R.L. Ramsay (Boston, 1907). Richard Stracke's new electronic edition of Alfred's prose Psalms, which has the Vulgate in parallel, is posted on the Internet at http://www.ac.edu/Augusta/arsenal/psalms/. For Alfred's authorship, see J. Bately, 'Lexical evidence for the authorship of the prose Psalms in the Paris Psalter', *ASE* 10 (1982) pp. 69–95.
57. P. O'Neill, 'Old English introductions to the prose Psalms of the Paris Psalter: sources, structure and composition', in J.S. Wittig, ed., *Eight Anglo-Saxon Studies* (Chapel Hill, NC, 1981) pp. 20–38.

called 'David's Psalm' 'because David in this psalm lamented and complained to the Lord about his enemies, both native and foreign, and about all his troubles. And everyone who sings this psalm does likewise with respect to his own enemies.'[58] King David, the anointed of God, was treated by ninth-century biblical exegetes as both the personification of earthly kingship and as a prefigurement of Christ. Alcuin's flattery of Charlemagne as a new David was only the most prominent example of what had by the end of the ninth century become a cliché of clerical sycophants.[59] Though Asser's preferred biblical exemplar for Alfred was Solomon, Alfred himself may have identified more with David. David offered Alfred an explanation for the trajectory of his own life, anointed to kingship as a child above all his brothers, a fugitive in hiding, and then, by the grace of God, a victorious king. One historian has even suggested that the mysterious figure on the Alfred Jewel, possibly the *æstel* that Alfred ordered attached to each copy of the *Pastoral Care*, is David, holding in his hands the *virga et baculus* or *gyrd and stæf*, the rod of judgement and the staff of comfort of Psalm 23.[60]

Augustine's *Soliloquies*, written by the saint while in retreat awaiting baptism in the winter of 387, was an odd choice for translation. The treatise was not popular in the early Middle Ages and remains among Augustine's least-read works today. What probably attracted Alfred to it was the questions it posed. The *Soliloquies* take the form of an interior dialogue between Augustine and his Reason about the possibility of knowledge of God and the self and the relationship between knowledge and the immortality of the soul. This provided Alfred with a framework for his own meditations. Augustine, still more of a philosopher than a theologian when he wrote the *Soliloquies*, explored the epistemological implications of the immortality of the soul. Alfred's interest, on the contrary,

---

58. Keynes and Lapidge, p. 153.
59. H.H. Anton, *Fürstenspiegel und Herrscherethos in der Karolingerzeit* (Bonn, 1968) pp. 419–33.
60. A. Crépin, 'L'importance de la pensée de Grégoire le Grand dans la politique culturelle d'Alfred, roi de Wessex (871–899)', in J. Fontaine, R. Gillet, and S. Pellistrandi, eds, *Grégoire le Grand* (Paris, 1986) p. 584. Crépin notes that Gregory concludes chapter six of his second book with exegesis on the meaning of the Psalm's *virga tua et baculus tuus*. But cf. below, p. 256.

was in the relationship between wisdom, God, and salvation. Perhaps because his chronic ill health was a constant reminder of the fragility of the body and the brevity of life, the *Soliloquies* have a sense of intimacy lacking from Alfred's other translations. For Alfred the central question was 'whether I shall live always; and then I would know whether I, after the parting of the body and the soul, shall ever know more than I know now of all that which I have longed to know; for I can not find anything better in man than that he know, and nothing worse than that he be ignorant'.[61]

To call the *Soliloquies* a 'translation' is rather misleading. Alfred used Augustine's text much as a fine jazz musician might play with a melody, improvising and weaving in new tunes until the source is transformed into an original composition. He stuck with Augustine's *Soliloquies* when they made sense to him, departed from them when they did not. His departures often took the form of supplementing Augustine with appeals to other authorities – notably Gregory the Great – and to his own commonsensical understanding of things. In some ways, Alfred is more conventionally Christian (at least in a ninth-century sense) than Augustine. Unlike the as yet unbaptized philosopher, Alfred's final answer to all questions of uncertainty is faith and authority. 'If your lord', Reason asks 'Augustine'

> whom you trust in all things better than yourself, should tell you something which you never heard before, or if he should say that he saw something that you yourself never saw, does it seem to you that you would doubt his statement at all, because you did not see it yourself?
>
> No, no, indeed! There is no story so incredible that I would not believe it, if he should tell me it.[62]

How much more, Alfred has Reason ask, should you trust your eternal lord? There are also other, less central, differences between Augustine's *Soliloquies* and Alfred's. Perhaps the most interesting is Alfred's unwillingness to repudiate wealth and friends as mere distractions from the pursuit of knowledge. As Alfred observed, God made 'two eternal things, angels and the souls of men, to which he has apportioned eternal gifts, such as wisdom and righteousness. . . . and to

61. *Alfred's Soliloquies*, ed. Carnicelli, p. 84; trans. Hargrove, p. 37.
62. *Alfred's Soliloquies*, ed. Carnicelli, pp. 87–8; trans. Hargrove, p. 39.

men he gives many and diverse good gifts in this world, although they are not eternal. They are, however, service-able while we are in this world.'[63] Earthly goods, wealth, honour, friends, although transitory, are nonetheless useful and necessary for a good life. The overall impression one receives from the *Soliloquies* is of a king who expected obedi-ence and deference from his followers, and of a conven-tionally pious man, impatient with metaphysical abstractions, but impassioned about the pursuit of wisdom.

As we have seen, Alfred's *Soliloquies* and his *Pastoral Care* differ considerably from their late antique Latin sources in minor and major ways. Scholars disagree about what these differences reveal about Alfred, his understanding of the texts he translated, and his purposes in translating them. One explanation is that Alfred and his helpers were trying to render faithfully the originals, but some of the ideas and arguments they encountered from an earlier and more cul-turally sophisticated age defeated them. They did the best they could to make sense of them within their own frame of reference.[64] A second view is that Alfred consciously altered what he was translating to reflect his own world-view. He intended the *Consolation of Philosophy* as a statement of his own personal beliefs concerning the nature of provid-ence and the meaning of suffering, and was not overly con-cerned about getting Boethius 'right'.[65] A third approach sees Alfred as a conventional ninth-century scholar whose translations reflected mainstream Carolingian and Insular intellectual thought about Boethius and Augustine.[66] These three explanations are not, of course, mutually exclusive. Indeed, they can – and ought – to be considered as comple-mentary. Alfred's understanding of his texts was, obviously, conditioned by the education he received and the world that he knew. The same is true for any translator, in the ninth century or today. Alfred's decision to abandon Augustine's dialectical investigation in favour of an appeal to authority

63. *Alfred's Soliloquies*, ed. Carnicelli, p. 82; trans. Hargrove, p. 32.
64. E.g., M. McC. Gatch, 'King Alfred's version of Augustine's *Soliloquia:* some suggestions on its rationale and unity', in Szarmach, ed., *Studies*, pp. 17–43.
65. E.g., F.A. Payne, *King Alfred & Boethius* (Madison, WI, 1968).
66. E.g., W.F. Bolton, 'How Boethian is Alfred's Boethius', in Szarmach, ed., *Studies*, pp. 153–68.

was a mark of his age. Augustine's philosophical demonstrations of the truth of propositions through logic were
profoundly alien to Alfred and to his helpers, who knew
that truth was to be found not in original thought, but by
understanding the meaning of authoritative texts. That is
why Alfred chose to translate rather than 'create' anew. It
also seems irrefutable that, on occasion, Alfred encountered
arguments in translating that he was simply unable to grasp.
(He was completely defeated by the geometrical analogies
offered by Augustine, though he did his best with them.) A
detailed analysis of the differences between Alfred's translations and the texts upon which they were based is beyond
the scope of this book. But it seems clear that Alfred was
attempting to do more than merely produce literal translations. His approach was more 'sense for sense' than 'word
for word', and sometimes his sense of what ought to have
been in the original led him to add to or subtract from it.
He stuck closely to a text if he agreed with what he was
reading, or if he considered it authoritative. In the case of
Boethius and Augustine's *Soliloquies*, he felt free to add what
amounted to his own commentary on the text. Many of the
changes Alfred introduced were merely to clarify abstruse
points in the Latin. Alfred, who seems to have been uncomfortable with abstract arguments, made the text's points
as concretely as he could. He also appreciated the efficacy
of teaching through analogy, and often drew upon his
own experiences as king or upon the collective learning of
his court scholars to come up with suitable metaphors. But
Alfred also brought his own ideas and biases to the translations. His treatment of the *Pastoral Care* is particularly instructive, because it is, on the whole, so faithful to the original.
Although following Gregory's text closely, Alfred consistently
softened Gregory's severe and unforgiving denunciations
of sinners.[67] Where Gregory speaks of penalties, Alfred writes
of God's mercy. By doing so, Alfred brought his *Pastoral Care*
more in line with the conception of Christian law that he
developed in the preface to his law code.[68] In short, Alfred
transformed the works that he translated so that they would
say what he believed they *ought* to have said.

67. Clement, 'Production of the Pastoral Care', pp. 136–7, 138.
68. See pp. 247–9 below.

. . .

ALFRED AND THE CHURCH

Despite his concern for the spiritual condition of his subjects, Alfred initiated no reform of ecclesiastical institutions
or religious practice in Wessex. Asser, it is true, lauds the
king's monastic foundations at Athelney and Shaftesbury.[69]
He praises Alfred not only for filling his monasteries with
monks from overseas, but, characteristically, for endowing
them 'with estates of land and every kind of wealth' and
devoting an eighth of his annual revenues to their upkeep.[70]
There is absolutely no reason to believe, however, that Alfred
planned a systematic monastic reform, certainly nothing along
the lines of King Edgar's sponsorship of SS Dunstan, Oswald,
and Æthelwold in the mid-tenth century. The two monasteries (in contrast to his thirty burhs) that Alfred established
look back to the age of Bede, when warrior-kings like Oswiu
founded religious houses to give thanksgiving for their victories and to house their daughters, rather than forward to
Ramsey or Ely.

Alfred's approach to Church reform within his kingdom
was personal. He dealt with problems, both in the spiritual
and secular realms, by appointing the right men for the job.
Though intent upon improving the quality of his episcopate, he was not dissatisfied with its organization and structure. His son, Edward the Elder, not he, redrew diocesan
lines within Wessex so that pastoral care could be offered
more readily and effectively. Nor, despite Asser's 'holy war'
rhetoric, did Alfred aggressively pursue the conversion of
the Danes, unless they were invading chieftains. As a consequence, the dioceses of East Anglia, the eastern Midlands
and Northumbria were severely disrupted and some of the
ancient sees disappeared. The passivity of the West Saxon
Church in the face of the resurgence of paganism over
much of England distressed some of the English enough for
them to complain about it to the papacy. Between 891 and
986, Pope Formosus sent a blistering letter to Archbishop
Plegmund and all the bishops of England excoriating their
lack of effort, even informing them that he had considered

69. Asser, chs 92–8.
70. Asser, chs 98, 102.

'thrusting [England] from the body of the Church of God with the sword of separation'.[71] Alfred, it seems, was content to restrict himself to the spiritual welfare of those Christians who had submitted to his lordship.

Alfred reigned long before the Investiture Controversy altered the fundamental relationship between the royal and ecclesiastical spheres. The bishops and abbots of Wessex were his thegns, his spiritual servants, whether they advised him in his court or acted on his behalf by fulfilling their spiritual duties in their sees. There was no doubt in his mind that he was at the head of this ecclesiastical organization or that his power, divinely granted, was the highest in the realm. Alfred saw nothing odd or unseemly about translating Gregory's *Pastoral Care* for the spiritual guidance of his bishops and their clergy; just as he lectured his dogkeepers and his fowlers about their craft, Alfred felt completely comfortable in teaching the clergy theirs. There was no native equivalent of Hincmar of Rheims in Alfred's England.

This helps explain an apparent paradox. Alfred's piety forms a leitmotif in Asser's *Life*,[72] yet Alfred was remembered by the twelfth-century monks of Abingdon as a 'Judas', a tyrant king who robbed their house of lands earmarked for the monks.[73] Nor is this an isolated incident. Alfred's relations with Canterbury before the accession of Plegmund were anything but harmonious. In around 877, Archbishop Æthelred of Canterbury, Plegmund's predecessor, complained to Pope John VIII about royal encroachment upon Christ Church. The Pope supported the archbishop, telling him that he had 'admonished your king to show due honour to you for the love of Jesus Christ the Lord, and to be anxious to preserve all the rights of your privilege in everlasting security and to keep them undiminished'.[74] The Pope's letter does not explain what Alfred had done to arouse the anger of the archbishop, but, given the past history of archiepiscopal–royal relations, the dispute most likely had to do with Alfred's

71. *EHD* I, no. 227.
72. Asser, ch. 88.
73. *Chronicon Monasterii de Abingdon*, ed. J. Stevenson, Rolls Series (London, 1858), I, p. 50. A.T. Thacker, 'Æthelwold and Abingdon', in B.A.E. Yorke, ed., *Bishop Æthelwold: His Career and Influence* (Woodbridge. 1988) pp. 45–6.
74. *EHD* I, no. 222, p. 883

claims to secular lordship over the Kentish minsters and their rich estates.[75]

That Alfred took land from churches seems as certain as his love of relics and the liturgy. For the defence of his realm, Alfred was more than willing to risk the wrath of monks, bishops, or even a people. The viking invasions left many churches smouldering ruins, and church lands depopulated waste, especially along the border with Guthrum's kingdom and the coastline of eastern Kent. Alfred appropriated extensive tracts of these strategically sited lands to endow his officials and followers.[76] Less sinister, but probably even more costly, were the financial charges that Alfred laid upon the Church. He pressed his bishops and abbots hard for their share of the geld paid to the Danes and for funds to build and maintain burhs. Bishop Ealhferth of Winchester was forced to hand over to the king two estates that King Æthelwulf had left to the Church in his will, because the bishop could not come up with his share of the geld to be paid to the Danes. Alfred paid the bishop's portion and took possession of the lands, which may have been the standard operating procedure.[77]

The king could also exert pressure on his bishops to exchange land with him. Often the goal was to obtain strategically located estates. The exchange of property vulnerable to viking attack for safer, if perhaps less valuable, lands benefited both king and clergy. Some of the king's dealings with his churchmen were more one-sided. One can only guess what the monks of Malmesbury gained by allowing Alfred to grant their land at Chelworth in Wiltshire to Dudi, a king's thegn, for the unusually long term of four lives.[78] A piteous charter survives from the reign of Alfred's son, Edward, in which Bishop Denewulf of Winchester informs his royal lord that he had persuaded the community to allow him to lease Beddington to the king, 'whether to use

---

75. Brooks, *Early History of the Church of Canterbury*, pp. 175–206.
76. R. Fleming, 'Monastic lands and England's defence in the Viking Age', *EHR* 100 (1985) pp. 247–65. Cf. D.N. Dumville, 'Ecclesiastical lands and the defence of Wessex in the first Viking Age', in his *Wessex and England*, pp. 29–54. See also Brooks, *Early History of the Church of Canterbury*, pp. 204–6.
77. S 354. Cf. S 385
78. S 356.

yourself or to let on lease to whomsoever you please'. The bishop went on to plead with Edward, for the love of God and for the holy Church, to take no more of Winchester's land, 'so God need blame neither you nor us for the diminishing in our days'.[79] As one historian has commented, 'In Wessex it would appear that religious foundations were more at risk from the depredations of the West Saxon kings than the Vikings.'[80]

Alfred, in short, dealt with the Church much as Charles Martel and his less-denigrated Carolingian rulers had.[81] While protecting the Church from external attack, he regarded its lands as at his disposal to defend it and the realm. Alfred, for all his undoubtedly sincere piety, was a pragmatist.

.   .   .

KING ALFRED'S POLITICAL THOUGHT

As Alfred's *Soliloquies* and the *Boethius* make clear, for him, wisdom was the source of all other virtues. Without it, a man could neither live a good life nor earn a place in heaven. Its very pursuit made a people worthy of God's favour and grace.[82] It may seem odd that a man as pragmatic and level-headed as Alfred should conceive of wisdom in so Gregorian or Augustinian a fashion.[83] But Alfred, in his mind, was being practical. All things, he knew, were subject to God's governance, even kings and the fate of nations. This was, after all, one of the prime lessons to be learned from seeking wisdom. How Alfred applied 'wisdom' to human affairs is best understood through an examination of his law

79. S 1444, *EHD* I, no. 101, pp. 543–4.
80. Yorke, *Wessex*, p. 122.
81. Charles Martel's reputation as a despoiler of Church lands may, in fact, owe less to his own rapacity than to ninth-century ecclesiastics projecting their grievances against later Carolingians safely back into a distant past. See P. Fouracre and J. Nelson in R. McKitterick, ed., *New Cambridge Medieval History*, pp. 90–2, 188–9.
82. E.g., *Alfred's Boethius*, ed. Sedgefield, ch. 27, p. 62; trans. Sedgefield, p. 67. See P.E. Szarmach, 'Alfred's *Boethius* and the Four Cardinal Virtues', in Roberts and Nelson with Godden, eds, *Alfred the Wise*, pp. 223–35.
83. P.E. Szarmach, 'Anglo-Saxon Letters in the Eleventh Century', *Acta* 1 (1974) p. 3; P. Wormald, 'The Uses of Literacy in Anglo-Saxon England and its Neighbours', *TRHS*, 5th ser., 27, p. 107.

code, especially its preface, which is, in effect, a short treatise on the relationship between divine and human law and authority.[84]

As Patrick Wormald has insightfully argued, Alfred's issuance of law was a public display of his regality. His law code was as much a political and ideological manifesto of kingship as it was a legal manual.[85] Though Alfred portrayed himself as a law-finder rather than a law-maker, harvesting the best laws from codes and capitularies issued by previous English kings, one ought not to underestimate his initiative or originality. Much as he did in his 'translation' of Augustine's *Soliloquies*, Alfred preserved what he found most congenial and omitted the rest, creating a document that reflected his own sense of justice.

The code's lengthy introduction, which includes a translation of the Decalogue, a few chapters of Mosaic law from the Book of Exodus, and the so-called 'Apostolic Letter' from the Acts of the Apostles (15:23–29), may best be understood as a meditation upon the meaning of 'law' and legislation among Christian peoples. Through its careful arrangement of texts, it expresses Alfred's sense of the essential continuity between God's gift of Law to Moses and his own issuance of law to his people. Alfred artfully related Exodus to the 'Apostolic Letter' with the observation that Christ 'had come not to shatter or annul the Commandments but to fulfil them; and he taught mercy and meekness' [Intro. 49.1]. He then explained how Christian law spread throughout the world, including England:

84. J.M. Wallace-Hadrill, *Early Germanic Kingship in England and the Continent* (Oxford, 1971) pp. 124–51; idem, *Early Medieval History* (Oxford, 1975) p. 190. The best introduction to Alfred's political thought is J.L. Nelson, 'The political ideas of Alfred of Wessex', in A.J. Duggan, ed., *Kings and Kingship in Medieval Europe*, Kings's College London Medieval Series 10, gen. ed. J. Bateley (Exeter, 1993) pp. 125–58. See also her '"A King across the sea": Alfred in continental perspective', *TRHS*, 5th ser. 36 (1986) pp. 45–68.

85. *The Making of English Law* (Oxford, forthcoming). I would like to thank Mr Wormald for his generosity in allowing me to read a draft of what promises to be an extremely important work. See also Patrick Wormald, '*Lex scripta* and *verbum regis*: Legislation and Germanic kingship, from Euric to Cnut', in P.H. Sawyer and I.N. Wood, eds, *Early Medieval Kingship* (Leeds, 1977) p. 132; Wallace-Hadrill, *Early Germanic Kingship*, pp. 148–50; and Keynes and Lapidge, p. 39.

> Afterwards, when it came about that many peoples had received the faith of Christ, many synods of holy bishops and also of other distinguished counsellors . . . then established, through that mercy which Christ taught, that for almost every misdeed at the first offence secular lords might with their permission receive without sin the monetary compensation, which they then fixed.[86]

Alfred, characteristically, 'translated' the idea of Christian mercy into his own cultural idiom, expressing it in terms of the wergelds and fines that figured so prominently in Continental and Insular 'barbarian' law codes, including his own. By doing so, he linked the holy past and the historical present. Alfred's code thus becomes a species of divine legislation and, by analogy, the West Saxons a new Chosen People fulfilling a covenant of rewards and punishments with a merciful but just God.[87]

To Alfred and his contemporaries, the brutal and turbulent political world depicted in the books of Samuel, Kings, and Chronicles must have seemed reassuringly familiar. They would have recognized themselves in biblical chieftains such as David who, aided by God and His holy men, ascended to kingship through the submission of the nobles and warred against foreign enemies and domestic rivals. If the great Mercian King Offa had pruned his family tree to secure the succession of his son, Ecgfrith, had not Solomon himself ordered the death of his older brother Adonijah and his followers? If the West Saxon King Caedwalla had contended for the throne by leading a warrior band in the wilderness, had he not followed in the footsteps of David? In Alfred's ordination as king, chrism was quite likely poured upon his head from a horn, in a literal borrowing from the Old Testament ritual of king-making, to the cry of 'Uncserunt

86. *Alfred* Intro. 49.7, trans. Keynes and Lapidge, pp. 163–4. The Anglo-Saxon text is edited by F. Liebermann in *Die Gesetze der Angelsachsen*, 3 vols (Halle, 1903–16) I, pp. 44–6, and by M.H. Turk, *The Legal Code of Ælfred the Great* (Boston, 1893).
87. Like Bede with the English people, ninth-century Carolingian ecclesiastical writers represented the Frankish people as 'a people of God' (*populus Dei*). See W. Ullmann, *The Carolingian Renaissance and the Idea of Kingship. The Birkbeck Lectures, 1968–9* (London, 1969) pp. 43–110; Wallace-Hadrill, *Early Germanic Kingship*, pp. 99–100, 98–125.

Salomonem', 'Thus they anointed Solomon'.[88] For Alfred the holy rulers and law-givers of the Old Testament, David, Solomon, Moses and Josiah, were practical exemplars.

Given Alfred's emphasis upon the divine origin of royal authority, one might expect to find in Alfred's law code, as we do in the writings of mid-ninth-century Carolingian ecclesiastics, an emphasis upon the sacral aspects of regality: grace, consecration and unction. That expectation, however, is not borne out by a reading of the text. Instead, we find that Alfred connected kingship with divine authority through the mediacy of lordship. In the laws, kingship is so closely tied to lordship that one cannot help but see the former as a species of the latter. Chapter four, for example, decrees that: 'If anyone plots against the king's life . . . he is liable for his life and all that he possesses', while '. . . he who plots against his lord's life is in return liable for his life and all that he possesses'.[89] The only difference between the two laws is in the size of the oath necessary to clear the accused of the charge: in the first case, it is to be equivalent to a king's wergeld and in the second, to that of the man's lord. The parallel construction clearly links kingship with lordship. Both clauses echo not only an earlier injunction against fulfilling oaths to betray one's lord [1.1], but a critical passage in Alfred's introduction.[90]

The mercy and forbearance that Christ taught and which holy synods and kings had translated into law extended to all wrongdoers but one: 'only for treachery to a lord did they dare not declare any mercy, since Almighty God adjudged none for those who despised Him, nor did Christ, the Son of God, adjudge any for the one who betrayed Him to death; and He commanded everyone to love his lord as

88. Nelson, *Politics and Ritual*, p. 354, 359. Cf. 1 Chron. 29:22–4; 2 Sam. 5:3; 1 Kings 1:39. On the importance of David and Solomon as royal exemplars in the early Middle Ages, see H.H. Anton, *Fürstenspiegel und Herrscherethos in der Karolingerzeit*, Bonn 32 (Bonn, 1986) pp. 101–4, 419–32. See also J. Nelson, *Charles the Bald* (London, 1992) pp. 15, 85.
89. Trans. Keynes and Lapidge, p. 165.
90. Cf. the injunction against conspiring to kill a king in chapter 12 of the capitulary issued by Pope Hadrian's Legates to the English in 786: 'Let no one dare to conspire to kill a king, for he is the Lord's anointed'. *EHD* I, no. 191, p. 838.

Himself'.[91] The crime of *hlafordsearwe*, treachery against one's lord, is made 'bootless' on the authority of Christ himself. Not only did Alfred connect the authority and person of the Lord Christ to that of his earthly ministers, the kings and the lords who serve them, but he underscored the high dignity with which God had endowed lordship by transforming Christ's Second Commandment from 'Love your neighbour as yourself' (Matt. 22:39–40) to 'Love your lord as you would love Christ Himself'. For Alfred, lordship was a sacred bond instituted by God himself for the governance of man. As he observed in the *Pastoral Care*, in a gloss that materially alters the meaning of Gregory's text, 'therefore when we offend against lords, we offend against God who created lordship'.[92]

Alfred's choice of political vocabulary in his *Pastoral Care* confirms that, to him, the sanctity of the king's person had less to do with his consecration than with the royal lordship with which God had endowed him. The king translated the text into his own cultural idiom, setting it firmly within a contemporary West Saxon political context. Pope Gregory I's *Pastoral Rule* had been written specifically as a model for bishops, but Gregory's language, especially his choice of the ambiguous *rector*, 'ruler', to connote 'bishop' and his use of Old Testament kings as exemplars, made it easy for Alfred to read the treatise as a work of general guidance for all men of authority. 'In Gregory's world', Robert Markus has observed, 'bishops and rulers were so alike that they could easily be thought of in the same vocabulary.'[93] If anything, Alfred's translation further blurred the distinction between secular and ecclesiastic authority. Gregory's *rector* and *praepositus* became *ealdormonn* or *sciremonn* (or, sometimes, a 'teacher', even where Gregory himself left this

91. Keynes and Lapidge, pp. 163–4.
92. *Alfred's Pastoral Care*, ed. Sweet, ch. 28, p. 201, l.2: '*forðam ðonne we agyltað wið ða hlafordas, ðonne agylte we wi(ð) ðone God ðe hlafordscipe gescop*'. Cf. Gregory the Great, *Regulae pastoralis liber*, ed. J.-P. Migne, *Patrologiae Cursus Completus Latinae* 77 (Paris, 1896), part 3, ch. 4, col. 56: '*Nam cum præpositis delinquimus, ejus ordinationi qui eos nobis prætulit obvimus*'.
93. R. Markus, 'Gregory the Great's *rector* and his genesis', in J. Fontaine, R. Gillet and S. Pellistrandi, eds, *Grégoire le Grand*, Colloques Internationaux du Centre National de la Recherche Scientifique (Paris, 1986) p. 138.

unsaid).[94] It is interesting how rarely Alfred used terms for kingship in this work and how often he added references to lordship to define and explain general relationships of superiority or of political rule in the original. An example appears in chapter 28 of the translation, which deals with how one ought to admonish rulers and subjects. Here Gregory held up as a model for behaviour David's refusal to kill King Saul when the latter was hunting him; David realized that, ill-use notwithstanding, 'it was not fitting to slay a king consecrated to God'. Alfred rendered this sentiment word for word, but added that 'David forbore slaying Saul [whom he characterized as David's 'old lord' [*ealdhlaford*]] for the fear of God and out of *his old allegiance* [*treowum*].[95] This reference to 'fear of God' has an echo in Alfred's recurring admonition in the *Pastoral Care* to 'fear one's lord'. To Gregory's meditations upon the divinely ordained equality of man and the humility with which a bishop ought to exercise authority even over transgressors, Alfred added, 'and yet it is necessary for a man to fear his lord [*his hlaford ondræde*], and a servant his master'.[96] To 'fear one's lord' was, for Alfred, a Christian duty; it was what St Paul had meant when he enjoined obedience to earthly authority.[97] The parallel between earthly lords and the Lord Christ was uppermost in Alfred's mind.

If Alfred found an image of Christian kingship to emulate in the Scripture, he found a second, and for him complementary, ideal in the vernacular poetry he loved. The

94. Compare, e.g., Gregory the Great, *Regulae Pastoralis Liber*, part 2, ch. 6, cols. 34–5, with *King Alfred's Pastoral Care*, ed. Sweet, ch. 17, pp. 107–8. Alfred also uses *lareowas*, teachers, to translate Gregory's *rectores* in this chapter.

95. *Alfred's Pastoral Care*, ed. Sweet, ch. 28, p. 197; cf. Gregory the Great, *Regulae Pastoralis Liber*, part 3, ch. 4, cols. 55–6.

96. *Alfred's Pastoral Care*, ed. Sweet, ch. 17, p. 108; cf. Gregory the Great, *Regulae Pastoralis Liber*, part 2, ch. 6, col. 34. Cf. Bede's commentary on the relevant biblical text, 1 Sam. 24:7, which emphasizes Saul's unction and provides an allegorical interpretation: *In Primam Partem Samuhelis libri* III, ch. 7, in *Bedae Venerabilis Opera: Opera Exegitica*, 2, ed. D. Hurst, *Corpus Christianorum, Series Latina* 119, pt. ii, 2 (Turnholt, 1962) p. 226. H. Maur's commentary on the four books of kings (ch. 24) also stresses unction and interprets the passage within a strictly allegorical and anagogical context.

97. *Alfred's Pastoral Care*, Sweet, ch. 62, p. 457; cf. Gregory the Great, *Regulae Pastoralis Liber*, part 3, ch. 38.

heroic aspect of Alfred's kingship is seen not only in the praise that Asser lavished upon his abilities as a warlord, but in his depiction of the king as the generous 'gift-giver'. Reciprocal gift-giving is one of the dominant themes and the 'open-handed lord' one of the stock characters in both Anglo-Saxon heroic poetry and the so-called wisdom literature. Alfred himself, when he tried his own hand at verse by translating Boethius's metres, visualized the author of the *Consolations* as 'a high-born chieftain, cherishing his lord . . . a giver of treasure, glorious ever', a characterization that probably would not have displeased the aristocratic scholar.[98] As we have already seen, both in heroic poetry such as *Beowulf* and in acts of statesmanship such as Alfred's gifts to his godson, Guthrum,[99] the giving of gifts created bonds of moral obligation.

' "God loves a cheerful giver" ', Asser intoned, quoting Scripture, and by this measure Alfred must have been one of the Lord's favourites. Alfred's generosity to those who frequented his court is a leitmotif in Asser's account, and it is no accident that the 'vessel' Alfred piloted to safety was 'laden with much wealth'. To Bishop Wulfsige, he was 'Alfred of the English, the greatest treasure-giver of all the kings he has ever heard tell of, in recent times or long ago, or of any earthly king he had previously learned of'.[100] Alfred regarded wealth as an essential resource of kingship, 'lent' him by God to be enjoyed in accordance with His will, to maintain his followers and reward the deserving.[101] Asser assures us that: 'With a cheerful disposition, he paid out [a sixth of the revenues received from royal taxation] to foreigners of all races who came to him from places near

98. *Alfred's Boethius*, trans. Sedgefield, p. 179. Cf. Nelson, 'Political Ideas', pp. 136–7. While Nelson is certainly right about Alfred using the idiom of Old English heroic poetry, one ought not to exaggerate the gulf between Boethius's and Alfred's cultural perspectives. Alfred's characterization of Boethius is fundamentally correct. The historical Boethius spent lavishly upon public games and distributed food and wealth to the Roman public when his sons were made consuls. The philosophic rejection of wealth for which he is now remembered came only at the end of an active civic life.

99. *Beowulf*, ll. 39–41; Asser, ch. 56. See discussion at pp. 38, 163 above.

100. Bishop Wulfsige's Preface to the translation of Gregory's *Dialogues*, trans. Keynes and Lapidge, p. 188.

101. See *Alfred's Boethius*, ed. Sedgefield, chs 6, 17, pp. 16–7, 41.

and far and asked money from him (or even if they did not ask), to each according to his particular station.'[102] Little wonder that Franks, Frisians, Gauls, heathen Danes, Irishmen, Bretons, and, of course, Welshmen, flocked to his court to be 'ruled, loved, honoured, and enriched'.[103]

In this Alfred was continuing the policy of his father, Æthelwulf, who, as we have seen, had distributed a tenth of the royal estate among his nobility and churchmen 'to the praise of God and his own eternal salvation' before he departed in 855 on pilgrimage to Rome. This merger of generous lord and Christian king is graphically represented by two finger rings, now in the British Museum, associated with Alfred's father, Æthelwulf, and sister, Æthelswith. The first bears the inscription Eth/eluulfr/x ('Æthelwulf rex') and bears a central design representing the Christian symbol of two peacocks flanking the Tree of Life. Scholars who have studied this ring and its companion in the British Museum, a second finger ring inscribed with the name of Alfred's sister, Æthelswith, Queen of Mercia, and decorated with a stylized *Agnus Dei* (a reference to John 1:29) flanked by the letters A and D, interpret them as 'gifts or as symbols of office bestowed upon faithful retainers'.[104] If so, we have in these rings material representations of Æthelwulf's and Alfred's ideology of kingship, a conception that placed traditional elements of barbarian lordship within the context of Christian kingship.

Wisdom for Alfred entailed not a repudiation of worldly wealth, as it had for Augustine or Boethius,[105] but the knowledge and virtue to use it well. No king, Alfred mused, can properly exercise authority or display his talents without the necessary human 'tools': a fully populated land and the services of praying men, fighting men, and working men. To maintain his instruments a king needed to provide 'land to dwell in, gifts, weapons, meat, ale, clothing, and whatever else the three classes need. Without these means he cannot keep his tools in order, and without these tools he

---

102. Asser, ch. 101, trans. Keynes and Lapidge, pp. 106–07.
103. Asser, ch. 76, trans. Keynes and Lapidge, pp. 91.
104. L. Webster, 'The Legacy of Alfred,' in J. Backhouse, D.H. Turner, and L. Webster, eds, *The Golden Age of Anglo-Saxon Art 966–1066* (Bloomington, 1984) p. 30.
105. See pp. 240–1 above.

cannot perform any of the tasks entrusted to him'.[106] In his generosity Alfred was practising the wisdom of good kingship, binding to him the helpers whom he needed to fulfil his obligations to God and to the men whom he 'has and holds'.[107]

He was also demonstrating his love for those who had taken him as their lord, offering not only material wealth but, more importantly, his friendship. 'With wonderful love he cherished his bishops and the entire clergy, his ealdormen and his nobles, his officials, as well as the members of his household.'[108] If a subject was enjoined to fear his lord, he was equally obliged to love him. For Alfred this was Christ's own commandment and formed the very foundation of the political world. This sentiment so informed the ideas of lordship and kingship in ninth- and tenth-century England that the proper manner of addressing a king was 'beloved' (*leof*), sometimes rendered as 'sire' or 'sir' by translators apparently uncomfortable with so great a degree of familiarity toward royalty.[109] As a gift looked for its return, so love, freely bestowed, was to be answered in full measure by the open-handed lord. Love, in this sense, was the essence of good lordship, and gifts were merely its manifestation. A thegn was enjoined to prefer the giver to the gift and to be willing to forfeit his worldly wealth if so commanded by his lord.[110] Alfred spoke of love in a number of his interpolations in his translations, especially in his very loose rendition of Augustine's *Soliloquies*, almost always in the context

---

106. E.g., *Alfred's Boethius*, ed. Sedgefield, ch. 17, p. 41. On the meaning of worldly riches to Alfred, see T.A. Shippey, 'Wealth and Wisdom in Alfred's *Preface* to the Old English *Pastoral Care*', *EHR* 94 (1979) pp. 346–55; J. Nelson, 'Wealth and Wisdom: the politics of Alfred the Great', in J. Rosenthal, ed., *Kings and Kingship*, Acta 11 (1984, publ. 1987) pp. 31–52; Nelson, 'Political Ideas', pp. 144–6, 157–8.
107. *Alfred's Soliloquies*, ed. Carnicelli, p. 72, ll. 16–17; p. 73, ll. 15–16.
108. Asser, ch. 76 (my translation).
109. *Leof* is the standard royal address in tenth-century letters, legal memoranda, and wills, e.g., S 1444, S 1445, S 1504, S 1504, S 1520; *III Aethlstan* Preamble. See S.D. Keynes, 'The Fonthill Letter', in M. Korhammer (with K. Reichl and H. Sauer), eds, *Words, Texts and Manuscripts. Studies in Anglo-Saxon Culture Presented to Helmut Gneuss on the Occasion of his Sixty-Fifth Birthday* (Cambridge, 1992) p. 63 n. 45.
110. *Alfred's Soliloquies*, ed. Carnicelli, pp. 62–63.

of true friendship or lordship. [111] In one of these Reason asks the speaker why he does not love the eternal Lord more than the temporal, since the latter is 'He who gives to you both the friendship of the worldly lord and His own. . . . The Lord is the ruler of you both, of you and your lord whom you so immeasurably love.'[112] From love for one's lord one could ascend to love of the Lord Christ. One cannot help but feel that for Alfred lordship remained a species of friendship, and that the king's thegns and servants were, in some sense, his true companions. This, I believe, is what Alfred meant by it being 'unjust' and 'unseemly' for a king to rule over a nation of slaves. Only free men could willingly return love and loyalty.[113] Alfred's answer to the ancient question posed of rulers: whether it is better to be loved or feared, would come closer to Cicero's answer than Machiavelli's.

In his oft-cited preface to Gregory's *Pastoral Care*, Alfred paired wisdom with both warfare and wealth. In this conjunction, I believe that we see best Alfred's conception of a good king. A ruler had to emulate Solomon by acquiring and practising wisdom. Such wisdom for Alfred combined both pragmatic skill and moral virtue, encompassing within it the virtues of prudence, temperance, courage, and justice.[114] A good king not only needed to be wise himself, but to be a teacher of wisdom, 'gently instructing, cajoling, urging, commanding' his bishops and nobles to prefer the 'general advantage of the realm' to their own private interests.[115] Not only did he have to be (in Asser's words) 'a painstaking judge in establishing the truth in judicial hearings, and this most of all in cases concerning the care of the poor',

---

111. See, e.g., *Alfred's Soliloquies*, ed. Carnicelli, pp. 62–3, 24–5, 60–1, trans. Keynes and Lapidge, pp. 142, 144, 149, 151–2; cf. *Alfred's Boethius*, ed. Sedgefield, ch. 24, p. 54; trans. Sedgefield, p. 57.
112. *Alfred's Soliloquies*, ed. Carnicelli, p. 63; trans. Hargrove, p. 16. Cf. *Alfred's Soliloquies*, ed. Carnicelli, pp. 88–9.
113. *Alfred's Boethius*, ch. 46, ed. Sedgefield, pp. 166–7.
114. Ibid., ch. 27, p. 67.
115. Asser, ch. 91, trans. Keynes and Lapidge, pp. 101–2. The idea of the king as teacher of divine wisdom and morality may be traced back to Charlemagne's English court-scholars, Alcuin and Cathwulf. A. Thacker, 'Bede's Ideal of Reform', in Wormald, Bullough, and Collin, eds, *Ideal and Reality*, p. 152; Wallace-Hadrill, *Early Germanic Kingship*, pp. 101–2.

but he was equally obliged to force his nobles to acquire the wisdom to judge well.[116]

But wise kings did not only maintain 'peace, morality, and authority at home. They also extended their territory abroad.' As Alfred observed, in the olden times kings succeeded in both warfare and in wisdom. And wisdom, in turn, brought with it the acquisition of wealth and the knowledge of how to use wealth properly.[117] Alfred's wisdom may have shared something of Augustinian *sapientia*; there is little doubt that for Alfred wisdom was indeed a moral and religious quality necessary for a Christian king.[118] Having said that, we are still left with the image of the wise king not only maintaining peace at home but extending his kingdom's borders at the expense of his neighbours, much like the 'good king', Scyld Scefing, in *Beowulf* or the God-favoured rulers in the Old English Orosius. The wealth that wisdom brought was not only the goods of the mind obtained from the study of books, but the material prosperity enjoyed by victorious people favoured by God. Alfred's appreciation of this duality is manifested by his attaching an *aestel* worth 50 mancuses – the value of fifty oxen (and more than the wergeld of a commoner) – to each copy of his translation of Gregory's *Pastoral Care*, and in the iconography of the Alfred Jewel in the Ashmolean Museum.[119] This was the wisdom learned not only from the writings of patristic and Carolingian theologians, but from Alfred's own meditations upon Scripture, especially upon the words and deeds

116. Asser, ch. 105–6, trans. Keynes and Lapidge, pp. 109–10.
117. *Alfred's Pastoral Care*, Preface, ed. Sweet, pp. 2–5.
118. P. Szarmach, 'Anglo-Saxon Letters in the Eleventh Century', *Acta* 1 (1974) p. 3; P. Wormald, 'The Uses of Literacy in Anglo-Saxon England and its Neighbours', *TRHS*, 5th ser., 27, p. 107.
119. *Alfred's Pastoral Care*, ed. Sweet, p. 5. It is not completely certain what an *æstel* was, but the context and the word's etymological roots suggest a pointer or bookmark. The Alfred Jewel is thought to have been one such *æstel*. Keynes and Lapidge, pp. 203–6. D. Howlett, 'The iconography of the Alfred Jewel', *Oxoniensia* 39 (1974) pp. 44–52, has plausibly suggested that the figure on the Jewel represents the Wisdom of Christ incarnate; other scholars have interpreted it as a representation of Sight (E. Bakka, 'The Alfred Jewel and Sight', *Antiquaries Journal* 46 (1966) pp. 277–82) or of King David as symbol of sacred kingship (above p. 239, n. 60). For the price of an ox, see *VI Æthelstan* 6 § 2.

of Solomon, in whom he and other early medieval rulers found the ideal of wise kingship. [120] For it was Solomon who declared that Wisdom endows with riches those who love her and fills their treasuries (Prov. 8:21), and it was he who explained in terms that Alfred could appreciate the many bounties that wisdom conferred upon a king who loved her:

> Through her, I thought, I will win fame with the crowds and honour among older men, as young as I am. When I sit in judgement, I shall prove myself acute, and the great men will behold with admiration and astonishment; when I am silent, they will hold themselves back, and when I speak they will attend, and though I hold forth at length, they will lay a finger to their lips and listen. Through her I shall have immortality, and shall leave an eternal memory to those who come after me. I shall rule over peoples, and nations will become my subjects. Horrid tyrants will be frightened when they hear of me; among my people I shall show myself to be good and in war, brave. When I come home, I shall rest with her; for there is no bitterness in her company, no pain in life with her, only gladness and joy. [121]

120. Anton, *Fürstenspiegel und Herrscherethos*, pp. 255–60, 430–1; Nelson, 'Wealth and Wisdom', p. 36.
121. Wisdom of Solomon 8:10–16. The translation is that of *The New English Bible* (New York, 1971) p. 105, though I have revised it in parts in accordance with the Vulgate.

Chapter 8

THE PRACTICE OF KINGSHIP

'What shall I say', asked Asser rhetorically, 'of his frequent expeditions and battles against the pagans and of the unceasing responsibilities of government?'[1] Asser knew exactly which of Alfred's governmental activities would impress his readers, in part because he had before him the model of Einhard's *Life of Charlemagne*. Like Charlemagne, Alfred was to be portrayed as a world figure, commanding the attention of rulers from 'the nations which lie from the Tyrrhenian Sea to the farthest end of Ireland', the recipient of letters and gifts even from Elias, patriarch of Jerusalem. And, again following the models of Charlemagne and Solomon, Alfred was to be held up as a builder. Asser draws to our attention the cities and towns Alfred had restored or built from scratch and the 'royal halls and chambers marvellously constructed of stone and wood' raised upon his command.[2] These marvellous constructions are now little more than post holes and earthen ramparts. But for Asser the thirty forts of the Burghal Hidage were nothing short of miraculous, wonders of craftsmanship that were the physical manifestations of Alfred's wealth, glory, and power.

The burhs, like his military and cultural accomplishments, were consequences of Alfred's ability to govern effectively, of his skill at binding his subjects to his will. Asser's litany of Alfred's accomplishments serves as a preamble to his description of how Alfred, that 'excellent pilot' of the ship of state, ruled, 'by gently instructing, cajoling, urging, commanding, and, in the end, when his patience was exhausted

1. Asser, ch. 91, trans. Keynes and Lapidge, p. 101.
2. Ibid.

258

by sharply chastising'[3] the recalcitrant and disobedient. Governance was personal rather than 'institutional', and 'the unceasing responsibilities of government' had less to do with the techniques of bureaucracy than with knowing when to praise and when to punish. 'Now no man can get full play for his natural gifts', Alfred wrote, 'nor conduct and administer government, unless he has fit tools, and the raw material to work upon. . . . A king's raw material and instruments of rule are a well-peopled land, and he must have men of prayer, men of war, and men of work. . . . Without these tools he cannot perform any of the tasks entrusted to him.'[4] To understand how Alfred ruled his kingdom, had his burhs built, defended his kingdom, preserved order and did justice, one must turn from the material artefacts that reflect his success to the human resources upon which it was based.

. . .

THE 'TOOLS' OF GOVERNMENT

'The [viking army] had not, by God's favour, afflicted the English people very greatly', reflected the Chronicler in his entry for the year 896. What had been a greater calamity during the previous three years, he thought, were the deaths of so many of the best king's thegns:

> Of those, one was Swithwulf, bishop of Rochester; and Ceolmund, ealdorman of Kent; and Beorhtwulf, ealdorman of Essex; and Wulfred, ealdorman of Hampshire; and Ealhheard, bishop of Dorchester; and Eadwulf, a king's thegn in Sussex; and Beornwulf, the town-reeve of Winchester; and Ecgwulf, the king's horse-thegn, and many besides them, though I have named the most distinguished.[5]

In this annal the Chronicler has given us a cross section of the men upon whom the king relied for the administration of his realm, his bishops, ealdormen, king's thegns, reeves, and court officials. Whether lay or ecclesiastic, in the Chronicler's eyes they were all 'king's thegns'. They served as Alfred's counsellors, the leaders of his armies, the custodians of his

---

3. Ibid.
4. *King Alfred's Version of the Consolations of Boethius*, trans. W.J. Sedgefield (Oxford, 1900) ch. 17, p. 41.
5. *ASC, s.a.* 896.

lands, and the executors of his justice. That the Chronicler found their deaths to be a greater affliction to the English people than the ravaging of the viking armies is eloquent testimony to the personal character of Anglo-Saxon governance. The safety of the realm depended upon men such as these, and, obviously, the Chronicler did not think that they would be easily replaced.

At the heart of the royal administration, as we glimpse it in the pages of Asser and in Alfred's own writings, were the king and his household, a fluctuating, peripatetic court that itinerated among the various royal and ecclesiastical estates of the realm. Alfred's *Soliloquies* explain how followers of the king sought him by various routes, some at a royal estate, some at an assembly or in the field with the army, and were received with differing degrees of familiarity and reverence. Some, Alfred explained, received virtually none, except that the king loved them all.[6] Alfred's world was strictly hierarchical; one's place was reflected not by the tariffs of wergeld and penalties that make up so much of Alfred's law code, but even by the sleeping arrangements at court, where, we learn, 'some men are in the chamber, some in the hall, some on the threshing-floor, some in prison, and yet all of them live through the one lord's favor'. One gets the impression, however, that royal favour could be as transitory as the location of the court itself.[7]

For the most part Alfred's court was populated by his immediate entourage, his officials, servants, chaplains, household warriors, foster sons, and blood kin, as well as any distinguished or interesting foreigners who happened to be visiting. The king's affinity, though, stretched from his court to the countryside, embracing not only the great royal agents, his ealdormen, bishops, and reeves, but local landowners as well, men who by the ninth century were already known as 'king's thegns'. When Alfred needed to decide important matters of state or resolve knotty disputes, he would summon to his side these lay and spiritual magnates for counsel and support, and his household would be transformed into an assembly of notables.

6. *Alfred's Soliloquies*, ed. Carnicelli, pp. 77, 96–7; trans. Hargrove, pp. 27, 43. See Keynes and Lapidge, pp. 143–4, 151–2.
7. Ibid.

Nineteenth-century historians, eager to provide the English Constitution and, in particular, the Parliament, with proper pedigrees, reified Alfred's consultations with his counsellors, his 'wise men' (*witan*), into a discrete organ of government which they termed the Witenagemot. The sources for Alfred's reign, however, should discourage any attempt to remake him into a constitutional monarch on the model of Prince Albert (or even the three Georges) presiding over meetings of a floating National Assembly. As used in Alfred's law code and other ninth-century diplomatic texts, the word *witan* is more a term of status than office, denoting a group of individuals deemed worthy of advising kings.[8] When a king sought their counsel on holy matters, they were a synod; on secular issues, an assembly. The composition of this coterie fluctuated greatly, as can be seen from the few charters of Alfred and his brothers that have survived. The appearance of ealdormen and bishops depended upon the occasion and the location of the court. If the surviving charter evidence is at all representative, Alfred's assemblies were mainly local affairs, where he would grant land or hear disputes attended by his immediate entourage and in the presence of an ealdorman or two, a few local bishops, perhaps a scattering of the shire's notables, and, of course, the interested parties.

When issues touched upon 'the common needs of the whole realm', Alfred would have called together 'all his counsellors' (though 'all' in these documents is more a term of art than a reflection of reality). While the occasions on which Alfred summoned 'all his *witan*' together were doubtless quite formal and impressive – Alfred himself wrote of kings 'seated on high seats, bright with many kinds of raiment, and girt about with a great company of their thegns, who are decked with belts and golden-hilted swords and war dress of many kinds'[9] – we should not fall into the anachronism of viewing such assemblies as proto-Parliaments. They were closer in spirit to the great councils of the Norman

8. Interestingly, the translator of Orosius used the Latin word *senatus* to designate the Roman Senate as a body, and *wita*/*witan* when referring to individual senators or (in two instances) a group of senators. *Old English Orosius*, ed. Bately, pp. 338, 404. Cf. S 367, 371 (Mercian charters of Edward the Elder, dated 903 and 904): *senatores Merciorum*.
9. *King Alfred's Boethius*, ch. 37, trans. Sedgefield, p. 128.

and Angevin kings, 'sessions of the king's court with a public face'.[10]

The sources, meagre as they are, afford some insight into Alfred's dealings with his counsellors and the conduct of such meetings. The Preface to Alfred's law code describes how he sought his magnates' advice when compiling the laws and then, upon completing his work, how he 'showed these to all his counsellors [*witan*], and they then said that it pleased them all to observe them'.[11] We also find the '*witan* of all the English race' agreeing to Alfred's treaty with Guthrum, and the Mercian *witan* witnessing, alongside Alfred, the arrangements devised by Ealdorman Æthelred and Æthelflæd for the building of fortifications at Worcester.[12] Alfred probably did not take any major step, whether military, civil, or religious, without consulting those men who would be most responsible for implementing the king's will.

An assembly of magnates was also an occasion for the expression of 'public opinion', or what passed for public opinion in the ninth century. As we have already seen, Alfred responded to his nephews' discontent over their inheritance by bringing the matter before an assembly at *Langedune*, where he had his father's will read aloud 'before all the counsellors of the West Saxons'. Alfred, swearing that he would bear no grudge against any man who spoke the truth, asked the assembled magnates 'to declare the customary law (*folcriht*) in such a case, lest any man should say that I had wronged my kinsfolk, whether of the older or the younger generation'. The *witan* responded by assuring the king that they could find 'no more just a title, nor find one in the will'. They then all solemnly gave their pledge and their sign manual.[13] What Alfred had sought, and obtained, was a public affirmation that he had dealt justly with his nephews. His exhortation to his counsellors to speak their mind freely without fear of retribution has a touch of the theatrical to it, almost like the formal preamble to a

10. W.L. Warren, *Henry II* (Berkeley, CA, 1973) p. 303.
11. *Alfred* Intro. 49.9–10, trans. Keynes and Lapidge, p. 164.
12. Treaty between Alfred and Guthrum, in Keynes and Lapidge, p. 171; S 223, trans. *EHD* I, pp. 540–1.
13. S 1507; Harmer, ed., *SEHD*, no. 11, pp. 15–19, 49–53. Cf. Keynes and Lapidge, p. 175; *EHD* I, p. 535.

public spectacle.[14] These proceedings were perhaps less a request for advice or a determination of law than the functional equivalent of a vote of confidence, manifested through the pledge and attestations that followed the rendering of judgement.

Great assemblies such as this were probably rare. Only two of the fourteen charters that purport to have been issued by Alfred are attested by more than two bishops or three ealdormen. The daily routine of central administration rested in the hands of the king, his household officers, and his entourage of clerics and thegns. Asser provides a rather idealized view of the workings of this body. Unsurprisingly, it resembles the households of the Carolingian and Capetian kings, with the confusion between domestic and public responsibilities so typical of the workings of early medieval administration. Asser tells us a good deal about his own activities and those of the other priests and chaplains of Alfred's household, John the Old Saxon, Grimbald of St-Bertin, and the Mercian priests, Plegmund, Æthelstan and Wærwulf. They instructed the king spiritually, educated him and his children in letters, read aloud to him and listened as he read to them, helped with his translations, and prayed for the well-being of his soul and his kingdom. Based on the consistency of formulas in his and his brothers' charters, they may also have functioned as a royal secretariat, corresponding in his name with foreign dignitaries, drawing up formal diplomas for those upon whom Alfred bestowed bookland and sealing orders of instruction to the king's agents.[15]

14. I suspect that the traditional formula for disclaiming partiality used the alliterative pair *leofran* and *laðran*, as did Alfred in his very free translation of Exodus 23.6, 'Do not make one judgement for those whom you love and another for those whom you loathe' *Alfred* Intro. 43, ed. Liebermann, *Gesetze* I, p. 40: 'Dem ðu swiðe rihte & swiðe emne. Ne dem ðu . . . oðerne ðam leofran and oðerne tham laðran ne dem ðu.' Alfred in his will, of course, does not admit that there are those who might not love him, so instead he tells them not to be swayed either by love (*for minan lufan*) or fear of him (*ne for minum ege*).
15. Asser, chs 77, 78, 88. On the likelihood of a central writing office under Æthelwulf and his sons, see S.D. Keynes, 'The West Saxon charters of King Æthelwulf and his sons', *EHR* 109 (1994) pp. 1131–49, and idem, 'Royal government and the written word in late Anglo-Saxon England', in R. McKitterick, *The Uses of Literacy in Early Medieval Europe* (Cambridge, 1990) pp. 244–5.

The secular element of the king's household was divided into two classes of followers, men of substance and property who served as officers of the household, and the humbler household warriors resident at court. The former possessed estates and households of their own; Alfred may have been thinking of them when in the *Soliloquies* he declared it better to respond to the letter and seal of one's lord than to linger behind so as to enjoy the wealth previously received as a reward.[16] As we have already seen, Alfred attempted to lighten the burden upon his landed thegns by dividing them into three cohorts, each of which would serve 'in various capacities' for a month in court, then return for two months to their own homes and attend to private affairs.[17] From the subscriptions to a charter, which survives only in a late medieval cartulary but has every indication of being genuine[18], we learn the names and offices of three of Alfred's household officials: Deormod, the 'cellerarius', who as the king's steward was responsible for provisions[19]; Ælfric, the 'thesaurarius', the keeper of the royal wardrobe and, by extension, of the treasure stored in a chest in the king's chamber[20]; Sigewulf, the 'pincerna', a royal butler who would later be raised to the rank of ealdorman of Kent. To these men we may add one more: the horse-thegn, Ecgwulf, whose death was mourned by the Chronicler and whose job it had been to care for the king's horses and, perhaps, to arrange

16. Ed. Carnicelli, p. 62; trans. Keynes and Lapidge, p. 141.
17. Asser, ch. 100, trans. Keynes and Lapidge, p. 106.
18. S 348 (dated AD 892), trans. Keynes and Lapidge, pp. 179–81 (comments, pp. 326–30). The charter is edited and discussed by D. Whitelock, 'Some Charters in the name of King Alfred', *Saints Scholars and Heroes: Studies in Medieval Culture in honour of Charles W. Jones*, ed. M.H. King, W.M. Stevens, Hill Monastic Manuscript Library, St John's Abbey and University (Collegeville, MN, 1979) pp. 77–98, at pp. 78–9.
19. Deormod witnessed charters for Alfred and Edward. S 345, 351, 352, 356, S 355, S 1445, S 362 (trans. *EHD* I, no. 541). Two men bear the title *cellerarius* in S 293, a grant by King Æthelwulf which survives in its original form.
20. Presumably Ælfric, the keeper of the wardrobe (*hrægglthegn*), who, according to a charter from Edward's reign, had been appointed by Alfred to investigate a legal dispute. See S 1445, trans. *EHD* I, no. 102, p. 544. He may also appear in S 351.

for transport for the court.[21] To modern ears such titles
might sound menial, and to be sure each of these men was
a servant of the king. But it was just this proximity to the
king's person that made them men of authority and prestige. One such was the king's thegn, Eastmund, who witnessed
a Kentish charter of Alfred's brother, King Æthelberht, dated
858 with the title '*pedesecus*'.[22] In classical Latin *pedisequus*
means something of the order of 'manservant' or 'lackey'.
The Anglo-Saxons apparently had higher regard for one
who attended at the feet of a king, for Eastmund's signature
appears immediately after Ealdorman Æthelmod's.[23] A decade later Eastmund was witnessing King Æthelred I's charters as ealdorman of Kent. Just as royal chaplains could
hope for an appointment to a episcopal see or abbacy, so
could a household official aspire to an ealdormanry – or
even to kinship with a king. Alfred, one might remember,
was himself the grandson of Oslac, 'King Æthelwulf's famous butler'.[24]

Of the sixty or so other thegns who witnessed charters of
King Alfred we know nothing more than their names. Many
of these men must have been household warriors, the other
main group of secular followers in Alfred's court. Fighting
men, Alfred declared, were, along with those who prayed
and those who worked, the necessary tools for a king's rule.[25]
In the turbulent years of Alfred's reign his household troops
played an especially important role. But one should not
think of them merely as 'tools' to be used in times of need.
They were also the king's hearth-companions, who feasted
at his table, slept in his hall, shared his delight in the
hunt, and followed him into the marshes of Somerset in
that dreadful and glorious winter of 878. We can glimpse

21. ASC s.a. 896. Keynes and Lapidge, 289 n. 34, suggest that he may be
    the same man who attests S 345 and S 356 and who is mentioned
    in Alfred's will (p. 175). Keepers of the king's horse (along with
    the keepers of his dogs and hawks) are mentioned in S 186 (*EHD* I,
    no. 83) as having the right to hospitality from landowners, presum-
    ably as they travelled on the king's business.
22. S 328; *EHD* I, no. 93, p. 531.
23. Cf. *Beowulf* ll. 499–500, where Unferth sits at the feet of King Hrothgar.
24. Asser, ch. 2. See above p. 48.
25. *King Alfred's Boethius*, trans. Keynes and Lapidge, p. 132.

their counterparts in the thegns who died at King Cynewulf's side rather than serve their lord's killer. Asser, influenced by his knowledge of Francia, called them *faselli*, 'vassals', which captures something of their intimacy with Alfred. The king's household men also played an important role in the civil administration of the realm in their capacity as royal messengers and emissaries. Ninth-century charters speak of *fæstingmen*, king's retainers, to whom hospitality was owed by those who held land from the king, presumably because they travelled on the king's business. Alfred's usual practice, as we learn from his own writings, was to send 'sealed letters' (*ærendgewrit and hys insegel*) of instruction to his landed retainers and local agents. In this way, he was able to summon his ealdormen, bishops and reeves to meetings and, to some extent, direct and oversee their activities.[26] Alfred's household men thus served as his eyes, ears and voice in his dealings with local government. Alfred rewarded his domestic servants and companions handsomely. He reserved one-sixth of his revenues for their use, paying them wages that reflected their rank and office. He remembered them also in his will, setting aside 200 pounds to be divided among them according to the manner in which they had been paid at the most recent Eastertide.[27]

The king's counsellors, his bishops and ealdormen, bridged the gap between central and local government. They, aided by the king's thegns and reeves, were responsible for administering justice, maintaining order, collecting the profits of justice and other royal revenues, and leading the king's armies. Asser regarded all of these men as invested 'after the Lord and the king, with the authority of the entire kingdom'.[28] Their compliance and collaboration were crucial to the successful implementation of Alfred's burghal policy. Alfred might command the building or refurbishing of 'cities and towns' and of 'royal halls and chambers marvellously

---

26. *Alfred's Soliloquies*, ed. Carnicelli, p. 62. Keynes, 'Royal government and the written word', pp. 244–5. F.E. Harmer suggests that Alfred's words ought to be taken as referring to writs, royal letters on administrative business to which seals were appended. *Anglo-Saxon Writs* (Manchester, 1952) pp. 1–3.

27. Asser, ch. 101, trans. Keynes and Lapidge, p. 106; Alfred's will, trans. Keynes and Lapidge, p. 177.

28. Asser, ch. 91, trans. Keynes and Lapidge, p. 102.

constructed of stone and wood', but it was up to local landowners and royal agents to bring the royal vision to fruition
by marshalling the necessary human and material resources
and finding the cash to pay for the work. As we have seen,
they were not always as enthusiastic about the task as Alfred
would have wished, and the king put a great deal of effort
into 'converting them to his will and to the general advantage of the realm'.

Though Alfred's spiritual and lay magnates differed in
wealth and power, they shared a personal relationship with
the king. This was as true of bishops as it was of ealdormen.
To each of the four bishops mentioned in his will Alfred left
the same bequest he made to his ealdormen, one hundred
mancuses (equivalent to 3,000 pennies), a monetary manifestation of the love he bore his spiritual thegns. Though
Alfred's bishops were great men in their own right, the king
seems to have regarded them as royal dependants and treated
them as such. They lacked the independence that their episcopal colleagues across the Channel had begun to enjoy. To
be sure, some engaged in political intrigue, and, as we have
seen, both King Egbert and King Æthelwulf eagerly sought
episcopal support for their choice of successors. Bishop
Ealhstan of Sherborne took a more direct hand in 'king-
making' when he conspired with King Æthelbald to prevent King Æthelwulf's return in 856. But even in this most
extreme of cases the bishop acted in the role of king's coun-
sellor, loyal to one of his lords if not the other. Though
Asser excoriated the betrayal of father by son and named
Ealhstan as one of the prime movers of the plot, the taint
of treason did not cling to the bishop. Rather, in his obituary notice Asser chose to characterize Ealhstan's fifty-year
rule as *honourable,* implicitly excusing his participation in the
treason much as the Chronicler forgave Cyneheard's thegns
for the murder of King Cynewulf.[29] What is perhaps most
remarkable is how amenable Alfred's bishops were to his
lordship. No Anglo-Saxon Hincmar of Rheims called Alfred
to account over his treatment of church lands (though
Archbishop Æthelred went behind his back to the pope), or
to remind him of his obligations to God. Rather, Alfred
exhorted *them* to be better pastors. Even as archbishops and

29. Asser, ch. 28, ed. Stevenson, p. 23. Cf. *ASC,* s.a. 867.

bishops, Asser, Wærferth, and Plegmund remained Alfred's thegns, frequenting his court, where they advised him, read to him, helped with translations, and, in short, shared the same activities as the royal chaplains. The main duties of a bishop, as Alfred reminded them in his *Pastoral Care,* were spiritual, and they served him best by serving the Lord well. They said prayers for the king and his loved ones, enforced church discipline upon priests and laity alike, and, undoubtedly, taught those in their charge the necessity of fulfilling their public oath to observe the law and obey their divinely ordained king. Nor should one underestimate the role they played in a legal system in which the boundary between sin and crime was indistinct. Oath-breakers risked not only their property and legal standing but their very souls. Wills and charters, with their spiritual preambles and anathema clauses, were as much religious as legal documents. It is little wonder that Alfred decreed in his laws (chapter 42) that disputes over the disposition of land held by book-right were to be heard in the presence of a bishop, and that a man who had foresworn himself was to be imprisoned on a king's estate and do penance as prescribed by a bishop (chapter 1.2).

In the bishop, as in the king, spiritual and secular authority commingled. Enjoying extensive holdings of land and lordship over numerous thegns and free and servile peasants, the princes of the Church were also lords of this world possessed of secular authority that, in some respects, bordered upon the regal. Eighth- and ninth-century archbishops enjoyed the prerogatives most associated with royal rule, the maintenance of justice, the making of law, and the issuance of currency. Alfred saw little to distinguish between the legislation produced by synods and royal assemblies, and there is even less to differentiate between the pennies struck in the names of the archbishops of Canterbury, Æthelred and Plegmund, and King Alfred, many with portraits based upon imperial Roman prototypes. Just as Gregory the Great's *Pastoral Rule* provided a model of authority equally relevant to secular and spiritual rulers, Alfred in his translation of this work thought it appropriate to describe St Peter as receiving from God the 'ealdordom' of the Holy Church, and by the reign of his grandson, King Æthelstan (924–939), bishops would play as explicit and central a role in the maintenance of order and punishment of criminals as ealdormen.[30]

The specific governmental duties and powers of Alfred's prelates are less certain due to the fragmentary nature of our sources. The secular activity of bishops most emphasized in the sources is military. As strange as it may seem, the battlefield exploits of Bishop Ealhstan of Sherborne and his successor, Heahmund, are better documented than their spiritual endeavours.[31] Whatever jurisdictional authority they had at this time may have come by way of grants from the king or his ealdormen. Ealdorman Æthelred of Mercia and his wife, Æthelflæd, according to a charter issued in their name sometime in the 890s, ordered the construction of fortifications at Worcester 'at the request of Bishop Wærferth their friend'. 'In the witness of King Alfred and of all the counsellors who are in the lands of the Mercians', they bestowed upon the bishop 'half of all the rights which [belonged] to their lordship, whether in the market or in the street, both within the fortification and outside; that things may be more honourably maintained in the foundation'. Whatever rights the bishop was to enjoy in his episcopal burh derived from and were to be shared with ealdorman Æthelred and Æthelflæd. Whether this meant that the bishop was to be responsible for overseeing the burh's court and collecting rents and fines as well as taking a cut of the profits is not clear.[32] What this charter does point up is that bishops, along with ealdormen, took a leading role in the establishment of Alfred's burghal system. Bishop Wærferth and Archbishop Plegmund were among the counsellors who met with Alfred at Chelsea in 898/899 to plan out the 'renovation' (*instauratio*) of the burh of London. At that assembly, as we have seen, Alfred granted to Wærferth and Plegmund estates in London near Ealdorman Æthelred's wharf (*Ætheredes hyd*, modern-day Queenhythe) along with market privileges and the right to moor ships. As Nicholas Brooks observes, 'The provision of burghal defences, and of

---

30. *Alfred's Pastoral Care*, ed. Sweet, ch. 17, p. 114. See *III Æthelstan* Preamble; *VI Æthelstan*; *II Edgar* 3.1; *III Edgar* 3, 5.2.
31. *ASC*, s.a. 845, 871.
32. *EHD* I, no. 899, pp. 540–1.

secure houses, streets and markets was of as much interest to the church as it was to the king. . . . If their churches were to be secure from Viking assaults in the future, the bishops had every reason to assist Alfred as best they could in creating effective burghal defences.'[33]

The greatest lay official in Alfred's kingdom was the ealdorman. The position of ealdorman seems to have originated in the governance of the subkingdoms that comprised early Wessex, but since the days of Ine in the late seventh century, the ealdormen of Wessex had functioned as royal administrators of the shires. By 871 there were probably eleven or so ealdormen at any one time in Wessex: two for Kent, an ancient kingdom traditionally divided into eastern and western districts, and one for each of the other nine shires. (We know nothing about the administration of Cornwall at this time.) During Alfred's reign some twenty-five men held the office of ealdorman, a rate of turnover reflecting in part the hazards arising from their military duties.[34] All were great men from ancient and distinguished lineages, and some could undoubtedly trace their ancestry back to Cerdic. But all of them were also the king's 'companions', his *comites*, bound to him by friendship and oath, and however independently an ealdorman may have acted, he was as much a king's man as the lowliest fighting man in the royal entourage. Some ealdormen even began their careers as king's thegns serving in the royal household. This was the case for Æthelmod, ealdorman of Kent under Æthelwulf and Æthelberht from 855 to 858, who prior to this had been a king's thegn and keeper of the royal cellar in Kent.[35] Similarly, Ceolmund, ealdorman of Kent, and Wulfred, ealdorman

33. N. Brooks, *The Early History of the Church of Canterbury. Christ Church from 597 to 1066* (Leicester, 1984) p. 154. For the charter see Harmer, ed., *SEHD*, no. 13, and discussion by A. Vince, *Saxon London: An Archaeological Investigation* (London, 1990) pp. 20–22.

34. The number is derived from the witness lists of the charters and from references in the *Anglo-Saxon Chronicle*. No attempt has been made to distinguish between 'authentic', 'interpolated', and forged charters. Simon Keynes identifies sixty-six West Saxon ealdorman in the ninth century, thirty-six of whom served the sons of Æthelwulf between 858 and 899. *An Atlas of Attestations in Anglo-Saxon Charters, c. 670–1066* (forthcoming), Table XXII.

35. S 315, 316, 1196, 328 (as ealdorman). Cf. S 293 (*cellararius*, Kent 843); S 289, 291, 296, 319 ('874' for 844).

of Hampshire, whose deaths are lamented by the Chronicler in the annal for 896, had long ministerial careers in the royal household before assuming the position of ealdorman. This, in fact, seems to have been a standard career path. Of the twenty-five ealdormen who served under Alfred, perhaps as many as fifteen previously witnessed charters in the capacity of king's thegns.

King Æthelwulf's ealdormen enjoyed higher dignity than all other nobles, and it is not unusual to find their attestations in royal diplomas preceding those of the king's own sons.[36] This was in large measure borrowed honour derived from their office rather than their lineage. It reflected their familiarity with the king and their role as the king's agents *par excellence.* King Alfred in his law code placed ealdormen on equal footing in terms of social status and legal protection with bishops (though below archbishops). The fine for breaking into the fortified residences of ealdormen and bishops was sixty shillings, only half as much as for a king's estate, but twice as much as for a nobleman's and ten times as much as for an ordinary commoner's.[37] There is also some evidence that ealdormen were protected by a double wergeld: 1,200 shillings for their noble birth and another 1,200 for their office.[38]

The ealdormen of the mid-tenth century were a close-knit group bound to each other, and to the king, by kinship, marriage, and friendship. The same was probably true of Alfred's ealdormen, though the prosopographical knowledge concerning them is scanty at best. Ordlaf, who became ealdorman of Wiltshire in the last years of Alfred's reign, was the grandson of Eanwulf, ealdorman of Somerset under both Æthelwulf and Æthelbald. The two ealdormen of Kent in 898, Alfred's former butler, Sigewulf, and Sigehelm, may well have been blood relations, since noble families identified themselves by sharing the leading element of their names and *Sige-* compounds were not that common at this time.[39] Sigewulf was certainly a kinsman of ealdorman Alfred (probably of Surrey), for he is mentioned in that Alfred's will,

---

36. E.g., S 316, 348.
37. *Alfred* chs 3, 15, 38–40.
38. *EHD* I, no. 97, p. 538 (reference to 'my two wergelds').
39. Sigewulf's son was named Sigeberht. *ASC,* s.a. 903.

and we can number among Sigehelm's relations King Edward the Elder, who married his daughter, Eadgifu.[40] In marrying an ealdorman's daughter, Edward was following in his father's footsteps. Alfred was the son-in-law of one Mercian ealdorman, the brother-in-law of a second, and, through the marriage of his daughter, Æthelflæd, to Æthelred, the father-in-law of a third. The 'Os-' predominated in Alfred's maternal lineage – his mother was Osburh, his grandfather Oslac, and he had kinsmen named Osferth and Oswald – so Osric, ealdorman of either Hampshire or Dorset in the 840s and 850s, was possibly also a blood-relation.[41]

The king used his ealdormen in various ways. Ninth-century charters speak of a right of hospitality for bishops, ealdormen, reeves, and other royal messengers when they crossed the realm on the king's business. That Alfred employed his ealdormen as special emissaries is clear from the *Chronicle*. He had Ealdorman Æthelhelm in 887 and Ealdorman Beocca in the following year carry alms to Rome.[42] Æthelnoth, ealdorman of Somerset, who had suffered with Alfred at Athelney and shared his triumph at Aller, was entrusted in 894 with a different sort of mission, either diplomatic or military, when he was sent to York at a time when that city was under viking attack.[43] Such missions, however, would have been exceptional: given the duties which came with the office, an ealdorman could not easily absent himself from his shire for too great a time. In war ealdormen were the king's chief military deputies, responsible for raising and leading the military forces of their shires. They were equally crucial to the civil administration of the kingdom. A sense of these more prosaic duties may be gained

---

40. S 350 (AD 898; Sigehelm *dux* is the beneficiary and *comes* Sigewulf witnesses); S 1508 (AD 871 X 889; will of ealdorman Alfred).

41. See J. Nelson, 'Reconstructing a family: reflections on Alfred, from Asser, chapter 2', in I. Wood and N. Lund, eds, *People and Places in Northern Europe, 500–1600. Essays in Honour of Peter Hayes Sawyer* (Woodbridge, Suffolk, 1991) pp. 51–4 (though the connection with Northumbria pushes the evidence).

42. *ASC,* s.a. 887, 888. Æthelhelm, described as Alfred's 'faithful ealdorman', is the beneficiary of a royal grant of land at North Newnton in his shire of Wiltshire in 892. Trans. Keynes and Lapidge, pp. 179–81.

43. Æthelweard's *Chronicle*, s.a. 894, trans. Keynes and Lapidge, p. 190. See H.R. Loyn, *The Governance of Anglo-Saxon England 500–1087* (Stanford, CA, 1984) p. 75.

from the immunity clauses of charters releasing 'bookland' from the 'domination of the ealdorman'. They included the collection of royal tribute, the levying of services (said to 'be exacted by force'), and the enforcing of 'penal matters, such as the capturing of thieves'.[44] In practice, a grant of this sort did not transform the favoured estate into a lawless area, as the words might imply, but meant that the responsibility for maintaining order, as well as the profits of justice, the point of the immunity, were to pass from the ealdorman and the royal reeves to the landholder. Among the secular burdens that were never remitted were the levying of soldiers for the king's army and the finding of labour for the repair of bridges and the upkeep of fortifications. An ealdorman's responsibility in towns included all of the above, with the addition of policing merchants and trade.[45]

Though ultimately the ealdorman was the king's deputy in the shire, the men who were actually most responsible for furthering and protecting the king's interests were his reeves. Theirs was the face of royal authority most familiar to the lesser thegns and commoners of the kingdom. By Alfred's day king's reeves had achieved sufficient social and political distinction to be singled out by Asser and to have their deaths noted in the *Anglo-Saxon Chronicle*. The reeves' primary charge was to oversee the king's estates and the villages and hamlets attached to them. As in centuries past, a king's reeve shared with the reeves of other nobles the responsibility for collecting renders, labour services, and food rents due from the free and servile peasants who belonged to the estate. In Alfred's day the military role of a reeve had become much more pronounced, as fortified royal vills were integrated into the defensive network centred upon the burhs.

King's reeves also played a critical role in the maintenance of law and order. Edward the Elder, in fact, addresses his first law code to them:

King Edward commands all [his] reeves: that you pronounce such legal decisions as you know to be most just and in accordance with the written laws [presumably referring to Alfred's law code]. You shall not for any cause fail to interpret the laws, and

44. E.g., *EHD* I, no. 93, p. 530.
45. E.g., *EHD* I, no. 99, p. 540.

at the same time it shall be your duty to provide that every case shall have a date fixed for its decision.[46]

In charging his reeves with knowing the law, Edward was simply following the practice of his father. In having them keep the court calendar he may have been innovating, especially given the provision in Edward's second code which decrees that 'every reeve shall hold a meeting every four weeks', but we cannot be sure.[47] Alfred's reeves, we know, were responsible for witnessing accusations of wrongdoing at public meetings distinct from those presided over by ealdormen. One cannot help but see in both Alfred's and his son's codes the genesis of what would later be known as the hundred courts. The reeve's responsibility for maintaining order probably accounts for the provision in Alfred's code that all foreign traders should report their presence to a king's reeve at a public meeting and bring with them all the men they planned to take with them on their travels. Given the grave concern expressed in the Alfred–Guthrum treaty about the possible misbehaviour of purported traders, this measure was probably intended less to regulate commercial activities than to ensure that a merchant would be legally accountable for any crimes committed by any of his company.[48] Alfred also entrusted his reeves with the care and feeding of those imprisoned on royal estates who did not have kinsmen to see to their needs.[49] The reeves of the late ninth and the early tenth century also led posses in pursuit of thieves and executed the king's orders by taking possession of the property of convicted criminals. In short, they were both judges and constables.

. . .

THE KING AND THE LAW

Much of what today would be the policing activities of the state did not, however, rest in the hands of ealdormen or

46. *I Edward* Preamble, trans. Attenborough, *Laws*, pp. 114–5. (The translation in the text discards Attenborough's archaisms.) The designations of Edward's codes as 'first' and 'second' are conventions of modern scholarship. See Keynes, 'Royal government and the written word', pp. 226–57, esp. 234–5.
47. *II Edward* 8.
48. *Alfred* 34; *Alfred and Guthrum* 5.
49. *Alfred* 1.3, 34.

reeves but in those of local landowners in their capacity as personal lords. Some of them held their lands in book-right, which by this time probably carried with it judicial responsibilities as well as fiscal privileges. Edward the Elder directed that 'everyone shall have always ready on his estate men who will guide others wishing to follow up their own [cattle]', and this practice may already have been in effect by the end of Alfred's reign.[50] But even those who did not hold by book-right were responsible for the good behaviour of their dependants and kinsmen. As early as the seventh century, King Ine had legislated on matters concerning the dealings of his men with their own dependants. However, in most instances these enactments arose from the king's rights over land and his claim to lordship over the tenants of the nobility.[51] In contrast, the laws of King Alfred present the king as standing above the lordship bond. Whereas Ine decreed that a man who left his lord without permission was to be returned and fined sixty shillings payable to the lord, Alfred restated this law two centuries later to emphasize royal authority, declaring that man could leave his lord with the cognizance of the king's ealdorman in whose shire he served.[52] If he departed without informing the ealdorman, any lord who accepted his services was liable to a fine of 120 shillings payable to the king. The point of these enactments was to make lords responsible for the activities of their men. Lordship for Alfred, as we have seen, was the force that held together the political world and through a hierarchy of authority connected the temporal world with the spiritual. Its centrality was such that Alfred decreed that men could fight for their lords without incurring vendettas and that no man could fight against his lord, even on behalf of a kinsman.[53] At the apex of the chain of lordship stood God and below him the king. Just as the king was responsible to God for justice being meted out to his men, so the king laid the charge upon those under his lordship to oversee the men who had sworn obedience to them. In practical terms,

50. *II Edward* 4. See discussion of the Fonthill suit below, in which a 'tracker' plays a prominent role.
51. *Ine* 40. See discussion in R.P. Abels, *Lordship and Military Obligation in Anglo-Saxon England* (Los Angeles and London, 1988) pp. 16–19, 87.
52. *Ine* 39; *Alfred* 37 § 1–2. Cf. II *Edward* 7; II *Æthelstan* 22.
53. *Alfred* 42 § 5–6.

someone was to be responsible and answerable for the behaviour of every man, whether free or slave. Alfred, in relying
upon lords to be responsible for the good behaviour of their
dependants, was moving toward the system of tithings that
would emerge in the tenth century and out of which would
grow that 'most tenacious and characteristic' of Norman
customs, the view of frankpledge.[54]

Alfred's code calls upon his subjects to exercise self-
restraint, but it also recognizes that the world is a place
of violence in which one must protect oneself and one's dependants. Perhaps the most surprising provisions in Alfred's
laws are those dealing with vendettas, chapter 42 and its
seven clauses. Because of the institutional limitations on
the police powers of the state, the vendetta, paradoxically,
was perhaps the most effective mechanism for the preven-
tion of violence and maintenance of order: the threat
of death to oneself or one's loved ones might well make a
man think twice before giving in to murderous impulses.
Consequently, Alfred did not seek to legislate the vendetta
out of existence but rather to regulate feuds and to bring
them under royal supervision if not control. He accepted
the necessity, and perhaps even the desirability, of self-help
remedies, but wished to make actual violence a course of
last resort. A man who knew that his enemy was at home, so
Alfred commanded, was not to fight him before he asked
for justice for himself. This meant that if he had sufficient
power he and his friends were to surround his enemy and
besiege him for seven days. As long as his foe chose to stay
peacefully inside, he was not to be attacked. If his enemy
was willing to lay down his weapons and surrender, the
captor was to send notice to his prisoner's kinsmen and
friends and keep him unharmed for thirty days, awaiting
their response. If the besieged enemy was unwilling to surrender or lay down his weapons, he could then be attacked
at will. The king's part in all of this was simply to referee
the dispute and to collect fines if someone refused to feud
according to the king's rules. The 'state' could take a more
active role, though, if the wronged party was too weak to

---

54. Loyn, *Governance*, p. 147. This view is advanced strongly by P. Wormald,
The Making of English Law: King Alfred to the Norman Conquest (Oxford,
forthcoming) ch. 9.

bring his enemy to justice. Then he was allowed to appeal for help to the ealdorman, who could chose to intervene or not. If the ealdorman refused aid, the plaintiff could take his case to the king. The king, like violence itself, was a last resort.

Alfred's acceptance of vendettas and his reliance upon the moral authority of secular lordship reinforces the general impression one receives from Alfred's law code of a state that lacked the mechanisms of coercive power. An authority greater than that of the king or an earthly lord was needed to ensure social order, and this was achieved through an appeal to a supernatural and communal sanction, the oath. The sanctity and efficacy of the solemn oath was taken so much for granted that the entire Anglo-Saxon legal system was founded upon it. A defendant's guilt or innocence did not depend upon an investigation into the facts of the case, as it would in a modern court of law, but upon his willingness to swear before God that he was innocent of the charge and his ability to produce the required number of oath-helpers to attest to his good faith. Little wonder that Alfred chose to begin his enactments with a series of laws concerned with the breaking of vows.[55] According to these, a man who failed to fulfil a rightful oath – Alfred is careful here to exclude vows of treachery against one's lord – was to submit to incarceration at a king's estate, where he was to endure for forty days whatever the bishop prescribed for him. If he refused to go, he was to be outlawed and excommunicated, thrust out of the society of man and God. The forsworn man was a man of ill-repute to be regarded with suspicion by his neighbours. More than that, to lose one's oath-worthiness was to become legally defenceless; a man such as this was at the mercy of all who bore grudges or harboured claims against his property.

This brings us to one of the most famous lawsuits in Anglo-Saxon studies, one in which King Alfred himself played a

---

55. *Alfred* 1 § 1–8. Cf. II *Æthelstan* ch. 26, which deprives a perjurer of the right to give oaths and decrees that he shall be buried in unconsecrated ground unless a bishop vouches that he made amends in accordance with the dictates of his confessor. P. Wormald, *The Making of English Law* (Oxford, forthcoming) contains a full discussion of the importance of oaths in Anglo-Saxon law.

decisive role, the dispute over the estate at Fonthill.[56] The story is preserved in a remarkable early tenth-century letter written in the first person, apparently by Ealdorman Ordlaf, and addressed to King Edward the Elder as testimony in an ongoing lawsuit that had begun in the last year of King Alfred's life. More than any other text of this period, the 'Fonthill Letter' provides a window into Anglo-Saxon legal procedure and illuminates the actual role of kings and nobles in resolving disputes.

'Leof,' 'Beloved,' it begins, 'I will inform you what happened about the land at Fonthill, the five hides which Æthelhelm Higa is claiming', and then goes on to describe the complicated legal history of this estate and of its previous owner, a criminal king's thegn named Helmstan. The author begins in mid-story after Helmstan, a king's thegn in Wiltshire, had stolen a belt and had been convicted of the crime: 'When Helmstan committed the crime of stealing Æthelred's belt, Higa at once began to bring a charge against him, along with other claimants, and wished to win the land from him by litigation.' Helmstan's guilt is assumed by the letter-writer and we learn nothing about his punishment. The penalty stipulated by Alfred's law code was the payment of a fine of 60 or 120 shillings, depending upon the value of the stolen property.[57] The unstated penalty was the loss of good reputation, which, as we have seen, carried with it serious consequences in an age in which law revolved around oaths and communal opinion. Helmstan was now a man of ill-repute, perhaps no longer even 'oath-worthy', and therefore vulnerable to all legal claims against him. Rather than acquit himself with a personal oath supported by compurgators, Helmstan could now only offer proof through the ordeal, which meant in practice appealing to 'public' opinion, which presumably would not favour him.

56. S 1445, in Harmer, ed., *SEHD*, no. 18, pp. 60–3; reprinted *EHD* I, no. 102, pp. 544–6. But now see S.D. Keynes, 'The Fonthill Letter', in M. Korhammer (with K. Reichl and H. Sauer), eds, *Words, Texts and Manuscripts. Studies in Anglo-Saxon Culture Presented to Helmut Gneuss on the Occasion of his Sixty-Fifth Birthday* (Cambridge, 1992) pp. 53–97. Cf. A.P. Smyth, *King Alfred the Great* (Oxford, 1995) pp. 393–400. My discussion follows Dr Keynes' translation and is based, in part, upon his insightful and comprehensive commentary.
57. *Alfred* 9.1, 9.2. Cf. *Ine* 10.

The scent of disgrace brought the predators out, and among them was Æthelhelm Higa, another king's thegn in Wilt-shire, who seized the opportunity to claim from Helmstan a five-hide estate at Fonthill.

Helmstan turned for help to the writer of the letter, Ealdorman Ordlaf, and begged him to intercede on his behalf, because the ealdorman had stood sponsor for him at his confirmation. Ordlaf responded to his godson's appeal by taking the matter up with his lord, and Helmstan's, King Alfred, who, as it happened, was then staying at (Old) Wardour, a royal estate or hunting-lodge only a few miles from Fonthill. Alfred was persuaded by Ordlaf's 'advocacy and true account' to allow Helmstan 'to prove his right', that is to defend himself in the legal proceedings, and appointed a group of thegns from his household, includ-ing Ordlaf, Wihtbord, Ælfric, 'who was then keeper of the wardrobe', Brihthelm, Wulfhun the Black of Somerton (in Somerset), Strica, Ubba, 'and many more men than I can now name', to reconcile the two parties. These men, some of whom we have already encountered as witnesses to a charter issued by Alfred in 892, listened to each party and decided that Helmstan should be allowed to 'come forward with the charters and prove his right to the land'.

As Alfred had done in his own dispute over inherit-ance with his nephews, Helmstan appealed to the written record. Helmstan swore that Fonthill had once belonged to Æthelfryth, who had obtained it from her husband, Æthelnoth, as a 'morning-gift', and that she had sold it to Oswulf 'at a suitable price'. Æthelfryth's charter recording the sale was then produced and read aloud. Its witness list, which had the names of King Alfred, Edward, Æthelnoth, Deormod, and 'each of the men whom one then wished to have', seems to have commanded special attention. The arbitrators then carefully examined the document and its attestations, and agreed that the evidence was such that 'Helmstan was nearer the oath'. In short, Helmstan had persuaded the arbitrators that his claim to the land was stronger than Æthelhelm's, and so obtained from them the right to prove his just possession with a personal oath sup-ported by a specified number of 'oath-helpers' swearing to the justice of his position. Æthelhelm, however, refused to consent to the judgement of the arbitrators 'until we went

in to the king and told him in every respect how we had
decided it and why we had decided it; and Æthelhelm himself stood in there with us'. The letter-writer now brings
Alfred on to centre stage.

> And the king stood in the chamber at Wardour – he was wash-
> ing his hands. When he had finished, he asked Æthelhelm why
> what we had decided for him did not seem just to him; he [the
> king] said that he could think of nothing more just than that
> he [Helmstan] should be allowed to give the oath if he could.
> I then said that he wished to attempt it, and asked the king to
> appoint a day for it, and he then did so.

Alfred's decision awarding Helmstan the oath would
ordinarily have concluded the matter; the giving of the oath
itself was in most cases a formality. Given his reputation,
however, Helmstan feared that he would not be able to find
sufficient oath-helpers. He turned once more to his godfather, Ealdorman Ordlaf. 'Then I said', wrote Ordlaf, 'that
I would help him to obtain justice, but never to any wrong,
on condition that he granted it to me; and he gave me a
pledge to that.' In other words, if Ordlaf helped find the
oath-helpers he needed to win the suit, Helmstan would
give him title to the land. The unstated second part of the
arrangement was that Ordlaf would then allow Helmstan to
enjoy the land on a life-long lease. Ordlaf had to be careful in
how he presented this. He needed to explain to King Edward
how Fonthill had come into his possession, but he had to be
careful lest he give the impression that he had been bribed
to pervert justice. The image he probably meant to project
was that of a dutiful godfather who extended an appropriate helping hand to a spiritual kinsman in need. Helmstan
had freely offered him the 'gift' of Fonthill in return for his
good services, and he had accepted both the offer and the
responsibility. But there was no bribe in this, since he aided
a man whom he believed to be in the right. As a result, on
the appointed day Helmstan, in the presence of Ordlaf,
Wihtbord, Æthelhelm, and Brihthelm, gave the oath. 'Then
we all said that it was a closed suit when the judgement had
been carried out.' Helmstan handed over his charter for
Fonthill to Ordlaf, and Ordlaf allowed him to use the land
as long as he lived, 'if he would keep out of disgrace'.

Apparently this was too much to ask. Two years later there was a new king and new troubles for Helmstan. This time he rustled some untended cattle at Fonthill and drove them to Chicklade, where he was caught. A tracker in the employ of either the owner of the stolen cattle or the lord of the estate where the crime had been committed had traced the cattle to Helmstan, who tried to deny the accusation, but was convicted in part on the basis of physical evidence, the tracks themselves and some fresh scratches from a bramble he had run into as he fled. Again Helmstan was found guilty of theft, and this time he not only forfeited his entire estate but was pronounced an outlaw as well. When the local reeve, Eanwulf Penearding, took possession of Helmstan's estate at Tisbury, Ordlaf, perhaps acting in his capacity as ealdorman, intervened and asked the reeve why he had done so, and was informed that because Helmstan was the 'king's man' his property had been adjudged to the king. Ordlaf did manage to retain Fonthill, because Helmstan had only been holding it on loan. More surprisingly, Helmstan was able to salvage something out of the affair. He fled to King Alfred's tomb at the Old Minster in Winchester and there apparently swore an oath vouching the deceased king to warranty and obtained a 'seal' to that effect. (What the text means by all of this is far from certain.) Helmstan brought the 'seal' to Ordlaf, who was with the king at Chippenham, and Ordlaf took it to King Edward on his behalf. The king forgave Helmstan his outlawry and restored to him an estate, to which the thegn withdrew.

Ordlaf subsequently gave the estate at Fonthill to the bishop of Winchester in exchange for five hides at Lydiard, Wiltshire. Some years later Æthelhelm Higa, who was as persistent as Helmstan was criminal, renewed his claims to Fonthill (hence this letter on behalf of the bishop and community at Winchester). Ordlaf concluded his missive with an appeal to his 'beloved' king Edward that all 'may remain as it now is arranged and was before'. After all, as the ealdorman pointed out, 'When will any suit be closed if one can end it neither with money nor with an oath? And if one wishes to change every judgement which King Alfred gave, when shall we have finished disputing?'

The Fonthill case does not revolve around 'folk-moots' and a community of free men applying folk-law. Nor was

its procedure as strictly formal as legal scholars of a generation or two ago believed Anglo-Saxon law to have been.[58]
Undoubtedly both Helmstan and Æthelhelm Higa swore
oaths and followed prescribed formulas, and the penalties
of the law may well have accorded with legal custom or even
the law-books of kings. But what is perhaps most striking
about the case is the role played by King Alfred, King Edward,
and their agents. Helmstan, perhaps because he was a king's
thegn of some substance, was able to appeal for aid to a
patron, Ealdorman Ordlaf, who used his influence with the
king to help obtain a desirable legal outcome. The decisions
in the case were rendered either by arbitrators acting as
royal agents or by the king himself. King Alfred is depicted
as the court of last appeal, and the informal manner in
which he rendered his judgement, while washing his hands,
is a reminder that law was not a matter of professionals or
technicalities as much as common sense. It was also a matter of who you were and whom you knew, as much as what
you had done.

Ealdorman Ordlaf went to great lengths in his letter to
assure King Edward that he himself had not abused justice
through his support of his godson. Helmstan may have been
a bad man addicted to crime, but in so far as Fonthill was
concerned, he was its legitimate owner. The homely story
about Alfred washing his hands while hearing the details of
the suit was a reminder to the king that the ealdorman had
been close to his father. It also underscored that the arbitrators' decision had been sanctioned by King Alfred himself.
Alfred approved of the way Ordlaf and the others had dealt
with the case. They had exercised prudence in their judgement. This was no small matter, for Alfred was not always so
well-disposed toward the judgements of his ealdormen and
reeves.

In the final two chapters of the *Life* Asser presents a portrait of Alfred as a Solomonic judge, calling his subordin-
ates to account for rendering poor judgements against the

58. The classic exposition on Anglo-Saxon legal procedure is by F. Pollock
and F.W. Maitland, *The History of English Law*, 2 vols, 2nd edn (1898;
reprinted Cambridge, 1978) I, pp. 37–52. See now P. Wormald, 'Charters, law and the settlement of disputes in Anglo-Saxon England', in
W. Davies and P. Fouracre, eds, *The Settlement of Disputes in Early
Medieval Europe* (Cambridge, 1986) pp. 149–68.

facts and against wisdom.[59] He himself, Asser assures us, was 'painstaking . . . in establishing the truth in judicial hearings', especially in cases concerning the poor, and he expected no less from those who did justice in his name. Often he found that suits brought before ealdormen and reeves at their assemblies ended in violent disagreements and complaints about the injustice of the judgements rather than in settlement and reconciliation. When the parties were in 'intransigent and obdurate disagreement', they were invited to come before the king, much as Æthelhelm had done in the Fonthill suit, and Alfred, being 'an extremely astute investigator in judicial matters as in everything else', would quickly arrive at the truth of the matter. Nor was Alfred shy about judging the judges. After inquiring 'politely, as is his wont', either in person or through one of his trusted men why they had arrived at decisions that were patently unjust, he asked the offending judges whether they were knaves or merely fools. If the latter, he ordered them to learn wisdom or lose their office. This meant, in part, to learn to read, and Asser presents us with the semi-comic picture of elderly ealdormen and nobles moaning and sighing as they practised their letters late into the night. Many, too old to begin, relied upon literate young kinsmen or servants to read to them.

Alfred, in short, was ordering his judges to follow the path that he himself had undertaken voluntarily. He was ordering them to seek after wisdom. Asser never mentions the law code, and from its jumbled arrangement and the problems presented by its incorporation of Ine's laws without attempt to reconcile discrepancies with Alfred's own promulgations, it would have been very difficult to use the code as a practical manual of law. What then did Alfred demand of his judges? Why should they become literate? The answer is to be found in what wisdom meant for Alfred. It was, for him, the *sine qua non* for good government. Wisdom made a man *worthy* of power; it taught him to care for the truth and to look to the common weal rather than to his own personal good.[60] 'I do not blame great works nor rightful power, but I blame a man for arrogance on that account;

59. Asser, chs 105–6, trans. Keynes and Lapidge, pp. 109–10.
60. Asser, ch. 105, ed. Stevenson, p. 92.

and I would strengthen the weakness of their hearts, and forbid the incompetent such desires, lest any of them presume to seize on power or the office of teaching so rashly, lest those attempt such a perilous ascent who cannot stand firmly on level ground.'[61] That is why Alfred, oppressed by viking invaders and the illness that plagued him throughout his life, devoted so much of his time and energy to translating Latin literature into English and promoting education throughout his realm.

61. *King Alfred's Pastoral Care*, ed. Sweet, I, ch. 4, p. 40.

Chapter 9

TRIUMPH AND DEATH, 892–899

Alfred's victory at Edington and the peace he made with Guthrum transferred the main operations of the viking raiders back once more to the Continent. What had been a nuisance to the rulers of Francia in the 870s became a major threat in the early 880s, as viking raiders streamed back to the Continent in search of easier prey. As viewed by the chronicler of the abbey of St-Vaast near Arras in the Pas-de-Calais, the devastation was little short of apocalyptic:

> Never do the Northmen cease to take captive and to kill Christian people, to destroy churches and ramparts, to burn out houses in flames. Through all the open streets the dead are lying – priests, laymen, nobles, women, youth and little children. Everywhere tribulation and sorrow meet our eyes, seeing Christian folk brought to utter ruin and desolation.[1]

Political chaos exacerbated the problem. The death of Charles the Bald in 877, quickly followed by the deaths of his son, Louis the Stammerer, in 879, and of his grandson, Louis III, and his nephew (and rival), Louis the Younger, in 882, made a volatile political landscape even more unstable. In his final entry in the *Annals of St-Bertin*, recorded under the year 882, an aged and bitter Archbishop Hincmar of Rheims criticized the lack of organized resistance offered by Frankish kings and counts against the Northmen. The archbishop watched helplessly as one fortress after another fell to the heathen invaders. When they burnt nearby Laon,

---

1. *Annals of St-Vaast*, s.a. 884, quoted in E.S. Duckett, *Death and Life in the Tenth Century* (Ann Arbor, MI, 1971) pp. 5–6; *Annales Xantenses et Annales Vedastini*, ed. B. von Simson, in *MGH, SRG* (Hanover, 1909) p. 53.

Hincmar, cradling the church's relics in his arms, fled the see he had served for thirty-seven years. Hincmar was certain that the vikings intended to bring the kingdom itself under their rule, but like the Anglo-Saxon Chronicler, he was probably crediting the hydra-headed enemy with more unity and strategic foresight than the marauders actually possessed.

Carolingian rulers tried as best they could to halt the despoliation of their lands, but the Scandinavian pirates proved too mobile and elusive. At times, they were simply too strong. In 886, while Alfred was occupying and restoring London, a massive Danish army, consisting of numerous warbands, surrounded Paris. From their perch atop the towers that guarded the city's two bridges, the defenders could see viking longboats clogging the Seine as far as the eye could see. Though the invaders failed to capture the city and its fortified bridges, they surrounded Paris and began a siege that lasted for more than a year. The Emperor Charles the Fat finally appeared with a relief army in the autumn of 886, but faced with the onset of winter, he chose to negotiate rather than fight. In exchange for a pledge to depart his realm by March 887, he promised the Northmen 700lb (318 kg) of silver and gave them permission to plunder the still virgin lands of Burgundy for provisions. The vikings returned to Paris within the year to collect the promised tribute, though, true to character, they failed to fulfil their part of the bargain.

To the author of the *Anglo-Saxon Chronicle*'s entries for the 880s, this mayhem on the Continent was not only a consequence of Alfred's victory in 878, but a prelude to the return of the vikings to England in 892. Simplifying a confusing military situation, the Chronicler wrote as if one great viking army, indeed, the same force that had departed Fulham for Ghent in 880, was responsible for all the devastation. He apparently believed that the viking army that drove Hincmar from his see and besieged Paris was the same force that had recently landed in Kent and was then pillaging southeastern England. This is why he so carefully recorded viking activities in Francia and gave a fuller record of Carolingian affairs in the 880s than of English. In particular, he noted the successes enjoyed by Christian armies, the victories won by a combined force of Old Saxons and

Frisians in 885, by the Bretons at St-Lô in 890, and, most dramatically, by Arnulf, king of East Francia, on the banks of the River Dyle in 891, in a battle so costly to the invaders that their corpses were said to have dammed the river. But a thoughtful Englishman should have found little comfort in viking defeats on the Continent, for as long as the Danes found it safe and profitable to plunder the lands of the Franks and Bretons, Alfred's kingdom was safe.

What finally persuaded the Danes to turn their attentions to English targets again was not the resistance of the Franks, but something far more relentless – a blight that devastated the fields of northeastern Francia after Easter in 892 and brought famine in its wake. Confronted with the prospect of starvation, the viking warbands made their way to the harbour at Boulogne, where, in the autumn of 892, the Franks provided them with as many as 250 ships, so that they could cross the Channel 'in one journey, horses and all'.[2] They entered the estuary of the Lympne in southeastern Kent near Rye, and rowed their ships some six kilometres upriver as far the great wood known as the *Andredesweald* or, more simply, the Weald. There they stormed a scarcely defended, half-made burh, which may have been the earthwork excavated at Castle Toll, Newenden, Kent.[3] The viking host then withdrew to make camp at Appledore on the edges of the Romney Marsh. Almost immediately after this, another eighty ships under the command of a veteran viking chieftain named Hasteinn (*Hæsten* in Old English) appeared at the mouth of the Thames estuary and set up base on the Swale marshes at *Middeltune,* now Milton Regis, near Sittingbourne, on the northern coast of Kent.[4]

Together these two viking fleets numbered as many as 330 ships. Since these ships were crammed with horses,

---

2. *ASC* s.a. 892.
3. N. Brooks, 'The unidentified forts of the Burghal Hidage', *Medieval Archaeology* 8 (1964) pp. 81–6; B.K. Davison, 'The Burghal Hidage fort at *Eorpeburnan*: a suggested identification', *Medieval Archaeology* 16 (1972) pp. 123–7.
4. Perhaps at Bayford Court, where archaeologists have found a three-sided earthwork enclosure. The defences, however, extended only about 300 metres, which seems too small to accommodate the crews, horses, and camp followers from eighty ships. Cf. J. Peddie, *Alfred the Good Soldier, His Life and Campaigns* (Bath, 1989) p. 168.

camp followers, and booty from Francia, they probably carried no more than a few thousand combatants.[5] Still, a few thousand seasoned warriors represented a major threat to Alfred's kingdom. To put matters in perspective, this new 'great army' was as large as the one that had conquered Northumbria, East Anglia and Mercia two decades before. Nor was this a mere raid, like the attack upon Rochester in 885. Vikings who had brought their families and goods clearly had no intention of returning to the famine-stricken lands of Francia. Hasteinn and his fellow captains looked to Guthrum and the sons of Ragnarr Loþbrok for inspiration, sea-kings who, through daring and luck, had won kingdoms for themselves and landed wealth for their followers. In short, for the third time in his twenty-one year reign, King Alfred faced a viking enemy bent on conquest. One wonders whether Alfred remembered the comet – 'the star with hair' (*feaxede steorra*) – that dominated the evening skies of the previous spring and summer, and if he did, what he made of that harbinger.[6]

Alfred acted quickly to contain the vikings in their camps at Appledore and Milton Regis, and in particular took steps to isolate them from outside help and from each other. He sent emissaries to the Scandinavian rulers of Northumbria and East Anglia demanding pledges that they maintain the peace with Wessex. The East Anglians even gave him six hostages as security that they would abide by their oath.[7] But, as in the past, oaths and hostages failed to bind the Northmen. As the Chronicler noted, whenever the newcomers went en masse on raids, vikings from the Danelaw would join in, either as part of their forces or on their own.[8] The import is clear: Alfred had to contend not only with the new invaders, but with opportunistic settlers from

---

5. N.P. Brooks, 'England in the ninth century: the crucible of defeat', *TRHS*, 5th series, 29 (1979) p. 7; A.P. Smyth, *King Alfred the Great* (Oxford, 1995) p. 121. Cf. P.H. Sawyer, *The Age of the Vikings* (London, 1962) pp. 124–5.

6. *ASC* s.a. 891 (A).

7. *ASC* s.a. 893.

8. That the Chronicler also observed that the two armies only came out in force from their encampments on two occasions, when they first landed, before Alfred had assembled his troops, and when they abandoned these camps because of Alfred's harassment, creates some consistency problems in his account. *ASC* s.a. 893.

Northumbria and East Anglia as well.[9] Indeed, in the autumn of 893, he and his ealdormen would find themselves fighting viking invaders in places as distant from one another as Exeter in Devonshire, Benfleet in Essex, and Buttington on the Welsh border.

Alfred's attempt to simplify matters by negotiating a separate peace with Hasteinn was only marginally more successful. Historians often treat the forces at Appledore and at Milton Regis as parts of a single army with a unified command, but this is far from certain. Nor should we assume that Alfred regarded them as such. Although the Chronicler creates the impression of a single foe by his repeated use of the phrase '*se here*', 'the army', in fact he is vague about the origin of the second force and its relationship to the first. All that he says is that the two armies landed in different places, the second soon after the first, and that the personnel of the two forces had merged by the end of 893. Given the history of viking raids and the difficulty of coordination, it is unlikely that this was a unitary invasion in two waves fulfilling a sophisticated strategic design.[10] The fleet of 250 ships that sailed from Boulogne landed at the mouth of the Lympne not as part of some master plan to detach eastern Kent from Wessex, but because it was the nearest English shore. The River Lympne, the old name for the Rother, was hardly a major access route into Kent, and they rowed up it largely in order to get their bearings. They established their camp at Appledore because the Weald and the Romney Marsh protected them there from surprise attack. We do not know the place of origin of the second fleet of eighty ships, but Hasteinn's decision to make camp at Milton Regis was strategically sound. Lying opposite the Isle of Sheppey, Milton Regis provided the invaders with an escape route by sea as well as control over the major lines of communication in eastern Kent. Milton lay along Watling Street between Canterbury, some twenty-five kilometres to the east of Milton, and Rochester, fifteen kilometres to the west. A nearby pre-historic trackway ran westward along the Downs to Selwood and beyond. In short, all of Wessex lay open to the invaders.

9. *ASC* s.a. 893.
10. Cf. F.M. Stenton, *Anglo-Saxon England*, 3rd edn (Oxford, 1971) pp. 266–7.

In contrast, there were no obvious lines of communication between Appledore and Milton Regis. The two bases were separated by some thirty kilometres of marsh, forest and hills, without any roads or paths leading directly from one to the other. Even if Alfred had not encamped between the two armies, messengers could not have easily shuttled between the two strongholds. To speak of a 'pincer movement' under such circumstances is pure fantasy.[11] The vikings at Appledore and Milton Regis look very much like two separate warbands with a common purpose. As we have seen, several viking armies, among them Hasteinn's company, were operating on the Continent in the 880s and early 890s. Famine in Francia made England the natural destination for hungry vikings in the autumn of 892.

The *Anglo-Saxon Chronicle* names only the leader of the eighty-ship fleet that based itself at Milton Regis, and this is probably because Alfred singled Hasteinn out for special attention. The Chronicle's 'Hæsten' was, presumably, the famous viking chieftain known to the eleventh-century Norman historians, Dudo of St Quentin and William of Jumièges, as *Hastingus*, the Latinized form of Old Norse Hasteinn.[12] By the time Dudo and William wrote about him, Hasteinn had become the archetypal viking, a cunning, savage and deceitful heathen capable of feigning baptism and even death to set a trap for unwary Christians. He was said to have burnt innumerable monasteries in northern France in the late 850s and to have sailed with his protégé Bjorn Jarnsiða, a son of Ragnar Loþbrok, into the Mediterranean in 860 on a famous expedition to capture Rome. Rome escaped destruction, according to the legend, only because Hasteinn mistook the small town of Luna, near Pisa, for the Eternal City.[13]

---

11. Cf. Peddie, *Alfred the Good Soldier*, pp. 168–70; Smyth, *Alfred the Great*, p. 123.
12. Or, possibly, Haddingr. See F. Amory, 'The viking Hasting in Franco-Scandinavian Legend', in M.H. King and W.M. Stevens, eds, *Saints, Scholars and Heroes: Studies in Medieval Culture in Honour of Charles W. Jones*, 2 vols (Collegeville, MN, 1979) II, pp. 265–86. See also Smyth, *King Alfred the Great*, pp. 116–19.
13. *The Gesta Normannorum Ducum* of William of Jumièges, Orderic Vitalis, and Robert of Torigni, ed. and trans. E.M.C. Van Houts, vol. 1 (Oxford, 1992) i, 4–10, pp. 17–27.

Little is known about the real man who gave rise to these extravagant stories. Frankish chronicles record that a viking chieftain named Hasteinn was among the leaders of a combined viking–Breton raid in 866 up the River Sarthe into Anjou. For a number of years after this, this same Hasteinn led a viking band based on the Loire, which profited not only from pillaging monasteries and villages but from offering its services to local counts in their interminable border wars.[14] The *Annals of St-Vaast* and the chronicler Regino of Prüm name Hasteinn as one of the viking captains active in northern France and the Lowlands in the 880s. He was sufficiently prominent for King Louis III of West Francia to buy peace from him in 882. In 890–891, as the leader of a band of vikings based at Argoeuves-sur-Sommes, he entered into a 'woeful compact' with the abbot of St-Vaast that allowed him to roam freely over the lands of the abbey in return for his promise to spare the monastery. The historical Hasteinn proved no more trustworthy than his legendary namesake; he used the 'peace' to prepare a surprise attack on the monks in connivance with a second viking band at nearby Noyon on the Oise. If the Hasteinn of the late 860s and of the 880s was the same man, Alfred was facing a veteran campaigner who had perpetrated mayhem across the fields and villages of West Francia and the Middle Kingdom for a quarter of a century.

Confronted by a two-front war, Alfred endeavoured to make peace with the enemy that appeared most dangerous to him. Fifteen years earlier he had converted Guthrum from an enemy into a friend by standing sponsor at his baptism. He hoped now to work the same magic on Hasteinn. While his troops were pursuing, with mixed success, small mounted raiding parties from Appledore, King Alfred and his son-in-law, Ealdorman Æthelred, met with Hasteinn. Prudence dictated that Alfred receive the viking chieftain in one of the king's burhs. Given the prominent role played by Æthelred in the proceedings and London's proximity to Milton Regis, the encounter may have taken place in the newly restored burh. There, in the shadow of London's refurbished Roman walls, Alfred would have done his best

14. Regino of Prüm, *Chronicon*, ed. F. Kurze, in *MGH, SRG* (Hanover, 1890; repr. Hanover, 1989) s.a. 867 [for 866], 874.

to impress upon Hasteinn the military strength of the kingdom that he had invaded. The ceremony itself, with its pomp and festivities, was designed to convince heathens of the power and glory of the Christian God. The king and his ealdorman each stood sponsor for one of Hasteinn's two sons. We are not told whether Alfred also received Hasteinn and his wife from the font, but it is likely that he did, unless, of course, the viking chieftain had previously accepted baptism as the price for doing business with Frankish kings and prelates. After he and his family were joined to Alfred through spiritual kinship, Hasteinn pledged peace with Alfred, and confirmed his oath with hostages. Alfred responded as a great king should, with generous gifts of money – and Hasteinn answered Alfred as he had the abbot of St-Vaast, by immediately breaking his pledge. For Alfred, the baptism of Hasteinn's family harked back to the heady days of Aller and Wedmore. To Hasteinn, on the other hand, the ceremony and its trappings were merely window-dressing for the taking of danegeld. Though Hasteinn did withdraw his army from Milton Regis, it was only to remove it to an even more defensible site, at Benfleet, Essex, on the northern banks of the Thames estuary. From there he continued to raid Alfred's territory, especially the Mercian lands entrusted to his other son's godfather, Ealdorman Æthelred. Alfred learned a lesson from his dealings with Hasteinn. What had bound Guthrum was not chrism, robe, and fillet, but the power that Alfred and his God had demonstrated in battle. Hasteinn and his compatriots in 892–893 still remained to be convinced.

Alfred's military actions proved more successful than his diplomatic manoeuvring. He could not risk an assault upon the viking strongholds. If he committed all his troops to a siege of one, the forces in the other would be free to pillage at will. If, on the other hand, he divided the *fyrd*, he risked being outnumbered. The strategic problem he faced, then, was to keep the two enemy forces from using their strongholds as bases to ravage the countrysides of Kent and Sussex, and to maintain contact with both so that neither could sneak past him into central Wessex. The solution was to encamp between Appledore and Milton Regis at the place where he thought he could most readily intercept either army if it tried to break out into the countryside.[15] The *Chronicle* does not tell us where Alfred made camp, but Maidstone on the River Medway would have been the logical choice. Commanding both a Roman road that ran north–south through the Weald and an east–west prehistoric trackway along the Downs, Maidstone offered the advantages of tactical mobility, the possibility of reinforcements from the burghal garrisons at Hastings and Rochester, and a fresh water supply.[16] From there Alfred could monitor his enemies through pickets along the Downs, while his patrols could seek out and destroy viking raiding parties. As critical as was the choice of a base, it was Alfred's ability to maintain his troops in the field that proved decisive. The military reforms that he had required of his subjects now proved their worth. Without a standing army and a network of garrisoned burhs on Roman roads to provide manpower and supplies, Alfred could not have adopted the patient strategy that circumstances dictated.

Our main source for Alfred's last war is the *Anglo-Saxon Chronicle*. Set apart by their density of detail, coherency and style, the annals for 893 to 896 clearly represent a separate stage in the compilation of the *Chronicle*. The author, whoever he was, composed these annals in 896 or shortly thereafter to celebrate Alfred's victory. He wrote what amounted to a 'single continuous narrative, structured in terms of campaigning years, with a basic opposition of winter and summer', which either he or someone else subsequently adapted to conform to the chronological framework of the pre-existing *Chronicle*.[17] Each entry of the sequence begins with the phrase 'in this year', and, except for the annal of 896, concludes with the formula 'and that was [so many months or years] after they had come hither across the sea'. The presentation of events is dramatic, vivid, and more than a little confusing. The author, at times, seems to have had difficulty making sense of the movements of various viking bands and of the chronology of the events he described. The text, as we have it, may also be truncated, referring

15. *ASC* s.a. 893.
16. Peddie, *Alfred the Good Soldier*, p. 170.
17. J. Bately, 'The compilation of the *Anglo-Saxon Chronicle* once more', *Leeds Studies in English* 16 (1985) pp. 7–26, at p. 15.

back to incidents that are missing from the surviving recensions.[18] The challenge the Chronicler set for himself was to integrate reports of sieges and engagements fought across the breadth of southern England and the western Midlands into a single campaign narrative, and like other military historians before and since, he made war seem more orderly and planned than it probably was. His theme, unsurprisingly, was Alfred's military greatness. For him, Alfred was the sole architect of the victory, and he took pains to place the king in the forefront of his narrative, even when it is clear from his own account that Alfred was hundreds of kilometres distant from the main action. As a result, Alfred 'steals the scene' from his generals, including his own son, the *ætheling* Edward. If it were not for a set of annals from Edward the Elder's reign preserved in the late tenth-century Latin chronicle of Ealdorman Æthelweard, we would not know how prominent a role the prince played in winning the war.

Harassed by Alfred's patrols, the viking army at Appledore broke camp around Easter of 893. Splitting their forces, they sent their ships north around the coast of Essex to the island of Mersea at the mouth of the River Blackwater, an area then probably in the hands of the viking rulers of East Anglia, and marched the bulk of their army overland to meet up with the fleet. Using the Weald for cover, they evaded the *fyrd*, then commanded by Alfred's elder son, Edward, and wound their way along forest paths until they found the great track that led west into Wessex. Their intention was ultimately to cross the Thames, probably at Reading or Wallingford, and then march back through East Anglia to Mersea. But their immediate goal was loot. Before Edward managed to catch up with them at Farnham in Surrey, about 140 kilometres west of Appledore, their raiding parties had pillaged and devastated farms and villages as far west as Hampshire and as far north as Berkshire.[19]

The vikings fell victim to their own success. The vast amount of booty that they seized as they followed their long, circuitous route to Essex so hindered their progress that they were outflanked by the English army. At Farnham in

---

18. T.A. Shippey, 'A missing army: some doubts about the Alfredian *Chronicle*', *In Geardagum* 4 (1982) pp. 41–55.
19. Æthelweard, *Chronicon*, ed. Campbell, p. 49; Keynes and Lapidge, p. 189.

Surrey, the vikings were forced to fight.[20] The battle commenced before Edward arrived, with local forces from the burhs in Hampshire and Surrey attempting to storm the makeshift defences thrown up by the vikings. As Æthelweard tells us, the appearance of the prince and his troops turned the tide in favour of the English: '[Prince Edward] came clashing in dense array into collision with the foemen at Farnham. There was no delay, the young men leaped against the prepared defences . . . they duly exulted, being set free [from care] by the prince's arrival, like sheep brought to the pastures by the help of the shepherd after the usual onslaught of predators.'[21] The unnamed 'king' of the Appledore Danes was badly wounded in the fray. Abandoning their booty, the panic-stricken survivors fled north along the River Wey across the Thames, without bothering to find a ford. They still lost the race. With the English army breathing down their necks, they took refuge on Thorney, a small island formed by the branching of the river near Iver, in Buckinghamshire.[22] Here the English surrounded them. Nursing their wounded and without food, the vikings huddled miserably on the islet, grimly waiting for their supplies to run out or the English to overwhelm them in a bloody assault. But, as it happened, the English could not capitalize on the vikings' dire circumstances. Edward's forces had also exhausted their own provisions. Worse yet, their terms of service had expired. Though Alfred was on his way with their relief, the prince had no option but to discharge his levies, who rode off to defend their homes and localities, leaving Edward to continue the siege with at most a few dozen personal followers. Ealdorman Æthelred rescued the day by arriving with forces from London. Fearing that the vikings might break out before Alfred arrived, Edward and Æthelred agreed to the vikings' request for a treaty. The terms of the

20. Ealdorman Æthelweard provides the fullest account of this battle, but the Latin of the received text is so convoluted and ungrammatical and its vocabulary so obscure and pretentious that it is difficult to make out precisely what the ealdorman intended to say. The frustration experienced by Keynes and Lapidge in trying to translate Æthelweard's narrative is evident in their commentary, pp. 334–8. It is instructive to compare their translation with Campbell's. Æthelweard, *Chronicon*, ed. Campbell, pp. 49–50; Keynes and Lapidge, pp. 189–90.
21. Æthelweard, *Chronicon*, ed. Campbell, p. 49.
22. Stenton, *Anglo-Saxon England*, p. 266.

peace were simple: the vikings would give hostages and immediately depart the kingdom. This particular band of vikings
had been battered badly enough to abide by their oaths. As
Æthelweard observed, 'They rightfully promise to go from
the realm of the aforesaid king [i.e. Ealdorman Æthelred].
Deed and word together are fulfilled at the same time.'[23]
Edward allowed them to cross safely into East Anglia. From
there the survivors straggled on, under protection of the
East Anglians, until they arrived at the island of Mersea
at the mouth of the River Blackwater in Essex, about sixty
kilometres up the coast from Benfleet. There, according to
Æthelweard, ships from Appledore awaited them.

The account of the battle of Farnham and its aftermath
in the main *Chronicle* differs significantly from Æthelweard's
version. It breaks off abruptly with the English abandoning
the siege, and the vikings immobilized on the islet, unable
to move their severely wounded king. The Chronicler fails
to explain how the vikings escaped. Indeed, the next we
hear of them they are with Hasteinn in Benfleet with their
ships. That Æthelweard was correct in asserting that the
Appledore vikings made camp on Mersea is clear from the
reference to a camp on that island in the *Chronicle*'s annal
for 894. The Chronicler, with his focus squarely on Alfred,
lost interest in the movements of the Appledore vikings
after their defeat. Intentionally or not, he leaves the impression that the Appledore vikings left their camp in order to
join with Hasteinn in his new stronghold. More likely, the
great army split after arriving on Mersea. Some remained
with their king, while others sailed south to Benfleet to
replenish the loot that they had lost at Farnham. This is
not to say that the forces on Mersea had seen the light and
were now willing either to return to Francia or settle down
in East Anglia. They too sought wealth and would not leave
before they had obtained it, but they had been badly mauled
and needed time to recover.

As Alfred advanced with his levies toward Thorney, news
reached him that the Danes in East Anglia and Northumbria had broken the peace. Apparently, the Appledore vikings
had been in contact with their compatriots in the Danelaw.
About the same time that the Appledore vikings broke camp,

23. Æthelweard, *Chronicon*, ed. Campbell, p. 50.

the Northumbrians and East Anglians assembled a fleet of a hundred ships and sailed south and then west along the coast of England. Their intention was to take advantage of Alfred's embroilment in the east to launch a surprise attack upon western Wessex. Forty ships rounded Cornwall to attack a fortress on the northern coast of Devon, perhaps Countisbury at the northern mouth of the Exe, where Ealdorman Odda had defeated a Danish army during the dark days of 878. The other ships remained behind to lay siege to Exeter. By taking the two fortresses and ravaging up and down the Exe, they hoped to split the local English defences and, perhaps, even gain control over western Devon and Cornwall. To complicate matters further, Hasteinn, emboldened by the arrival of new recruits from the other viking army at Mersea, began to pillage eastern Mercia from his stronghold at Benfleet. Alfred responded by dividing his forces. Sending a small detachment on to London, the king immediately turned west with the bulk of his forces and began a 225-kilometre march to relieve Exeter.

Alfred's troops brought the Londoners news of the extension of the war to the western shires. They could not depend upon the fyrd to deal with the rising menace at Benfleet. The English leaders in London, the bishop, reeves and king's thegns, and, perhaps, Ealdorman Æthelred, if he had already returned from Thorney, resolved to raise an army from London and nearby burhs to burn out this new hornets' nest. Hasteinn was out with a raiding party when the English troops arrived. Lulled by their successes and, perhaps, by Alfred's attempts at accommodation, the viking army at Benfleet were caught completely unawares by the sudden approach of the English. Sweeping down upon Benfleet, the English killed or drove off all those unlucky enough to be caught in the open and stormed the Vikings' defences. Confused and leaderless, the vikings fell back as the English poured into the enclosure. The viking stronghold fell after a brief but intense struggle. Vikings fled with their wives, children and whatever goods they could, as the Londoners began to reap the harvest of their victory. The English recovered much of the loot stored at Benfleet. They also captured human booty, women and children who could be either sold as slaves or ransomed for a handsome profit. Among the captives were Hasteinn's wife and his two sons, the godsons of King Alfred and Ealdorman Æthelred. They were separated from the rest and held for Alfred's personal judgement. As for the viking longboats, the Londoners sailed the most seaworthy to London or Rochester and smashed up or burnt the rest on the spot. They then levelled the ramparts at Benfleet and returned home in triumph.

Though dramatic, the fall of Benfleet proved indecisive. Too many men, including Hasteinn, had escaped. The viking chieftain's response was to order a new fortress to be built on the coast of Essex at Shoebury, about seventeen kilometres east of Benfleet. There he assembled what remained of his original followers, augmented by vikings from Appledore. His prospects were brightened by the arrival of 'a great reinforcement' from the settlers of both East Anglia and Northumbria, lured to Shoebury by the prospect of plunder.[24] The new fortification was not intended to be a base from which to raid the already exhausted eastern shires, but a refuge for the camp followers and a place to safeguard booty and ships. Still intent upon filling his coffers, Hasteinn decided upon a bold strike across the breadth of England to the yet unplundered lands of western Mercia. Though the Londoners had not persuaded Hasteinn to abandon his predatory ways, they had taught him to respect English military power. What the viking chieftain now sought was safety for his dependants and fresh fields to plunder, as far from burghal garrisons and fyrds as he could manage.

Leaving behind their women and children, Hasteinn and his forces pushed up the Thames as quickly as they could. Apparently, Alfred had not yet learned the value of building double burhs connected by fortified bridges, because the viking fleet was able to sail safely past burghal forts at Southwark, Sashes, Wallingford, Oxford, and Cricklade. Turning north up either the River Coln or the River Churn, the raiders made their way to the Severn, and then followed the river to Buttington near Welshpool.[25] There, surrounded by hills in a gap in Offa's Dyke, they made a fortified camp, possibly on an islet in the Severn. They had traversed Alfred's realm from east to west, but they had not escaped his military system. Whereas it is unlikely that the various bands of

24. *ASC* s.a. 893.
25. Stenton, *Anglo-Saxon England*, p. 267, n. 1.

marauders in England coordinated their movements, there is little doubt that the English forces that opposed them did. As Æthelred pursued the vikings from the east, Alfred's veteran ealdormen in Wiltshire and Somerset, Æthelhelm and Æthelnoth, moved to meet them from the south. Æthelhelm, an experienced commander who been with Alfred since Athelney, led a troop of mounted infantry that tracked the movements of the enemy and reported upon them to his fellow commanders. As a result, the English knew precisely where to find Hasteinn's base. The entire available forces of Wessex, Mercia and Powys converged on the viking stronghold. Instead of the rich and undefended farms and villages they had expected to find when they began their dash across England, Hasteinn and his men now faced a huge army made up of 'all the king's thegns who were then at home from every borough east of the Parret, and both west and east of Selwood, and also north of the Thames and west of the Severn, and also some portions of the Welsh people'.[26]

The combined English and Welsh forces occupied both banks of the Severn and began a siege that lasted for a number of weeks. After the trapped vikings had devoured their horses and had begun to starve, they made a desperate attempt to break out, attacking the part of the army on the eastern shore. The fighting was intense. The English experienced heavy losses (though only one casualty, the king's thegn Ordheah, was deemed worthy of mention), but the vikings suffered even more. The Christians, Æthelweard exults, had a triumph that was still vaunted by old men a century later.[27]

Undoubtedly the English had won a great victory as measured by body count and possession of the field, but a large part of the viking army managed to survive, either by flight (as asserted by the *Chronicle*) or by, yet again, making peace and giving hostages (as Æthelweard maintained). The remnants of the army straggled back to Essex. Despite the imminent approach of winter, they decided to try once more. Again they recruited warriors from among the East Anglians and Northumbrians, and, sending their women, children, goods and ships to safety in East Anglia (probably to the

26. *ASC* s.a. 893; Æthelweard, *Chronicon*, ed. Campbell, p. 50.
27. Ibid.

stronghold on Mersea), they force-marched day and night again across Mercia. English forces pursued, but the raiders managed to occupy and refurbish the defences of Chester, then a deserted Roman ruin on the River Dee at the junction of a network of Roman roads. The arrival of the English forces ended any hope they had of wintering at Chester. Alfred's generals now acted as he had at Chippenham back in 878. They killed the men and seized all the cattle they caught outside the walls. Then they surrounded the fortress, and for two days systematically burnt or fed to their horses the harvest from the entire region. This scorched earth strategy worked. Unable to sustain themselves at Chester for the winter, the viking army withdrew into Wales. In the early months of 894, they plundered the territory of their erstwhile ally and recent enemy, King Anarawd ap Rhodri of Gwynedd and Powys. When they had obtained sufficient booty to justify the expedition, they returned to Mersea, showing their respect for English military power by following a northerly route through Northumbria and East Anglia rather than risk another engagement. The raiding expedition had proved successful, but the cost and dangers had been far greater than any had imagined when they first landed at Appledore and Milton in Kent in the autumn of 892.

Around the spring of 894, King Alfred's persistence finally wore down the joint Northumbrian–East Anglian army in Devonshire. With Alfred and his army in the field, the prospect of plunder or conquest became ever more remote. The leaders of the expeditionary force (among them, perhaps, the piratical Northumbrian king, Sigeferth[28]), deciding there was little to be gained by remaining, departed for home. Along the way, they landed on the coast of Sussex, only to be driven off by the garrison from the burghal fort at Chichester, who 'killed many hundred of them, and captured some of their ships'.[29] Some of the fleet probably dispersed, while others made their way to Mersea.

28. Æthelweard, *Chronicon*, ed. Campbell, p. 50. See A.P. Smyth, *Scandinavian York and Dublin: The History and Archaeology of Two Related Kingdoms*, 2 vols (Dublin, 1975–9) I, pp. 33–7. Cf. F.M. Stenton, 'Æthelweard's account of the last years of King Alfred's reign', in his collected papers, *Preparatory to Anglo-Saxon England*, ed. D.M. Stenton (Oxford, 1970) pp. 10–11; Keynes and Lapidge, p. 337, n. 32.
29. *ASC* s.a. 894.

His western shires now safe, Alfred returned east. By late autumn 894 he was in London. Among the captives the Londoners brought back with them from Benfleet were Hasteinn's wife and two sons, the godsons of Alfred and Ealdorman Æthelred. Now they were brought before King Alfred. Rather than punish the sons for the sins of the father, Alfred chose to teach his viking kinsman in Christ a lesson in Christian charity and fidelity. Acknowledging his and Æthelred's obligations as godfather, Alfred generously returned the boys and their mother to Hasteinn.[30] How Hasteinn responded to this gesture is not known. The Chronicler appears to have been somewhat embarrassed by the entire affair. The only part of it that he deemed worthy of mention is Alfred's saint-like forbearance. It may or may not be significant that Hasteinn disappears from the Chronicler's narrative after the annal for 893.

What brought Alfred to London was a new threat from the Danish army on Mersea. In the early winter of 894, the Danish army, accompanied by their women and children, abandoned their stronghold on Mersea, entered the Thames, and rowed up the River Lea. They made camp about thirty-three kilometres north of London, in the vicinity of Hertford, and, as was their custom, fortified it with ditches and ramparts.[31] Some months later, during the summer, the garrison of London marched against the stronghold, but were driven off with losses; among the dead were four king's thegns. By autumn the problem had become critical, as the Danes now threatened to deprive the Londoners of the harvest. As the late Roman military writer, Vegetius, had observed, famine is more savage than the sword. What was at stake, quite simply, was the survival of the burh. Alfred responded quickly. He marched his army to London, encamped north of the burh, and ordered his warriors to stand guard over the peasants as they reaped their crops. This solved the immediate problem, but Alfred could not leave the vikings in possession of a base so close to London. Perhaps the 'heroic' thing would have been to assault the stronghold, but Alfred was intelligent enough to realize that the loss of the harvest placed the vikings in an untenable situation. All he had to do

30. *ASC* s.a. 893.
31. *ASC* s.a. 895.

was bottle them up in their camp and wait for their supplies to run out.

The military problem, then, was not how to drive them out of their camp, but how to keep them in it. This was easier said than done. Experience had taught Alfred how slippery a viking army could be. The Chronicler's explanation of how Alfred solved this problem sheds a great deal of light upon the king's military thinking and his own understanding of the tactical function of the 'double burhs' and bridges that he and his children ordered to be built upon the banks of the navigable rivers of Wessex and Mercia. If the Danes abandoned their stronghold on the Lea and rowed downriver to the Thames estuary, they would be free to raid the coastal areas at will, at least until his mounted forces caught up with them again. The prudent course was to finish it now. Along the banks of the River Lea, Alfred looked for a place downstream of the Danes where he could most easily block the river and thereby entrap their ships. He found what he was looking for, moved his camp to this site, and ordered his soldiers to excavate ditches and construct ramparts for burhs on each bank. As soon as the English began to dig, the vikings realized what was afoot. Apparently, they were well acquainted with this tactic from their experiences with fortified bridges in West Francia, and though the Chronicler would lead us to believe that he hit upon this ingenious solution on the spot, it is likely that Alfred was also drawing upon Frankish military lessons. The Danish leaders knew that if they waited until the double burh was complete, they would be trapped on the upper reaches of the Lea. Rather than chance an open battle against a superior force, they abandoned their ships and struck out overland. Sending their women and children to safety in East Anglia, the men made their way westward across Mercia, not stopping until they came to Bridgnorth in Shropshire, some 200 kilometres from where they had started. The *fyrd* went in pursuit, while the citizens of London triumphantly seized the ships left behind.

As had been so often the case, Alfred achieved only a partial victory. True, he had defended London's harvest and had forced the Danes to evacuate a stronghold that menaced the burh, but the careful language of the Chronicler cannot conceal the fact that the viking army managed to escape. Nor had they been so discouraged as to abandon hopes of future gains. Stripped of camp followers, the viking forces were more mobile and potentially more dangerous than before. They made their way overland, along the frontier that Alfred had established with Guthrum more than two decades before, until they arrived at Bridgnorth on the Severn. There they established their winter camp. But the political climate itself had changed. In the previous year Alfred had sent Ealdorman Æthelnoth to York to negotiate a peace with their King Gunfrith, who had become more receptive to Alfred's overtures since he had entered into his own war over Rutland with his Scandinavian neighbours.[32] After three years of hard effort with little to show for it, what remained of the viking army finally dispersed in the summer of 896. Those who had obtained sufficient wealth settled alongside their compatriots in Northumbria and East Anglia. Their less fortunate companions obtained ships and, under the leadership of an otherwise unknown viking chieftain named Huncdeus, crossed the Channel to the Seine in search of plunder. By then their numbers had dwindled to the point that their entire force could be embarked on only five large ships.[33]

Reviewing the course of the war, the Chronicler reflected, 'The army, by God's grace, had not on the whole afflicted the English people very greatly; but they were more seriously afflicted in those years by the mortality of cattle and men, and most of all in that many of the best king's thegns who were in the land died in those three years.'[34] This was perhaps an odd judgement, given the attention he had lavished upon the military events of the preceding years. But, on the whole, the Chronicler was right: Alfred's people had weathered the storm well. And if the West Saxons and Mercians suffered more in these years from natural than human causes, it was the result of Alfred's hard work and planning. King Alfred had had little to do directly with the great victories enjoyed by the English in 893–896. His son,

---

32. Æthelweard, *Chronicon*, ed. Campbell, p. 51. I follow here Keynes and Lapidge's translation, p. 190. What precisely Æthelnoth was doing at York is unclear, but it is more likely that he was on a diplomatic mission than a military expedition, especially given the distances involved and Æthelweard's uncharacteristic silence about the outcome.
33. *Annals of St-Vaast* s.a. 896. See Keynes and Lapidge, p. 288, n. 25.
34. *ASC* s.a. 896.

Edward, and his ealdormen, in particular his son-in-law, Æthelred, had won the glory. For much of this time, Alfred had been engaged in the less dramatic, but, to him, perhaps more important job of defending Devonshire. Of course, while he had immobilized the enemy, his own forces had been equally tied down by what amounted to a long, drawn-out siege of the besiegers. The king's physical distance from the centre of military action in 893 proved awkward for the Chronicler, who went so far as to suppress any mention of the exploits of Prince Edward so as not to overshadow the father's accomplishments.

Though Alfred had not won the heroic glory celebrated in vernacular poems, in a larger sense, the victories had been his. Hasteinn and the others had failed, not because the English commanders were cleverer or their men more resolute, but because of a complex and sophisticated military *system* that permitted the English to fight a multi-front war. The vikings had discovered that English towns were no longer easy prey. It was dangerous to leave a garrisoned burh intact, but it was equally dangerous to attempt to take one. Possessing neither siege engines nor doctrine, they could not storm burhs protected by ditches, earthworks strengthened by wooden revetments, and palisades. If they attempted to starve a town into submission, the hunter was likely to become the hunted, as the *fyrd* and garrisons from neighbouring burhs would come to the relief of the besieged. Alfred's system, in short, had worked precisely as he conceived it would. The very geography of his last war attested to its effectiveness. In 871, 876, and 878, the Great Heathen Army had attacked and ravaged the heartland of Wessex (see Map 6, p. 356). In 892–894, an even larger army, with allies in Northumbria and East Anglia, had to content itself with raiding along the frontiers of Wessex and Mercia (see Map 7, p. 357). Only once had viking raiders penetrated the country-side of Surrey or Hampshire, and those marauders had paid for their daring at Farnham. When the men of Somerset and Wiltshire fought, it was well beyond the borders of their shires. Alfred had proved to his enemies and his friends alike the wisdom of his demands 'with regard to the building of fortresses and the other things for the common profit of the whole kingdom'.[35]

35. Asser, ch. 91; *EHD* I, no. 7, p. 299.

The Chronicler responsible for the narrative of Alfred's final campaigns against the vikings concluded his writing with the annal for 896. Either he, or more likely another of Alfred's clerics, added to the annal a final note, concerning the king's experiment with a new naval design. Among the more enduring Alfredian myths is that Alfred was the 'Father of the Royal Navy'. The founders of the American Navy were so certain of this, that they named the first flagship of the infant United States the *Alfred*, which became one of the vessels commanded by John Paul Jones. To commemorate the thousandth anniversary of Alfred's death, the royal navy in 1901 christened one of their new armoured battlecruisers the HMS *Alfred*. As with other Alfredian myths, there is a grain of truth in this. King Alfred did contemplate naval defence, and even went so far as to design warships according to his own specifications, though here his ingenuity almost proved costly.

The dispersal of the Great Heathen Army had ended the threat to the kingdom but not all raiding. The years of war bred lawlessness, and throughout the summer of 896 small fleets, some of whose ships were quite old, continued to sail from ports in Northumbria and East Anglia with freebooters in search of plunder. Alfred had been long interested in matters of naval defence. Years before, in 884, he had gone out personally to sea to fight, and win, a battle against the crews of four viking longboats.[36] During the recent campaigns, he had experienced the disadvantages of attempting to defend against a maritime threat without a navy. His solution to the problem of seaborne raiding was now to order the construction of a fleet of 'longships' to oppose the older and smaller Danish warships. Characteristically, Alfred decided to improve upon the standard ship types of the day. His ships would conform neither to the Danish nor the Frisian pattern, but would be of his own design, incorporating whatever elements he deemed most useful. On the theory that bigger is better, they were to have sixty oars, some even more, and be nearly twice the length of an ordinary viking ship. The Chronicler, clearly reflecting his patron's evident pride of accomplishment, boasted that Alfred's ships were not only larger, but swifter, steadier, and rode higher in

36. See p. 172 above.

the water than other warships. In conception, they were far superior to anything they might encounter. In practice, however, they proved less sound than desired.

Before the summer of 896 was over, Alfred's new model fleet, manned by a mixed crew of Englishmen and professional Frisian sailors, had an opportunity to prove its worth against an enemy fleet of six ships that had wreaked havoc on the Isle of Wight and along the southern coast as far as Devon. In the naval engagement that ensued, Alfred's fleet won, but did so in spite of, rather than because of, the new ship design. The Danish vessels, with their shallow drafts, had been designed for use on the rivers. Alfred's were not. When Alfred's fleet of nine ships came upon the enemy in the mouth of an unidentified river along the coast of southern England, it immediately moved to block the estuary from the seaward end. The Danes had beached half of their ships, either to rest the rowers or to forage for food. The crews on the other three boats realized the danger they were in and tried to break through the English lines. Only one made it. Alfred's ships intercepted the other two. Lashing the viking boats to their own, the mixed English and Frisian crew boarded the enemy's vessels and proceeded to kill everyone on board. Even the one ship that escaped lost all but five of its crew, and it managed to get away only because all of Alfred's ships ran aground.

What Alfred had gained by size, he lost in manoeuvrability. The situation was particularly awkward, since three of Alfred's ships lay near the beached Danish ships, while the other six were stranded on the opposite shore, unable either to get at the enemy or to help their comrades. With the tide ebbing, the Danes, though outnumbered, decided it was better to attack the three ships within their reach than chance fighting all nine together when the tide rose once more. Slogging along on foot, they advanced on the English. The English and their Frisian allies poured out of their ships to meet the vikings on the shore. In the hand-to-hand fighting that followed, the English and Frisians lost sixty-two men, including a king's reeve and a member of Alfred's household. The Danes lost 120. Before the English could finish them off, however, the tide rose. The Danes rushed back to their boats, which being lighter, with shallower drafts, were freed before Alfred's ships. Helplessly, the English watched as the Danes rowed past them. But the pirates had suffered so many casualties that they had difficulties putting out to sea. Two of the ships were driven against the Sussex shore, while the third barely made it back to East Anglia. The shipwrecked sailors, many of them wounded, were taken captive and brought before Alfred, then at Winchester. He did not extend to these common ruffians the mercy he had shown to Hasteinn's sons. As far he was concerned, they were pirates and, even worse than that, oathbreakers. He had them hanged.

The *Anglo-Saxon Chronicle* says little about Alfred's final years, recording only the deaths of a few prominent individuals. We can presume that Alfred spent his days hunting and working on his translations, for he now had the leisure to pursue his passions. Peace also raised long-deferred questions. With the king approaching his fiftieth birthday, an old man by the reckoning of the day, the hungry *æthelings* at court began to look to the future. Alfred's two sons and those of his older brother, Æthelred, were now grown men. One of them, each knew, would be the next king. Alfred's elder son, Edward, had to be the front runner. The prince had proved his worth as a commander and warrior. By 898, he was also the father of a young, albeit illegitimate, son, the future King Æthelstan. That Alfred had favoured Edward to succeed him is amply demonstrated by the king's will: Edward was to receive all of his father's bookland in Kent and estates spread throughout Wessex, a far greater bequest than any other. We do not know whether in these final years Alfred advanced the interests of his elder son more directly, by pressuring the magnates of Wessex and Mercia to accept him as his heir, or by conferring upon him an underkingship in Kent, as King Æthelwulf had done for his sons. A strange charter drawn up by a Rochester cleric in 898 that survives in contemporary, or near-contemporary, form confers upon Edward the title *rex*, and places his name in its witness list immediately beneath Alfred's (also *rex*), but whether this reflects political reality or merely the whims of its drafter is debatable.[37] Nor does it seem entirely consistent that Alfred, having created the ideal of a unified kingdom of the Angles and Saxons, would have allowed even his

37. S 350.

son to rule part of that kingdom as *rex*. That the tensions and intrigues in the court were real, however, is evidenced by the subsequent revolt of the *ætheling* Æthelwold.

There is nothing more to be said about Alfred's final years. On 26 October 899 King Alfred died. He was either fifty or fifty-one years old and had reigned twenty-eight and a half years. The details of his passing are unknown. The notice of his death in the *Anglo-Saxon Chronicle* is surprisingly restrained, evidence that it was written long after the event, probably by one of King Edward's clerics, who was far more interested in the military exploits of the son than the past glory of the father. All it says is that 'in this year died Alfred, son of Æthelwulf, six nights before All Hallows' Day. He had been king over the whole English people except that part which was under Danish rule'. Alfred himself appreciated how transitory is the glory of this world. Though later medieval and early modern authors would come to appreciate his greatness, to the generations that came immediately after, his accomplishments paled before those of his son and grandsons, who built upon his foundations to transform his idea of a kingdom of the Anglo-Saxons into the reality of an 'England'. In their vision of history, he played the role of an English Charles Martel to his grandson, Æthelstan's, Charlemagne. But Alfred was not forgotten. Nearly a century after his death, Ealdorman Æthelweard, a descendant of Alfred's brother, Æthelred, gave Alfred a fitting tribute:

> Then, in the same year, passed from the world the magnanimous Alfred, king of the Saxons, unshakable pillar of the people of the west, a man full of justice, active in war, learned in speech, and, above all, instructed in divine learning. . . . His body rests in peace in the city of Winchester. Now say, reader, 'O Christ our Redeemer, save his soul.'[38]

38. Æthelweard, *Chronicon*, ed. Campbell, p. 52.

. . . . .

CONCLUSION: 'MY MEMORY IN GOOD WORKS'

For many years an obscure quotation from an equally obscure Victorian general, Sir William Butler, graced the bulletin board outside the offices of the Division of Humanities and Social Sciences at the school where I teach, the United States Naval Academy. It read:

> The nation that will insist upon drawing a broad line of demarcation between the fighting man and the thinking man is likely to have its fighting done by fools and its thinking by cowards.[1]

Butler's insistence that academe and the military must go hand in hand is a sentiment that today seems quaint if not archaic. A hundred years and two World Wars ago, things were quite different. There was nothing even faintly comic about the notion of a scholar soldier, of a Benjamin Jowett in spurs. What made King Alfred 'England's Darling' even more in the nineteenth century than in the ninth was the general acknowledgement that he was the first native of the British Isles to combine in his person the moral, physical and intellectual virtues of the 'model Englishman'.[2] That he did so while serving his nation as a conscientious and indefatigable king seemed particularly fitting in the England of Queen Victoria and her 'Saxon' consort Prince Albert. This

1. Col. W. Butler, *The Life of Charles George Gordon* (London, 1891) p. 85.
2. Thus Charles Dickens: 'under the GREAT ALFRED, all the best points in the English character were first encouraged, and in him first shown'. *A Child's History of England*, vol. 15 of *The Complete Works of Charles Dickens*, 20 vols (New York, n. d.) p. 25, cited in C.A. Simmons, *Reversing the Conquest: History and Myth in Nineteenth-Century British Literature* (New Brunswick, NJ, 1990) p. 40.

was the ideal that found material expression in the wonderfully romantic statues of Alfred that now stand on the High Street of Winchester and in the marketplace of Wantage. As the Right Hon. J. Bryce, MP, enthused in a speech given in 1898 to promote a national commemoration in celebration of Alfred's forthcoming millenary: 'He was a man valiant in war, but also just and lenient in peace. . . . But though much of his life was spent in fighting, he was also the first of our kings who set himself deliberately to work to promote learning, education, and culture in the people, still fierce and rude. . . . He showed that union of force & strength & courage with wisdom & piety & the love of letters which was the note of all the greatest men in the Dark and the Middle Ages.'[3]

Some historians of the post-World War II era have had a more difficult time in reconciling Alfred 'the simple, great-hearted warrior' (as Vivien Galbraith characterized him) with the philosophical Alfred of the Boethius or Augustine translations or the saintly Alfred of Asser's *Life*.[4] Not so the Victorians. The *speculum regis* for Alfred devised by Charles Plummer, Thomas Hughes, and Beatrice Lees may now seem hopelessly old fashioned, but these writers did perceive a basic unity in Alfred's various actions and writings that, I believe, was quite real. The dichotomy that Galbraith and others perceived between Alfred the warlord and Alfred the seeker of wisdom is a false one. Alfred himself made this clear in the preface to his translation of Gregory the Great's *Pastoral Care*, in which wisdom is alliteratively portrayed as a precondition to both the wealth of a people and their success in war. Any attempt to comprehend Alfred's views on the nature of kingship must fuse the theocratic king with the warlord. The same man who impetuously rushed into

---

3. A. Bowker, *The King Alfred Millenary. A Record of the Proceedings of the National Commemoration* (London: Macmillan & co., 1902) p. 14. Cf. C. Plummer, *The Life and Times of Alfred the Great, being the Ford Lectures for 1901* (Oxford: The Clarendon Press, 1901) pp. 197–203.
4. V.H. Galbraith, 'Research in Action: Who Wrote Asser's Life of Alfred?', in *An Introduction to the Study of History* (London: C.A. Watts & Co., 1964) pp. 127–28; J.L. Nelson, 'The Political Ideas of Alfred of Wessex', in *Kings and Kingship in Medieval Europe*, ed. A.J. Duggan, King's College London Medieval Studies 10, gen. ed. J. Bately (London, 1993) p. 130.

battle at Ashdown and traded sword blows with vikings on the decks of their own ships mused and wrote about the immortality of the human soul. The new Moses of the law code was also a pragmatic judge who decided disputes while washing his hands in his chamber and a 'politician' who knew how to cajole, persuade and intimidate.

It is from Asser and Alfred's own writings that we know him best. But what they teach us is less about the man as he actually was than about what he aspired to be and how he wished others to see him. That Alfred was pious is beyond doubt. His abiding faith and burning interest in matters relating to Christian theology informed all of his writings, including his law code. Nor should we doubt Asser's report that Alfred loved the Psalms and the divine offices. His translation of the Psalms and his personal, if derivative, introductions confirm what Asser tells us. But we must also be wary of accepting Asser's (or even Alfred's own) portrait too uncritically. The *Life* was intended not only for the pleasure of the king but for the edification of Asser's brethren in St David's. As such, Asser wrote it as much to be an *apologia* for his own service to a foreign king as an encomium for a patron. Drawing upon models provided him by Einhard's Charlemagne and, probably, Thegan's and the Astronomer's Louis the Pious, he depicted Alfred as the ideal Christian prince, one who, like Solomon, crowned renown and wealth with piety.[5] Alfred's love of learning; the friendship he freely gave to his chaplains, bishops and priests; his great generosity, demonstrated so amply through the lands and honours that he bestowed upon Asser himself; and his power, sufficient to defend the monks of St David against even their *bête noire*, the rapacious King Hyfaidd of Dyfed, made him a prince to be honoured, obeyed and loved.[6] Alfred thus became the Saxon Charlemagne and Asser his Welsh Alcuin.

One of the stories that Asser tells of Alfred involves the king's attempt to invent a device to tell time so that he could dedicate, 'in so far as his health and resources and abilities would allow', half of his hours to thoughts of and

---

5. Asser, ch. 76, ed. Stevenson, pp. 60–1: *pius et ipinatissimus atque opulentissimus.*
6. Asser, chs 79, 81, ed. Stevenson, pp. 65, 67–8.

services to God.[7] What follows is an elaborate account of how Alfred arrived at a useful and prudent solution to the problem. He ordered his chaplains to gather wax, which he had them weigh against the weight of pennies upon a two-pound balance. When they measured out a quantity equal to the weight of seventy-two pennies (about 4 ounces (113g)), he ordered them to divide the wax equally and make six (extremely thin) twelve-inch candles, carefully marking the inches on each. He intended to place the candles before the holy relics that he always carried with him, and have them burn, one after the other, day and night so that he would know when twenty-four hours had passed. (Apparently he had determined that each candle would burn precisely for four hours.) Unfortunately, his churches and tents proved so draughty that the candles either were blown out by the wind or they burnt more quickly than they should have. Alfred considered the matter carefully and hit upon a solution. He intelligently and skilfully devised a plan. The candles would be placed in a lantern constructed out of wood and ox-horn, so finely shaved that it became as translucent as glass. Thus shielded against the wind, his candles burnt the proper length of time. Alfred not only had his time-measuring device but had, in the process, invented the horn lantern.

William Henry Stevenson, Asser's greatest editor, and Alfred Smyth, his most recent denier, both spilled a good deal of ink over the plausibility of the story.[8] For the former the question was whether the details made sense. Certainly, a modern twelve-inch candle made from about two-thirds of an ounce (19g) of wax would not only be flimsy but would burn far too quickly, being consumed (according to my experiments) in about twenty minutes. Stevenson discusses such matters as the material used for wicks in the ninth century (linen or flax) and whether we can necessarily rely upon the accuracy of the details (we cannot). Smyth, on the other hand, dismisses this entire line of enquiry. For him it is far more important to consider the purported reason for Alfred's invention of this timepiece:

---

7. Asser, ch. 104, ed. Stevenson, pp. 90–1; trans. Keynes and Lapidge, pp. 108–9.
8. Stevenson, *Asser's Life of King Alfred*, pp. 339–41; A.P. Smyth, *King Alfred the Great* (Oxford, 1995) pp. 321–4.

The notion of Alfred's desire to offer half his life in the service of God, having become so obsessive to the point of wanting to calculate that time with exactitude 'by means of some enduring principle', depends on our acceptance of the hagiographical view of Alfred as a saint. If we accept this story, then we must view Alfred as a frustrated saintly astronomer-king, who, failing to read the time from the sun and stars, was driven to invent a candle clock to satisfy his obsession with giving half of his life up to prayer and to God.[9]

Such a 'vision does not tally' with Smyth's understanding of Alfred, but there is nothing improbable about the story. Given Alfred's love of the pursuit of 'wisdom', which for Smyth is key to understanding the man, a resolution of this sort is not difficult to imagine. Nor is it implausible that a king who made two pilgrimages to Rome as a youth, whose father left a bequest to the papacy for the purchase of oil for lamps in the churches of SS Peter and Paul, and whose chroniclers boasted about a gift of relics sent him by the pope should have burnt his candles in front of his favourite relics.[10] One cannot understand Alfred without first grasping the role that prayer, relics and pilgrimage played in his world and his life. And if Alfred even toyed with the idea, urged on perhaps by Asser and his other spiritual helpers, the king's biographer would have reported it. It fits in with his theme and his conception of the king. But what also comes out strongly in Asser's narrative is Alfred's fascination with solving problems. Indeed, this is the main theme of the chapter. The king, confronted with the question of how to know when half of the hours of the day have passed, devises an ingenious time-keeping device. When it does not work as planned, he considers the problem and comes up with a practical solution. This is the same Alfred who divided his army into rotating halves and his landed court attendants into three alternating contingents, who devised a pay ladder for his household warriors according to the favour in which he held them, who created a tripartite taxonomy for the human 'tools' of a king and who created an elaborate budget for his expenditures. The story of the horn lantern, in short, is consistent with what we know of the

9. Smyth, *King Alfred the Great*, pp. 321–2.
10. Cf. ibid., pp. 323–4.

man, his obsession with details, his delight in finding practical solutions to problems, and, certainly, with the piety and practical turn of mind demonstrated in page after page of his writings. As one scholar put it, Alfred's true genius lay in his 'inspired commonsense' and that is precisely what this story is really about.[11]

What emerges from reading Alfred's own works is the sense of engaging a wonderfully inquisitive, practical intelligence, and one that was not easily awed by the authority of others. 'I dared not presume', he humbly tells the audience for his law code, 'to set down in writing at all many of my own [edicts], since it was unknown to me what would please those who should come after us.'[12] Yet, Alfred did presume to emend Holy Scripture itself so that it would make better sense to him and his subjects. This entailed not only changing the word 'Hebrew' to 'Christian' in his translation of passages from Exodus, but in eliminating injunctions to help one's enemy, a command profoundly alien to an ethos that accepted the feud as necessary and, if regulated, even desirable.[13] Alfred not only translated Latin texts into English but transformed them in accordance with his understanding of the nature of divine and human authority. In Alfred's hands 'Augustine' becomes a secular lord, concerned for the welfare of his dependants and friends and unshaken in the love he bears for his own worldly lord. Running through all of Alfred's writings is the conviction that the political and social hierarchy he knew so intimately was not simply the way of the world, but was a manifestation of the divine order. God Himself, Alfred maintained, had established lordship among men and set kings above all other lords. To betray a lord was to betray Him. But the authority of a king was equally circumscribed by his duty to obey God, the Lord of all men, and His ordinances. 'He rules the kings who have the most power on this earth – who like all men are

11. M. Dolley, 'Ælfred the Great's abandonment of the concept of periodic recoinage', in C.N.L. Brooke, B.H.I.H. Steward, J.G. Pollard and T.R. Volk, *Studies in Numismatic Method presented to Philip Grierson* (Cambridge, 1983) p. 157.
12. *Alfred* Intro. 49.9, trans. Keynes and Lapidge, p. 164.
13. Exod. 21:2; 22:9, 23:5. Cf. *Alfred* Intro. 11, 28, 42. See M.H. Turk, ed., *The Legal Code of Ælfred the Great* (Boston, 1893) pp. 35–8. Cf. P. Wormald, *The Making of English Law* (Oxford, forthcoming).

born, and also perish like other men.'[14] Nor was obedience
to a lord servitude. Alfred insisted that the relationship
between a lord and his man was freely chosen, reciprocal
and founded upon love as well as duty. Alfred prided himself upon being the king of free men; to rule over slaves
was neither fitting nor honourable.[15]

Alfred's self-proclaimed 'sense for sense' translation of
Boethius profoundly reshaped the *Consolation* to reflect
his own ideas about human freedom, man's accountability
to God and divine providence. Alfred, the king, refused to
accept the philosopher's repudiation of earthly wealth and
fame as mere vanity. For Alfred the challenge was to use
wealth and power properly, and to earn through good works
a lasting memory of virtue. Like Gregory the Great, Alfred
embraced the responsibilities of rulership as a divine duty,
to be fulfilled with all the skill that one could bring to the
task. Wisdom, Alfred taught, confers upon those who love
her the virtues necessary to exercise authority properly: prudence, temperance, courage and justice. Conversely, power
without wisdom is mere tyranny. But even 'wisdom', Alfred
knew, did not guarantee 'success' in one's earthly endeavours. He had known failure as both a king and a general.
He had seen his brothers rise to the heights of earthly
glory, only to suffer untimely deaths. And he knew how
difficult it was to preserve the tranquillity of one's mind
when the body is wracked with pain. To endure and to
strive was Alfred's counsel. In this life, it was all that one
could do.

Alfred strove as mightily to learn and to understand as
he did to defeat his enemies and enhance the power of
his house. If, as Alfred believed, power and fame are the
earthly rewards of wisdom, he also taught that knowledge is
worthwhile for its own sake, and that all earthly goods are
but pale reflections of the highest good that man obtains
through wisdom, an eternal home in God's kingdom. 'I think
that man very foolish and exceedingly wretched who will
not increase his understanding while he is in this world,
and also wish and desire that he may come to the eternal

14. *Alfred's Soliloquies*, ed. Carnicelli, p. 86; trans. Hargrove, p. 37.
15. *Alfred's Boethius*, ed. Sedgefield, ch. 41, p. 142; trans. Sedgefield,
   p. 166.

life, where nothing is hidden from us.'[16] There is nothing startling or original in such thoughts. They are commonplace in the writings of early medieval thinkers. What is astonishing is not that Alfred thought them, but that he, a king, should have written them. This, more than anything else, roused the wonder and admiration of the chronicler, Ealdorman Æthelweard, in the late tenth century and of John of Worcester, William of Malmesbury and Gaimar in the twelfth.

Alfred reveals himself equally to us through his works and actions. In the burghal system that he devised and the ships he designed, we see the many facets of Alfred's mind. Here is the problem-solver, the systematizer, the general and the canny early medieval politician who knew how to coax, reward and intimidate his subjects into fulfilling his will. We see him in the carefully laid-out streets of ninth-century Winchester, in the wharfs of a restored City of London, in the restoration of a debased coinage to fine silver. In a more private moment, we see him as the chronic (and a trifle obsessive) teacher lecturing his dogkeepers on the fine points of their craft. Nor must we forget the battlefield. The law-giver who prided himself on his Christian mercy also waged bloody and ruthless war. He not only presided over massacres on the battlefield, but killed captives and summarily hanged wounded viking prisoners. These acts did not embarrass his eulogists. On the contrary, they exulted in their hero's bloody deeds. Yet, the man who massacred Danes outside Chippenham was also the gift-giver who bestowed treasures upon defeated enemies. What we are finally left with is an impression of a man who did not transcend his age, but embodied its ideals. No matter how superior we might feel toward the past, we ought not to make the mistake of thinking of it as a simpler time. It was not. Nor was Alfred a simple man. He combined within himself the complexities and contradictions of his age.

Alfred, I believe, would have been pleased with the statues erected in his honour at Winchester, Wantage and Alfred, New York – not because of the beauty of their proportions or the accuracy of their details, but because they preserve the memory of his good works. Like his own writings they

16. *Alfred's Soliloquies*, ed. Carnicelli, p. 97; trans. Hargrove, p. 47.

are monuments to a moral ideal, which for Alfred, after all, was the true purpose of writing history.

> Why will you not inquire after the wise men and those that coveted honours, what manner of men they were that came before you? And why will you not, when you have found out their manner of life, copy them with might and main? For they strove after honour in this world and set themselves to win good report with good works, and wrought a goodly example for those that came after. Therefore by virtue of their good deeds they now are dwelling above the stars in bliss everlasting.[17]

17. *Alfred's Boethius*, ed. Sedgefield, ch. 40, pp. 162–3; trans. Sedgefield, p. 139.

APPENDIX ON THE AUTHENTICITY OF ASSER'S *LIFE OF KING ALFRED*

Asser's biography of King Alfred is a source of inestimable value for understanding Alfred and his times, but it is also a work fraught with difficulties, some of them intrinsic to the text and genre, and others created by enterprising historians. To begin with, there is no extant medieval manuscript of the *Life*. An early eleventh-century copy at least twice removed from the original survived until 1731, when it was destroyed in the fire that ravaged the priceless Anglo-Saxon collection of Sir Robert Cotton, then stored in Ashburnham House, Little Dean's Yard, Westminster. What we know today as Asser's *Life of King Alfred* is a reconstruction of that lost manuscript, Cotton MS Otho A.xii, based on transcripts and early modern editions, supplemented and corrected by collation with extracts from the *Life* incorporated into Byrhtferth of Ramsey's late tenth- or early eleventh-century 'Historical Miscellany', John of Worcester's *Chronica Chronicarum*, composed ca. 1130, and the anonymous Annals of St Neots, compiled at Bury St Edmunds in the 1120s or 1130s. The most useful transcript (Cambridge Corpus Christi College MS 100) was made by order of a previous owner of the manuscript, Matthew Parker, Master of Corpus Christi College, Cambridge (1544–53), and subsequently archbishop of Canterbury (1559–75), in preparation for an edition printed in 1574. Parker annotated the manuscript heavily, and his edition 'improved' the text by incorporating material from other sources. Among these was the story of the burnt cakes, taken from the *Annals of St Neots*, which Parker believed incorrectly to have been also authored by Asser. William Camden reprinted Parker's edition in 1602, adding a passage that credited Alfred with the foundation of

Oxford University. Francis Wise's edition of 1722 strove to be scholarly, but was undermined by Wise's decision to base it on Parker's edition rather than on the Cotton manuscript, which he apparently never examined. He did, however, consult with the palaeographer Humphrey Wanley about the state of the Cotton manuscript, who reported to him that it was written by several hands, the oldest of which resembled that of a charter of Æthelred the Unready, dated 1001. Wise also employed an antiquary, James Hill, to collate the Cotton manuscript against Camden's edition, and Hill most valuably undertook to draw a facsimile of the opening page of the manuscript, which Wise subsequently printed. This rough-drawn facsimile supports Wanley's conclusions about the dating of the manuscript to around the year 1000. In 1848 Henry Petrie produced an edition that tried to distinguish between what was and was not in the Cotton manuscript. This was superseded in 1904 by a truly first-rate scholarly edition by W.H. Stevenson that reconstructed the 'genuine' Asser as best as the evidence then allowed.[1] Stevenson's edition and extensive commentary, though not the last word, are the basis for modern studies of Asser and Alfred, including Simon Keynes's and Michael Lapidge's excellent English translation and edition of the *Life* and even Alfred Smyth's iconoclastic *King Alfred the Great.*[2]

Given this manuscript history, it is little wonder, perhaps, that some historians have doubted the authenticity of the work. In recent times two historians, V.H. Galbraith and,

---

1. W.H. Stevenson, ed., *Asser's Life of King Alfred together with the Annals of Saint Neots Erroneously Ascribed to Asser* (Oxford, 1904). Cf. the comments of D.N. Dumville, *The Annals of St Neots with Vita Prima Sancti Neoti*, ed. D.N. Dumville and M. Lapidge; *The Anglo-Saxon Chronicle: A Collaborative Edition*: vol. 17, gen. eds D.N. Dumville and S.D. Keynes (Cambridge, 1985) p. xlii, and the response by A.P. Smyth, *King Alfred the Great* (Oxford, 1995) p. 160.

2. Stevenson, *Asser's Life of King Alfred*, pp. xi–lxv; D.G. Scragg, ed., *The Battle of Maldon* (Manchester, 1981) pp. 1–4; Keynes and Lapidge, pp. 223–7; Smyth, *King Alfred the Great*, pp. 155–6. For the use of Asser by medieval chroniclers, see *The Annals of St Neots*, ed. D.N. Dumville and M. Lapidge, pp. xxxix–xliii; M. Lapidge, 'Byrhtferth of Ramsey and the early sections of the *Historia Regum* attributed to Symeon of Durham', *ASE* 10 (1982) 97–122; *The Chronicle of John of Worcester*, vol. II: The Annals from 450 to 1066, ed. R.R. Darlington and P. McGurk (Oxford, 1995) pp. lxxii, 260–334, and, more generally, E. Conybeare, *Alfred in the Chroniclers* (London, 1900).

most recently, Alfred Smyth, have argued that the *Life* is
a forgery. Galbraith, a specialist in the Domesday Book
and Anglo-Norman administrative history, was troubled by
a number of aspects of the work. He found its relation of
Alfred's illness in chapters 74 and 91 muddled, contradict-
ory and implausible; its portrayal of Alfred as a 'neurotic
invalid' hagiographical nonsense; and its content an amal-
gam of ninth-century sources mixed with popular lore. But
what clinched the matter for Galbraith were the apparent anachronisms. Of these, Galbraith focused on two, the
author's designation of Alfred as 'king of the Anglo-Saxons'
(*rex Angul-Saxonum*) and his use of the term *parochia*, 'diocese' in medieval Latin, to describe Alfred's gift to Asser of
the lands and properties of the church of Exeter. The latter
suggested to Galbraith the identity and motive of the forger.
The *Life*, he concluded, was an invention of Leofric, bishop
of Devon and Cornwall from 1046 to 1072, who fabricated it
to provide historical support for his translation of the see
from Crediton to Exeter in 1050.[3]

Though it created a stir in the scholarly community,
Galbraith added actually very little to earlier debates over the
authenticity of the *Life*, echoing a number of points made
by Thomas Wright a century before.[4] Dorothy Whitelock,
a distinguished Anglo-Saxon scholar and editor, responded
in detail, answering Galbraith's arguments to the satisfaction
of most.[5] *Parochia*, she pointed out, often denoted in Celtic
Latin writings the jurisdiction of a monastery over its depend-
ent lands. She admitted that the shortage of genuine, contemporary charters from Alfred's reign made judgements
about the range of Alfred's royal styles uncertain, but found
nothing implausible about Asser's designation of the king
as *Angul-Saxonum rex*. (Whitelock in later years came to
accept the authenticity of a number of the charters in which

3. V.H. Galbraith, 'Who wrote Asser's Life of Alfred?', in his *An Introduction to the Study of History* (London, 1964) pp. 88–128.
4. T. Wright, 'Some historical doubts relating to the biographer Asser',
   Archaeologia 29 (1842) 192–201; Stevenson, *Asser's Life of King Alfred*,
   pp. xci–cviii; Smyth, *King Alfred the Great*, p. 150.
5. D. Whitelock, *The Genuine Asser*, Stenton Lecture 1967 (Reading, 1968),
   reprinted in D. Whitelock, *From Bede to Alfred: Studies in Early Anglo-
   Saxon Literature and History* (London, 1980) no. 12.

Alfred was styled 'king of the Anglo-Saxons'.[6]) In other words, there were no anachronisms. The agreed upon dating of the scribal hand to ca. 1000, moreover, meant that the manuscript of the *Life* existed half a century before Leofric was supposed to have concocted it. This last point was substantially strengthened by the discovery that the early section of the *Historia Regum* which includes the extracts from the *Life*, the so-called 'Historical Miscellany', was not composed by the twelfth-century monk Symeon of Durham, as was once believed, but by Byrhtferth of Ramsey in the late tenth or the early eleventh century.

The last observation is the jumping-off point for Alfred P. Smyth's recent investigation of Alfred and his biographer. Practically every one of the 602 pages of Professor Smyth's dense, polemical and idiosyncratic *King Alfred the Great* is coloured by his 'discovery' that the *Life* is an elaborate forgery concocted by Byrhtferth or one of his circle at the monastery of Ramsey in order to lend Alfred's prestige to the Benedictine monastic reform movement of the late tenth century.[7] Though Smyth revived a number of Wright's and Galbraith's criticisms, his argument rests upon an analysis of the elaborate, 'hermeneutic' Latinity of the *Life*, which Smyth thought to be characteristic of the late tenth-century school of Ramsey. According to Smyth, the similarities between the vocabulary of the *Life of King Alfred* and that of Byrhtferth's Latin hagiographies proves that Byrhtferth not only used the *Life* in putting together his 'Historical Miscellany' but composed it as well. To those who pointed out that all the sources upon which the *Life* drew were either ninth century or earlier, Smyth responded by arguing that the model for the *Life of King Alfred* was the *Life of St Gerald of Aurillac*

6. See D. Whitelock, 'Some charters in the name of King Alfred', *Saints, Scholars and Heroes. Studies in Medieval Culture in Honour of Charles W. Jones*, ed. M.H. King and W.M. Stevens (Collegeville, MN, 1979) I, pp. 77–98; Keynes and Lapidge, pp. 227–8, n. 1, where the numismatic evidence is also discussed. The charters in question are S 346, 347, 348, 354, 355, 356. Galbraith's case is also undermined by the observation that *Angul Saxonum rex* was the normal style used by Alfred's son, Edward the Elder, and that it had long fallen out of use by the late tenth century. S.D. Keynes, 'The West Saxon charters of King Æthelwulf and his sons', *EHR* 109 (1994) pp. 1147–9.

7. Smyth, *King Alfred the Great*, pp. 149–367.

written by Odo of Cluny ca. 930.[8] Whereas Stevenson and Whitelock were impressed by the author's knowledge of Alfred's personal history, life in his court, and political doings in ninth-century Wessex and Wales, Smyth dismissed the historical value of the *Life* as an independent source for Alfred's reign. The only 'hard' information in the *Life of King Alfred*, Smyth asserted, comes from the *Anglo-Saxon Chronicle*. The rest, according to Smyth, is a tissue of wandering folk tales and motifs, miracle stories, and sheer invention, owing more to the obsessions of Byrhtferth than to the deeds or personality of Alfred. Any names mentioned by Asser that do not come from the *Chronicle* or from the Preface to Alfred's *Pastoral Care* were made up, and the charters and letters that seem to corroborate them are dismissed as forgeries based upon the forged *Life*.[9] (Smyth allowed, however, that the 'Pseudo-Asser' possessed some lost sources for the history of ninth-century Wales, though he muddled the details in the retelling.) All this, Smyth contended, is apparent to anyone who looks at the evidence with an unjaundiced eye. Unfortunately, few have done so, because 'The study of Alfred, unlike that of any other Anglo-Saxon ruler – unlike even studies of the Conqueror – has long become enmeshed in polemic and the politics of academe.' The 'establishment', Smyth averred, had and has a stake in preserving the fiction. From medieval kings and Protestant bishops to Victorian imperialists and twentieth-century patriots, the *Life*

8. Smyth, *King Alfred the Great*, pp. 205–7, 208–10, 272–4, 279, 323–4. Smyth fails to demonstrate any verbal borrowings by the putative forger other than a few common 'Frankish' Latin words. In fact, the two works are structurally and stylistically very different, and many of the 'shared' stories are used to quite different purpose and effect. (To say, for example, that the story of the battle of Ashdown, in which Alfred is forced to fight alone because his brother lingered in his tent hearing mass, derives from a story about how St Gerald proved victorious because he acted like Alfred's pious brother, seems to me to miss the point of Asser's presentation.) Asser's and Odo's use of Scripture (*pace* Smyth) also tells heavily against the reliance of the former upon the latter. Asser quotes or paraphrases the Bible ten times; Odo, ninety-three. Only once do they cite the same passage, Matt. 6.33, which Asser quotes and Odo paraphrases. The similarities between the two works, in short, are the superficial ones one might expect given that both works were written in the same early medieval milieu by monks as panegyrics to holy laymen.
9. See, e.g., Smyth, *King Alfred the Great*, pp. 13–4, 253–4, 269, 383.

has served as propaganda and a source of English national-
ist images and myths. In the romantic and imperial age of
nineteenth-century Britain, Asser's 'Super-King of Wessex'
provided historical justification for the 'divine destiny for the
British Empire'. For Sir Frank Stenton, writing in the early
1940s, Alfred's longships were 'a symbol of an embattled
island's defences against the Reich'.[10] Stenton's acceptance
of the authenticity of the *Life* and the scholarly authority of
Stevenson, guaranteed that Dorothy Whitelock, a friend and
admirer, would rise in defence of Asser against Galbraith's
assault. Once the prestige of Whitelock had been placed
behind the authenticity of the *Life*, it became a 'sacred canon'
which 'no scholar with an eye to reputation or patronage'
dared assail.[11] For Smyth, then, a putative scholarly conspiracy
by a cast of romantic imperialists, nationalists, and lackeys
has foisted an 'obvious' fraud upon an unwitting public.

Perhaps it is not surprising that the academic 'establishment' has not found Smyth's arguments persuasive. The
reviews in academic journals have not been kind. The leading authorities on the Latinity of Byrhtferth and other Anglo-
Latin authors have dismissed Smyth's lexical analysis as naive,
amateurish and fatally flawed.[12] Historians have criticized
Smyth's understanding of politics, monasticism and military practice in ninth-century England.[13] Archaeologists have
weighed in by observing that the topographical details Asser
provides about Athelney and the West Country would not
have been known by a monk of Ramsey in the late tenth

---

10. Smyth, *King Alfred the Great*, pp. 152–3, citing the second edition
   (1947). The point is perhaps strengthened by the dating of the first
   edition, 1943.

11. Smyth, *King Alfred the Great*, pp. xxii, 14, 153–4.

12. M. Lapidge, 'A king of monkish fable?', *The Times Higher Education
   Supplement* (8 March 1996), p. 20; D. Howlett, *EHR* 112 (1997),
   pp. 942–4. See also the comments of E.G. Stanley, 'On the Laws of
   King Alfred', in J. Roberts and J.L. Nelson with M. Godden, eds,
   *Alfred the Wise: Studies in Honour of Janet Bately on the Occasion of her
   Sixty-Fifth Birthday*, (Woodbridge, Suffolk, 1997) pp. 215–16. Cf. the
   more positive reviews by J. Campbell, 'Alfred's Lives', *TLS* (26 July
   1996) p. 30, and, especially, M. Altschul, in *American Historical Review*
   102 (1997) pp. 1463–4.

13. S.D. Keynes, 'On the authenticity of Asser's *Life of King Alfred*', *Journal
   of Ecclesiastical History* 47 (1996) pp. 529–51; B. Bachrach, in *Journal of
   Military Studies* 61 (1997) pp. 363–4.

century. The geographical focus of the work upon the western shires of Wessex and Wales, the author's Welsh glosses on place-names, and his failure to mention Ramsey or any places associated with that monastery tell against Smyth's attribution of authorship to Byrhtferth.[14] Smyth's explanation of the purpose of the forgery has also been challenged. The agenda of the tenth-century Benedictine Reform was to remake minsters into monasteries by ousting canons in favour of monks. Though the author of the *Life* presents Alfred as interested in reviving the monastic life in England, he does not contrast the virtues of monks with the vices of canons. The controversies of the late tenth century, in short, are not the concerns of the author of the *Life*, though political disputes within late ninth-century Wessex were.[15]

For my part, I accept the authenticity of the *Life*. It reads to me like a genuine ninth-century work. Neither Galbraith nor Smyth, try as they might, could produce a credible 'smoking gun' that would prove the *Life* to have been written after Asser's death.[16] The author's Latinity and the texts that he quotes are consistent with a late ninth-century dating. The 'Alfred' that emerges from a reading of the *Life* owes a great deal to the 'Alfred' of his translations and law code. (Smyth admits as much. Indeed, he contends that the image of Alfred as a 'neurotic invalid' was suggested to the forger by his reading of the prefaces that Alfred wrote for Bishop Wærferth's and his own translations and by the prayer with which he concluded his translation of Boethius's *Consolation of Philosophy*![17]) The concerns that underlie Asser's work – the need for loyalty to lords and kings, the paramount importance of wisdom for Christian rulers, the Gregorian doctrine of duty and patience – are precisely those one finds in Alfred's law code and translations and in the *Chronicle*.[18]

14. D. Hill, 'Asser not a forgery', *British Archaeology* 9 (1995): Letters.
15. Keynes, 'On the authenticity of Asser's *Life*', pp. 538–9; B. Yorke, 'Faked cakes', *History Today* 46 (1996) p. 58; Stanley, 'On the Laws of King Alfred', p. 216.
16. See, e.g., note 8 above.
17. Smyth, *King Alfred the Great*, pp. 213–16.
18. See, e.g., A. Scharer, 'Zu drei Themen in der Geschichtsschreibung der Zeit König Alfreds (871–899)', *Ethnogenese und Überlieferung: Angewandte Methoden der Frühmittelalterforschung*, ed. K. Brunner and B. Merta, Veröffentlichungen des Instituts für Österrechische Geschichtsforschung 31 (Vienna, 1994) pp. 200–8.

Asser's insistence upon Alfred's superiority to his brothers and his occasional digs at Mercians would have meant little to a late tenth-century audience, but it was the very stuff of court politics in the 890s, when the coming of age and lingering resentments of the sons of Alfred's older brother, King Æthelred, threatened the stability of the realm, and age-old enemies mingled with one another and jostled for the favour of the king.

But it is what the *Life* lacks as much as what is in it that persuades me of its authenticity. Miracle stories about Alfred and St Cuthbert and St Neot current in the late tenth century play no part in the *Life*. The only saint whose powers are touted by the author is St Gueriir, a Welsh holy man so obscure that Asser's is the only notice we have for his cult. St Neot, it is true, is mentioned by Asser as 'now' buried in Gueriir's church, but it was to Gueriir that Alfred is said to have prayed.[19] Could Byrhtferth or one of his circle at Ramsey have resisted mentioning the martyrdom of St Edmund of East Anglia at the hands of the vikings to underscore the terrors that Alfred faced? And why should he have? Indeed, one of the changes that Byrhtferth made to the *Life of Alfred* when he excerpted it for his 'Historical Miscellany' was to add a reference to St Edmund's glorious martyrdom.[20] Even odder are the historical events in Alfred's life that are left out. The *Life* follows the *Anglo-Saxon Chronicle* only to 887, and says nothing about Alfred's final victory over the vikings in 893–6. From this Smyth concludes that Byrhtferth possessed only a truncated copy of the *Anglo-Saxon Chronicle* ending in ca. 892–3. Even so, one would have expected the forger to have mentioned the return of the

---

19. Asser, ch. 74. Keynes and Lapidge, pp. 254–5, nn. 141–2. Gilbert Doble suggested that Gueriir is a corruption of Guenyr. St Gwinear was an Irish saint credited with evangelizing the Welsh. G.H. Doble, *St Neot*, Cornish Saints Series 21 (Exeter, 1929) pp. 39–40; Doble, *The Saints of Cornwall*, vol. 1 (1960) pp. 100–10. Stevenson, *Asser's Life of King Alfred*, pp. 55, 297, suggested, though without good cause, that the reference to St Neot was a later interpolation.

20. Lapidge, 'Byrhtferth', p. 115. Abbo of Fleury composed his *Passion of St Edmund* at the behest of Archbishop Dunstan during Abbo's stay at the newly refounded monastery of Ramsey, around 986–7. Smyth sees the *Life of King Alfred* as 'part of the same hagiographical programme which produced the *Life* or *Passio* of St Edmund'. *King Alfred the Great*, pp. 213, 275–6.

vikings, described in the entry for 892, especially since a late tenth-century author would surely have known how the story turned out. Nor does the author mention Alfred's law code or his programme of translation, though Smyth's forger is represented as well acquainted with Alfred's writings; indeed, his very choice of a persona, supposedly, came from reading the preface to Alfred's *Pastoral Care*.[21]

In the final analysis, one's judgement of the authenticity of Asser rests upon how one understands Alfred himself. Smyth wishes to rescue the historical Alfred from the hands of a 'hagiographer' who transformed a tireless warrior-king and erudite scholar into a nearly illiterate, neurotic invalid. But such a characterisation of Asser's 'Alfred' is a caricature of the ideal that the Welsh monk wished to portray. His Alfred is no 'neurotic invalid'; nor is he an illiterate miraculously enlightened. The Alfred of the *Life* is, rather, a ninth-century ideal of Christian kingship: a victorious warrior-king who rules his people with justice, who, with the help of friends such as Asser, strives after wisdom and learning, and who bears patiently, as did Gregory the Great, the pains and tribulations that were his lot. That the 'real' Alfred was not the perfect Christian king of Asser's (or Plummer's) biography is obvious. But that Alfred wished to be seen that way seems to me to be equally evident. As Dorothy Whitelock observed many years ago, the character of Asser's 'Alfred' is familiar to anyone who has read Alfred's own writings. Asser's dutiful king and the man who claimed that he only 'desired to live worthily' and leave to posterity his 'memory in good works' share the same traits and obsessions. One recognizes Asser's champion of justice for the poor in the Alfred who legislated on behalf of helpless dependants and slaves and who excerpted Exodus for his law code so as to elaborate upon an injunction to judge poor and rich alike while leaving out another passage forbidding judges to favour the poor.[22] In short, Asser's 'Alfred' rings far truer to Alfred, at least as he wished to be seen, than do either Galbraith's or Smyth's.

21. Smyth, *King Alfred the Great*, pp. 215–16, 224–5.
22. Asser, ch. 105; *Alfred*, Intro. 41, 43, ed. F. Liebermann, *Die Gesetze der Angelsachsen*, 3 vols (Halle, 1903–16) I, pp. 40–1. Cf. Exodus 23.3, 6. Note also the fifty pounds he left the poor in his *Will*. Keynes and Lapidge, p. 177.

FURTHER READING

. . .

SOURCES

The best collection of primary sources in translation is *Alfred the Great: Asser's Life of King Alfred and Other Contemporary Sources*, translated with an introduction and notes by Simon Keynes and Michael Lapidge (London, 1983), readily available in paperback from Penguin Books. The notes and commentary by Keynes and Lapidge are an indispensible guide to the scholarly problems and issues surrounding these works. *English Historical Documents, vol. I: c. 500–1042*, ed. Dorothy Whitelock, 2nd edn (London, 1979), a massive compendium of translated sources with authoritative introductions, includes an excellent translation of the *Anglo-Saxon Chronicle*. Among other translations of the *Anglo-Saxon Chronicle*, G.N. Garmonsway's *The Anglo-Saxon Chronicle* (London, 1955) is notable for its layout, which follows Charles Plummer, ed., *Two of the Saxon Chronicles Parallel*, 2 vols (Oxford, 1892–99). Plummer's edition, long the standard, has been now superseded by *The Anglo-Saxon Chronicle: A Collaborative Edition*, gen. eds D.N. Dumville and S.D. Keynes, 23 vols (Cambridge, 1983–).

Along with the *Anglo-Saxon Chronicle*, Asser's *Life of King Alfred* is the most important narrative source for Alfred's reign. The standard edition remains W.H. Stevenson, ed., *Asser's Life of King Alfred together with the Annals of Saint Neots erroneously ascribed to Asser* (Oxford, 1904). Stevenson's notes on Asser and Plummer's on the *Chronicle* continue to be invaluable resources for students. J. Campbell, 'Asser's *Life of Alfred*', in C. Holdsworth and T.P. Wiseman, eds, *The*

Inheritance of Historiography, 350–900, Exeter Studies in History 12 (Exeter, 1986), pp. 115–35, is the best general introduction to Asser's text. See also Anton Scharer, 'The writing of history at King Alfred's court', *Early Medieval Europe* 5 (1996), pp. 185–206. Alfred P. Smyth, *King Alfred the Great* (Oxford, 1995), attempts to demonstrate that the *Life* is an early eleventh-century forgery. (For the debate over the authenticity of this important text, see the appendix and references there.) King Alfred, unsurprisingly, figures prominently in later medieval English chronicles and histories. Edward Conybeare's *Alfred in the Chroniclers* (London, 1900) translates the relevant passages in the chronicles dealing with Alfred's reign, beginning with Asser's *Life.* Conybeare's critical judgements and translations, however, are not always reliable, and it is best to consult recent editions of the Latin chronicle sources. Ealdorman Æthelweard's late tenth-century Latin version of the *Anglo-Saxon Chronicle* is edited and translated by Alistair Campbell (Oxford, 1962). Campbell's translation of Æthelweard's difficult and often obscure Latin ought to be read in conjunction with that offered by Keynes and Lapidge in *Alfred the Great.*

Alfred's charters, both genuine and forged, are catalogued in P.H. Sawyer, *Anglo-Saxon Charters: An Annotated List and Bibliography* (London, 1968). Sawyer provides information on manuscripts, editions, translations, and bibliography for scholarly discussions of the charters. Sawyer's book is now being revised and updated by Susan Kelly; the revision is scheduled to be published in electronic format on Cambridge University's 'Anglo-Saxon Charters on the Web' (see below). The standard edition for Anglo-Saxon charters issued before 975 remains W. de G. Birch, ed., *Cartularium Saxonicum,* 3 vols (London, 1885–93). A.J. Robertson, ed. and trans., *Anglo-Saxon Charters* (Cambridge, 1956), contains the handful of charters written in Old English that date from this period, including the Burghal Hidage. The British Academy and the Royal Historical Society are co-sponsoring an ongoing project to re-edit the corpus of pre-Conquest charters, arranged by archive, but given the deliberate pace at which this project is advancing, it will be some time before Birch is finally retired. Perhaps the most interesting and significant new resource for the study of Anglo-Saxon charters is 'Anglo-Saxon Charters on the Web', a website (http://www.trin.ca,.ac.uk/users/sdk13/chartwww/ASChart-Homepage.html) maintained by Simon Keynes at Trinity College, Cambridge, under the auspices of the British Academy–Royal Historical Society Joint Committee on Anglo-Saxon Charters. Among the materials that are now available at this site is a 'Regesta Regum Anglorum' that includes an electronic edition of Alfred's charters. Critical study of King Alfred's charters begins with Dorothy Whitelock's 'Some charters in the name of King Alfred', in Margot H. King and Wesley M. Stevens, *Saints, Scholars and Heroes: Studies in Medieval Culture in Honour of Charles W. Jones*, 2 vols, (Collegeville, MN, 1979) I, pp. 77–98. Simon Keynes, 'The West Saxon charters of King Æthelwulf and his sons', *EHR* 109 (1994), pp. 1109–49, discusses the diplomatic tradition of ninth-century West Saxon charters and comments upon the authenticity of those that survive in later copies.

Alfred's literary endeavours are unique among Dark Age kings. They are of inestimable value for the light they shed upon the thoughts, beliefs, and personality of a man who died eleven hundred years ago. The excerpts from Alfred's writings in Keynes and Lapidge's *Alfred the Great* are well chosen. Alfred's translations, however, are most profitably read in their entirety. The only attempt to render the entire corpus into modern English was an 1858 'jubilee edition' of *The Whole Works of King Alfred the Great*, 2 vols (London, 1858; repr. New York 1969), edited by John A. Giles, an ambitious but flawed effort that reflects the state of the scholarship of the day. Editions and modern English translations of Alfred's works include: *King Alfred's West Saxon Version of Gregory's Pastoral Care*, ed. and trans., Henry Sweet, 2 vols., Early English Text Society, Original Series 45 & 50 (London, 1871–72); *King Alfred's Old English Version of Boethius De Consolatione Philosophiae*, ed. Walter John Sedgefield (Oxford, 1899); *King Alfred's Version of the Consolations of Boethius Done into Modern English, with an Introduction*, trans. Walter John Sedgefield (Oxford, 1900), with Alfred's 'additions' in italics; *King Alfred's Version of St. Augustine's* Soliloquies, ed. Thomas A. Carnicelli (Cambridge, MA, 1969); *King Alfred's Old English Version of St. Augustine's* Soliloquies *Turned into Modern English*, trans. Henry Lee Hargrove (New York, 1904); *Liber Psalmorum, The West Saxon Psalms*, ed. J.W. Bright and R.L. Ramsay (Boston, 1907). Richard Stracke's annotated electronic edition of Alfred's Psalms, with the Vulgate in parallel, may be accessed at http://www.ac.edu/Augusta/arsenal/psalms.

Alfred's law code and his treaty with King Guthrum are edited and translated by F.L. Attenborough, *The Laws of the Earliest English Kings* (Cambridge, 1922). Attenborough, however, omits Alfred's important introduction. The preface and the complete text of Alfred's laws can be found in Milton H. Turk, ed., *The Legal Code of Ælfred the Great* (Boston, 1893), and in F. Liebermann, *Die Gesetze der Angelsachsen*, 3 vols (Halle, 1903–16): vol. I, text; vol. II, glossary; vol. III, notes and commentary. Liebermann edits not only the Old English texts, but also includes in parallel a twelfth-century Latin translation of Alfred's law code and his own (German) translation. Excerpts from the preface and the law code appear in Keynes and Lapidge, *Alfred the Great*, and in *English Historical Documents*, vol. I. John A. Giles's literal translation of the full preface and law code for *The Whole Works of King Alfred the Great*, II, pp. 119–40, preserves, sometimes to the point of obscurity, the flavour of the original.

Archaeologists, numismatists, and art historians have done a great deal to help us understand the material culture of ninth-century England. David M. Wilson, ed., *The Archaeology of Anglo-Saxon England* (London, 1976, paperback edn, Cambridge, 1986), is a good, if somewhat dated, introduction to that topic. The periodical *Anglo-Saxon England* (1972–) has a convenient annual bibliography of excavation reports, articles, and books on Anglo-Saxon archaeology. Numismatics, the study of coins, is of particular importance for understanding royal power and ideology, as well as economic development, in the early Middle Ages. Philip Grierson and Mark Blackburn, *Medieval European Coinage with a Catalogue of the Coins in the Fitzwilliam Museum, Cambridge. I. The Early Middle Ages (5th–10th Centuries)* (Cambridge, 1986), provides a good overview of West Saxon coinage in the ninth century. Its discussion of Alfred's coinage, however, draws heavily upon R.H.M. Dolley and C.E. Blunt, 'The chronology of the coins of Ælfred the Great 871–899', in R.H.M. Dolley, ed., *Anglo-Saxon Coins* (London, 1962), pp. 77–95, an interpretation of the evidence that Mark Blackburn has since challenged. For Blackburn's revised chronology of Alfred's issues and its historical implications, see his and Simon

Keynes's articles in M.A.S. Blackburn and D.N. Dumville, eds, *Kings, Currency, and Alliances: The History and Coinage of Southern England, AD 840–900* (Woodbridge, forthcoming). The artistic achievements and craftsmanship of Alfredian England are surveyed in 'The Age of Alfred' in Leslie Webster and Janet Blackhouse, eds, *The Making of England: Anglo-Saxon Art and Culture AD 600–900* (London, 1992), pp. 254–89. This handsomely illustrated volume includes not only photographs and iconographic analyses of the Alfred Jewel and the Fuller Brooch, but also valuable descriptions of ninth-century manuscripts and coins.

.   .   .

GENERAL

As the result of the Victorian 'cult of the Anglo-Saxons', uplifting biographies of Alfred the Great, both 'serious' and 'popular', abounded in late nineteenth-century England. The trend climaxed around the turn of the century with the millenary celebration of Alfred's death. Two early twentieth-century biographies are still worth reading: Beatrice A. Lees's *Alfred the Great, The Truth Teller, Maker of England 848–899* (New York and London, 1915), and Charles Plummer's *The Life and Times of Alfred the Great, Being the Ford Lectures for 1901* (1902, reprinted New York, 1970). Beatrice Lees's vivid and underrated narrative stands up remarkably well after eighty years and remains, in many ways, the most satisfying of the many previous biographies of Alfred. The celebration of England's 'Germanic' roots ended with the onset of World War I. Though Winston Churchill clearly shared the Victorian admiration for Alfred, the popular appeal of this Dark Age king clearly waned in the decades following his millenary. The only major biography of Alfred that has appeared since Lees's is Alfred P. Smyth's massive *King Alfred the Great* (Oxford, 1995). Smyth's book is less a traditional biography than an extended and highly controversial reconsideration of the sources for Alfred's life and reign. More suitable for undergraduates and general readers are Eleanor Shipley Duckett's popular account *Alfred the Great and his England* (London, 1957), and John Peddie's *Alfred the Good Soldier: His Life and Campaigns* (Bath, 1989). Duckett's book focuses on Alfred's cultural achievements and Peddie's on his military activities. The best general overview of Alfred's life, accomplishments, and subsequent reputation is Keynes's and Lapidge's introduction to their *Alfred the Great*. Alfred and his reign, of course, figure prominently in general surveys of Anglo-Saxon history. Of these, the best are Sir Frank Stenton's magisterial *Anglo-Saxon England*, 3rd edn (Oxford, 1971); R.H. Hodgkin, *A History of the Anglo-Saxons*, 2 vols, rev. edn (Oxford, 1952); and J. Campbell, P. Wormald and E. John, *The Anglo-Saxons*, ed. J. Campbell (Oxford and Ithaca, N.Y., 1982) (the chapter on the ninth century is written by Patrick Wormald). The last is lavishly illustrated. Alfred's subsequent treatment in literature is well discussed by Louis Wardlaw Miles in his *King Alfred in Literature* (Baltimore, 1902), which is to be supplemented by Eric Stanley, 'The glorification of Alfred King of Wessex (from the publication of Sir John Spelman's *Life*, 1678 and 1709, to the publication of Rheinhold Pauli's, 1851)', *Poetica* 12 (1981), pp. 103–33; and Keynes and Lapidge, pp. 44–8. The Victorian cult of Alfred, exemplified by Alfred Bowker's *The King Alfred Millenary: A Record of the Proceedings of the National Commemoration* (London, 1902), is discussed by Clare A. Simmons, *Reversing the Conquest: History and Myth in Nineteenth-Century British Literature* (New Brunswick, NJ, and London, 1990), chap. 6. Simon Keynes, 'A tale of two kings: Alfred the Great and Aethelred the Unready', *TRHS*, fifth ser., 36 (1986), pp. 195–217, explores how Alfred's court helped shape his subsequent historical reputation.

For further reading on Alfred, consult J.T. Rosenthal, *Anglo-Saxon History: an Annotated Bibliography 450–1066* (1985), and Simon Keynes's on-line, 'Anglo-Saxon History: A Select Bibliography', Richard Rawlinson Center for Anglo-Saxon Studies and Research, Medieval Institute of Western Michigan University, http://www.wmich.edu/medieval/rawl/keynes1/home.htm.

.   .   .

CHAPTER 1: ALFRED'S WESSEX

The best general study of West Saxon history is Barbara Yorke, *Wessex in the Early Middle Ages*, Studies in the Early History of Britain Series, Nicholas Brooks, gen. ed. (London & New York, 1995). For the shaping of the West Saxon landscape and its importance for the history of the region, see B. Cunliffe, *Wessex to* AD *1000* (London and New York, 1993), chap. 9. David Hill, *An Atlas of Anglo-Saxon England* (Toronto and Buffalo, 1981), is an indispensible resource for the historical geography of ninth-century England. On kingship and kingdoms in eighth- and ninth-century England, see Barbara Yorke, *Kings and Kingdoms of Early Anglo-Saxon England* (London, 1990); D.P. Kirby, *The Earliest English Kings* (London, 1991); and Patrick Wormald's important essay 'Bede, the *Bretwaldas* and the origins of the *Gens Anglorum*', in Patrick Wormald, Donald Bullough, and Roger Collins, eds, *Ideal and Reality in Frankish and Anglo-Saxon Society: Studies Presented to J.M. Wallace-Hadrill* (Oxford, 1983), pp. 99–129. Diplomatic and numismatic evidence for relations between the West Saxons and the Mercians in the ninth century is examined in detail by Simon Keynes, 'King Alfred and the Mercians', in M.A.S. Blackburn and D.N. Dumville, eds, *Kings, Currency, and Alliances: The History and Coinage of Southern England*, AD *840–900* (Woodbridge, forthcoming). For the West Saxon domination of Kent, see Simon Keynes, 'The control of Kent in the ninth century', *Early Medieval Europe* 2 (1993), pp. 111–31; Nicholas P. Brooks, *The Early History of the Church of Canterbury* (Leicester, 1984), chaps 7–9; Robin Fleming, 'History and Liturgy at Pre-Conquest Christ Church,' *Haskins Society Journal* 6 (1995 for 1994), pp. 67–82; and Richard Abels, 'The devolution of bookland in ninth-century Kent: a note on BCS 538 (S 319)', *Archaeologia Contiana* 99 (1983), pp. 219–23. The structure and bonds of ninth-century Anglo-Saxon society are discussed and debated by Stenton, *Anglo-Saxon England*, pp. 277–318; H.R. Loyn, *Anglo-Saxon England and the Norman Conquest*, 2nd edn (London and New York, 1991); Eric John, *Orbis Britanniae and Other Studies* (Leicester, 1966); H.P.R. Finberg, 'Anglo-Saxon England to 1042', in Finberg, ed., *The Agrarian History of England and Wales*, vol. 1, bk. 2 (Cambridge, 1972), chap. 4; Richard P. Abels, *Lordship and Military Obligation in Anglo-Saxon England* (Berkeley, Los Angeles and London, 1988).

．　．　．

CHAPTER 2: MEMORIES OF CHILDHOOD, 848–858

For an interesting discussion of how royal genealogies in eighth- and ninth-century England were used to legitimate royal authority and address contemporary political issues, see D.N. Dumville, 'Kingship, genealogies and regnal lists', in P.H. Sawyer and Ian Wood, eds, *Early Medieval Kingship* (Leeds 1977), pp. 72–104. For speculation about Alfred's possible maternal family connections, see Janet Nelson, 'Reconstructing a royal family: reflections on Alfred, from Asser, chapter 2', in Ian Wood and Niels Lund, eds, *People and Places in Northern Europe 500–1600: Essays in Honour of Peter Hayes Sawyer* (Woodbridge, Suffolk, 1991) pp. 47–66. Ninth-century West Frankish history is best approached through Janet Nelson's *Charles the Bald* (London and New York, 1992) in Longman's The Medieval World series. Nelson has also translated the *Annals of St-Bertin* for the Manchester Medieval Sources series (*Ninth-Century Histories, Volume 1*, Manchester and New York, 1991). See also in the same series the translations of the annals of Fulda by Timothy Reuter (1992). The Latin text of the *Annals of St-Bertin* is edited by F. Grat, J. Viellard and S. Clémencet, with introduction and notes by L. Levillain (Paris, 1964). The letters of Abbot Lupus are edited by Peter K. Marshall, *Servati Lupi Epistolae*, Bibliotheca Scriptorum Graecorum et Romanorum Teubneriana (Leipzig, 1984), and translated by Graydon W. Regenos, *The Letters of Lupus of Ferrières* (The Hague, 1966). Paul E. Dutton, ed. and trans., *Carolingian Civilization: A Reader* (Peterborough, Ontario, and Lewiston, New York, 1993), is a convenient collection of eighth- and ninth-century Frankish sources in translation. For Anglo-Saxon pilgrimages to Rome, see W.J. Moore, *The Saxon Pilgrims to Rome and the Schola Saxonum* (Fribourg, 1937), and, more generally, Veronica Ortenberg, *The English Church and the Continent in the Tenth and Eleventh Centuries: Cultural, Spiritual, and Artistic Exchanges* (Oxford, 1992). For Brescia's 'Liber Vitae' and its evidence for Alfred's pilgrimages, see H. Becher, 'Das königliche Frauenkloster San Salvatore/San Giula in Brescia im Spiegel seiner Memorialüberlieferung', *Frühmittelalterliche Studien* 17 (1983), pp. 299–392, and Simon Keynes, 'Anglo-Saxon Entries in the "Liber Vitae" of Brescia,' in Jane Roberts and Janet Nelson with Malcolm Godden, eds, *Alfred the Wise: Studies in Honour of Janet Bately on the Occasion of her Sixty-Fifth Birthday* (Cambridge, 1997), pp. 99–119. For the importance of spiritual affiliation in the ninth century, see Joseph H. Lynch, *Godparents and Kinship in Early Medieval Europe*

(Princeton, NJ, 1986). The topography and architecture of Rome in the early Middle Ages are described by Richard Krautheimer, *Rome, Profile of a City, 312–1308* (Princeton, 1980). Articles by Dvaid Whitehouse and by Paolo Delogu in Richard Hodges and Brian Hobley, eds, *The Rebirth of Towns in the West AD 700–1050*, Council for British Archaeology Report 68 (London, 1988) survey the archaeological and documentary evidence for population and material conditions in Rome at the time of Alfred's pilgrimages. M.J. Enright, 'Disease, royal unction, and propaganda: an interpretation of Alfred's journeys to Rome, 853 and 855 AD', *Continuity* 3 (1982), pp. 1–16, relates Alfred's first childhood pilgrimage to Rome to his illness. The same author's 'Charles the Bald and Æthelwulf of Wessex: the alliance of 856 and strategies of royal succession', *Journal of Medieval Studies* 5 (1979), pp. 291–302, and Pauline Stafford's 'Charles the Bald, Judith and England', in Margaret T. Gibson and Janet L. Nelson, eds, *Charles the Bald, Court and Kingdom*, 2nd edn, revised (Great Yarmouth, Norfolk, 1990), pp. 139–53, examine the possible political connection between Æthelwulf's marriage to Judith and Æthelbald's rebellion. For the status of the king's wife in ninth-century Wessex, see Pauline Stafford, 'The king's wife in Wessex', *Past and Present* 91 (1981), pp. 5–27.

·   ·   ·

CHAPTER 3: SCOURGES OF GOD, 858–868

The status of *æthelings* and principles of royal succession are the subjects of D.N. Dumville, 'The ætheling: a study in Anglo-Saxon constitutional history', *ASE* 8 (1979), pp. 1–33. For Anglo-Saxon medical knowledge and practice, see M.L. Cameron, *Anglo-Saxon Medicine* (Cambridge, 1993). G. Craig, 'Alfred the Great: a diagnosis', *Journal of the Royal Society of Medicine*, 84 (1991), pp. 303–5, attempts to diagnose Alfred's illness on the basis of modern medical knowledge. 'Bald's Leechbook' is in Oswald Cockayne, ed., *Leechdoms, Wortcunning, and Starcraft of Early England*, 3 vols (London, 1864–6), II, pp. 174, 290.

Studies of the vikings, both popular and scholarly, abound. Else Rosedahl, *The Vikings* (London, 1987), is especially good on the archaeological evidence for Scandinavian society and culture. Gwyn Jones, *A History of the Vikings*, 2nd edn (Oxford, 1984), is an entertaining narrative that draws heavily upon the sagas. Peter Sawyer, *Kings and Vikings* (London, 1982), provides an excellent introduction to the problem of sources. James Graham-Campbell, ed., *Cultural Atlas of the Viking World* (Abingdon, Oxfordshire, 1994), combines sound scholarship with beautiful illustrations, as does Peter Sawyer, ed., *The Oxford Illustrated History of the Vikings* (Oxford, 1997). *The Vikings*, ed. R.T. Farrell (London and Chichester, 1982), is an outstanding collection of scholarly articles on viking history, art, archaeology, and literature. The vikings are perhaps best understood through their own words. The primary sources for viking history, religion and society are collected, translated and discussed in R.I. Page, *Chronicles of the Vikings: Records, Memorials and Myths* (Toronto, 1995). H.R. Loyn's *The Vikings in England* (Oxford, 1994) is a good, basic survey. Alfred P. Smyth's stimulating and controversial *Scandinavian Kings in the British Isles, 850–880* (Oxford, 1977) relates the activities of viking armies in England and Ireland, and attempts to identify the leaders on the basis of the evidence of medieval sagas.

· · ·

CHAPTER 4: 'A VERY GREAT WARRIOR', 869–879

The best study of Alfred's generalship is John Peddie's *Alfred the Good Soldier: His Life and Campaigns* (Bath, 1989). Though Peddie is not a professional medieval historian and makes some questionable assumptions about the organization of Anglo-Saxon and viking armies, his emphasis upon the importance of geography, lines of communication, and logistics for determining the movement of armies brings a refreshing touch of realism to the subject. For Anglo-Saxon military organization and warfare, see Richard Abels, *Lordship and Military Obligation in Anglo-Saxon England* (Los Angeles, Berkeley, and London, 1988); C. Warren Hollister, *Anglo-Saxon Military Institutions* (Oxford, 1962); N. Hooper, 'The Anglo-Saxons at War', in S.C. Hawkes, ed., *Weapons and Warfare in Anglo-Saxon England* (London, 1989), pp. 191–202. For early medieval warfare in general, see Karl Leyser, 'Early Medieval Warfare', in Janet Cooper, ed., *The Battle of Maldon, Fiction and Fact* (London, 1993), pp. 87–108, an important essay that makes a number of interesting observations about the viking approach to warfare and the problems it presented to their Frankish opponents. Paddy Griffith's *The Viking Art of War* (London, 1995) is more systematic and detailed in its analysis of viking warfare and less persuasive in its conclusions. On the military threat posed by the vikings, see Nicholas Brooks, 'England in the ninth century: the crucible of defeat', *TRHS*, 5th series, 29 (1979), pp. 1–20. See also P.H. Sawyer, *The Age of the Vikings* (London, 1962) and Simon Coupland, 'The Vikings in Francia and Anglo-Saxon England to 911', in *The New Cambridge Medieval History*, vol. II, ed. R. McKitterick (Cambridge, 1995), pp. 190–201. R.H.C. Davis, 'Alfred the Great: propaganda and truth', *History* 56 (1971), pp. 169–82, and Dorothy Whitelock, 'The importance of the Battle of Edington AD 878', in *From Bede to Alfred: Studies in Early Anglo-Saxon Literature and History* (London, 1980) no. 13, debate the gravity of Alfred's military and political situation in 878 and the character of the *Anglo-Saxon Chronicle*.

My discussion of Alfred's negotiations with viking leaders draws upon my article, 'King Alfred's peace-making strategies with the Danes', *Haskins Society Journal* 3 (1992), pp. 23–34. Carolingian payments of danegeld are surveyed by Einar Joranson, *The Danegeld in France* (Rock Island, Illinois, 1923). For other interpretations of Alfred's treaty with Guthrum, see R.H.C. Davis, 'Alfred and Guthrum's frontier', *EHR* 97 (1982), pp. 803–10, reprinted in Davis, *From Alfred the Great to Stephen* (London, 1991), and D.N. Dumville, 'The treaty of Alfred and Guthrum', in *Wessex and England from Alfred to Edgar* (Woodbridge, 1992) pp. 1–28. For the Danish settlement of East Anglia, see D.M. Hadley, ' "And they proceeded to plough and to support themselves": the Scandinavian settlement of England', *Anglo-Norman England* 19 (1997), pp. 69–96.

．　．　．

CHAPTER 5: KING OF THE ANGLO-SAXONS, 880–891

Simon Keynes, 'King Alfred and the Mercians', in M.A.S. Blackburn and D.N. Dumville, eds, *Kings, Currency, and Alliances: The History and Coinage of Southern England, AD 840–900*

(Woodbridge, forthcoming), examines the political significance of Alfred's 'kingdom of the Anglo-Saxons'. The best study of Alfred's daughter, Æthelflæd, remains F.T. Wainwright, 'Æthelflæd, Lady of the Mercians', *Scandinavian England*, ed. H.P.R. Finberg (Chichester, 1975) pp. 305–24. Patrick Wormald has written extensively on Bede's ideal of a *gens Anglorum* and the growth of a sense of English identity. See his 'Bede, the *Bretwaldas* and the origins of the *Gens Anglorum*', in Patrick Wormald, Donald Bullough, and Roger Collins, eds, *Ideal and Reality in Frankish and Anglo-Saxon Society: Studies Presented to J.M. Wallace-Hadrill* (Oxford, 1983) pp. 103–4, 121; '*Engla Lond*: the making of an allegiance', *The Journal of Historical Sociology* 7 (1994), pp. 10–15; and 'The Making of England', *History Today* (February 1995), pp. 26–32. See also Sarah Foot, 'The making of *Angelcynn*: English Identity before the Norman Conquest', *TRHS*, Sixth Series, 6 (1996), pp. 25–49. For Wales in the ninth century, see J.E. Lloyd, *A History of Wales from the Earliest Times to the Edwardian Conquest*, 2 vols, 3rd edn (London, 1939) I, pp. 324–30; Wendy Davies, *Wales in the Early Middle Ages* (Leicester, 1982).

CHAPTER 6: THE DEFENCE OF THE REALM

For Alfred's military military reforms, see Richard Abels, *Lordship and Military Obligation in Anglo-Saxon England* (Los Angeles and Berkeley, 1988) especially pp. 58–78; and idem, 'English logistics and military administration, 871–1066: the impact of the Viking wars', in Anne Nørgård Jørgensen and Birthe L. Clausen, eds, *Military Aspects of Scandinavian Society in a European Perspective, AD 1–1300. Papers from an International Research Seminar at the Danish National Museum, Copenhagen, 2–4 May 1996,* Publications from the National Museum Studies in Archaeology & History, 2 (Copenhagen, 1997), p. 258, n. 6. For a different view of the development of military obligations in early England and of Alfred's reforms, see Nicholas Brooks, 'The development of military obligations in eighth- and ninth-century England', in P. Clemoes and K. Hughes, eds, *England Before the Conquest: Studies in Primary Sources Presented to Dorothy Whitelock* (Cambridge, 1971), pp. 69–84, and idem, 'England in the ninth century: the crucible of defeat', *TRHS*, 5th ser., 29 (1979), pp. 1–20. For the text of the Burghal Hidage and discussions of the system, see David Hill and Alexander R. Rumble, eds, *The Defence of Wessex: The Burghal Hidage and Anglo-Saxon Fortifications* (Manchester, 1996). Bernard Bachrach and R. Aris, 'Military technology and garrison organization: some observations on Anglo-Saxon military thinking in light of the Burghal Hidage', *Technology and Culture* 31 (1990), pp. 1–17, speculates about the weaponry and manpower required to defend Alfred's burhs.

For the planning and layout of Alfred's burhs, see David A. Hinton, *Alfred's Kingdom: Wessex and the South 800–1500* (London, 1977); Martin Biddle, 'Towns', in David Wilson, ed., *The Archaeology of Anglo-Saxon England* (1976), pp. 124–34; Jeremy Haslam, ed., *Anglo-Saxon Towns in Southern England* (Chichester, Sussex, 1984). For Alfred's role in the development of London, see Alan Vince, *Saxon London: An Archaeological Investigation*, The Archaeology of London series, gen. eds John Schofield and Alan Vince (London, 1990); Tony Dyson, 'Two Saxon grants for Queenhithe', in J. Bird, H. Chapman and J. Clark, eds, *Collectanea Londiniensia*, London & Middlesex Archaeological Society Special Paper 2 (1978), pp. 200–15; idem, 'King Alfred and the restoration of London', *The London Journal* 15 (1990), pp. 99–110; Brian Hobley, 'Lundenwic and Lundenburh: two cities rediscovered', in Richard Hodges and Brian Hobley, *The Rebirth of Towns in the West, AD 700–1050* (London, 1988) pp. 73–6; Gustav Milne, 'King Alfred's plan for London?', *London Archaeologist* 6 (1990), pp. 206–7.

The importance of Alfred's reign for the economic development of Anglo-Saxon England is explored by J.R. Maddicott, 'Trade, industry and the wealth of King Alfred', *Past & Present* 123 (1989), pp. 3–51; S.R.H. Jones, 'Transaction costs, institutional change, and the emergence of a market economy in later Anglo-Saxon England', *Economic History Review* 41 (1993), pp. 658–71; and Richard Hodges, *The Anglo-Saxon Achievement: Archaeology & the Beginnings of English Society* (Ithaca, N.Y., 1989). For objections to Maddicott's views and his response to them, see Ross Balzaretti, Janet Nelson, and J.R. Maddicott, 'Debate: trade, industry and the wealth of King Alfred, I', *Past & Present* 135 (1992), pp. 142–88.

CHAPTER 7: THE REIGN OF SOLOMON

The purposes and significance of Alfred's programme to renew religion and learning are discussed by J.M. Wallace-Hadrill in 'Charles the Bald and Alfred', in his *Early Germanic Kingship in England and the Continent* (Oxford, 1971), pp. 124–51, and by D.A. Bullough in 'The educational tradition in England from Alfred to Ælfric: teaching *utriusque linguae*', *Settimane di Studio del Centro Italiano di Studi sull'Alto Medioevo*, 19 (1972), pp. 453–94, repr. in his *Carolingian Renewal: Sources and Heritage* (Manchester and New York, 1991), pp. 297–334. One should also consult: Jennifer Morrish, 'King Alfred's Letter as a source on learning in England in the ninth century' in P.E. Szarmach, ed., *Studies in Earlier Old English Prose* (Albany, N.Y., 1986), pp. 87–107; H. Gneuss, 'King Alfred and the history of Anglo-Saxon libraries', in P.R. Brown, ed., *Modes of Interpretation in Old English Literature: Essays in Honour of Stanley B. Greenfield* (Toronto, 1986), pp. 29–49; Keynes and Lapidge, *Alfred the Great*, pp. 25–41 (and notes); Alfred P. Smyth, *King Alfred the Great* (Oxford, 1995) pp. 455–602; and David N. Dumville, *Wessex and England from Alfred to Edgar: Six Essays on Political, Cultural, and Ecclesiastical Revival* (Woodbridge, 1992), pp. 55–139, 185–205.

The best general introduction to Alfred's literary works is Allen J. Frantzen, *King Alfred*, Twayne's English Authors Series (Boston, 1986). Dorothy Whitelock, 'The prose of Alfred's reign', in Eric Stanley, ed., *Continuations and Beginnings: Studies in Old English Literature* (London, 1966), pp. 67–103, remains fundamental reading. Janet Bately has done more than anyone to establish the corpus of Alfred's own writings upon the basis of lexical analysis. See especially her 'King Alfred and the Old English Translation of Orosius', *Anglia* 88 (1970), pp. 433–60; 'The compilation of the Anglo-Saxon Chronicle, 60 BC to AD 890: vocabulary as evidence', *Proceedings of the British Academy* 64 (1980 for 1978), pp. 93–129; 'Lexical evidence for the authorship of the Prose Psalms in the Paris Psalter', *ASE* 10 (1982), pp. 69–95. Bately has also written a series of important articles placing Alfred's translations within their cultural context. See her *The Literary Prose of King Alfred's Reign: Translation or*

Transformation?, Inaugural Lecture, University of London King's College (London, 1980), repr. with *addenda* in the *Old English Newsletter Subsidia*, ed. Paul Szarmach, vol. 10 (Binghamton, NY, 1984); 'Old English prose before and during the reign of Alfred', *ASE* 17 (1988), pp. 93–139; 'Those books that are most necessary for all men to know: the Classics and late ninth-century England: a reappraisal', in Aldo S. Bernardo and Saul Levin, eds, *The Classics in the Middle Ages* (Binghamton, NY, 1990), pp. 45–78. Paul Szarmach, ed., *Studies in Earlier Old English Prose* (Albany, NY, 1986), is an important collection of essays on Alfred's works. For Alfred's Boethius, see also Anne Payne, *King Alfred and Boethius: An Analysis of the Old English Version of the Consolation of Philosophy* (Madison, Wisconsin, 1968), a speculative and stimulating 'Germanic' reading of the text; T.A. Shippey, 'Wealth and wisdom in King Alfred's *Preface* to the Old English *Pastoral Care*', *EHR* 94 (1979), pp. 346–55; Joseph Wittig, 'King Alfred's *Boethius* and its Latin sources: a reconsideration', *ASE* 11 (1983), pp. 157–98; Jonathan Frakes, *The Fate of Fortune in the Early Middle Ages: The Boethian Tradition* (Leiden, 1988).

The case for Alfred's seizure of strategically sited ecclesiastical estates is argued most forcefully by Robin Fleming, 'Monastic lands and England's defence in the Viking Age'. *EHR* 100 (1985), pp. 247–65. See also David Dumville, 'Ecclesiastical lands and the defence of Wessex in the first Viking Age', in his *Wessex and England*, pp. 29–54. For Alfred's dealings with his archbishops and clergy, see N. Brooks, *Early History of the Church of Canterbury: Christ Church from 597 to 1066* (Leicester, 1984); David Dumville, 'King Alfred and the tenth-century reform of the English Church', in his *Wessex and England*, pp. 185–205.

The pioneering study of King Alfred's political thought is J.M. Wallace-Hadrill's 'Charles the Bald and Alfred' in his *Early Germanic Kingship* (cited above), which places Alfred in Carolingian perspective. Janet L. Nelson has written three stimulating and insightful articles on Alfred's conception of kingship: 'The political ideas of Alfred of Wessex', in Anne J. Duggan, ed., *Kings and Kingship in Medieval Europe*, King's College London Medieval Studies 10, gen. ed. Janet Bately (Exeter, 1993), pp. 125–58; '"A King across the sea": Alfred in continental perspective', *TRHS*, 5th ser. 36 (1986), pp. 45–68; 'Wealth and Wisdom: the politics of Alfred the Great', in

J. Rosenthal, ed., *Kings and Kingship*, Acta 11 (Binghampton, NY, 1986 for 1984), pp. 31–52. Patrick Wormald's forthcoming *The Making of English Law: King Alfred to the Twelfth Century* contains the fullest exposition of Alfred's law code as an expression of his ideology of kingship. Possible Carolingian antecedents for Alfred's 'three orders' are discussed by Timothy E. Powell, 'The "Three Orders" of society in Anglo-Saxon England', *ASE* 23 (1994), pp. 103–32. H. Anton, *Fürstenspiegel und Herrscherethos in der Karolingerzeit*, Bonn 32 (Bonn, 1986), is a thorough exploration of Carolingian political thought.

. . .

CHAPTER 8: THE PRACTICE OF KINGSHIP

The best overview of royal of government in ninth-century England is H.R. Loyn, *The Governance of Anglo-Saxon England 500–1087* (Stanford, CA, 1984). The importance of the written word in Anglo-Saxon administration is emphasized by Simon Keynes, 'Royal government and the written word in late Anglo-Saxon England', in Rosamond McKitterick *The Uses of Literacy in Early Medieval Europe* (Cambridge, 1990) pp. 226–57. Patrick Wormald's forthcoming *The Making of English Law: King Alfred to the Twelfth Century* promises to be the fundamental work on Alfred's law code and concept of justice. For the Fonthill suit, see Simon Keynes, 'The Fonthill Letter', in Michael Korhammer (with Karl Reichl and Hans Sauer), ed., *Words, Texts and Manuscripts. Studies in Anglo-Saxon Culture Presented to Helmut Gneuss on the Occasion of his Sixty-Fifth Birthday* (Cambridge, 1992) pp. 53–97.

. . .

CHAPTER 9: TRIUMPH AND DEATH, 892–899

See the works on military history and the viking raids cited in the bibliography for chapters 3 and 4. Eleanor Shipley Duckett, *Death and Life in the Tenth Century* (Ann Arbor, MI, 1971), provides a vivid account of viking activity in Francia in the late ninth century.

GENEALOGICAL TABLE,
MAPS AND FIGURES

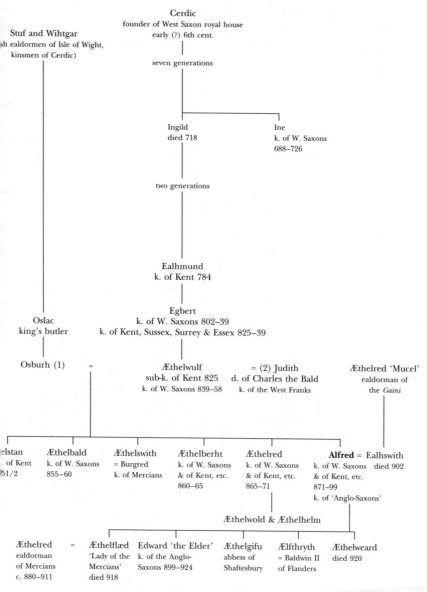

Alfred's family and genealogy

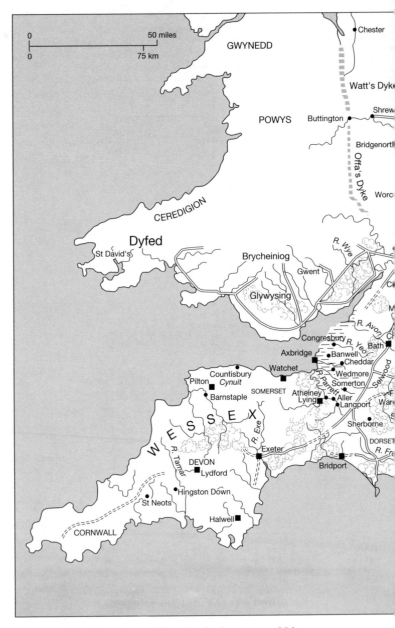

Map 1: The kingdom of the Anglo-Saxons c. 890
After Alfred P. Smyth, *King Alfred the Great* (Oxford, 1995) and
David Hill, *An Atlas of Anglo-Saxon England* (Oxford, 1981)

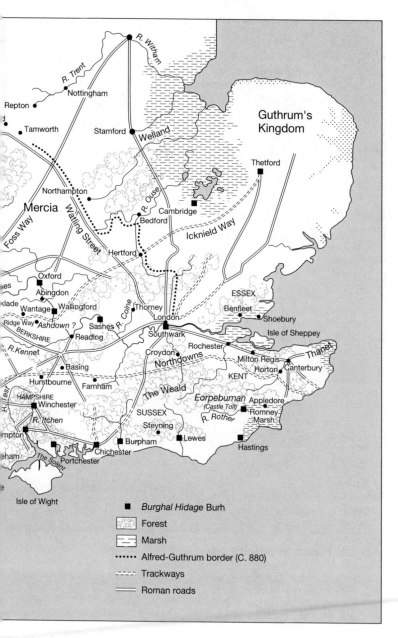

Guthrum's Kingdom

Mercia

Repton
Tamworth
Nottingham
Stamford
Welland
Thetford
Northampton
Cambridge
Bedford
Hertford
Icknield Way
Oxford
Abingdon
Wantage
Wallingford
Thorney
ESSEX
Benfleet
Shoebury
Ashdown ?
Sashes
London
Ridge Way
Reading
Southwark
Isle of Sheppey
Croydon
Rochester
Northdowns
Milton Regis
Thanet
R.Kennet
Basing
Horton
Canterbury
Hurstbourne
Farnham
KENT
HAMPSHIRE
Winchester
The Weald
Eorpeburnan
(Castle Toll)
Appledore
R.Itchen
SUSSEX
Steyning
R. Rother
Romney Marsh
mpton
Burpham
Lewes
Hastings
Chichester
Portchester
The Solent
Isle of Wight

BERKSHIRE

R. Trent
R. Witham
Foss Way
Watling Street
R. Ouse
R. Colne

■ *Burghal Hidage* Burh
Forest
Marsh
•••• Alfred-Guthrum border (C. 880)
----- Trackways
—— Roman roads

0 · · · · 50 miles
0 · · · · 75 km

STRATHCLYDE

NORTHUMBRIA

GWYNEDD

Offa's Dyke

LINDSEY

POWYS

MERCIA

EAST ANGLIA

DYFED

CEREDIGION

GWENT

BRYCHEINIOG
GLYWSYSING

ESSEX

BERKSHIRE

SURREY

KENT

WESSEX

SUSSEX

CORNWALL

▨ Acquired by Egbert and Æthelwulf, 825-848

Map 2: Britain at Alfred's birth, 848

Map 3: Britain at Alfred's death, 899

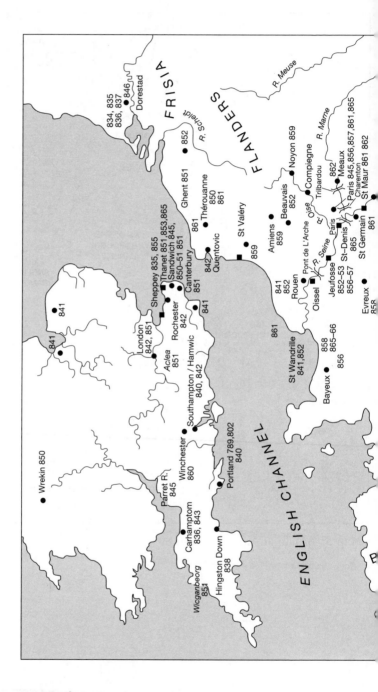

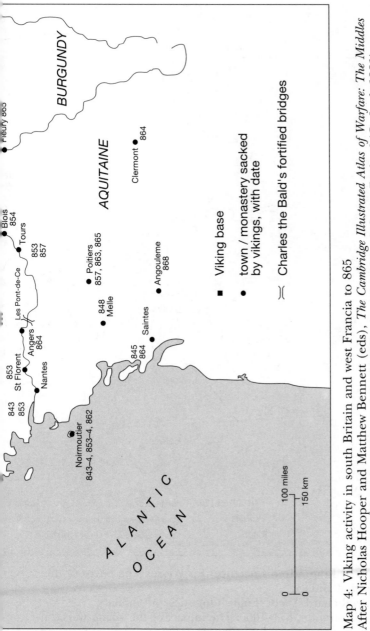

Map 4: Viking activity in south Britain and west Francia to 865
After Nicholas Hooper and Matthew Bennett (eds), *The Cambridge Illustrated Atlas of Warfare: The Middles Ages, 769–1487* (Cambridge, 1996) and David Hill, *An Atlas of Anglo-Saxon England* (Oxford, 1981)

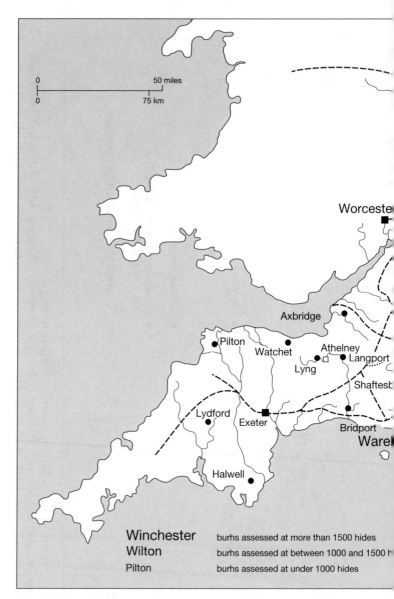

Map 5: King Alfred's defences for Wessex: the burhs of the
Burghal Hidage
After Richard Abels, 'English logistics and military
administration, 871–1066: The impact of the viking wars', in
A.N. Jorgensen and B.L. Clausen, *Military Aspects of Scandinavian
Society in a European Perspective, AD 1–1300* (Copenhagen, 1997)

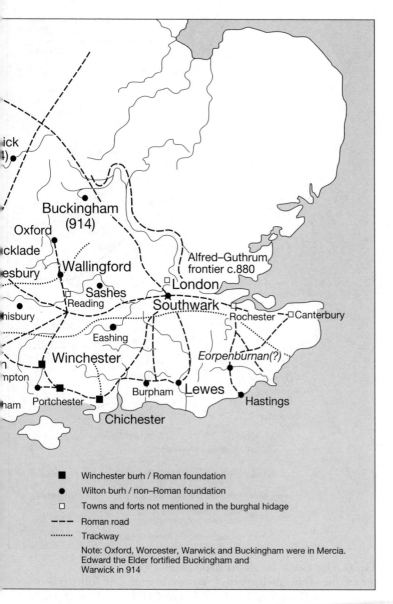

ick
4)

Buckingham
(914)

Oxford

cklade

esbury   Wallingford

Alfred–Guthrum
frontier c.880

London

Sashes
Reading

Southwark

hisbury

Rochester   Canterbury

Eashing

Winchester

Eorpenburnan(?)

npton

Burpham   Lewes

ham   Portchester

Hastings

Chichester

■   Winchester burh / Roman foundation

●   Wilton burh / non–Roman foundation

□   Towns and forts not mentioned in the burghal hidage

– – –   Roman road

·········   Trackway

Note: Oxford, Worcester, Warwick and Buckingham were in Mercia.
Edward the Elder fortified Buckingham and
Warwick in 914

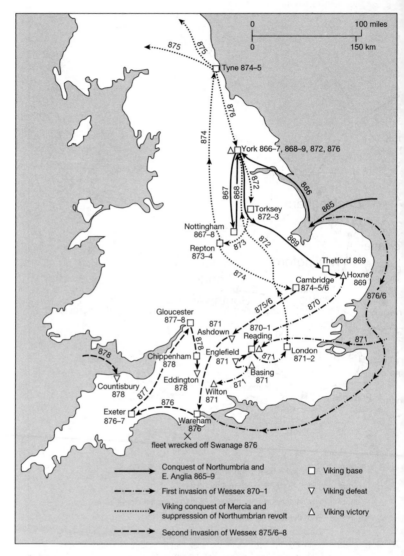

Map 6: The Great Heathen Army, 865–79
After James Campbell, Patrick Wormald and Eric John, *The Anglo-Saxons* (London, 1982) and David Hill, *An Atlas of Anglo-Saxon England* (Oxford, 1981)

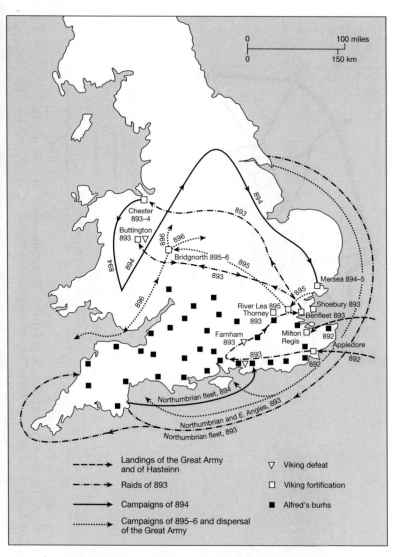

Map 7: Alfred's final campaigns, 892–6
After James Campbell, Patrick Wormald and Eric John, *The Anglo-Saxons* (London, 1982) and David Hill, *An Atlas of Anglo-Saxon England* (Oxford, 1981)

357

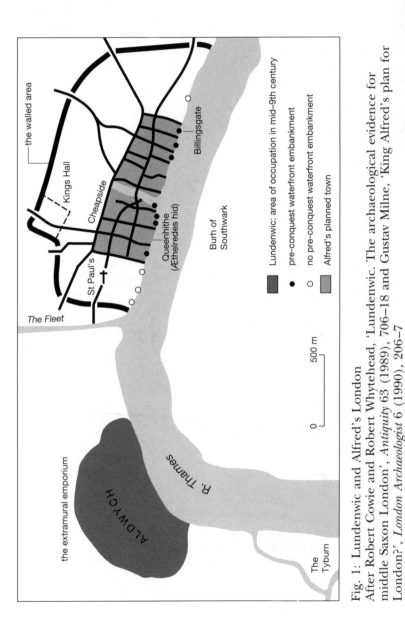

Fig. 1: Lundenwic and Alfred's London
After Robert Cowie and Robert Whytehead, 'Lundenwic. The archaeological evidence for middle Saxon London', *Antiquity* 63 (1989), 706–18 and Gustav Milne, 'King Alfred's plan for London?', *London Archaeologist* 6 (1990), 206–7

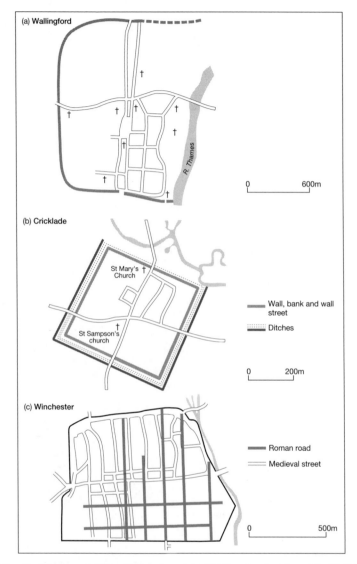

Fig. 2: Three of Alfred's burhs: (a) Wallingford. After M. Biddle and D. Hill, 'Late Saxon Planned towns', *Antiquaries Journal* 51 (1971), 70–85 and David A. Hinton, *Alfred's Kingdom: Wessex and the South 800–1500* (London, 1977). (b) Cricklade. Based on the 1841 Tithe Award map. (c) Winchester. After M. Biddle and D. Hill, 'Late Saxon Planned towns', *Antiquaries Journal* 51 (1971), 70–85 and David A. Hinton, *Alfred's Kingdom: Wessex and the South 800–1500* (London, 1977)

INDEX

361